Best Kept Secrets of the Gospel of Jesus Christ

Best Kept Secrets of the Gospel of Jesus Christ

Celestial Concepts in a Telestial World

Lawrence D. Gardner

Library of Congress Number:		2005910013
ISBN:	Hardcover	1-4257-0245-7
	Softcover	1-4257-0244-9

This book was printed in the United States of America.

To order additional copies of this book, contact:
Xlibris Corporation
1-888-795-4274
www.Xlibris.com
Orders@Xlibris.com
31348

Contents

ACKNOWLEDGMENTS 9

KEY TO ABBREVIATIONS 11

FOREWORD 13

INTRODUCTION—A NON-DISCLAIMER 15

1 WHERE TO STOP OR DAMNATION? 23

2 ELUSIVE TRUTH, WHERE ART THOU? 53

3 KNOW THE ONLY TRUE GOD 109

4 OTHER ATTRIBUTES OF GOD 127

5 THIS THING CALLED LOVE? 155

6 LIFE, WHAT MEANEST THOU? 187

7 WHO'S THE BOSS? 213

8 PROPHECY OR THE FUTURE IS NOW 231

9 THE ZION LIFE, A PICTURE OF PARADISE 233

10 GRACE AND LETTING GO 269

11 THE GREAT SECRET 291

INDEX 345

Dedication

In loving dedication to my wonderful wife Lana, to my children Letische, Lawrence II, Leslie, Lee, and Lanae, who through the failures, never stopped believing in me.

Acknowledgments

Special thanks to Letische whose comments and editorial skills made this book possible, but especially for her integrity, her understanding of me, and our mutual love and respect.

Special thanks to Bruce W. Inglis for the many hours of intimate discussions, and for being the catalyst of many of my greatest discoveries.

Thanks to Lynne and Gary Summerhays, Owen Stewart, Allen and Marilyn Parker, Michelle Davidson, John Van Driel, Daniel Lambson, Betty Petersen, and Bill Johnson for their valuable contributions as well as their treasured friendships.

Key to Abbreviations

B of M	*The Book of Mormon*, a compilation of translated ancient writings of the inhabitants of the American continents from 1200 BC to 420 AD by Joseph Smith (The Church of Jesus Christ of Latter-day Saints, Salt Lake City).
DBY	*The Discourses of Brigham Young*, The Church of Jesus Christ of Latter-day Saints (Deseret News Press, Salt Lake City).
D&C	*The Doctrine and Covenants*, a collection of revelations from God to Joseph Smith and other modern prophets (The Church of Jesus Christ of Latter-day Saints, Salt Lake City).
DHC	*The Documentary History of The Church* (Church Historian's Office, The Church of Jesus Christ of Latter-day Saints, Salt Lake City).
HC	*History of The Church of Jesus Christ of Latter-day Saints*, by B. H. Roberts, Church Historian (The Church of Jesus Christ of Latter-day Saints, Salt Lake City, 1932-1951).
JD	*Journal of Discourses*, by George Q. Cannon (Latter-day Saints' Book Dept., London, 1854-1886).
MD	*Mormon Doctrine*, by Bruce R. McConkie (Book Craft, Salt Lake City).
P of GP	*The Pearl of Great Price*, a compilation of translations from ancient scrolls, Joseph Smith's History, some inspired Biblical translations, and other modern writings (The Church of Jesus Christ of Latter-day Saints, Salt Lake City).
TPJS	*Teachings of the Prophet Joseph Smith*, selected by Joseph Fielding Smith (Deseret Book Company, Salt Lake City, 1938).

Foreword

Daniel B. Lambson
Co-editor

This book has become a personal study guide and companion to the scriptures in my search for truth and enlightenment in the gospel of Jesus Christ.

I have rarely found a work that finishes concepts as thoroughly as this book. Lawrence Gardner has gone to great lengths to not leave loose ends and make sure no stone is unturned. All of the principals he covers herein bring the reader to logical conclusions, not to precipices. Thorough are the topics in their treatment, inspiring in their depth, yet one marvels at the simplicity.

Because of the authors inspired application of resources and references and his down to earth approach to life, this book will catch the reader off guard at times and reach to the core of his soul. I found myself re-examining every aspect of my life with more clarity and purpose, because of the bold and honest approach taken in the treatment of the doctrine.

This book is a must for the library of every disciple of Jesus Christ, and a boon to every person who desires to unlock and understand the mysteries of God.

There is no need for me to say more. I cannot do this work justice no matter what I espouse, or how eloquently I might state it. I urge everyone to read this book, prayerfully, and begin to unlock the secrets of the gospel of Jesus Christ!

Introduction
A Non-Disclaimer

I Never Said That!

Before I teach any class (particularly on religious or philosophic subjects) or give talks, speeches, or lectures, I generally insert a disclaimer. Those of you who have had experience with legal documents will know that a disclaimer is a particular statement placed somewhere in the document (sometimes in the fine print, but these days up front in plain view) that basically says the party writing the document may not be held responsible for what is said therein.

We find such disclaimers printed on nearly every product we buy. Radio and TV ads include a narrator rattling off exclusions or exceptions to the rule in a low monotone voice, too quickly to be properly heard, let alone understood. TV ads often flash words at the bottom of the screen so briefly and in print so small as to render them unintelligible to anyone but a small percentage of speed-readers with magnified vision. Of course, any good attorney will certainly leave him/herself as many outs as possible by the installation of one or more hefty and comprehensive disclaimers in every document they write.

Although I am no attorney (on the contrary, I'm an artist), I have, over the years, inserted these disclaimers in my talks, lessons, and writings. Sometimes they were extensive and specific, sometimes short and general, but always with ample or at least sufficient rhetoric to absolve myself of any responsibility relative to what I might say.

I thought I would start this book the same way, with a huge disclaimer declaring all my weaknesses and lack of credentials, as well as all the reasons why you should pay no attention to me whatsoever. In fact I had it all written out that way—but have since had second thoughts. *I have decided* ***not*** *to include a disclaimer within these writings.*

While it is true enough that I am not all that smart, accomplished, clever, cultured, enlightened, educated, or otherwise endowed with any unusual gifts;

and while it is also true that I do not consider myself, in general, to be any more or less moral or righteous than any other person; nor entitled, any more or less than any other person, to personal revelations, let alone revelations for others; and further, while it is true that I have never had any out of body experience, seen beyond the veil,[1] heard thundering voices from heaven declaring to me any great revelations, or anything like that; still, God has given me knowledge and understanding of various principles of the Gospel of Christ and I would indeed be an unworthy servant should I seek to circumvent my responsibility to proclaim these things to others. I may actually enlighten someone, thereby bringing them closer to God. God has given me some gifts and I feel an obligation to pass them on to others. I cannot discharge that obligation by the use of a disclaimer, no matter how comprehensive it might be.

He's Just A Fool

In the past, my reasons for including the disclaimers were two fold. First, I found that it disarmed my audience. It made it easy for those with their minds already made up to dismiss or discard me and/or the concepts I promote. I handed them all they needed right up front. It also discouraged those who might have felt duty-bound to take me more seriously than I deserved to be taken. And further, pious folks, who felt obliged to counter my thinking with all fervor, would consider me an unworthy opponent. Where is the victory in converting this man? He is, after all, just a fool. Those with a more humble view toward me could feel sorry for me, a poor misguided soul in want of their compassion. Whatever the case, I discovered that, as a result of my disclaimers, my audiences seemed not to be driven quite so easily to argument.

Passing The Buck

Second, and far more important, my disclaimers would free me to express myself without fear that what I said may not be entirely correct. The disclaimers put the responsibility of discerning truth where it should be, squarely upon the shoulders of those who might have been within earshot of my words. My disclaimers would declare that no one should deem any of my feelings, beliefs, or opinions any more deserving of attention or more valid than anyone else's, nor should anyone assume that all or even any of my personal spiritual insights need be rightly applied to his or her life.

Although I still feel very strongly that it is not only the right but also the obligation of each individual to discover truth for themselves by listening to the Holy Ghost, the testifier of all truth, I now realize that my disclaimers were the cowards' way out. They were evidence of my lack of faith, my reluctance to commit fully to God's work. I was afraid of what people might think. What if they misunderstand? What if they do not agree with me? What if they condemn me or try to censor me? In short *I was afraid to stand boldly for the truths that God has given me.* I was afraid to expose myself, to lay bare for the world to see, some of the deepest thoughts and feelings of my soul.

Who Is This Guy?

You see; I am basically a "back row person" more inclined to be an observer of life than a participant. Notwithstanding the fact that I am often found in front of large groups of people as a teacher, actor, director, or in some other leadership role, I am a very private individual, painfully shy and bashful. It always amazes me to find that others are afraid and threatened by me when in fact; I am the one who is inhibited. Perhaps it is my size; I am nearly 6 ft. 4 in. and 250 pounds, or perhaps it is my feigned show of confidence. Maybe it is my arrogant, opinionated style that frightens people. I don't know. Honestly speaking, I am over my head and scared to death most of the time and those who really know me know that about me. Who am I after all? I am not a giant success at anything, certainly not in my chosen career field of filmmaking. In fact, filmmaking has never been especially lucrative for me. This has forced me to take work wherever I may to earn an often, meager support for my family, leaving me comfortable to say, "I am merely a *common laborer.*" Again in short, I am but a common man. Yet, notwithstanding my flaws and lack of certification, I have felt spiritually compelled for some time, years in fact, to write this book. God has given me these things that I might be a witness of them and I realize that I must somehow muster the courage to boldly testify, no matter how difficult it is for me or no matter what the consequences. Accordingly, if I am to be truly, fully, dedicated to the Lord's work, I can no longer cowardly hide behind a disclaimer. I must be willing to take full responsibility for what I say, what I know to be true, even what I *believe* to be true.

I am a member in good standing of The Church of Jesus Christ of Latter-day Saints (The Mormon Church)[2], and have been from my youth. Although I am not a General Authority[3] nor have I ever been a Stake President, Bishop, or served in any administrative position of authority in The Church, I have served for many years as Adult Gospel Doctrine Teacher, Teacher of Youth Sunday School, and Teacher of Priesthood Quorums. In the course of that service, I have found that a number of fundamental and extremely important concepts are not clearly understood by members of The Church. For whatever reason, despite their best study efforts and the abundance of scriptural resources, many members are stuck on some basic principles rendering them unable to move on to higher ones. It has been one of my greatest joys as a Gospel Doctrine Teacher to help my students reach more exalted concepts.

Please understand that although I served a two year voluntary mission for The Mormon Church in England and I am a graduate (BA in Art) of Brigham Young[4] University,[5] I am not a noted religious professor at any great university, nor am I a professor at all. I am not trained in the ministry, nor do I consider myself a theologian or scriptorian of any kind. I probably couldn't quote five scriptures if my life depended upon it. The truth is, I have to look up every reference when I need it. I have always been a full tithe[6] payer and a temple[7] recommend holder. I have been married in the temple[8] to my good wife for thirty-eight years and I have five wonderful children who love the gospel of Christ and are true and faithful.

Now, should any of the above qualify me to write a book? Of course not. Additionally, I do not represent or speak for anyone but myself, and certainly not The Church of Jesus Christ of Latter-day Saints. I speak with **no** authority. I repeat; I **do not** represent The Church of Jesus Christ of Latter-day Saints or any other organization. Since, save for the quotes found herein, it is only my personal opinion, you *may*—no, you ***must*** feel no obligation (on this basis at least) to agree or disagree with whatever concept is put forth. You and you alone must take responsibility for what you believe to be true. Therefore, should you discover any truth to my testimonies herein, it must be upon the merits of that truth and not just because you deem me a credible witness. That being said, you will note again there is **no** disclaimer found herein. I will gladly take full responsibility for what is written and I will bear witness to the truths of the concepts as they are unfolded in this book, bearing in mind that my only real qualification is that the spirit has constrained me to write. So, on we go!

Notwithstanding the above, I promise to write only that which I ***know*** to be true. Or ***believe*** is true . . . or ***think*** is true? How's that?

Please Put Away Those Rocks

Will you stone me if, within these pages, I present something new or contrary to what you now hold as true? Well, before you start gathering stones for that purpose, remember the words of the Prophet Joseph Smith[9] when he said, "Many men will say, 'I will never forsake you, but will stand by you at all times.' But the moment you teach them some of the mysteries of the Kingdom of God that are retained in the heavens and are to be revealed to the children of men when they are prepared for them they will be the first to stone you and put you to death. It was this same principle that crucified the Lord Jesus Christ, and will cause the people to kill the prophets in this generation." (*TPJS, pg. 309*)[10]

Fear not that I may be in danger of revealing any great heavenly truths, that should not be divulged as such are only received by personal witness of the Holy Ghost. What I present herein is basics and already revealed in God's word, but hopefully a deeper understanding of the same. Like Joseph Smith, I only ask that you not be narrow of mind. For your comfort and my protection, I promise I will stick close to the scriptures and the revealed word.

If It Doesn't Taste Good, Don't Eat It

Relative to the non-Mormons who, for whatever reason, find themselves reading this material, I would like to welcome you. I do hope there are many non-Mormons that will find some enlightenment within the covers of this work. I shall endeavor to pay special attention to you. I recognize that like the Catholic, Jewish, Protestant, Eastern and other religious persuasions, the Mormon culture has its own vocabulary and phraseologies that only those who have been associated with them for a time can interpret. For this reason, I will attempt to make my rhetoric understandable on any level and from any point of view. For the sake of those not familiar with some of the resources I may use herein, I will attempt explanations of the same in the endnotes and provide a key with full titles for any abbreviations used. With that being said, *I make no excuse for the use of resources that are only found within and/or accepted by The Mormon Church.* I do not intend, by any means, to ignore a vast and comprehensive supply of spiritual revelations found in such literary sources just because the rest of the world is not familiar with or perhaps does not accept them as truth. My advice to those of you not familiar with my sources is to search them out and determine their validity for yourselves.

Of course, you are not bound to accept such resource materials just because I use them in this book. I hope that you will consider this book as a buffet, where you may take what tastes (feels) good to you and pass on the rest. It seems to me, however, that much of the confusion and conflict in the world today is due to the lack of truths, truths that are unavailable only because we refuse to look at them before we judge them to be false. In so doing, we ignore possible solutions and explanations to this confusion and conflict. I have come to subscribe to Joseph Smith's statement, "I believe all that God ever revealed, and I never hear of a man being damned for believing too much; but they are damned for unbelief." (*TPJS pg. 373*) Damnation is the state of being stopped up, not going far enough. One may, for a time, be led in a direction that is not correct, but if the mind is open and accepting, it is my belief that a person will come full circle, back to the truth of any given matter. This is the basic reason why I do not feel compelled to argue with others over what they believe. As Bruce R. McConkie[11] said, "I have the truth and know that truth will prevail. Why should I contend against others and their views? Such true principles as they possess shall prevail and all else will vanish away in due course, for truth only is eternal." (*Doctrinal New Testament Commentary, by Bruce R. McConkie, Vol.2, pg. 63*) Like McConkie, I am not given to contending or trying to prove anything to anyone. If the doctrines I preach do not feel good, don't accept them. I am not looking for an argument on any issue presented herein—discussion yes, argument no. I believe firmly that "he that hath the spirit of contention is not of me [Christ], but is of the devil, who is the father of contention, and he stirreth up the hearts of men to contend with anger, one with another." (*3 Nephi 11:29*)[12] If you say, "I do not understand," I will keep talking. If you say, "I understand but cannot accept," then I have nothing more to say.

So, whether you are a Mormon or not, the responsibility is yours to seek out the truth. If you are fortunate enough to find some herein, take it home and leave the rest. It is your choice. Let the Holy Spirit guide.

So What's The Secret?

At this point in my writing, so that we don't waste each other's time, let me reveal some of what you may expect from this composition. If perhaps you supposed from the word secret in the title of this book that I would expose some deeply hidden scandalous operations, shocking history, clandestine ordinances, disgraceful policies, or any other such hitherto unknown shameful activities by The Mormon Church or its members, you are mistaken. If that is what you were looking for, you may now put down this book, not bothering to read on. If indeed there are such secrets, I am not at all privy to them. Having been, as stated above, a life-long member of The Mormon Church, I can honestly say that, so far as I know, any and all black marks, embarrassing facts, or events of this kind that may be associated with the Mormons have already been dragged into the light by the enemies of The Church and are open for the world to view. Although it is not The Church's policy to air their dirty linen in public, I do not believe there are any cover-ups in the Mormon Church. In fact, I have never been member to any organization that is as open and divulging as The Mormon Church. This leaves me to believe that there are no such hidden events or facts of any consequence yet to be disclosed. Should there be, the antagonists of The Mormon Church will find them long before I and, no doubt, make them public, with commentary. Therefore, if you have come to this volume in hopes of finding something slanderous to hold against the Mormons, well, you have my apologies, as you will not find it here.

I will also state here at the opening of this text that *it* ***is not my intention, in any way, to criticize the leaders of The Church of Jesus Christ of Latter-day Saints***. It is not they who are keeping truths secret from the rest of the membership of The Church or the world in general. On the contrary, they are they who have struggled with all fervor for generations to get the members and the world to see, understand, and accept these concepts. I believe we have excellent leaders, called and inspired of God, and these leaders, general and local, are doing an excellent job.

Although you may conclude from my style of presentation, my occasional impertinent manner that I am being overly critical of the membership of The Church, I don't mean to be. I love The Church, its leaders, and its members. They are some of the finest people God has ever created. I am, in no way, ashamed to be numbered among them. Further, I do not wish to be like a professor that I once had who started his lecture nearly every day by saying, "If I offend any of you, I want you to know I meant to." I do not mean to insult or offend you in any way. I, therefore, beg your forgiveness should I do so.

"Then," you might rightly ask, "What are some of these great secrets of the gospel of Christ that are best kept, even by The Mormon Church? What do you plan to reveal?" You will find the answers to those questions in the ensuing chapters, read on. And let me say here that despite the loftiness of the concepts presented herein, (hence, the second part of my title, *Celestial Concepts in a Telestial World*), they are accessible to us all, member and non-member alike.

Be assured that *it is my intention* to reach to the heavens in search of the highest level of ideas, concepts, and truths. I shall not presume to condemn any man to a lower level of thinking because I judge him not able to understand or unwilling to accept. I will let him do that. Let all men go as far to heaven as their own mind, heart, and resolve will take them.

---

1 **The veil, as often referred to by Mormons, generally means the separation of mortals from God and the spirit world. It also refers to the accompanying forgetting of any pre-earthly existence.**

2 **The Church of Jesus Christ of Latter-day Saints (LDS) is often referred to, by members and non-members alike, as The Mormon Church. Those who belong to The LDS church are called Mormons. This is a nickname derived from the Mormons'**

belief in a book of scripture called *The Book of Mormon* (see endnote on *The Book of Mormon*). A *Saint* is generally accepted to mean simply a member of The Church, not a canonized leader, and The Mormons consider that we are living in the latter-days of the earth's mortal time, hence the *Latter-day Saints*.

[3] **A General Authority in The LDS Church would be the Prophet of The Church, his counselors (usually two in number), the Twelve Apostles, Presiding Bishop with his counselors (usually two in number), a member of the First Quorum of Seventies (varies in number, about 40 but no more than 70), or the Second Quorum of Seventies (also varies in number). Although these men hold no more priesthood than many of the lay members of the church, they have been set apart and given keys to administer the affairs of the church on a full-time basis and have been blessed as special witnesses of Christ to testify to the world of revealed truths.**

[4] **Brigham Young was the second Prophet of The LDS Church from 1847 to 1877.**

[5] **Brigham Young University, established by Brigham Young (originally the Brigham Young Academy), is a private university owned by The LDS Church. It is located in Provo, Utah.**

[6] **Mormons believe in giving, as a contribution to The Church, one tenth of their income. This is called a tithe.**

[7] **The Mormon Church builds temples for holy worship, higher learning, and the performance of sacred ordinances for the living and the dead. Although it is not necessary to have a "temple recommend" to be active and in full fellowship, any member who is recommended (by the local leaders) and deemed worthy to enter the temples is considered to be so.**

[8] **A temple marriage is believed by Mormons to be not just for time but also for all eternity.**

[9] **Joseph Smith (Jr.) was the first prophet and founder of The LDS Church from 1830 to 1844.**

[10] **(TPJS), *Teachings of the Prophet Joseph Smith*, compiled by Joseph Fielding Smith, contain some of Joseph's writings taken from various sermons during his ministry.**

[11] **Bruce R. McConkie was an apostle of the LDS Church from 1972 to 1985.**

[12] **3 Nephi is a book in *The Book of Mormon* (see note on *The Book of Mormon*) covering the period from 1 AD to 35 AD. The book is named after a prophet of God that lived at that time. It includes an account of Christ's appearance to the ancient natives of North, South, and Central America.**

1
Where to Stop or Damnation?

I Don't Wanna Hear It

"But there has been a great difficulty in getting anything into the heads of this generation. It has been like splitting hemlock knots with a corndodger for a wedge, and a pumpkin for a beetle. Even the Saints are slow to understand." (*TPJS, pg. 331*)[13] This statement made by Joseph Smith[14] is more than descriptive. Hemlock wood is considered to be one of the hardest. To try splitting a knot of such a hard wood using a corncob for a wedge and a pumpkin for a hammer does indeed conjure up a most vivid picture in one's mind.

He further stated, regarding the unwillingness of the Saints to learn, "I have tried for a number of years to get the minds of the Saints prepared to receive the things of God; but we frequently see some of them, after suffering all they have for the work of God, will fly to pieces like glass as soon as anything comes that is contrary to their traditions, they cannot stand the fire at all. How many will be able to abide a celestial law, and go through and receive their exaltation, I am unable to say, as many are called, but few are chosen." (*TPJS, pg. 331*)

Is this so? Do we really resist change? Do we categorically reject new concepts? Yes we do! History has documented that. As individuals, as groups, as entire societies and cultures, our first reaction is to close our minds to almost everything new, especially new ideas, concepts, and beliefs. In a moment I will suggest a few reasons why this is so but first, for those not truly convinced that this is true, let me give a couple of examples of how completely we reject new things.

The "Atomic Theory" (that all things are made of unseen tiny particles called Atoms) put forth by Dalton in 1808 took over one hundred years to be generally accepted by the scientific community. They scorned and attempted to disprove his theory, which is now a basic truth of life taught to every grade school student.

In the 1840's a Hungarian physician by the name of Dr. Ignas Semmelweis was appalled by the high rate of death to women giving birth in hospitals. The death rate to both women and their newborn children was over thirty percent and he became obsessed with finding out the cause of the infections and disease that was killing them. He noticed that many of the doctors were coming straight from the morgue where they were working with cadavers who had died from a multitude of diseases. After conducting anatomy classes and examinations they would go directly into the delivery rooms without washing their hands, often in their street clothes, and performed the childbirth. Semmelweis suspected that they were carrying something on their hands that caused the infections and in one hospital instituted a policy of having the doctors wash their hands and dip them in a chlorine solution before delivering any babies. The death rate in that hospital dropped right away to almost zero but the foreign medical community of the day condemned his idea by cutting off his research funding, ostracizing, and finally discharging him from his positions in maternity hospitals. Even the American medical community condemned Dr Semmelweis's practice of washing hands because they thought it was witchery to be afraid of something that could not be seen. The newly formed American Medical Association threatened to withdraw the licenses of any doctor caught washing his hands before a procedure. So, because of their reluctance to accept a new concept, untold women suffered and died. It wasn't until the advent of the microscope in the 1880's, some 40 years after Dr. Semmelweis's assertion, that doctors could finally see bacteria and his theory was proven. Distraught by the fact that thousands of unnecessary deaths continued, the poor doctor died of insanity in 1865.

Performing a medical procedure today without washing hands and disinfecting equipment would be unthinkable but doctors through the turn of the century were still calling for more evidence before they would believe. Notwithstanding the above information, Louis Pasteur encountered great resistance when he put forth his theory of germ disease. But then it is as Albert Einstein said, "Great spirits have always encountered violent opposition from mediocre minds."

Albert Einstein himself, one of the greatest scientific minds of our day, suffered constant criticism from his fellow scientists. A group of them collaborated on a publication against his theory of relativity. It was called "One-hundred Against Einstein". When Einstein learned of the publication he said, "If they were right, one would be enough."

It is truly incredible how utterly universal and comprehensive this phenomenon really is on this planet. I am sure you can think of many examples of mans reluctance to accept new ideas and concepts. It was said by Max Planck (a Nobel Prize winner of 1903), "An important scientific innovation rarely makes its way by gradually winning over and converting its opponents; what does happen is its opponents gradually die out and the growing generation is familiarized with the idea from the beginning."

Even the Lord Himself had to lead the children of Israel in the wilderness until an entire generation died off, leaving a more accepting youth to enter the promised land. History has proven time and time again that "a man convinced against his will is of the same opinion still."

I wonder what great truth of tomorrow we are rejecting today?

Also, remember the words of the Prophet when he said your best friends will turn on you and stone you when you reveal something new about the mysteries of the Kingdom of God. (see *TPJS, pg. 309*) We just don't seem to be able to accept new things.

Good Quality Wood

Why? Why is it so hard for us to accept new concepts? We can list a number of reasons, among which would certainly be personal characteristics such as pride, vanity, piety, fear, laziness, apathy, arrogance, egotism, etc. It is true that the need to be right runs deep in our souls. I hope not just because we want to be right, (that is pride) but rather because truth is what we seek diligently for and want to be associated with. Truth, as we will discuss in an ensuing chapter, is more than just very important. Truths are the planks we use to construct our scaffolding to heaven. We can't afford to weaken such a vital structure with boards that are mere sawdust lest it should fall and leave us in a place we never planned or wanted to be.

Although our adverse personal traits are deterrents to our acceptance of new truths, I suspect there is a process we are all going through which is equally destructive to our ability to receive truth. It starts when we are very young and has to do with the methods or procedures we develop that enable us to discern truth from lies. It is at the foundation of our discernment process, or our personal scaffolding to heaven as it were, where we sometimes fail to lay the blocks of simple truths. It is here, at the footing, that we must learn and accept the basics, the fundamentals. This is an absolute necessity and in nothing that I may write herein do I mean to infer that the basic truths are not essential nor do I mean to diminish their importance in any way. On the contrary, I feel that those who neglect or disregard the fundamental truths will meet the same fate as those Jews referred to by Jacob[15] in *The Book of Mormon* (B of M)[16] when he said (italics for emphasis), "But behold, the Jews were a stiff-necked people; and they despised the words of plainness, and killed the prophets, and sought for things that they could not understand. Wherefore, because of their blindness, *which blindness came by looking beyond the mark,* they must needs fall; for God hath taken away His plainness from them, and delivered unto them many things which they cannot understand, because they desired it. And because they desired it God hath done it, that they may stumble." (*Jacob 4:14*)[17]

We can never skip ahead of the foundational truths, for upon these truths we build others. One of our means of discovering new truths is to measure them against or compare them to those we have already placed at the foundation of our structure. The more truth we have in our scaffolding, the easier it is to discern new truths and be confident in our findings. Since all truths complement and support each other, our scaffolding becomes stronger and stronger. When we leave too many false planks in our construction, the integrity of the structure suffers and we become confused, unable to tell new truths from lies. Now this may be an oversimplification of the operations we use to find truths, but it serves to illustrate the point I am about to make.

I Haven't The Teeth For It

Relative to this process of building our scaffolding to heaven upon the foundation of basic truths, the apostle Paul had this to say to the Hebrews, "For when for the time ye ought to be teachers, ye have need that one teach you again which be the first principles of the oracles of God; and are become such as have need of milk, and not of strong meat. For everyone that useth milk is unskillful in the word of righteousness: for he is a babe. But strong meat belongeth to them that are of full age, even those who by reason of use have their senses exercised to discern both good and evil." (*Hebrews 5:12-14*) Said Paul to the Corinthians (italics for emphasis), "When I was a child, I spake as a child, I understood as a child, I thought as a child: but when I became a man, I put away childish things. *For now we see through a glass, darkly*; but then face to face: now I know in part; but then shall I know even as also I am known." (*1 Corinthians 13:11-12*) Paul further taught the Corinthians that not only is our immaturity a cause of our distorted views (seeing through dark glasses), but our carnal minds have the same effect. "And I, brethren, could not speak unto you as unto spiritual, but as unto carnal, even as unto babes in

Christ. I have fed you with milk, and not with meat: for hitherto ye were not able to bear it, neither yet now are ye able. For ye are yet carnal: for whereas there is among you envying, and strife, and divisions, are ye not carnal, and walk as men?" (*1 Corinthians 3:1-3*)

I for one, and I think most people, will not take issue with the belief that when we are babes we must be fed philosophical, doctrinal, and spiritual milk. It is absolutely vital that we understand the truths we lay at the foundation of our process of deciphering truth and untruth, else how shall we measure against misunderstanding and confusion? Without the teeth to chew or the facility to digest, it would be more than detrimental to be fed meat. It could be fatal. We could very well choke! Accordingly, even teachers must study the first principles of God until they are *of full age* (old) in the gospel and *have their senses exercised to discern both good and evil,* otherwise they are *unskillful in the word of righteousness*. Further, we must reach a place where our minds are no longer *carnal* but *spiritual,* otherwise we have no capacity to understand, let alone expound the greater spiritual truths. The carnal man will see through carnal eyes and his seeing will be tainted by his carnal desires.

And what are the attributes of the carnal man that will taint his vision? Some are *envying, strife, and division*. The carnal man will not see clearly enough to judge righteously. For these reasons Christ has said, "And I command you that you preach naught but repentance, and show not these things unto the world until it is wisdom in me. For they cannot bear meat now, but milk they must receive; wherefore, they must not know these things, lest they perish. Learn of me, and listen to my words; walk in the meekness of my Spirit, and you shall have peace in me. I am Jesus Christ; I came by the will of the Father, and I do His will." (*Doctrine and Covenants [D&C] 19:21-24*)[18] What will qualify us to eat meat? He said, "Learn of me, and listen to my words; walk in the meekness of my Spirit." When we have grown old doing that, when we, as Paul says, *are of full age* in spiritual things, we may move on to meat, and not before. Laying the basics of the Gospel of Christ as foundation stones of our scaffolding is essential and not withstanding the statement to follow, I firmly testify that if we fail to do so our whole structure will, at some point, inevitably fall.

Give me Meat

But, it is more than that we ***may*** move on to meat, we ***must*** move on to meat. If we do not, we remain babes, refusing to grow up to greater concepts and thinking, rendering us never able to understand the mind and will of

God. "For my thoughts are not your thoughts, neither are your ways my ways, saith the Lord. For as the heavens are higher than the earth, so are my ways higher than your ways, and my thoughts than your thoughts." (*Isaiah 55:8-9*) As we construct our scaffolding to heaven, we must, eventually, raise our *thoughts* as well as our *ways* closer to the place we hope to end up. There is no way around this. We cannot reach heaven while our thoughts are immature. We are inevitably earth bound.

Well, you ask, when and where do I change from milk to meat? Who am I to give you such personal counsel? I believe the answer to that question is embedded in the fabric or planks of our own scaffolding of truths. As we learn the basic truths and lay them securely at our foundation, there is a natural desire to move on to higher concepts and thoughts. Anyone who is close to a child recognizes how inquisitive he or she is as they grow. They very often annoy their parents by asking question after question. It is too bad, indeed shameful, that we often smother that questioning side of a child. Those children, who manage to maintain that questioning spirit, despite their environment, are the ones who become our greatest inventors, scientists, artists, and leaders.

Like a child, the best indicators that it is time to move on to higher truths are the questions themselves. There are spiritual reasons why questions come to our minds. If we don't disregard them, they give us our best clue that we should reach for higher issues and understandings. Out of laziness, pride, fear, tradition, arrogance, piety, elitism, or some other not so virtuous trait, we stop asking. We even pretend the questions don't exist, let alone look for the answers. If we are not asking questions we are asleep. So, wake up!

If we do not smother our spiritual curiosity, but continue in our questioning, we will continue to receive answers. It's a simple basic concept. You see, the more questions one asks, the more answers one gets. **Wow! Huh**? You may not get all the answers at first, but you will get more than those who don't ask. It is, after all, a *process* (too often a slow one). "—assuredly as the Lord liveth, who is your God and your Redeemer, even so surely shall you receive a knowledge of whatsoever things you shall ask in faith, with an honest heart, believing that you shall receive . . . . Yea, behold, I will tell you in your mind and in your heart, by the Holy Ghost, which shall come upon you and which shall dwell in your heart. Now, behold, this is the spirit of revelation; behold, this is the spirit by which Moses brought the children of Israel through the Red Sea on dry ground." (*D&C 8:1-3*) "Ask, and it shall be given you; seek, and ye shall find; knock, and it shall be opened unto you: For every one that asketh receiveth; and he that seeketh findeth; and to him that knocketh it shall be opened." (*Matthew 7:7-8*)

How Many Times Do I Have to Tell You?

As an aside, let me say that in my search for the above scripture references, I was astounded to find so many references with not only the same theme, but also the same or nearly the same wording. I would venture a guess that these phrases are perhaps some of the most often stated in the scriptures. What does that tell you?

To press the admonition, I have decided to take the time to include a few of them here. Please be patient. "And I say unto you, Ask, and it shall be given you; seek, and ye shall find; knock, and it shall be opened unto you." (*Luke 11:9*) "If any of you lack wisdom, let him ask of God, that giveth to all men liberally, and upbraideth not; and it shall be given him." (*James 1:5*) "Ask, and it shall be given unto you; seek, and ye shall find; knock, and it shall be opened unto you. For every one that asketh, receiveth; and he that seeketh, findeth; and to him that knocketh, it shall be opened." (*3 Nephi 14:7-8*)[19] "Therefore, ask, and ye shall receive; knock, and it shall be opened unto you; for he that asketh, receiveth; and unto him that knocketh, it shall be opened." (*3 Nephi 27:29*) "Ask, and ye shall receive; knock, and it shall be opened unto you . . ." (*D&C 4:7*) "Therefore, if you will ask of me you shall receive; if you will knock it shall be opened unto you." (*D&C 6:5*) "But ye are commanded, in all things to ask God, who giveth liberally . . . . Therefore, if you will ask of me you shall receive; if you will knock it shall be opened unto you." (*D&C 11:5*) "Therefore, if you will ask of me you shall receive; if you will knock it shall be opened unto you." (*D&C 12:5*) "Therefore, if you will ask of me you shall receive; if you will knock it shall be opened unto you." (*D&C 14:5*) "Behold, I say unto you, go forth as I have commanded you; repent of all your sins; ask and ye shall receive; knock and it shall be opened unto you." (*D&C 49:26*) "—Be patient in affliction. Ask, and ye shall receive; knock, and it shall be opened unto you." (*D&C 66:9*) "Let them ask and they shall receive, knock and it shall be opened unto them, and be made known from on high, even by the Comforter, whither they shall go." (*D&C 75:27*) "Draw near unto me and I will draw near unto you; seek me diligently and ye shall find me; ask, and ye shall receive; knock, and it shall be opened unto you." (*D&C 88:63*) Let me finish my list with my favorite. "Behold, I stand at the door, and knock: if any man hear my voice, and open the door, I will come in to him, and will sup with him, and he with me." (*Revelation 3:20*) There are more but let me get back to the subject at hand.

I Said, Give Me Meat

We don't suddenly say one day, "Oh, I can now throw over the milk, give me steak," anymore than a growing child can take solid foods exclusively when the child hasn't grown the teeth for it. On the other hand, one would not attempt to keep a young child solely on milk through his teen years and on to adulthood. Such a child would probably not receive sufficient nourishment to make it to adulthood. The point, I hope I have made by now, is that some are ready—perhaps past ready—to receive meat. One must, when ready, move on to higher thoughts and concepts. To not do so is to stunt one's spiritual growth. The higher thoughts and concepts to which I refer are not secret, neither are they far out in some distant realm of thinking unrelated to the human condition or otherwise useless information. They are still the basic concepts, only a greater understanding and deeper level of the same.

The Riddle

I once had a religion professor at Brigham Young[20] University (BYU)[21] who, at the beginning of each semester, was fond of asking each new class, "What is the best kept secret of The Mormon Church?" Many put forth their guess that it was priesthood ordinances, temple[22] work, or some such thing as that. He would declare all such answers amiss and would then make this statement, "The best kept secret of The Mormon Church is the Gospel of Jesus Christ!" Naturally, we were all appalled. We, above all, as a church, are missionary minded and spend a very large portion of our means, time, and effort propagating the Gospel of Jesus Christ. How could that be a secret? His follow-up question was, "Well then, what is the Gospel of Jesus Christ?"

As I have often times asked this same question of my Gospel Doctrine classes (an adult Sunday School class in The Mormon Church), I have received many and varied answers. The answer my professor was looking for is, faith in Jesus Christ (not just faith, but faith in Jesus Christ), repentance, baptism of water (for the remission of sins), and Baptism of Fire (the reception of the Holy Ghost). "Wait!" you say, "We have discussed those concepts in nearly every Sunday School class we've attended since our youth." The question is not *what* we discuss, but to what *level* of thinking and understanding we discuss it. I submit, as we will consider in the following chapters, that most of the *mysteries* of the Gospel of Christ, the great secrets of heaven itself, are embedded in those first most basic principles.

Oh, No! I Used That Unsanctioned Word: Mysteries

I cannot say how non-Mormons feel about the mysteries of the Kingdom of God, but it has been my experience as a member of The Mormon Church, that "*we do not delve into the mysteries*." Something about that has stuck in my craw from a very young age. I am not sure how or why we Mormons became so resolute in our determination to stay away from the *mysteries*. Perhaps it was a teacher or even a well-meaning leader who cautioned us against wasting our time on tenets of doctrine that are *not essential to our personal salvation*.

I can't think of any doctrine that does not impact our salvation. Possibly a subject of curiosity alone would not be essential to our salvation, something like the exact width and length of Noah's Ark or what were the colors on Joseph's coat of many colors. Though such facts might be interesting to possess, I must admit they have little, if anything, to do with our eternal salvation. Further, it is doubtful that God would satisfy our curiosity by filling in such small spaces. On the other hand, it might be argued that most, if not all, earthly studies are so infantile and inaccurate when compared to God's knowledge as to render them also a waste of time. But should we not continue to seek? And isn't it true that "—if a person gains more knowledge and intelligence in this life through his diligence and obedience than another, he will have so much the advantage in the world to come.", (*D&C 130:19*) as it is also true that "It is impossible for a man to be saved in ignorance"? (*D&C 131:6*) Does not all truth, no matter what that truth concerns, improve our lives, at least a little, and isn't that improvement worth the study? Does not all truth testify of Christ? "And whatsoever thing is good is just and true; wherefore, nothing that is good denieth Christ, but acknowledgeth that He is." (*Moroni 10:6*)[23] Also, since truths are so inter-related, doesn't one truth inevitably lead to another? Isn't that a good thing? At the very least, the search for and discovery of truth, of any kind, will help us develop our ability to find other, more important truths. I testify that **all** truth is ultimately **essential**, if not for the salvation,[24] then for the exaltation of our souls.

Trivial Pursuit Or How Did It All Get Started?

Perhaps subjects that might be classed among the forbidden mysteries would be, can God build a rock so big He can't lift it? Or who created God or the first God, whichever the case may be? Such brain teasers do more than show our ignorance or lack of capacity to understand, indeed, they prove that our thoughts are not His [God's] thoughts. (see *Isaiah 55:8-9*)

I understand that it is God's plan that we all live by faith, at least at first. According to Moroni, such faith is requisite to knowing. "—I would show unto the world that faith is things which are hoped for and not seen; wherefore, dispute not because ye see not, for ye receive no witness until after the trial of your faith." (*Ether 12:6*)[25] I understand the propriety of not knowing some things at first, and readily admit that there are things God simply does not want us to know right now or while in this life, things that if revealed to us, we would not be capable of understanding, things like the *first great cause of all things*. Bruce R. McConkie put it right. "We do not now know, nor can the mortal mind discern, how all things came to be. We have the divine promise that if we are faithful in all things, the day will come when we shall know 'all things' (*D&C 93:28*) and 'comprehend even God.' (*D&C 88:49*) But for the present our finite limitations shut out the view of the infinite. How element, matter, life, organized intelligence and God Himself first came into being, we can no more comprehend than we can suppose that life, the earth, and the universe shall vanish away." (*The Promised Messiah, by Bruce R. McConkie, pg. 10-pg. 11*)

Brigham Young[26] also gave us some very good advice about seeking for the *first great cause* of things but still admonished us to call upon God and explore the best books in search of greater truths. He said, "Many have tried to penetrate to the First Cause of all things; but it would be as easy for an ant to number the grains of sand on the earth. It is not for man, with his limited intelligence, to grasp eternity in his comprehension. There is an eternity of life, from which we were composed by the wisdom and skill of Superior Beings. It would be as easy for a gnat to trace the history of man back to his origin as for man to fathom the First Cause of all things, lift the veil of eternity, and reveal the mysteries that have been sought after by philosophers from the beginning. What then, should be the calling and duty of the children of men? Instead of inquiring after the origin of Gods—instead of trying to explore the depths of eternities that have been, that are, and that will be, instead of endeavoring to discover the boundaries of boundless space, let them seek to know the object of their present existence, and how to apply, in the most profitable manner for their mutual good and salvation, the intelligence they possess. Let them seek to know and thoroughly understand things within their reach, and to make themselves well acquainted with the object of their being here, by diligently seeking unto a super-power for information and by the careful study of the best books." (*Discourses of Brigham Young, [DBY] pg. 25*)

Certainly, if subjects like the *first great cause* are the kinds of mysteries that are referred to by those telling us to stay away from the mysteries, then I might agree and say that we all just misunderstood the admonition and are once again still free to search out the mysteries of the Gospel of Christ.

Mystery? What's That?

Please note that I said, "Search out the mysteries." I did not say ***speculate*** on them; there is a great difference. When we enter the realm of speculation we are trying to skip the requirements, the prerequisites. Like those stiff-necked Jews who looked beyond the mark (see *Jacob 4:14*), we are trying to skip ahead of the plain and basic truths and failing to lay a solid foundation for our scaffolding to heaven. By so doing, we defeat ourselves at the start. An unstable foundation will teeter and certainly fall. Further, one need not speculate, as all necessary truth is as available as our ability to find it. As I will show later, the gift of truth is available to each individual, not just members of The Church or any other select few. Each of us can find it by seeking, by knocking, by asking, and by searching that which has already been revealed and by developing and preparing ourselves, through righteousness, to receive the gifts of God, one of the greatest being the gift of revelation.

Mysteries, after all, are just things we don't understand. I believe McConkie expressed it well when he said, "A mystery is something which cannot be explained, either because it is beyond human comprehension in general, or because some particular man has not learned enough to understand it. Accordingly, some matters of doctrine, philosophy, or science may be a mystery to one person and not to another. When a thing is understood it is no longer a mystery. In the eternal sense there are no mysteries; all things are known to and understood by Deity; and there will be no mysteries among exalted beings, for they too shall know all things." (*Mormon Doctrine [MD] pg. 523*)[27] "All gospel mysteries become plain and simple and easy to understand once the light of heaven sheds its darkness-dispelling rays into the hearts and souls of sincere seekers of truth." (*The Promised Messiah, by Bruce R. McConkie, pg. 5*)

Since I believe the great mysteries of heaven are found within the first principles of the Gospel of Christ, being told to stick to the basics still frees me to pursue such mysteries. If any are telling us not to study, or search after the mysteries of God, I believe them to be misled. Occasionally, I hear members of The Church quoting Joseph Fielding Smith[28] who was quoting Joseph Smith when he said, "Leave the mysteries alone." To put this in context I refer to the Prophet Joseph's own statement. "Oh, ye elders of Israel, hearken to my voice; and when you are sent into the world to preach, tell those things you are sent to tell, preach and cry aloud, Repent ye, for the kingdom of heaven is at hand; repent and believe the Gospel. Declare the first principles, and let mysteries alone, lest ye be over thrown." (*TPJS, pg. 292*)

He was referring to what the missionaries are to preach when they take the Gospel of Christ to the world. This is entirely consistent with what the Savior Himself said, "And I command you that you preach naught but repentance, and show not these things unto the world until it is wisdom in me. For they cannot bear meat now, but milk they must receive; wherefore, they must not know these things, lest they perish." (*D&C 19:21-22*) To the apostles He admonished, "—Because it is given unto you to know the mysteries of the Kingdom of Heaven, but to them it is not given." (*Matthew 13:11*) In days of old as today, we are told to preach the basics to the newcomers and unbelievers. In fact, the Lord spoke in parables so the rest of the world could not hear or understand. This was explained by Joseph Smith, "And the disciples came and said unto Him, 'Why speakest thou unto them in parables?' I would here remark, that the 'them' made use of in this interrogation, is a personal pronoun, and refers to the multitude. 'He answered and said unto them, that is unto the disciples, because it is given unto you, to know the mysteries of the Kingdom of Heaven, but to them, that is, unbelievers it is not given; for whosoever hath, to him shall be given, and he shall have more abundance; but whosoever hath not, from him shall be taken away even that he hath . . . . Therefore,' says the Savior, 'speak I unto them in parables because they, seeing, see not, and hearing, they hear not, neither do they understand; and in them is fulfilled the prophecy of Esaias, which saith, By hearing ye shall hear, and shall not understand; and seeing ye shall see, and not perceive.'" (*TPJS, pg. 94-95*)

One cannot go on to higher truths without accepting the basics. Said Christ to Nicodemus, "If I have told you earthly things, and ye believed not, how shall ye believe, if I tell you of heavenly things?" (*St. John 3:12*) Again McConkie explains, "That is to say, parables are for non-members of The Church, for those outside the kingdom, or, at best, as we shall see, for those who are weak in the faith; who are not prepared to receive the truth involved in plain words; from whom the full truth must, as yet, remain hidden. To the Twelve, Mary Magdalene, and the other faithful disciples, both male and female, who traveled and ministered with Him, to all of the believing Saints of His day—to them it was given to know the doctrine; from them it need not be hidden in a parable." (*Bruce R. McConkie, The Mortal Messiah, Vol.2, pg. 239*) So it is necessary that all newcomers first drink milk, the basics, before moving on.

Moving On

Once we *have* received, understood, and accepted those basic truths and laid them firmly at the foundation of our scaffolding, we ***must*** move on to greater understanding, even the *mysteries* of God. I fear that, for whatever reason, the vast majority of us, especially old members of The Church (after all, we already have it all don't we?—or do we?), stay on the surface of the doctrines. It is no wonder that they are mysteries to us. Said Joseph Smith (italics for emphasis), "How vain and trifling have been our spirits, our conferences, our councils, our meetings, our private as well as public conversations—too low, too mean, too vulgar, too condescending for the dignified characters of the called and chosen of God, according to the purposes of His will, from before the foundation of the world! *We are called to hold the keys of the mysteries of those things that have been kept hid from the foundation of the world until now.*" (*James R. Clark, Messages of the First Presidency, Vol.1, pg.* 95)[29]

Go Run Against The Wind

Too often we come to our religion classes spiritually famished, supposedly ready for the word of God, and yet we go away hungry. Apostle Jeffrey R. Holland,[30] in his April 1998 conference talk, expressed his concern for the quality of teaching in The Church by asking, "Are we giving them a kind of theological Twinkie—spiritually empty calories?" He further stated, "President John Taylor[31] once called such teaching 'fried froth,' the kind of thing you could eat all day and yet finish feeling totally unsatisfied." ("*A Teacher From God*"—*The Ensign*[32] *May 1998, pg. 26*) It reminded me of my grandfather's comment when asked why he did not like sponge or angel food cake. He said, "You might as well put a funnel in your mouth and go run against the wind!"

Same Ol'—Same Ol'

Week after week we attend our religion classes and stay comfortably on the surface of the same old subjects. Our comments are mostly clichés, true but old and trite (milk not meat). I know, it's boring, but it is also *safe*, or so we think. It is as if we are afraid to *think*. Of what are we afraid? Are we afraid we will be wrong? Most of us are wrong already or at the very least, infantile in our knowledge and understandings. So what? Maybe we think we know it all and that the Lord has nothing left to reveal to us. Oh boy! Perhaps we are just plain lazy or feel that we must wait until God reveals more, not even knowing what He has already revealed. Or, perhaps we have failed to read all those scripture references we quoted above, asserting it is our responsibility to seek, knock, ask, and search in order to find. Some believe that it is all in the *doing*, that is to say, if they will keep obeying the outward commandments, greater knowledge and revelations will come. It will not. These are the same who busy themselves with so much activity in The Church that they have no time to turn around let alone to examine and/or *contemplate* the doctrines. I call this *hyperactivity* and it is often just another way to hide from our duty to our self to personally seek, study, and understand. Of course it is important to be engaged in good causes. "Verily I say, men should be anxiously engaged in a good cause, and do many things of their own free will, and bring to pass much righteousness." (*D&C 58:27*) It is also imperative that we stay in tune with the spirit by keeping the commandments, but that is only half the process. It is a combination of *thinking* **and** *doing*. Do we not understand that we *must* be seeking, searching, and knocking or we will not find? Do we not understand that *thinking* is requisite to understanding? Duh? We must find—no ***make***—time to meditate upon heavenly subjects. Pondering spiritual concepts is nothing less than praying, communicating with God.

In any case, we seem to sit comfortably through our religious discussions, giving little consideration to higher concepts and thoughts or rather deeper understanding of the old basic concepts. That this should *not* be the case, Joseph Smith made clear when he exhorted (italics for emphasis), "I advise all to go on to perfection, and search deeper and deeper into the *mysteries* of Godliness. A man can do nothing for himself unless God direct him in the right way; and the Priesthood is for that purpose." (*TPJS, pg. 364*) "Brethren beloved, continue in brotherly love, walk in meekness, watching unto prayer, that you be not overcome. Follow after peace, as said our beloved brother Paul, that you may be the children of our Heavenly Father, and not give occasion for stumbling, to saint or sinner. Finally, brethren, pray for us, that we may be enabled to do the work whereunto we are called, that you may enjoy the *mysteries* of God, even a fullness; and may the grace of our Lord Jesus Christ be with you all. Amen." (*TPJS, pg. 20*)

Brigham Young also preached this same doctrine. "There is one principle that I wish the people would understand and lay to heart. Just as fast as you will prove before your God that you are worthy to receive the *mysteries*, if you please to call them so, of the Kingdom of Heaven . . . as quick as you prepare to be entrusted with the things of God, there is an eternity of them to bestow upon you." (*DBY, pg. 93*) John Taylor also explains that, "The Melchizedek[33] priesthood holds the *mysteries* of the revelations of God. Wherever that priesthood exists, there also exists a knowledge of the laws of God; and wherever the gospel has existed, there has always been revelation; and where there has been no revelation, there never has been the true gospel." (*DHC, 13:231, May 6, 1870*)[34] Even Joseph Fielding Smith, quoted above as one saying, "Leave the mysteries alone," preached that, "The promise has been made to all those who will receive the light of truth and through their research and obedience endeavor to acquaint themselves with the gospel, that they shall receive line upon line, precept by precept, here a little and there a little, until the fulness of truth shall be their portion; even the hidden *mysteries* of the kingdom shall be made known unto them; 'For every one that asketh receiveth; and he that seeketh findeth; and to him that knocketh it shall be opened.'" (*Joseph Fielding Smith, Doctrines of Salvation, Vol.1, pg. 303*)

The Promise

It is apparent that these prophets taught that we are not only entitled to search after the mysteries, it is our duty to do so. Let me say again that ***it is not necessarily our leaders who are keeping these things secret****. It is our own reluctance to search them out and accept them. It is our own fear, insecurity, indifference, apathy, pride, and unbelief that keep the mysteries mysteries* (*secret*). The Lord Himself said (italics for emphasis), "Seek not for riches but for wisdom, and behold, the *mysteries* of God shall be unfolded unto you, and then shall you be made rich. Behold, he that hath eternal life is rich." (*D&C 6:7*) "And if thou wilt inquire, thou shalt know *mysteries* which are great and marvelous; therefore thou shalt exercise thy gift, that thou mayest find out *mysteries*, that thou mayest bring many to the knowledge of the truth, yea, convince them of the error of their ways." (*D&C 6:11*) "If thou shalt ask, thou shalt receive revelation upon revelation, knowledge upon knowledge, that thou mayest know the *mysteries* and peaceable things—that which bringeth joy, that which bringeth life eternal." (*D&C 42:61*) "But unto him that keepeth my commandments I will give the *mysteries* of my kingdom, and the same shall be in him a well of living water, springing up unto everlasting life." (*D&C 63:23*) "For thus saith the Lord—I, the Lord, am merciful and gracious unto those who fear me, and delight to honor those who serve me in righteousness and in truth unto the end. Great shall be their reward and eternal shall be their glory. And to them will I reveal *all mysteries*, yea, all the *hidden mysteries* of my kingdom from days of old, and for ages to come, will I make known unto them the good pleasure of my will concerning all things pertaining to my kingdom. Yea, even the wonders of eternity shall they know, and things to come will I show them, even the things of many generations. And their wisdom shall be great, and their understanding reach to heaven; and before them the wisdom of the wise shall perish, and the understanding of the prudent shall come to naught. For by my Spirit will I enlighten them, and by my power will I make known unto them the secrets of my will—yea, even those things which eye has not seen, nor ear heard, nor yet entered into the heart of man." (*D&C 76:5-10*) "And this greater priesthood [Melchizedek] administereth the gospel and *holdeth the key of the mysteries of the kingdom*, even the key of the *knowledge of God*." (*D&C 84:19*) "He that keepeth His commandments receiveth truth and light, until he is glorified in truth and *knoweth all things*." (*D&C 93:28*) Could more power be put into a promise? No.

To Whom Is The Promise Given?

It is evident from the above references that the *mysteries* are open and available to *all who will seek after them*, not just a select few. The mysteries of God are not just for those who are General Authorities of The Church, or those evolving from any particular ethnic roots, nor are the mysteries only for those who wear white shirts and ties, have a particular hair style, or any other particular outward appearance, or those who are bishops, or have some other service calling in The Church. You don't even have to be a member of The Church at first, although it is my testimony that as you embark on the road of eternal life, that road will lead you through the earthly ordinances (such as baptism, etc.) necessary for the reception of the above stated endowments of spiritual knowledge. ***Every person* has not only the right, but also the obligation to seek after and find the mysteries of heaven!** *Every person* has within his or her reach, the knowledge of God if they will but seek, knock, open, and obey, if their heads are not like "*hemlock knots*," if they will "*not fly to pieces like glass as soon as anything comes that is contrary to their traditions*."

Sacred Things

Those who have been given to know and understand some of the mysteries of heaven must be very careful to keep what has been entrusted to them sacred, telling others only upon the prompting of the Holy Spirit. "Remember that that which cometh from above is sacred, and must be spoken with care, and by constraint of the Spirit, and in this there is no condemnation, and ye receive the Spirit through prayer; wherefore, without this there remaineth condemnation." (*D&C 63:64*) Brigham Young also said, "If the Lord Almighty should reveal to a High Priest, or to any other than the head, things that are true, or that have been and will be, and show to him the destiny of this people twenty-five years from now, or a new doctrine that will in five, ten, or twenty years hence become the doctrine of this Church and Kingdom, but which has not yet been revealed to this people, and reveal it to him by the same Spirit, the same messenger, the same voice, the same power that gave revelations to the Prophet Joseph Smith when he was living, it would be a blessing to that High Priest, or individual; but he must rarely divulge it to a second person on the face of the earth, until God reveals it through the proper source to become the property of the people at large. Therefore when you hear Elders say that God does not reveal through the President of the Church that which they know, and tell wonderful things, you may generally set it down as a God's truth that the revelation they have had is from the Devil, and not from God. If they had received from the proper source, the same power that revealed to them would have shown them that they must keep the things revealed in their own bosoms, and they seldom would have a desire to disclose them to the second person." (*DBY pg. 338*) Further, we are admonished, relative to those who refuse to accept the truth, to "cast not our pearls before swine" or "Give not that which is holy unto the dogs." (see *Matthew. 7:6; 3 Nephi. 14:6.*)

It should be said here that the Prophet Joseph understood well the importance of keeping hallowed things sacred and secret from those who would degrade them. "But great and marvelous are the works of the Lord, and the mysteries of His kingdom which He showed unto us, which surpass all understanding in glory, and in might, and in dominion; *Which He commanded us we should not write while we were yet in the Spirit, and are not lawful for man to utter*; *Neither is man capable to make them known*, for they are only to be seen and understood by the power of the Holy Spirit, which God bestows on those who love Him, and purify themselves before Him; To whom He grants this privilege of seeing and knowing for themselves." (*D&C 76:114-117*) Joseph Smith knew that the only way to understand or see these things is *by the power of the Holy Spirit, which God bestows on those who love Him and purify themselves before Him.* Again, those who have eyes to see and ears to hear will be the only ones that will receive the mysteries.

I do not worry that I might be seeking after forbidden things because *if* I am not supposed to have something, it will not be revealed. Also, I don't believe I am in danger of revealing, within these writings, any forbidden thing for if "*man is not capable of making them known*," I certainly am not. Further, all of which I speak has already been revealed and, as I stated before, I will stick close to the scriptures and the revealed word. They will be my protection. Since these concepts are readily found throughout the revealed word, I feel not only licensed to study them, but compelled to do so. Apostle McConkie minced no words when he said, "That scriptures dealing with all these and a host of other Messianic matters might easily be misconstrued, as they have been by the learned in an apostate Christendom, is perfectly clear. Our problem is to come to a proper understanding of their meaning. We cannot brush them aside as though they were an unnecessary part of revealed writ. The mere fact that the Lord has preserved them for us in the scriptures is a sufficient witness that He expects us to ponder their deep and hidden meanings so that we shall be as fully informed about His eternal laws as were the Saints of old." (*Bruce R. McConkie, The Promised Messiah, pg. 8*)

My purpose and hope, in writing this book, is that I may perhaps inspire and enhance others' understanding of some of these eternal, celestial principles; those same principles of God that Joseph Smith (and I must add, all of the prophets since) tried for a number of years to get into the hemlock knot heads of the Saints. I will herein attempt to comply with the commandment given by our Lord as recorded in *The Doctrine and Covenants*, "And I give unto you a commandment that you shall teach one another the doctrine of the kingdom. Teach ye diligently and my grace shall attend you, that you may be instructed more perfectly in theory, in principle, in doctrine, in the law of the gospel, in all things that pertain unto the kingdom of God, that are expedient for you to understand;" (*D&C 88:77-78*)

Say It Again

At the risk of being redundant in my attempt to make it abundantly clear that once we have received the basics we ***must search out the mysteries,*** let me leave a few more testimonies.

Paul said to the Corinthians (italics for emphasis), "But as it is written, Eye hath not seen, nor ear heard, neither have entered into the heart of man, the things which God hath prepared for them that love Him. But God hath revealed them unto us by His Spirit: for the Spirit searcheth all things, yea, *the deep things of God* . . . But the natural man receiveth not the things of the Spirit of God: for they are foolishness unto him: neither can he know them, because they are spiritually discerned. But he that is spiritual judgeth all things, yet he himself is judged of no man. For who hath known the mind of the Lord, that he may instruct him? But we have the mind of Christ." (*1 Corinthians 2:9-10, 14-16*) He further said, "Let a man so account of us, as of the ministers of Christ, and stewards of the *mysteries* of God." (*1 Corinthians 4:1*) From the ancient prophets of the American continents we receive the same testimony. Nephi[35] taught us, "For he that diligently seeketh shall find; and the *mysteries of God shall be unfolded unto them*, by the power of the Holy Ghost, as well in these times as in times of old, and as well in times of old as in times to come; wherefore, the course of the Lord is one eternal round." (*1 Nephi 10:19*)[36] Jacob tells us, "Behold, great and marvelous are the works of the Lord. How unsearchable are the depths of the *mysteries* of Him; and it is impossible that man should find out all His ways. And no man knoweth of His ways save it be revealed unto him; wherefore, brethren, *despise not the revelations of God.*" (*Jacob 4:8*) King Benjamin,[37] in a great prophetic speech to his people, said, "And these are the words which he spake and caused to be written, saying: My brethren, all ye that have assembled yourselves together, you that can hear my words which I shall speak unto you this day; for I have not commanded you to come up hither to trifle with the words which I shall speak, but that you should hearken unto me, and open your ears that ye may hear, and your hearts that ye may understand, and your minds that the *mysteries of God may be unfolded to your view*." (*Mosiah 2:9*)[38] Alma[39] also taught this doctrine. "And now Alma began to expound these things unto him, saying: It is given unto many to *know the mysteries* of God; nevertheless they are laid under a strict command that they shall not impart only according to the portion of His word which he doth grant unto the children of men, according to the heed and diligence which they give unto Him. And therefore, he that will harden his heart, the same receiveth the lesser portion of the word; and he that will not harden his heart, to him is given the greater portion of the word, until it is given unto him to *know the mysteries of God* until he know them in full." (*Alma 12:9-10*)[40] "Yea, he that repenteth and exerciseth faith, and bringeth forth good works, and prayeth continually without ceasing—unto such it is given to *know the mysteries of God*; yea, unto such it shall be given to reveal things which never have been revealed; yea, and it shall be given unto such to bring thousands of souls to repentance, even as it has been given unto us to bring these our brethren to repentance." (*Alma 26:22*) "Seek not for riches but for wisdom; and, behold, *the mysteries of God shall be unfolded unto you*, and then shall you be made rich. Behold, he that hath eternal life is rich." (*D&C 11:7*)

In the interest of saving space, the above references are but a few that I have compiled over the years. My motivation for preparing such a list of related references was born out of my need to save time and smooth out interruptions when teaching Gospel Doctrine Class.[41] More than occasionally, someone would say that "we should not delve into the mysteries," at which time I would simply hand them a copy of my comprehensive list and go on with the particular lesson at hand. I never had a student come back with the same statement after they studied the references.

Who Can Believe? Who Can Know?

I hate to say this and I am grateful that it does not happen very often but unfortunately some church members, even some leaders, for reasons that are not entirely clear to me, feel compelled to censor the information to which other church members may have access. They seem bound to protect others from exposure to anything they deem contrary to what they think and believe is, or should be, church doctrine. Even some that may agree with the doctrines take it upon themselves to determine whether the rest of us *are ready* for such mysteries, as if we are so devoid of the spirit of discernment that we are without the ability to make these choices for ourselves. This seems a little like an old familiar program to remove our God-given agency. What is worse, a few of these self-appointed monitors, too often out of insecurity, feel compelled to "fix" anyone whose views, beliefs, and traditions differ from their own. On occasion they even seem obliged to make enemies of those who do not conform to their own standards or beliefs. This is most unfortunate and certainly not in keeping with the spirit of brotherly love that should prevail.

I here testify that the mysteries of the Kingdom of God are not promised only to a select few, General Authorities, Bishops, or the like. This is a promise to **all** who will humble themselves, rid themselves of all vanity, fear, and unbelief. "And we know also, that sanctification through the grace of our Lord and Savior Jesus Christ is just and true, *to all* those who love and serve God with all their mights, minds, and strength." (*D&C 20:31*) The mysteries are accessible to all. They are promised to all. They are promised to you!

Over My Dead Body

We somehow readily accept the idea that at our death we will suddenly be zapped into being righteous people worthy enough to know the mysteries of God and to stand in His presence. The irony is that if we don't find righteousness at some point in life, after death we will not be privileged to know the mysteries either, not until we become righteous in that state of being. "And then cometh the judgment of the Holy One upon them; and then cometh the time that he that is filthy shall be filthy still; and he that is righteous shall be righteous still; he that is happy shall be happy still; and he that is unhappy shall be unhappy still." (*Mormon 9:14*)[42]

For some reason we still refuse to believe that it is possible to know the mysteries of God while in the flesh (italics for emphasis). "But great and marvelous are the works of the Lord, and the mysteries of His kingdom . . .— they are only to be seen and understood by the power of the Holy Spirit, which God bestows on those who love Him, and purify themselves before Him; To whom He grants this privilege of seeing and knowing for themselves; That through the power and manifestation of the Spirit, *while in the flesh*, they may be able to bear His presence in the world of glory." (*D&C 76:114, 116-118*)

Our reluctance to believe that we could actually receive the mysteries of God while in the flesh may give us a hint as to our perception of our personal state of worthiness. But the more *worthy* we feel, the easier it is to accept that such a thing is possible. Actually, the more *humble* we feel, the more likely it *will* happen (more on this later). **We *must come to believe*** that we may have the privilege of receiving the mysteries of the kingdom or be condemned not to have it happen. Why do we not believe?

Condemnation?—Who?

Unfortunately, we, the so-called *Saints of Zion*,[43] are under condemnation as a result of this unbelief (italics for emphasis). "And your minds in times past have been darkened *because of unbelief*, and *because you have treated lightly the things you have received* . . . Which *vanity and unbelief* have brought the whole church under condemnation. And this condemnation resteth upon the children of Zion, even all. And they shall remain under this condemnation until they repent and remember the new covenant, even *The Book of Mormon* and the former commandments which I have given them, not only to say, but to do according to that which I have written . . . That they may bring forth fruit meet for their Father's kingdom; otherwise there remaineth a scourge and judgment to be poured out upon the children of Zion." (*D&C 84:54-58*)

Now this is no idle condemnation. The Lord is telling us that because of our *vanity and unbelief* and because we have treated lightly the things we have received, we are under condemnation. He was *not* talking to the world in general here. He was talking to the *children of Zion*, the members of the restored church. This revelation was given in 1832, only two years after The Church was organized. We remain under this condemnation, scourge, and judgment to this day, despite the invitation, proclamation, and blessing of a living Prophet in a General Conference[44] on April 6, 1986, to come out from under it. In that conference, the Prophet Ezra Taft Benson[45] disclosed again why we must turn our attention to the study of *The Book of Mormon* when he said, "Now, in our day, the Lord has revealed the need to reemphasize *The Book of Mormon* to get The Church and all the children of Zion out from under condemnation—the scourge and the judgment. This message must be carried to the members of The Church throughout the world . . . . *The Book of Mormon* declares that 'everything which inviteth and enticeth to do good, and to love God, and to serve Him is inspired of God . . . . And whatsoever thing . . . persuadeth men to do evil, and believe not in Christ, and deny Him, and serve not God, then ye may know with a perfect knowledge it is of the devil.' (*Moroni 7:13-17*) . . . Now, in the authority of the sacred priesthood in me vested, I invoke my blessing upon the Latter-day Saints and upon good people everywhere. I bless you with increased discernment to judge between Christ and anti-Christ. I bless you with increased power to do good and to resist evil. I bless you with increased understanding of *The Book of Mormon.* I promise you that from this moment forward, if we will daily sup from its pages and abide by its precepts, that God will pour out upon each child of Zion and The Church a blessing hitherto unknown—begin to lift the condemnation—the scourge and judgment. Of this I bear solemn witness." (*Ensign, May 1986, pg. 78*) These are the words of a living prophet to you and to me. Let us give ear that we may receive "a blessing hitherto unknown."

What is this vanity? It is pride. It is *treating lightly the things that God has already given us*. And what has He already given us? The *Gospel of Jesus Christ*, His priesthood power, the opportunity to know the mysteries of the Kingdom of God. What have we done with this opportunity to know the mysteries? Have we, who have already had the milk, moved on to the meat of the Gospel? I fear we have not. We, the so-called *Saints*, are dawdling around with lesser laws, truths, doctrines, carnal commandments, and outward performances when the Lord wishes, in fact *has* revealed to us, to those of us who hopefully have eyes to see and ears to hear, a much greater light. Those who have been ordained to the higher Melchizedek Priesthood, and/or received their temple endowments presumably are ready to move on to this greater light. "And this greater priesthood [Melchizedek] administereth the gospel and *holdeth the key of the mysteries of the kingdom*, even the key of the *knowledge of God*." (*D&C 84:19*) To receive the mysteries of the kingdom and the knowledge of God is what the endowment is. That is what the Melchizedek Priesthood is for. That is why we go to the temple of our God, to learn how to receive this transfer of His heavenly powers. The temple teaches us about it. We go through the outward ordinance (our temple endowment) to prepare us to actually receive the mysteries of the kingdom and meet God. Just as the outward ordinance of baptism prepares us to receive the inward power, the spiritual Gift of The Holy Ghost, receiving our temple endowment prepares us to actually receive the gift of eternal life. Do we understand this? Are we actively seeking, asking for it, or as a result of apathy, vanity, and unbelief do we blind ourselves to greater light by *lightly treating the things that God has already given us*? Apparently the Lord thinks that is precisely what many of us are doing. "But behold, verily I say unto you, that there are many who have been ordained among you, whom I have called but few of them are chosen. They who are not chosen have sinned a very grievous sin, in that they are walking in darkness at noon-day." (*D&C 95:5-6*)

What is this, not just sin, not just *grievous sin*, but ***very grievous sin***? Please note: the Lord is not saying because of sin we are walking in darkness at noon-day. He is saying *that **is** the sin*, to be walking in darkness at noon-day. In other words, the light of Christ is cast upon us yet we refuse to see it, we don't believe we can actually be chosen. We do not believe we can know the mysteries of God nor do we believe we can know Him, God. "The light shineth in darkness, and the darkness comprehendeth it not . . . ." (*D&C 88:49*)

It is not that the light is not there. In fact, it is the law and property of light that it cannot be extinguished by darkness. That is to say, you cannot put darkness in a lighted place and expect that darkness to overtake and extinguish the light. On the contrary, a single candle can be put in the darkness of the immensity of space and that darkness has not the ability to quench the light. It shines on. The light is there and radiates through that space. We can however, cover that light or hide our eyes from it. Nevertheless, the light is there. God's light is always there in abundance but we blind ourselves and choose to walk in darkness at noon-day. This is a *very grievous sin.* Because of our *vanity* and *unbelief*, because we, in our vanity, think we have already arrived, we pass on the opportunity to know, to *actually know* the mysteries of the kingdom.

See My Pretty Keys

To *not* seek after the mysteries is to deny the very purpose of the priesthood. Let me say again, that to *not* seek after the mysteries of heaven is to deny the very purpose of the Melchizedek Priesthood, which holds these keys. Unlike the lesser or Aaronic Priesthood which holds the keys of the ministering of angels and to administer in outward ordinances (see *D&C 107:20*), "the power and authority of the higher, or Melchizedek Priesthood, is to hold the keys of all the spiritual blessings of The Church. *To have the privilege of receiving the mysteries of the kingdom of heaven, to have the heavens opened unto them,* to commune with the general assembly and church of the Firstborn, and *to enjoy the communion and presence of God the Father, and Jesus the mediator of the new covenant.*" (*D&C 107:19*) Presumably, if we have been endowed or have received this Melchizedek Priesthood we ***should*** be seeking after the mysteries of the kingdom. This is the *purpose* of that Priesthood. This is the reason God gave it to us. This is the key; these are the tools. Really!

In the words of my good friend Dan Lambson, "Oh we have the keys all right. We fondle them a lot but seldom use them to open any doors to the mysteries of heaven."

To not seek after the mysteries is a notion I have found not only foreign to what God expects of us, but I believe it to be a cop out by those of us too lazy or fearful to explore the thoughts of God.

Fear, How Debilitating

We have only ourselves to blame for laziness but I might say that I understand the fear element. To be given an understanding of the mysteries of heaven might shake the socks off anyone. On top of that, "For of him unto whom much is given, much is required, and he who sins against the greater light shall receive the greater condemnation." (*D&C 82:3*) It is not only easier but *safer* to continue quibbling about the lesser laws, carnal commandments, and outward performances such as the Word of Wisdom,[46] keeping the Sabbath day holy, paying our tithes and offerings[47], keeping the 10 commandments, and etc. It might be said that like the scribes and Pharisees, we omit the weightier matters of the law. "Woe unto you, scribes and Pharisees, hypocrites! for ye pay tithe of mint and anise and cummin, and have omitted the weightier matters of the law, judgment, mercy, and faith; these ought ye to have done, and not to leave the other undone." (*Matthew 23:23*) "But before faith came, we were kept under the law, shut up unto the faith which should afterwards be revealed. Wherefore the law was our schoolmaster *to bring us* unto Christ, that we might be justified by faith. But after that faith is come, we are no longer under a schoolmaster. (*Galatians 3:23-25*)

Two Gospels

We are doing the same thing today. We muddle around in argument about what laws we are bound to keep and which we are not, and how to go about it. We think it is safer to keep only to these outward performances than to reach to the heavens for greater light, knowledge, and gifts. I testify that these are lesser laws. The gospel of repentance, baptism of water and obedience to the carnal commandments and performances is the *lesser gospel*. "And the lesser priesthood continued, which priesthood holdeth the key of the ministering of angels and the preparatory gospel; Which gospel is the gospel of repentance and of baptism, and the remission of sins, and the law of carnal commandments, which the Lord in His wrath caused to continue with the house of Aaron . . . ." (*D&C 84:26-27*). Not that this gospel and these laws are not important; on the contrary, they are our foundation, they are the schoolmaster and should be strictly obeyed, if we can (more on this later). But when shall we study or at least take notice of the greater gospel? Must we hear the same old rhetoric, year after year, in Gospel Doctrine class? Where is the depth? Where is the new? Where is the change? Where is the progress? How may we expect to progress if we are clinging to the old at the exclusion of the new? Let us take those same doctrines and go to a greater level of understanding.

We might subconsciously think that if we don't study or learn a higher law, we will not be held accountable for living that law. Said George Q. Cannon,[48]

"God does not hold people accountable for that which they do not know, or that which they have not had an opportunity of knowing. Where there is no law, there is no transgression. Transgression commences when the law is received and men reject it." (*Journal of Discourses, George Q. Cannon, Vol. 20, pg. 247*) Though it is true that we are not held accountable for laws which we do not know, it is also true that *we will never be sanctified nor glorified by those laws either* (see *D&C 88:21-24*). As we will learn in an ensuing chapter, even the Mormons are lulling themselves into a false sense of security by adhering to what they think are the highest celestial laws, when in fact, they are lesser laws. Whether wittingly or unwittingly, we are hiding from greater responsibility and consequently higher blessings. We think because we have complied with the lesser laws, are paying a full tithe, living the Word of Wisdom, attending meetings, even attending the temple,[49] we *have it made*. We don't!

There is a *greater gospel*. We must find out what it is and we must live it. "*And this greater priesthood administereth the gospel and holdeth the key of the mysteries of the kingdom, even the key of the knowledge of* God. Therefore, *in the ordinances thereof, the power of godliness is manifest*." (*D&C 84:19-20*)

Like baptism itself, there are the outward parts of all ordinances (baptism by water) and inward or spiritual parts (Baptism of Fire and the Holy Ghost). One without the other is only half a baptism. The same is true relative to the temple ordinances, as well as other commandments and performances. How many will be shocked at the last day when they discover that *continual progress* was as important as any other principle? "How many will be able to abide a celestial law, and go through and receive their exaltation, I am unable to say, as many are called, but few are chosen." (*TPJS pg. 331*)

Then there is the matter of being held accountable for the *opportunity of knowing*. All men must one day stand before God and answer for themselves concerning what they chose to accept or reject, even the opportunity of the same. In this author's mind, hiding behind ignorance is only another form of damnation. Remember that the Lord said, "It is impossible for a man to be saved in ignorance." (*D&C 131:6*) Where is the forward progress? Where is the change? Without change, there is no progress. Do we expect to have a different experience without *doing something different*?

Danger, But Not Ahead

Still, as I said before, I can certainly understand the apprehension associated with learning higher concepts and principles. It's like staying far away from a door that leads to an unknown room so there's little chance of being harmed by what might be on the other side. On the other hand, if we fail to try the door, how will we ever know what *good* thing may be waiting there? The Lord has guaranteed us that He waits on the other side of the door. All we need to do is believe Him, knock, and enter.

There is a great danger in not advancing in truth as expressed by Bruce R. McConkie when he said, "Those who harden their hearts against gospel truth soon become engulfed in total spiritual darkness in which they know nothing concerning God and His mysteries; and then they are taken captive by the Devil, and led by his will down to destruction. Now this is what is meant by the chains of hell."(*MD pg. 120*) We must split our hemlock knot heads and let in new things.

Of course higher laws are *new things*. Do we expect that advancement or progress will not require the acceptance of *new things*? How absurd. We must face the new—new concepts, new ideas, new laws, new understandings—**or** face damnation.

It seems that our eternal progress, our hope of reaching to the heavens, depends on accepting new truth and more of it. We must keep moving forward or be dammed in our progress and, by default, fall back. Many, due to laziness, don't bother to even *think* about moving on to higher concepts, let alone make the effort to put such thoughts into practice. Like the Israelites of old, they methodically move through life, not even understanding the laws they are living and consequently, never gaining the ability to live higher ones. Again, by default, they fall back. "Wherefore, now after I have spoken these words, if ye cannot understand them it will be because ye ask not, neither do ye knock; wherefore, ye are not brought into the light, but must perish in the dark." (*2 Nephi 32:4*)

Also because of our vanity (see *D&C 84:54-58*) we think we have already arrived. Believe it or not, some of us actually think we know enough and that the Lord has nothing left to reveal to us. This is truer than most of us would like to admit. Such a vain posture (whether admitted or not) causes us to pass on the opportunity to know, to actually know the mysteries of the kingdom.

The Lord told Nephi this would be the condition of the Saints in the latter-days, "For behold, at that day shall he [the Devil] rage in the hearts of the children of men, and stir them up to anger against that which is good. And others will he *pacify, and lull them away into carnal security*, that they will say: *All is well in Zion*; yea, Zion prospereth, all is well—and thus the devil cheateth their souls, and leadeth them away carefully down to hell. Therefore, *wo be unto him that is at ease in Zion!* Wo be unto him that crieth: All is well! Yea, wo be unto him that hearkeneth unto the precepts of men, and *denieth the power of God, and the gift of the Holy Ghost!* Yea, wo be unto him that saith: *We have received, and we need no more!* And in fine, wo unto all those who tremble, and are angry because of the truth of God! For behold, he that is built upon the rock receiveth it with gladness; and he that is built upon a sandy foundation trembleth lest he shall fall. Wo be unto him that shall say: *We have received the word of God, and we need no more of the word of God, for we have enough!* For behold, thus saith the Lord God: I will give unto the children of men line upon line, precept upon precept, here a little and there a little; and blessed are those who hearken unto my precepts, and lend an ear unto my counsel, for they shall learn wisdom; for unto him that receiveth I will give more; and from them that shall say, We have enough, from them shall be taken away even that which they have." (*2 Nephi 28:20-22, 24-30*) Again, the Lord is not speaking to the world at large here. He is speaking to us, the members of The Church. How many of us, because we have received so much, think we have received enough and need no more? How many of us have taken on the values of men and deny the power of God to receive His mysteries? How many of us even become angry when more truth is presented to us?

Don't Stop!

Living on the edge is frightening indeed, as one runs the risk of falling, but our scaffolding is there, and if it is secure, it will bear us up. We must have faith in God, that He will give us the gift of discernment of truth and gradually reveal what is right for us to know as we carefully increase the height of our scaffolding on a firm foundation of basic truths. Then we must learn to trust in our scaffolding, to hold tight to it as we contemplate the mysteries of God and build on.

So where do we decide to stop? When do we say, "We have received the word of God, and we need no more of the word of God, for we have enough!" (*2 Nephi 28:29*) Wherever it is, that is our damnation. We need to ask ourselves where we draw the line? Where is our own personal damnation?

Let us not choose either consciously or unwittingly to stop seeking, knocking, and receiving more truth, higher laws, and new things, even the mysteries of God. Let us open our minds and hearts to the many things God has to reveal to us, as Brigham Young said, ". . . an eternity of them to bestow upon us."

"Since it is impossible for a man to be saved in ignorance of God and His laws, and since man is saved no faster than he gains knowledge of Jesus Christ and the plan of salvation, it follows that men are obligated at their peril, to learn and apply the true doctrines of the gospel." (*Mormon Doctrine, Preface* by Bruce R. McConkie) What more can I say upon this subject?

---

[13] **(TPJS), *Teachings of the Prophet Joseph Smith*, compiled by Joseph Fielding Smith, contain some of Joseph's writings taken from various sermons during his ministry.**

[14] **Joseph Smith (Jr.) was the first prophet and founder of The LDS Church from 1830 to 1844.**

[15] **Jacob was a prophet living on the South American continent approximately 544 BC.**

[16] ***The Book of Mormon* (B of M) is a history of the ancient inhabitants of the American continents (the forefathers of the American, Central, and South American Indians) from 1200 BC to 420 AD and God's dealing with them. The book is named after one of the ancient prophets who lived approximately 400 years AD. *The Book of Mormon* was written on plates of gold, which were given to Joseph Smith (the first latter-day prophet of The Church of Jesus Christ of Latter-day Saints) in 1827 by an angel of God. He then translated them by the power of God into what is now *The Book of Mormon*, which is accepted by The LDS church as scripture equal to *The Holy Bible* in importance.**

[17] **The book of Jacob can be found in *The Book of Mormon*, which is a record of many such prophets kept by their hand (see above note).**

[18] ***The Doctrine and Covenants* (D&C) is a collection of modern day revelations from God to Joseph Smith and other latter-day prophets. It is considered by The LDS Church as scripture.**

[19] **3 Nephi is a book in *The Book of Mormon* (see note on *The Book of Mormon*) covering the period from 1 AD to 35 AD. The book is named after a prophet of God that lived at that time. It includes an account of Christ's appearance to the ancient natives of North, South, and Central America.**

[20] **Brigham Young was the second Prophet of The LDS Church from 1847 to 1877.**

[21] **Brigham Young University, established by Brigham Young (originally the Brigham Young Academy), is a private university owned by The LDS Church. It is located in Provo, Utah.**

[22] **The Mormon Church builds temples for holy worship, higher learning, and the performance of sacred ordinances for the living and the dead.**

[23] **The book of Moroni is found in *The Book of Mormon* and covers the period from 400 AD to 421 AD. Moroni was the last prophet to write in *The Book of Mormon*, as his people had become so wicked that they ceased to keep a written record.**

[24] **It is generally accepted as Mormon doctrine that salvation is to be saved in The Kingdom of God in the heavens and that exaltation is to be in the highest part of that kingdom.**

[25] **The book of Ether is found in *The Book of Mormon*. Ether was the last prophet of a people called Jaredites. They came to the South American continent from the Tower of Babel when the tongues were confounded. Their civilization grew into a great nation but they began to war with each other and finally completely destroyed themselves. Their record was preserved by the hand of God and found by a later group of people called Nephites. (See Note 28)**

---

[26] **Brigham Young was the second Prophet of The LDS Church from 1847 to 1877.**

[27] ***Mormon Doctrine* (MD): written by Bruce R. McConkie.**

[28] **Joseph Fielding Smith was the 10th prophet of The LDS Church from 1970 to 1972.**

[29] **This was a message from Joseph Smith sent March 25, 1839, to the membership of The LDS Church. Joseph was being unjustly held with his brother and some of his friends in the Liberty Jail, Liberty, Missouri. This and many other messages of the first presidency of The LDS Church down through the years were compiled and published in 1964 by James R. Clark, a Brigham Young University (BYU) religion professor.**

[30] **Jeffrey R. Holland is a current member of the Counsel of the 12 Apostles.**

[31] **John Taylor was the third prophet of The LDS Church from 1880 to 1887.**

[32] ***The Ensign* is a Church produced and sanctioned, monthly publication containing conference reports, inspiring stories, and articles on other Church-related information.**

[33] **There are two divisions to the priesthood of God in The LDS Church, the Aaronic, or lesser, and the Melchizedek, or higher.**

[34] ***The Documentary History of the Church* (DHC) vol. 13 pg. 231, May 6, 1870.**

[35] **Nephi was a prophet to his people on the South American continent approximately 600 BC. A portion of his people were named after him (Nephites). A more rebellious group was named after his brother Laman, the Lamanites. These two groups warred against each other throughout most of the history of *The Book of Mormon*.**

[36] **The book of 1 Nephi is a book in *The Book of Mormon*; written by Nephi, covering the history of the ancient inhabitants of the South American continent from the time they left Jerusalem in 600 BC to 570 BC.**

[37] **King Benjamin was a king and prophet to his people on the South American continent approximately 125 BC.**

[38] **The book of Mosiah is a book in *The Book of Mormon* covering the history of the ancient inhabitants of the South American continent from 130 BC to 91 BC.**

[39] **Alma was a great prophet to his people on the South American continent approximately 80 BC.**

[40] **The book of Alma is a book in *The Book of Mormon*, written by Alma, covering the history of the ancient inhabitants of the South American continent from 91 BC to 53 BC.**

[41] **The Gospel Doctrine Class is one of the adult Sunday School classes in the LDS Church**

[42] **There is a book of Mormon found in *The Book of Mormon* written by the hand of Mormon, a prophet who died 401 AD. When he died, the book was finished by his son Moroni. The book covers the history of the ancient North, Central, and South American Indian or native inhabitants from 322 AD to about 400 AD when his people became so wicked that they warred and destroyed each other in great numbers.**

---

[43] **Whether a single person, a group, or a place, Zion is generally considered to be the place where God's accepted, righteous, pure in heart people dwell.**

[44] **The Church holds General Conferences semi-annually, where the apostles and prophets of the presiding leadership issue counsel, teachings, new doctrines, and revelations to the membership.**

[45] **Ezra Taft Benson was the 13th prophet of the church, 1985 to 1994.**

[46] **The Word of Wisdom is a health law given by the Lord in 1833 to Joseph Smith for the benefit of The Saints. It prohibits the use of tobacco, tea, coffee, and alcohol, as well as prescribing the proper use of many other substances. It is found in full in D&C 89.**

[47] **The Mormons believe that the law of the tithe requires them to give, as a free will offering to The Church, a tenth of their worldly income. Other offerings may include offerings specifically to benefit the poor, missionaries, or some other special need.**

[48] **George Q. Cannon was an apostle of The LDS Church from 1860 to 1901 and served as counselor to four prophets (Brigham Young, John Taylor, Wilford Woodruff, and Lorenzo Snow).**

[49] **The Mormons build temples wherein they go to comply with higher priesthood ordinances and covenants, which will qualify them for exhalation, a greater endowment from God than salvation alone.**

2
Elusive Truth, Where Art Thou?

Your Choice

Some years ago I had a friend who was an atheist. We worked at the same location and would carpool for a thirty-minute commute each morning and afternoon. This gave us time to talk and we would often debate philosophy and religion. I somehow felt compelled to try to convert him to a belief in God. We had many deep and wonderful discussions but he was very secure in what he believed and I could not arouse in him a need to see things differently. I would spend much time researching various topics, looking for proof that I could use to convince him of the error of his way, but failed in my attempts. I found myself feeling a certain responsibility, even guilt, for what he believed and my inability to convince him of the truth.

In our attempt to find common ground upon which to build a case, the subject matter of the discussions became more and more basic. Finally, we came down to the concept of truth itself and there we stayed until my friend made the following statement, "Well," he said, "you know, we all believe what we choose to believe regardless of what is true." To others this statement may not mean much. It shocked me at the time and has haunted me ever since. I had always felt that I didn't really have a choice. Once a truth came to my awareness, I was then duty bound to accept it and to put it into operation, so to speak. I have, since that time, come to the conclusion that I was taught one of the greatest truths of my life by an atheist.

This realization, that *we all believe what we* ***choose*** *to believe*, has impacted my thinking and my life beyond my ability to express. It has proven to be one of the basic truths or foundation planks in my heavenward scaffolding. It has freed me from the guilt or responsibility I have felt from time to time for what others believe; after all, it is their choice to believe what they will. It has given me greater insight into my own need and responsibility to properly discern truth.

Prior to understanding this principle, I thought that *if I* believed something, it *must* be true, because, of course, I am committed to believing only that which is true. I did not realize that what I believe is *what I choose to believe*. I guess I assumed that since I believed a certain thing, it had to be true because I would never be able to believe something unless it was true. I had it backwards. It wasn't that something was true and then I believed it. It was as if I first believed something and that belief was evidence of its truth. In my mind my belief and the truth were one and the same. I now recognize that *what I choose to believe, and what is truth, can be two entirely different things*. For the first time in my life, I realized **I could be wrong!** Shock, huh? Somehow, this had never occurred to me previously. I now know that our motivations, our desires, control the choice of what we believe.

Since I have come to this realization the old saying, "A man convinced against his will is of the same opinion still," has taken on new meaning. Further, I now recognize that if you wish to change someone's beliefs, you must first change his or her motivation for that belief, and then you have a chance of changing the belief itself. This is very difficult to do as often our motivations for our beliefs are deeply hidden, frequently in our subconscious. Often we don't even know ourselves, why we believe what we believe.

At the very least, this knowledge has caused me to seriously review my motivations for what I have ***chosen*** to believe.

In our ensuing discussion about truth, please keep in mind that, for whatever reasons we have; *we believe what we* ***choose*** *to believe, regardless of what is true.*

The Simple Truth

I feel it is necessary, before we progress to any other subject, that we spend some time on the concept of truth. As determined as we Mormons are to find truth and lay hold upon it, the properties and characteristics of truth remain a great secret to us. This seems very strange, especially in light of all that the Lord has revealed on the subject to modern prophets.

As discussed in the previous chapter, it is paramount, for the sake of stability that we place at the foundation of our scaffolding to heaven, solid blocks or planks of truth upon which, or against which, we will weigh all other truths. Let us start by defining truth. I have yet to find a better definition than that given us by the Lord Himself. "And Truth is knowledge of things as they are, and as they were, and as they are to come." (*D&C 93:24*) In other words, truth is having a cognizance of what *really is*, what *really was*, and what *really will be*. I will refer to this definition many times in the coming pages.

An Absolute Maybe

Notwithstanding our definition, the characteristics of truth can be confusing, like, why is truth so hard to come by? Why is something true in one situation and not in another, or is it? Where is truth found? How do we get it? How do we know it, and is truth relative to the situation or absolute? Most religious people will say that truth is absolute, no matter what the situation, otherwise their beliefs become subject to the change of the situation.

For the sake of discussion, let us examine some *absolute* religious truths. "Thou shalt not bear false witness . . . ." (*Exodus 20:16*) "Thou shalt not lie; he that lieth and will not repent shall be cast out." (*D&C 42:21*) We all know that we should not lie. This is a basic, somewhat self-evident truth. Still, you will remember that Abraham lied about his wife Sarah, so that he would not be killed. He said she was his sister (see *Genesis 12: & 20:2*). Though a lie, this was not considered a sin. Also, you will have probably heard the scenario where a frantic young woman comes to your door crying that there is a rapist murderer chasing her and she pleads for help and protection. You let her in and give her refuge. Soon the murderer comes to the door and asks you if the young woman is inside. Of course you say, "no." By definition, this is a lie. It certainly is *not* things as they really are. There is no way to get around that, yet who in their right mind would condemn you for so saying? The question is not whether or not the lie is a sin, but why a lie is a sin in one situation and not another? At any rate, if our scenario is a true situation, we cannot say it is true *absolutely*, that "Thou shalt not lie."

Perhaps one of the surest truths is the commandment, "Thou shalt not kill." That seems straightforward enough, safe enough. Yet when we examine the history of killing in a religious setting, we find that David killed Goliath (*1 Samuel 17:49*) and the act was not only accepted, it was praised. The Lord commanded the children of Israel "Thou shalt not kill," yet before they entered the Land of Canaan, after their 40-year hike through the wilderness, they were commanded to kill *all living things*. (see *Deuteronomy 3:7, 7:1-3* & *Joshua 12*) The Mormons are very familiar with a similar incident in the history of the ancient South American inhabitants. While still in Jerusalem where they came from, a Prophet by the name of Nephi, in order to obtain a record of his people and a copy of their religious law to take with him to his new world (South America), was compelled by an angel of the Lord to kill a man called Laban (see *1 Nephi 4:18*). Then there is war, where fighting and killing our enemy is, at times (for many people at least), a necessity and not wrong. God wiped everyone from the face of the earth, save eight souls, during the great flood of Noah's time. Isn't God breaking His own commandment? Apparently, the truth, "thou shalt not kill," is not true absolutely. Or again perhaps the question should be, how can killing be right in one situation and wrong in another?

These are just a few examples I use to make my point. There are many other, so-called religious truths that under scrutiny do not hold up any better and we can play this game with each. "Wait," you say, "these are exceptions to the rule." But when you open the door of exceptions to the rule, absolute truth flies out. Suddenly, truth becomes elusive, a mirage in the desert. We have hundreds of religions, even hundreds of Christian religions, throughout the world, all believing different things, and all claiming to have the truth. But remember, belief and truth can be different things; so which or who, if any, are true?

Let us move on to material truths. Take a basic law of physics. What goes up must come down. That is, if you throw a rock into the air, gravity dictates that it must come down. Well, not if you throw it high enough. If it leaves the earth's atmosphere it can keep going, theoretically, indefinitely. This is the plight of scientists and their theories. No sooner do they find an absolute rule, than they find an exception to it. Again, where is absolute truth?

Well, perhaps we can do better with a more exact science, mathematics. Two plus two is always four, right? You put two raindrops together with two others and you have what? One. Not four. "But," you say, "that was relative to a certain situation." Of course, but don't you see? To say so is to make truth relative and here we go again.

Let us try something that is indisputable. Everyone must die! Surely that is true? So what about Enoch and his city? He and his entire city of hundreds of thousands, perhaps millions of people, were "translated that they should not see death." (*Hebrews 11:5, Moses 7:21*)[50] The same thing happened to John the Beloved. (*D&C 7:2-3*) And then there were the three apostles[51] that Christ blessed when He appeared to the ancient natives in the South Americas about 34 AD. (*3 Nephi 28:8*) Like John the Beloved, they were spared death. They were translated and are presumably walking this earth today. Anyway, so much for everyone must die.

If one should need more proof, that truth is not so easy to come by, just contemplate the multitude of opinions and beliefs that exist in the world on any given subject. By now you may think I'm just playing a silly game. Well, if it is a game, it is not silly. Much of the trouble in the world stems from our inability to discern truth or more correctly, our reluctance to *accept* truth. I am not trying to further confuse an issue that it is inherently confusing. I am only trying to make a point. But we'll get back to my point. Let us depart, for a moment in an attempt to get a handle on truth.

High School Again or Who Is Euclid?

Those of you who have taken high school geometry should be familiar with a man named Euclid. The Greeks, born of a need to keep track of taxes, property, and trade, were generally credited for inventing the science of mathematics and geometry during the Classical period, though much of what they organized and recorded came from the Egyptians and Babylonians. The Greeks converted this limited information into a vast, systematic, and thoroughly deductive structure. They could, by deductive reasoning, prove from a few basic facts many other unknowns. About 300 BC a man named Euclid organized the best results of dozens of fine mathematicians during the period from 600 BC to 300 BC and published a book called *Euclid's Elements*. There he put forth ten axioms, basic *self-evident* truths, upon which all subsequent reasoning and truth could be based. Through deductive reasoning, Euclid proved 467 theorems (other truths) relative to points, lines, circles, triangles, physical objects, space, and etc. These ten basic truths are as follows:

AXIOM 1 — The shortest distance between two points determine a unique straight line.

AXIOM 2 — A straight line extends indefinitely far in either direction.

AXIOM 3 — A circle may be drawn with any given center and any given radius.

AXIOM 4 — All right angles are equal.

AXIOM 5 — Two lines in the same plane, that are parallel, will never meet at any common point.

AXIOM 6 — Things equal to the same thing are equal to each other.

AXIOM 7 — If equals are added to equals, the sums are equal.

AXIOM 8	If equals were to be subtracted from equals, the remainders are equal.
AXIOM 9	Figures that can be made to coincide are equal (congruent).
AXIOM 10	The whole is greater than any part.

If you weren't asleep or busy passing notes to that cute person sitting behind you, you may, by now, be remembering that high school geometry class where you first saw these axioms. By use of these obvious, self-evident truths, many other truths about the world we live in and must relate to, have been deduced. The Greeks reasoned that the way to build sound systems of thought in any field was to start with these truths and then apply deductive reasoning carefully and exclusively, thus obtaining an unquestionable body of thoroughly reliable and usable conclusions, **new knowledge**, or **new truths**. Cattlemen were able to deduce the needed length of fencing. Farmers were able to figure the acreage in a given piece of land. Architects were able to build complex structures. Ship builders were able to design great vessels for the sea. Navigators were able to pilot the seas. Astronomers were able to plot heavenly courses, and on and on. Euclid's ten truths were so effective in proving other theories and finding other truths in all the sciences and arts, that they were soon the basis of philosophical, political, as well religious theory. Remember too, in those days a scholar did not choose a single discipline but was schooled in all known information which was not so extensive or specialized that they could not become knowledgeable in all the colleges. Euclid's truths were used as the foundation of truth in all disciplines and their contribution to molding the course of Western civilization was enormous to the extent that these principles are still in wide use today. For over two thousand years, Euclid has not only been accepted as the father of the science of logic, but his geometry has become the ***foundation of all truth*** about the physical world in which we live. These truths are so clear, so evident, that no one in his right mind could question them.

Ah, Finally We Have A Handle On Truth, But No

Now why would I be harrowing up those dreadful high school memories by telling you all this stuff about Euclid? I am telling you as a background for what happened in about 1820. A man by the name of Karl Friedrich Gauss, one of the greatest inventors, astronomical observers, and mathematicians of his time (his systems and instruments for measurement of the earth's magnetic field are still in use today), made a discovery. Though he was not the first, he detected a problem with Axiom 5 in particular (the parallel axiom), as well as axiom 2. Looking at your ten axioms, can you see the problem? They involve an assumption about what happens out in the far off regions of space. In other words, they don't reflect man's **actual** experience. Not only are they not *self-evident*, in fact, ***we can't even prove them***. How do we know these two axioms are true? Could it be that Euclidean geometry was not necessarily the correct description of physical space way out there somewhere? Others prior to Gauss had made the same discovery and tried in vain to delete, replace, or re-state these axioms so that they could be used without the nagging doubt. Gauss also failed but took it a step further. He *assumed* the parallel axiom to be *un-provable*. He then asserted that since they had been used so effectively for such a long time (2000 years), even though they could not be proven by man's practical experience, he was logically free to adopt other axioms that were different from Euclid's whether or not they were theoretical or could be proven. One could then use these new axioms to find and prove other truths, and further, that those new axioms and newfound truths may be an even better description of physical space than were Euclid's. This is what Gauss and others who came after him did. They set up other basic axioms and used them to prove a vast number of theorems. These new geometries were called *Non-Euclidean geometries*.

Non What? Who Needs It?

Most mathematicians regarded non-Euclidean geometry as an exercise in futility as they were thought to have no practical use. Two thousand years of believing in and using Euclid's geometry had caused a mindset too ingrained, in some, to be easily shaken. Again, with new concepts, change comes hard and slow. Ultimately, however, it was discovered that these geometries were, in some cases, more accurate depictions of physical space. When Einstein's theory of relativity made use of non-Euclidean geometry, the world was forced to accept it as legitimate and valid. Einstein, by necessity, had to include the factor of time making his non-Euclidean geometry four-dimensional.

It was found that many of these new, non-Euclidean geometries were a better, truer, description of our physical space. Take, for instance, the earth itself. It is a round sphere or orb, and if you draw a straight line (the shortest path between two points) on its surface, we can clearly see that the line is not straight like a ruler, but curved over the radius of the orb. Also, we find that this *shortest path between any two points* is only a shorter arc of the great circle formed by continuing the line through the points, around the orb's surface until what? Lo and behold, we learn that the line doesn't go indefinitely in either direction, as it did in Euclid's geometry, but *must* come around the orb to meet itself. This is true in every case of the straight line in this non-Euclidean geometry of the orb. Yet it is still, by definition, a straight line (the shortest path between two points).

If we put *two* straight lines on the surface of the same orb (the shortest paths between two points), we find they *cannot* be parallel to each other. We also find that they *must* meet each other at two points. In other words, the law, truth, or axiom was discovered that there are no parallel lines on the surface of an orb. (The latitude/longitude lines on the globe are not *straight* lines as they are not the shortest paths between two points.) Unlike Euclid's geometry where all angles of a triangle must total 180 degrees, in this non-Euclidean geometry of the orb we find that whatever the size or shape of the triangle, the sum of the three angles *must* be *greater* than 180 degrees. Other axioms were discovered like; all perpendicular lines to any given line on an orb must meet at a single point. Like the Earth's longitude lines, perpendicular to the line of the equator, all meet at the north (and south) pole.

As this new non-Euclidean geometry, the orb, developed, more and more axioms, truths, laws, and theorems governing it were discovered. In short, here was a physical shape, a common physical shape, which non-Euclidean geometry described better than Euclid's geometry. A whole geometry, with its axioms (basic self-evident truths) and deductive truths, can and has been worked out to fit this shape. But what is even more abstruse, amazing, or complex is that one may take a cone shape, or saddle shape, or any other shape and discover its axioms and from them deduce many other truths. In fact, a multitude, even an infinite number of new, non-Euclidean, geometries can be built.

More and more uses were found for non-Euclidean geometries. Men were no longer tied to proving things from one set of truths. They could now pick and choose what truths would be relevant to their particular situation. These non-Euclidean geometries have been used to put men on the moon and send our satellites to the outer reaches of space. Because of unique shapes involved, the bending of light rays (a fact more recently discovered, historically speaking), and the element of time, they are more accurate and useable descriptions of our physical space than Euclid's geometry. Moreover, it has been discovered that in many cases, Euclid's geometry did not fit at all.

So What?

More profound than their uses was the impact that non-Euclidean geometry had on the body of truth accepted for over two thousand years. **The advent of**

other possible geometries caused the greatest ideological revolution in history. The fact that Euclid's truths could no longer be trusted to accurately describe our environment, that other geometries were *truer*, was like cutting loose the anchor, casting adrift *all truth*. The implication is that man no longer has a means of discovering *absolute truths* and that indeed *absolute truth* may not exist. This concept unavoidably affects all thought. Whether or not we believe absolute truth is unattainable (and I don't, for reasons I shall later explain), it revolutionized the thinking of Western civilization. It became more accurate to say that man is surest of what he believes than to say that he believes what is sure. My friend's words come echoing, "We all believe what we choose to believe."

Most of the world interpreted this revolution as shattering all hope of ever obtaining a single truth. It is my testimony that it, in fact, *freed us to find* ***all truth****!* We were previously tied to one truth (one geometry) whether or not it fit the particular situation. Now we are free to explore and discover truths without constraint.

I have inserted this bit of geometric history into my text not as an analogy, and not just as a ***true example***, but to show how truth really works. This multiplicity of geometries is how truth actually functions.

Most of the Mormon community (myself included), as well as the rest of the world, I include in this next statement. For whatever reason, pride, laziness, tradition, insecurity, fear, stubbornness, the need to be right, or whatever, we cling so tightly to the truths that have come to us, that we fail to understand that God's creations are *not just* ***one*** *geometry*! In fact, they are infinite. Let me explain this by referring to the Lord's own statement to Joseph Smith, "All truth is independent in that sphere in which God has placed it, to act for itself." (*D&C 93:30*) "And again, verily I say unto you, he hath given a law unto all things, by which they move in their times and their seasons." (*D&C 88:42*) In other words, truth (in its proper sphere or realm) exists eternal, *a knowledge of things as they* ***are****, and as they* ***were****, and as* ***they are to come***. Past, present, and future truth will always remain the same ***in the realm, sphere, or geometry to which it relates!*** It isn't that nothing is absolute. ***All*** is absolute. What changes is the ***sphere*** or ***realm, (the geometry)*** in which it is placed.

All law and truth remain constant within their own geometry. Though the geometry may change, the truths relating to any particular geometry remain true and constant in that geometry. Our confusion comes from the fact that many realms (geometries) are interacting around us at any given time. This means that different sets of truths, those truths assigned by God to those realms, are coming into play at different times and in different situations. Problems arise because we have not developed our ability to correctly assess the particular realm, the geometry; nor have we learned the truths assigned to it.

How Many Geometries, Laws, And Realms?

Once more, this is not an analogy, not just a true example, but it is the way truth operates. I refer, again not as an analogy but as a true example, to another statement by the Lord to Joseph Smith, "And they who are not sanctified through the law which I have given unto you, even the Law of Christ, must inherit another kingdom, even that of a terrestrial kingdom, or that of a telestial kingdom.[52] For he who is not able to abide the law of a celestial kingdom cannot abide a celestial glory. And he who cannot abide the law of a terrestrial kingdom cannot abide a terrestrial glory. And he who cannot abide the law of a telestial kingdom cannot abide a telestial glory; therefore he is not meet for a kingdom of glory. Therefore he must abide a kingdom which is not a kingdom of glory." (*D&C 88:21-24*) Here the Lord is telling us that there are at least four major realms of governing laws, truths, or geometries that we are associated with. But are the truths of these realms or kingdoms really different? Absolutely! For a detailed description of the requirements or laws of each realm and the kind of people that will inherit or be sanctified by them, I refer you to D&C 76. In the interest of space, I will give only a synopsis of these different laws and kingdoms.

I will follow the example the Lord set and start with the highest celestial degree of law, realm, geometry, truth, or glory. As an aside, please note in the above scripture, that the Lord does not say to you that He would reveal the lowest law, the telestial, and when you are able to live that, He would give you a higher law, the terrestrial, and when you live that, He would give you the highest, celestial law. No, it is the other way around. Even when the Mormon missionaries go out and are admonished to teach the basics, they are instructed to teach the basics of the *celestial law*, not the basics of any of the lower laws. We are the ones that choose a course of progression from lower to higher, and this concept has given us the impression that God starts us at the bottom and we then work our way up. That could not be farther from the truth. God always *offers* us the *best gift*, and then if we refuse to take it, He offers us the lesser. "For what doth it profit a man if a gift is bestowed upon him, and he receives not the gift? Behold, he rejoices not in that which is given unto him, neither rejoices in him who is the giver of the gift." (*D&C 88:33*) God always gives us the *highest law*, and if we are unable to live it, then He gives us a *lower law*. A grand example of this was the children of Israel. Moses tried to get the children of Israel prepared for the higher law but they would not, and were cursed by God to live the lesser law of carnal commandments and performances. "Now this Moses plainly taught to the children of Israel in the wilderness, and sought diligently to sanctify his people *that they might behold the face of God*; but they hardened their hearts and could not *endure His presence*; therefore, the Lord in His wrath, for His anger was kindled against them, swore that they should not enter into His *rest* while in the wilderness, *which rest is the fulness of His glory*. Therefore, He took Moses out of their midst, and the Holy Priesthood also . . . ." (*D&C 84:22-25*)

Fortunately, we are living in the *Dispensation of Fullness of Times*.[53] We have all three levels of law available to us and may pick and choose which we will live. Unfortunately, we tend to do just that, pick and choose. We take a little from this realm of law and a little from that, bouncing back and forth between all three levels. This will not work. At some point we will be judged. When we are, we can only be sanctified by the law we lived. "And again, verily I say unto you, that which is governed by law is also preserved by law and perfected and sanctified by the same. And unto every kingdom is given a law, and unto every law there are certain bounds also and conditions. Ye who are quickened by a portion of the celestial glory shall then receive of the same, even a fulness. And they who are quickened by a portion of the terrestrial glory shall then receive of the same, even a fulness. And also they who are quickened by a portion of the telestial glory shall then receive of the same, even a fulness. And they who remain shall also be quickened; nevertheless, they shall return again to their own place, to enjoy that which they are willing to receive, because they were not willing to enjoy that which they might have received." (*D&C 88:34, 38, 29-32*)

So a *little* obedience to *some* of the celestial laws will not get it. We must live enough of the law to be sanctified by it or, by default; we will need to be sanctified by the lesser.

Four Basic Laws or Geometries

Celestial laws require that you believe in Jesus Christ, repent of all wrong doing, be baptized by water in His name, by His authority, and then keep His commandments to the best of your ability. So that you might be washed clean of your sins by the Baptism of Fire or the Holy Ghost which the Father sheds forth upon all those who are just and true. You must overcome all by faith in Christ. You must live by the spirit of truth and be ready and worthy to receive God's glory, His mysteries. You must be just and true and having repented of your sins, God will forgive them and eventually make you perfect (see *D&C 76:50-70* and *92-95*).

Terrestrial laws do not require a person to receive a testimony of Christ or if they have, to be valiant in that testimony. They are those who would not accept or live the gospel ordinances of repentance and forgiveness and must, for a period at least, suffer for their own sins but will eventually be retired to a place of glory. The law requires that they be honorable men of the earth, but may have allowed themselves, because of pride, to be blinded by the craftiness of men. If your heart is set too much upon the things of this world, you are likely operating in a terrestrial realm (see *D&C 76:71-80*).

Telestial law includes liars and those who love to make lies, adulterers, rapists, power and war mongers, murderers, whoremongers, sorcerers, idolaters, and those who plunder and keep their fellow men in one form of bondage or another. Eventually these will confess that Jesus is Christ and receive a lesser glory but not before they suffer the torments of hell for their unrepentant sins (see *D&C 76:31-48, &: 81-88 &: 103-106*).

The fourth place, which is described above as a place without glory, Mormons call *outer darkness*. "Then said the king to the servants, Bind him hand and foot, and take him away, and cast him into outer darkness; there shall be weeping and gnashing of teeth." (*Matthew 22:13*) "And then shall it come to pass, that the spirits of the wicked, yea, who are evil—for behold, they have no part nor portion of the Spirit of the Lord; for behold, they chose evil works rather than good; therefore the spirit of the Devil did enter into them, and take possession of their house—and these shall be cast out into outer darkness; there shall be weeping, and wailing, and gnashing of teeth, and this because of their own iniquity, being led captive by the will of the Devil." (*Alma 40:13*) In other words, these are those persons who are described as perdition, devils, or servants to the Devil. They may have many of the traits listed in the telestial realm but have gone a step further. They have chosen a law that makes them enemies to God and void of truth. Although they knew the truth they denied it and thereby the Holy Ghost which is the embodiment of all truth. This is the unpardonable sin, to deny the Holy Ghost.

Why all the realms, or spheres? Why not just one? Simply stated, we are all on different levels. Where one person may be willing and desire to live one law, another person may choose to live a higher or lower one. So God, in His wisdom, has given us free agency[54] to choose between these levels of law by creating a situation where we *can* choose. Whatever level of law, what ever geometry (truths), we decide to live, we will be *judged* and *sanctified* by the same. Although in the Lord's house are many mansions, all people, as well as all laws and choices, fall generally into these four categories: celestial, terrestrial, telestial, or outer darkness. Even the above brief descriptions of the laws governing each give you the ability to generally separate or discern which realm you are operating in when you make your choices.

A Matter of Choice

Whenever I teach a religious class, I like to ask the students, "Which of the three laws of glory do they want me to teach, celestial, terrestrial, or telestial?" Of course, anyone with the desire to know and serve God will say they want to live the highest celestial laws. The point is, **we make the choice** of not only which level of law we will live, but the level of truth we will accept. We are not only free to choose whatever course we **will** to take, we are free to choose which geometry we **will** to live in as also which truths we **will** to believe.

This point is paramount to understand. When we realize that it is **our** God-given choice, **our** agency, **our** freedom to choose, we begin to take responsibility for our actions and stop making useless excuses for our choices. It is equally important to realize that God has given us the ability (at least before we are resurrected) to progress from one realm or level of law or truth to another, until we hopefully, find ourselves in His celestial realm. What a beautiful program. Man himself, through his God-given agency, is put at the helm. It is not a matter of intelligence or being smart. We don't have to be smart to be righteous—only obedient in the choices given us to make. Man is free to choose but must remain confined to those geometries he will accept. Agency is having choices and the more correct choices you make the more choices God gives you. Conversely, every wrong choice limits your further choices and accordingly, your agency. "They shall return again to their own place, to enjoy that which they are willing to receive, because they were not willing to enjoy that which they might have received." (*D&C 88:32*) My friend's words again, "We all believe what we choose to believe." So, every man *can* receive what he ***will*** receive.

Am I Wrong Or Right?

And now I shall make a statement *of which I am sure.* I am, however, equally certain you will probably not understand this assertion and will most likely object. The statement is: ***whatever level of law, truth, and glory (celestial, terrestrial, or telestial) you choose, you are not wrong. It is not a matter of right or wrong but a matter of choice.***

God has given you the agency, the opportunity to choose whatever level of law you want to live and be sanctified thereby. Of course He would like to see us all choose the highest celestial law, so that we might know the greatest joy, but he will not force us to do so. That He cannot do.

I speak for myself when I say that from time to time I would like to grab hold of certain people and somehow shake the truth into them or shout it in a voice that they could not deny. I feel like that song that talks about, "If I ruled the world every man would be good and all would be right." Even the great Prophet Alma realized this could not be when he wished he could have the power of an angel to speak with the trump of God, that his voice would shake the whole earth and cause people to repent. He too wanted to *fix* every soul, that is, force them to choose the highest level of law and truth, but he realized that he sinned in his wish. He said (parenthesis, italics, and bold for emphasis), "For I know that He (God) granteth unto men according to **their *desire***, whether it be unto death or unto life; yea, I know that He allotteth unto men, yea, decreeth unto them decrees which are unalterable, *according to* ***their wills***, whether they be unto salvation or unto destruction . . . but he that knoweth good and evil, to him is given according to **his *desires***, whether he desireth good or evil, life or death, joy or remorse of conscience." (*Alma 29:4-5*)

It is a matter of choice. It is a matter of what we *desire* most. "But," you say, "it's God's will that we choose the highest glory." No, it is God's will that we find the greatest joy that we *can*, or should I say, *want* or *will* to find. Should you choose a lesser law, the Lord, by virtue of the law itself, is obliged to allow you to live that level. It is, of course, *not the best*, but **it is *not wrong*. It is merely *your choice*.**

What *would* be wrong is our being thrust into the presence of God when we are not living His celestial law. We would not only be uncomfortable there, we would be very unhappy. In fact, we would be looking for a place to hide or a mountain to fall upon us. On the other hand, if God put us in an environment with liars, cheaters, and murderers when we were not living that lesser law, we would again be very uncomfortable and unhappy. That would be wrong indeed. Nevertheless, what ever we choose, it is not wrong but our choice.

You are probably fighting this concept right now, as it seems to eliminate right and wrong completely. Let me give you an out but still keep to the truth that what we choose is not wrong but merely a choice. Should you choose, or rather commit, to live, say, the highest law, the celestial Law of Christ, and you then do something that is against that law you have done something wrong. Relative to your original choice and the law governing the results of that choice, you have done wrong. You cannot expect the laws of the lesser choice to yield the blessings of the higher law. The same is true of those who choose a lesser glory, say, the terrestrial, and then do something that is telestial in nature. They will have made a mistake and done something wrong. Do you see the difference? In this sense there is right and wrong. But then our daily choices are what evidence our *real* intentions, our real commitment, our real desires, and the glory or law we are *really* choosing to live. So, we are back to choice, not right or wrong.

That's Good Enough For Me

This truth was once again driven home to me not long ago when I was working on a project with a fellow in San Francisco. He is a really nice guy and although he is quite worldly, I have learned to appreciate his honesty and integrity, and we have become very good friends. Since we were staying in the city through the week and going home on the weekends, we were spending a great deal of time together in traffic, which gave us time to talk. On occasion, I would take the opportunity to try and bend the conversations to meaningful topics with spiritual significance. As we were headed back to the hotel one evening, we got on the subject of higher and lower laws and glories. He, not only being a non-member, but not religious in any way, listened intently as I carefully and concisely explained the three degrees of glory and the rules and laws associated with each. I explained that the celestial people would be the ones that would live with God in eternal glory; that the terrestrial people would be those who were honorable but men who set their hearts upon the things of this world; I then explained about the telestial glory which would be made up of the evil people of the world; and finally, that outer darkness would be reserved for those who made themselves enemies to God. After I was all through with my explanation, he turned to me and said, "Hummm, what was that second place—you called it the terrestrial place? I like the sound of that. That's where I want to go when I die. It sounds good to me, especially if they let you play basketball and go fishing."

Well I don't know if Terrestrial people will be able to go fishing, but I know they will be happy doing things they like. At any rate, I was stunned at his statement. It had never occurred to me that someone would want to settle for less right from the start. Of course I always thought that I, or others, might fall short of our goal to achieve the best, but I never thought of someone wanting less from the onset. I must applaud my friends' honesty and integrity, but I have since recognized that many people are, wittingly or unwittingly, doing the same thing. They are settling or wanting less than the best. Of course, less is less, but can we condemn these people for choosing what they want to choose? No, nor will God. He gives them the choice, they make it, and that's it. As Alma said, they will be rewarded according to their desires, even though it is less, perhaps far less than what they could have had. To us, those who presumably have chosen better, it seems that these people are wrong but to God they are not wrong. Again, it is not a matter of right or wrong, but of choice.

No Pushing Please

If you can understand and accept this principle, you will see how presumptuous and impertinent it is for each of us to attempt to force our own standards (geometry) or level of law on others, or they on us. To usurp others' agency, even our own children's, is to take the role of Satan himself who wanted to force all to be good. This was shown to Moses in a vision of the souls of men where our brother, Satan, was a leading participant. In describing the vision he said (parenthasis and italics added), "And he (Satan) came before me, (God) saying—Behold, here am I, send me, I will be thy son, and I will redeem *all mankind, that one soul shall not be lost*, and surely I will do it, wherefore give me thine honor." (*P of GP, Moses 4:1*)

We cannot coerce, condemn, or even look down on others for their choices. From our perspective, we may consider their choices *wrong* and for us those choices may, in fact be wrong; but for them, those choices may be right. Further, their choices may be the best they can possibly make for the level of law they have selected to live. It is not for us to make that judgment. We can only judge or choose for ourselves what is right for us. All we can do is use our best influence, usually by example, to entice them to reach higher. In the case of our children, our influence is greater than that which we have over others and this gives us a greater responsibility to teach them correct principles. Still, they will ultimately make their own choices. If we want to be like God Himself, we must accept that others may choose, *according to their own will*; to live in a lesser geometry, realm of law, or glory. A person may be operating on a lesser level and be doing quite well therein. Again, *from God's perspective, although it is not the best,* ***it is not wrong***. It is simply their choice.

I often see members of The Church judging and condemning others, even nonmembers, because they are not living Church standards. How preposterous! Most have never heard of some of the laws we have been given in the latter-days let alone make the choice to live them. Yet we look down on these people and often disassociate ourselves from them because they drink, or smoke, or are not living other laws we think they should. How can we presume to judge these people when God does not? Remember that our thoughts and ways are not as high as His. We are **all** operating on a lower level than God. From His vantage point, most, if not all, our choices *could* be considered wrong. Still, I have the belief, as well as the hope, that He considers our choices infantile and not wrong, as we may be doing right for the level we are on or the geometry we are in. Assumedly, hopefully, we will continue in our progression to a higher geometry or realm until our thoughts and ways are as high as God's. At any rate, I feel certain we have stepped across the line when we superimpose our standard, our geometry upon others.

The Law And The Geometry

With all this said about other geometries, realms, glories, or spheres, with different levels of laws and truths, we can clearly see why a thing may be right in one situation and wrong in another. Said the Prophet Joseph (parentheses added for emphasis), "That which is wrong under one circumstance, may be, and often is, right under another. God said, 'Thou shalt not kill.' At another time He said, 'Thou shalt utterly destroy.' This is the principle on which the government of heaven is conducted—by revelation adapted to the circumstances (sphere, realm, or geometry) in which the children of the kingdom are placed. Whatever God requires is right, no matter what it is, although we may not see the reason thereof till long after the events transpire . . . even things which might be considered abominable to all who understand the order of heaven only in part, but which in reality were right because God gave and sanctioned by special revelation." (*TPJS, pg. 255-6*)

We can now understand why it is not right to lie yet in some cases, the only proper choice. Accordingly, is it not comprehensible that God might give a personal revelation to one individual and yet just the opposite to another, depending on the level of the respective persons and what God deems their needs at the time.

We are all subject to many of the same laws as we are generally in the same geometry, yet, because of our varied and individual situations (our *personal geometries*), we are all living subject to different sets of laws, like Nephi was living under a different law and geometry when he slew Laban. "Abraham was commanded to offer for a sacrifice his son Isaac; nevertheless, it was written; Thou shalt not kill. Abraham, however, did not refuse, and it was accounted unto him for righteousness." (*D&C 132:36*) These were different geometries and laws than we are normally commanded to live. Certainly, the "thou shalt not kill" law, in general, holds true. "And now, behold, I speak unto the church. Thou shalt not kill; and he that kills shall not have forgiveness in this world, nor in the world to come." (*D&C 42:18*) My whole point here is that what is true in one situation or geometry, may not be in another.

If that is so, and I testify that it is, then we would all do better if we would stop trying to impose our personal geometries upon each other. Simply put, since we are on different levels, what is true for you may not be for me. Like God, I believe we must *offer* the best we have and let others seek their own level. Again, to attempt to force anyone else to a higher level of law or glory is to take the role of the Devil, who wants to relieve us of our God-given free agency.[55] Let us not condemn others for their choices.

Perhaps now, the following passage of scripture has more meaning to us (as you read this scripture, try changing the word time to geometry): "To every thing there is a season, and a time to every purpose under the heaven: A time to be born, and a time to die; a time to plant, and a time to pluck up that which is planted; A time to kill, and a time to heal; a time to break down, and a time to build up; A time to weep, and a time to laugh; a time to mourn, and a time to dance; A time to cast away stones, and a time to gather stones together; a time to embrace, and a time to refrain from embracing; A time to get, and a time to lose; a time to keep, and a time to cast away; A time to rend, and a time to sew; a time to keep silence, and a time to speak; A time to love, and a time to hate; a time of war, and a time of peace." (*Ecclesiastes 3:1-8*)

Absolute Truth—Different Geometries—The Key To Agency

You see; God does not manipulate truth. All truth remains constant, ***absolute***, throughout eternity. Even God cannot change truth, it is things as they are, were, and will be. He does however; manipulate the spheres or realms, bringing other *different geometries* or *truths* into play. This is wholly within His right; He is, after all, God. "For behold, by the power of His word man came upon the face of the earth, which earth was created by the power of His word. Wherefore, if God being able to speak and the world was, and to speak and man was created, O then, why not able to command the earth, or the workmanship of His hands upon the face of it, according to His will and pleasure?" (*Jacob 4:9*)

The fact remains that because God knows all the realms and geometries that exist (and they must be many, if not infinite), and all the laws and truths relative to those realms, He is *free* to work with or within whichever He chooses. God, therefore, has ***ultimate freedom***. He is no more bound to operate according to our earthly laws, than we are bound by the lesser Mosaic laws that were fulfilled in Christ. "Behold, I say unto you that the law is fulfilled that was given unto Moses. For behold, the covenant which I have made with my people is not all fulfilled; but the law which was given to Moses hath an end in me." (*3 Nephi 15:4* and 8)

I used the word "bound" above and said God is *not bound*, a better word is *governed*, that is He is not governed by anyone or anything. He is free. Totally free to choose, but whatever law He chooses to work within; He is bound by the properties of that law. There is a marked difference. Let me put it this way, *God is bound by the laws He chooses to live but because He is free to choose the laws He will live, He is therefore, not bound at all.* God can do exactly according to His own good will and pleasure, to operate in whatever realm of law and with whatever truths apply thereto, that He may choose. This is why He can command us not to kill; yet He can utterly destroy. This concept also gives new meaning to the scripture, "Then said Jesus to those Jews which believed on Him, If ye continue in my word, then are ye my disciples indeed; And ye shall know the truth, and the truth shall make you free." (*John 8:31-32*) The more truths or geometries we know and understand, the freer we become until, like God, we may choose the geometries within which we will work. Since we are stuck in a very few of these geometries, we are a long way from being as free as God to do just what we will. It is not that God operates *without law*, He operates *with* ***all*** *law*, which makes it seem as if He is without or beyond any and all law (more to come on this concept of ultimate freedom without the law, or rather with all law, and how it applies to us).

As said above, God has also given us a certain amount of freedom to choose in what realm we will operate (celestial, terrestrial, telestial, and etc.). For us, the only problem is that we know but a few laws and truths and probably accept even less than those we know.

The Wrong Geometry Can Be Fatal

So you see, this revolution of non-Euclidean geometries does not shatter our hope of obtaining truth, it enhances it; nor does it destroy any truths we already have. We don't throw out old truths; we put them in their proper sphere and build upon them. We accept that any new, seemingly contradictive truth may apply to another sphere, hopefully a higher one. We don't have to give up Euclidean geometry to accept and use others. The key is to ***not*** hold so tight to the geometries we know, our testimony of the lesser truths, that we exclude the greater ones the Lord is ready to reveal to us.

I am reminded of a story I heard a long time ago, and I am not even sure of its source, but for some reason, it has stuck with me. The story tells of a small town in some far away land many years ago. It seems that whenever a problem arose in the town, the old wise man was summoned to bestow his great wisdom, thus giving solution to the problem. One day a man was working on the roof of a small two-story house. As he finished the roof, he closed off the place where he had climbed through, leaving no place to get down. He yelled for help but none of his friends knew how to get him down. The wise man was called and upon much contemplation, he told them to get a rope. This they did, and he further instructed them to put five strong men at one end and throw the other end up to the man on the roof. Then he told the man on the roof to tie the end around his waist, which he did. He told the five strong men on the ground that when he gave the signal they were to pull with all their might. He then gave the signal to pull. The five men pulled, the man was jerked off the roof, and fell to his death. Everyone stood around in astonishment that the wise man's answer to the problem had resulted in the death of the man. The old wise man said, "I don't understand! It worked last time—to get a man out of a well."

You see; it was the right process but the wrong geometry. If we can only accept one or a few geometries, we cannot make progress, or worse, like the man on the roof we could be in trouble. I am sure that we've all heard that a little knowledge can be dangerous and so it can, if we are unwilling to accept the further light and knowledge that gives meaning and relevance to that which we already have. It is a matter of applying the proper law to the particular situation, realm, or geometry. As Joseph Smith said, the key is ***not*** to "fly to pieces like glass as soon as anything comes that is contrary to [our] traditions."

The Priesthood, A High Geometry

It is appropriate to say here that to reach a celestial glory, one must take advantage of the blessings of the Melchizedek Priesthood. Priesthood we will here define as the power and authority of God conferred upon man. To God, this power, His power, is the respect, honor, fear, reverence, homage, and obedience that all people and things pay to Him. The Lord tells us (italics for emphasis), "That Satan . . . came before me, saying—Behold, here am I, send me, I will be thy son, and I will redeem all mankind, that one soul shall not be lost, and surely I will do it; wherefore give me thine *honor*." (*Moses 4: 1*) "For he rebelled against me, saying, Give me thine *honor, which is my power*." (*D&C 29:36*) God gets His power from us, that is, all people and things that give Him honor and obey him. This is His power and priesthood, and it is this priesthood that is the vehicle given man to reach such a glory or obtain such power. Said Bruce R. McConkie as he quotes the prophets, "This higher priesthood is designed to enable men to gain exaltation in the highest heaven in eternity. Paul says it is ordained after the power of an endless life. (*Hebrews. 7:16.*) The Prophet Joseph says, 'The power of the Melchizedek Priesthood is to have the power of endless lives; for the everlasting covenant cannot be broken.' (*TPJS pg. 322.*) Perfection can be gained only in and through and because of this priesthood. 'I advise all to go on to perfection, and search deeper into the mysteries of godliness,' the Prophet said. 'A man can do nothing for himself unless God direct him in the right way; and the priesthood is for that purpose.' (*TPJS pg. 364.*) Through this priesthood men become joint-heirs with Christ, receiving and possessing the fulness of the Father's kingdom. 'And all those who are ordained unto this priesthood are made like unto the Son of God, abiding a priest continually.' (*Inspired Version*[56], *Hebrews 7:3*)" (*MD, pg. 480*) So, sooner or later, in order to receive the highest blessings, one must learn about and learn to work within this geometry, with this power of God which is called His priesthood. This is the law and governing power of the highest as well as all other kingdoms.

Again, for us, confusion reigns until we, by faith, learn to sort out the various geometries or realms, and the laws that are relevant to them. It may be more accurate to say that confusion reigns until we quit messing around between different realms and commit to living God's highest. "No man can serve two masters: for either he will hate the one, and love the other; or else he will hold to the one, and despise the other. Ye cannot serve God and mammon." (*Matthew 6:24*) It is my observation that most of us, unfortunately, muddle around in the confusion of a pool of terrestrial laws and truths mixed with some telestial and some celestial. Far too seldom do we operate exclusively in a celestial realm of laws and truths. Why is this so? Probably because of our worldly desires, but perhaps it is because we are unaware of these higher laws or geometries.

What Will Get Us There?

How do we come to know the celestial laws? Well, this is what the Lord has been trying to tell us over the Millennia. He has communicated the way through His prophets down through time. "Surely the Lord God will do nothing, but He revealeth His secret unto His servants the prophets." (*Amos 3:7*) The word of the Lord is recorded in the scriptures, *The Holy Bible, The Book of Mormon, The Doctrine and Covenants,* and *The Pearl of Great Price*. Although many geometries are spoken of and many levels of laws are given (even some laws and geometries that we are no longer required by God to live), the word of God, that is, the Gospel of Jesus Christ, is contained within these scriptures, and we must seek, by study, in order to find. The significance of the word of God is as important as any other instruction book, only in this case the instructions are how to get back to God.

This point was amply made to Lehi and his son Nephi in a dream or vision they had concerning the *Tree of Life* and the *fountain of living waters*. In this vision they saw a tree and fountain of water. They were given to understand that the fruit of the tree and the water was the love of God. They also saw a large gulf of water and a mist of darkness separating the tree from a large building. This building represented the pride of the world. A mist of darkness and a gulf of water represented the temptations of the Devil and hell. There were multitudes of people in the large building who were in the act of scoffing and ridiculing the people who were trying to work through the darkness to the tree. Lehi and Nephi saw that a path led to the tree but many strayed off the path and got lost in the darkness or fell into the gulf of water. They also saw that there was a rod of iron, representing the word of God (which word is truth) that went along the path leading to the tree. Those who took hold of the truth, the rod, or the word of God, and did not let go, did eventually get down the path to the tree and were able to taste of its fruit, or the love of God, which tasted sweet above all other fruits (see *1 Nephi 8-15*).

The importance of knowing the word of God or truth is essential, but as expressed before, the truth comes on different levels and is found in different geometries. To some it is milk and to others it is a parable that only the spiritually discerning mind can understand. I am not here to determine what level you are on or what level you should be on, but I will testify that if you hold to the iron rod, truth, you will *eventually* go from one level to another until you get to the prized tree. It is a process of growth as we walk the path, sometimes blindly, through mists of darkness. Don't give up and don't let go of the rod of iron (the word of God, truth) but remember to keep your mind open to new truths as you go from one step to another.

Shift Into A Higher Gear

We must expose our minds to new geometries. As Einstein said, "You can't solve tomorrow's problems with the mindset that created them today." We must have a paradigm shift. If we are to progress, if we are to get more truth, *new truths* and *new geometries*, we must accept and act upon those that we do have without becoming locked into them. Joseph Smith said (italics for emphasis), "Happiness is the object and design of our existence; and will be the end thereof, if we pursue the path that leads to it; and this path is virtue, uprightness, faithfulness, holiness, and keeping all the commandments of God. But we cannot keep all the commandments without first knowing them, and we cannot expect to know all, or more than we now know *unless we comply with or keep those we have already received*." (*TPJS, pg. 255*) And Brigham Young said, "The laws that the Lord has given are not fully perfect, because the people could not receive them in their perfect fullness; but they can receive a little here and a little there, a little today and a little tomorrow, a little more next week, and a little more in advance of that next year, *if they make a wise improvement upon every little they receive*; if they do not, they are left in the shade, and the light which the Lord reveals will appear darkness to them, and the kingdom of heaven will travel on and leave them groping. Hence, if we wish to act upon the fullness of the knowledge that the Lord designs to reveal, little by little, to the inhabitants of the earth, *we must improve upon every little as it is revealed*." (*DBY, pg. 4*) Alma tells us that we receive knowledge of the mysteries of God according to the heed and diligence, which we give to God and that which we have already received. "And therefore, he that will harden his heart, the same receiveth the lesser portion of the word; and he that will not harden his heart, to him is given the greater portion of the word, until it is given unto him to know the mysteries of God until he know them in full. And they that will harden their hearts, to them is given the lesser portion of the word until they know nothing concerning his mysteries; and then they are taken captive by the devil, and led by his will down to destruction. Now this is what is meant by the chains of hell." (*Alma 12:10-12*)

But no, we seem to accept and reject truth as if there were some virtue in being wishy-washy, and so confusion reigns within us and we wonder why we can't get a handle on truth. We wonder why we are confused and unhappy. I will go out on a limb here and state that *if you are not happy, if you do not have inner peace, it is because you are fighting a truth, or perhaps many*. The Devil is in a place where there is little or no truth and there is much weeping, wailing, and gnashing of teeth. The cause of the Devils misery, as well as our own, is the rejection of truth. Also remember, "misery loves company". The Devil confuses simple things so that those who do not reverence truth will reject it.

I have heard people say that it is a struggle to accept truth. I do not believe it. The struggle comes because we are fighting the truth, instead of accepting it. If we are open to new truths and accept them as fast as they come, there is no struggle, and what is more, our progression on the road to knowledge and glory is rapid. This is how Christ lived. "And He received not of the fullness at first, but continued from grace to grace, until He received a fullness." (*D&C 93:13*) He did not fight truth when it came and I am sure, save His remorse for others, He was a happy, contented man.

Discerning of Truth

I have probably said enough in this chapter about the great secret "truth" and perhaps what I will say now is anticlimactic, but I feel it needs saying.

The main mistake that Euclid and his followers made was in believing that a study of known truths and deductive reasoning is the only road or source of other truths. Although it is a very good means (we've already talked about the importance of checking our new truths against the foundation truths at the base of our scaffolding) it is not the only way to obtain truth, nor is it the best. You see; if we fail to correctly recognize the realm or geometry the truth is in, we could discard it on the grounds that it contradicts our previously established truths. Further, it is unlikely that God will reveal again, to each individual, that which He has already revealed to all. For this reason, we give a heavy measure of weight to the need to study the scriptures and other sources of revealed truth.

However, on a higher level, in order to obtain truth, one must go to the source. As Moroni testified, the source is God Himself or His Holy Spirit, which is the testifier of all truth (italics and bold for emphasis). "And when ye shall receive these things, I would exhort you that ye would ask God, the Eternal Father, in the name of Christ, if these things are not true; and if ye shall ask with a sincere heart, with real intent, having faith in Christ, He will manifest the truth of it unto you by the power of the Holy Ghost. And *by the power of the Holy Ghost ye may know the truth of all things*." (*Moroni 10:4-5*) Appealing to the Holy Ghost is the ultimate standard of measurement, the best and most reliable way to obtain truth. "But he that believeth these things which I have spoken, him will I visit with the *manifestations of my Spirit*, and he shall know and bear record. For *because of my Spirit he shall know* that these things are true; for it persuadeth men to do good." (*Ether 4:11*) Said Brigham Young (italics and bold added), "Now, my friends, brethren and sisters, ladies and gentlemen, how do you know anything? Can you be deceived by the eye? You can, you have proved this; you all know that there are men who can deceive the sight of the eye, no matter how closely you observe their movements. Can you be deceived in hearing? Yes; you may hear sounds but not understand their import or whence they came. Can you be deceived by the touch of the fingers? You can. The nervous system will not detect everything. What will? The revelations of the Lord Jesus Christ, *the spirit of truth will detect everything, and enable all who possess it to understand truth from error, light from darkness, the things of God from the things not of God.* **It is the only thing that will enable us to understand the Gospel of the Son of God, the will of God, and how we can be saved.** Follow it, and it will lead to God, the fountain of light, where the gate will be open, and the mind will be enlightened so that we shall see, know and understand things as they are." (*DBY, pg. 34*)

Joseph Fielding Smith also had this to say on the subject, "When a man has the manifestation from the Holy Ghost, it leaves an indelible impression on his soul, one that is not easily erased. It is spirit speaking to spirit, and it comes with convincing force. A manifestation of an angel, or even the Son of God himself, would impress the eye and mind, and eventually become dimmed, but the impressions of the Holy Ghost sink deeper into the soul and are more difficult to erase." (*Answers to Gospel Questions, Joseph Fielding Smith, 2:151*)

Revelation from God to the spirit will burn a stronger testimony into our souls than can be obtained with our own eyes, ears, and other physical senses. These senses can be deceived as well as lose their conviction, but a revelation to the soul is irrefutable, save by our own will to deny that revelation. In a very personal sense, we must appeal to God for truth. He knows what level of truths we are ready for and need. If we fail to seek personal revelation of the Holy Ghost in our search for truth; if we fail to be patient enough to wait on God's witness to us; if we listen only to our own inner desires and physical senses; we fall victim to misinterpretations, false perceptions, and faulty definitions (a bag of bugaboos we all, unfortunately, bring to the table with every thought we possess).

My Perception, My Truth

I have been in discussions with people who believe *perception* is truth. This notion was popularized in the sixties by the pseudo-intellectuals of that day. They say that our perception is truth. No, a thousand times no! I believe others cling to this concept because they don't understand what we've just discussed about non-Euclidian geometry, the different geometries with different but absolute truths attached. Our perceptions are ***a*** truth but not necessarily ***the*** truth. It may very well be that our perception of something is true, if we have perceived it correctly. It may also very well be that another person has a true but differing perception of the same thing because they are in a different geometry. Take, as an example, a room that is 78 degrees Fahrenheit and a person walks into the room from a colder outdoors. This person's perception is that the room is hot, whereas a person who just walked into the room from, say, a hot kitchen, would perceive the room to be cold. Now which is true? Coming from their unique vantage point or geometry, both are true, that is to say, it is true that to the first the room *feels* hot and it is also true that to the second, the room *feels* cold. These are perceptions. This is consistent with the *reality* they are both experiencing. It is also consistent with our concept of different geometries having different truths. However, if that first person, who thought the room was hot, perceived it to be 90 degrees, he or she would be wrong as anything more or less than 78 degrees is not true (things as they are). Further, notwithstanding the second person's true perception of the room being cold, if that person perceived it to be 60 degrees, he or she would be wrong.

Should either person have perceived the room to be 78 degrees, they would now have hold of not only the truth of their perception of its relative hot or cold, but also have a second truth that the room is 78 degrees. If your perception of something is wrong, though it is true in itself that that is your perception, you still have no *knowledge* of things as they really are, were, or will be. You have only *a false perception*.

We all have differing perceptions. In fact, it would be difficult for any two people to have exactly the same perception, as there are many factors that put us all in different geometries such as physical variances, individual perspectives, personality traits, insights, abilities, experiences, personal history, environments, and etc. We are as different as snowflakes, and unless we are relating in general terms, we are probably going to perceive things differently. Does this make us right or wrong? That depends on whether or not our perception is correct. If, whether wittingly or unwittingly, our perceptions are false, no matter how real it may seem to us, we are laboring under a falsehood and will be bound, not free, because we do not *know things as they really are*. The magician's tricks *seem* real too, but are illusions.

Our false perceptions can, and do, get us into trouble more often than we even know. For instance, say you watch a magician put a woman in a box and, with a large saw, he saws her in half. Then he magically makes her whole again. Who has not seen this trick? Our good sense tells us that this is an illusion, that it is not real. But what if we acted on our perception rather than our good sense? What if we went home and tried to saw a person in half. Obviously, someone is going to get hurt, or in other words, our perception of what is true could give us grief.

This is happening to all of us all the time, on many levels, as our perceptions are polluted, tainted by all manner of untruth. A friend of mine recently wrote a very fine book called *Life Without Cheap Sunglasses,* in which he tells of how, while on vacation, he and his wife visited a beautiful flower garden. Upon strolling through the garden for most of a day he could not understand his wife's half-hearted reaction to the beauty of the flowers until they discovered that the true color and beauty had been dampened and distorted by the cheap sunglasses she had been wearing. Unfortunately, they were unable to go back through the garden again so the flowers' splendor and elegance was lost to her. Likewise, whether by choice or default, we are all, unfortunately, viewing the world through more or less distorted, discolored, cloudy glasses. Paul's statement comes to mind, "*For now we see through a glass, darkly*; but then face to face: now I know in part; but then shall I know even as also I am known." (*1 Corinthians 13:11-12*).

So, **our** perception is ***a*** truth, in and of its self, but may not reflect the truth of the thing it relates to. Our *reality*, that is, what we *perceive* to be true (what seems real to us), does not make it so, ***but it seems so to us***. Still, any perception we have, though possibly false, should be considered valid to some degree or at least important, because that perception is what is real or what seems true to us, and that truth in itself, is ***a*** truth worthy of attention. Nevertheless, such a perception should not *necessarily* be considered truth, at least not *just because* they are our perceptions.

Since we all work from our perceptions, that is what seems real or true to us (our *reality*), we must pay close attention to each other's realities so we can relate to each other. But, we must also be careful not to *necessarily* accept each other's perceptions as truth. Even though each other's perceptions may be true, we might be in a different geometry requiring a different truth. Again, what is true to us *may* not relate to or resemble in any way, things as they *are perceived by others*. And again, no matter what the geometry, the only sure way to know truth is to become one with the spirit of truth itself. "Howbeit when He, the Spirit of truth, is come, He will guide you into all truth . . . ." (*John 16:13*) A spiritual revelation is certain when our perceptions may not be. But let us get back to why truth is so elusive.

Who Said That?

My nephew Bevan and I have a very comfortable relationship. We are able to discuss just about any subject and often do. We were at lunch one day discussing a subject that I will cover in a following chapter, when he turned to me and said, "Where did you get this? What General Authority[57] said that?" The implication was that if I hadn't received this bit of truth from a sanctioned source, namely a General Authority, then he could not accept it as being true. Further, the implication is that if it *did* come from a General Authority, it *must* be true. I am sure that anyone who has sat through a gospel doctrine class in The Mormon Church has heard the above statement or a similar one. What is worse, when it comes to doctrine, we in The Church have a tendency to classify even General Authorities according to believability, credibility, or acceptability. Occasionally, General Authorities will disagree with each other, which gives us the opportunity to quote only those who support our views, to the exclusion of those who differ. If I were a General Authority, I would hate to have the responsibility of absolutely speaking the truth every time I opened my mouth. In their writings, many have declined this responsibility by saying that it is only their opinion. My question is; what difference does it make if *it is only their opinion*? If what they are saying is true, it is true!

Remember too, that the General Authorities, by virtue of their position, must often speak to The Church and the public in generalities. Further, it depends on our understanding the geometry or realm in which the truth is given as well as understanding the geometry or realm in which it is received. Remember, they must speak to those who are in need of milk as well as those who are in need of meat. If you could sit in counsel with them, what they might say to you on a personal basis, in accordance with your individual need, could be entirely different from the counsel they give to the whole Church. Still, I would search my soul deeply if I found myself receiving personal revelation that ran counter to the admonitions of the prophet to the general membership.

Safety In Numbers

Some of us seem to side with the majority, no matter what the issue or the argument. The reasoning here is of course, that the greater numbers can't be wrong. But they can be and historically have been over and over again. Of course it is easier to make a defense of your position when you have the weight of the majority behind you. Still, I am reminded of Albert Einstein's statement in regards to the book published against his theories, *100 men against Einstein*. He remarked, "If they were right, one would be enough."

Truth, A Personal Responsibility

One must realize that although their callings may require General Authorities to be in tune with truth, as much as is humanly possible, it does not make them infallible or any more entitled to truth than the rest of us. These are men attempting to traverse the same path the rest of us must travel, namely faith, repentance, baptism, and reception of the Holy Ghost. They simply have a different calling than the rest of us. They are doing the best they can, and an excellent job I might hasten to add. But even they are varied in their gifts of the spirit and their doctrinal understandings.

Of course, should one whom we have sustained and accepted as a Prophet of God say, "Thus saith the Lord," we would be naturally bound to give his words all due respect. After all, isn't that his job and authority, to receive the word of the Lord for His people? Yes, and he does. The Prophet is the only person with the authority to speak on behalf of the Lord, to receive revelations *for the whole Church. He is* ***not****, however, the only person with a right* ***to know truth***. That is for individuals to seek out and find for themselves.

General Authorities are in the same process of discovering for themselves, that which is true. The notion that by virtue of their callings, General Authorities are more righteous than anyone else can possibly be, or more entitled to personal revelation than any of the rest of us, is simply not true. The Lord, in His wisdom, has chosen some very good and valiant men (and thankfully so) to represent Him and His Church but we all, *individually*, have not only the same responsibility, but the same opportunity to come to know God. Said Brigham Young, ". . . and if you want the mind and will of God at such a time, get it, it is just as much your privilege as of any other member of The Church and Kingdom of God. It is your privilege and duty to live so that you know when the word of the Lord is spoken to you and when the mind of the Lord is revealed to you. I say it is your duty to live so as to know and understand all these things." (*DBY pg. 163*) He even went further when he said, "My knowledge is, if you will follow the teaching of Jesus Christ and his Apostles, as recorded in the New Testament, *every man and woman* will be put in possession of the Holy Ghost; *every person will become a Prophet, Seer, and Revelator, and an expounder of truth.* They will know things that are, that will be, and that have been. They will understand things in heaven, things on the earth, and things under the earth, things of time, and things of eternity, according to their several callings and capacities." (*DBY pg. 161*) But let us remember, and I repeat that Brigham Young also said, "If the Lord Almighty should reveal to a High Priest, or to any other than the head, things that are true, or that have been and will be, and show to him the destiny of this people twenty-five years from now, or a new doctrine that will in five, ten, or twenty years hence become the doctrine of this Church and Kingdom, but which has not yet been revealed to this people, and reveal it to him by the same Spirit, the same messenger, the same voice, the same power that gave revelations to Joseph Smith when he was living, it would be a blessing to that High Priest, or individual; but he must rarely divulge it to a second person on the face of the earth, until God reveals it through the proper source to become the property of the people at large. Therefore when you hear Elders say that God does not reveal through the President of the Church that which they know, and tell wonderful things, you may generally set it down as a God's truth that the revelation they have had is from the Devil, and not from God. If they had received from the proper source, the same power that revealed to them would have shown them that they must keep the things revealed in their own bosoms, and they seldom would have a desire to disclose them to the second person." (*DBY pg. 338*)

We should never feel that we are less righteous or spiritually inferior to those who are called to serve us as leaders. Spirituality and righteousness is a function of personal obedience, not station, calling, or status in The Church or life in general. Some of the most spiritual and righteous men and women I have ever known have been regular members of The Church with no particular status at all. This goes for non-members as well. Still, I often hear members say that

General Authorities, stake presidents, bishops, and other leaders are on a higher plain of spirituality than are the rest of the membership. If they are, it is because they have individually struggled to become so, not because they have, by virtue of their callings, any spiritual entitlements that the rest of us cannot have. The path is the same. The process is the same for all men.

Joseph Smith made this point when asked if he believed that he was a prophet. "Yes and every other man who has the testimony of Jesus, for the testimony of Jesus is the spirit of Prophecy." (*TPJS pg. 119* see also *Revelation 19:10*) You see; personal revelation from the Holy Spirit is the foundation stone of truth and the Gospel of Jesus Christ (they are really one in the same). We should not take pride in our personal revelations, but we should not subordinate them to a place that is less than any other truth from God. Most certainly, we should not feel that we are less than those who are called to serve us.

The General Authorities, by virtue of their callings, must constantly be careful not to abuse their powers. Make no mistake. They have great influence. Can you imagine what would happen if the Prophet said, "It is time to march back to Independence, Jackson County, Missouri,[58] to establish the Zion Society"?[59] (More to come on the Zion Society.) Why, it would throw The Church, if not the entire nation, into a panic. Most Mormons are so willing to do what the Prophet says that they would forsake all to comply. Although, frankly speaking, the same members continually disregard the Prophet's counsel to stay out of debt, put up their food storage, stop drinking caffeine drinks, keep the Sabbath day holy, do their home teaching, study *The Book of Mormon*, pray daily, and the like. Go figure! At any rate, the Prophet and his counselors must be in tune with the spirit of truth constantly else they would cause the members to do the wrong thing at the wrong time.

Because one is personally responsible for what he or she believes, it behooves us all to take it to *the source* and try the promise that "by the power of the Holy Ghost ye may know the truth of all things." (*Moroni 10:5*) Regarding this personal responsibility, Brigham Young said (italics for emphasis), "I am more afraid that this people have so much confidence in their leaders that they will not inquire for themselves of God whether they are led by Him. I am fearful they settle down in a state of blind self-security, trusting their eternal destiny in the hands of their leaders with a reckless confidence that in itself would thwart the purposes of God in their salvation, and weaken that influence they could give to their leaders, did they know for themselves, by the revelations of Jesus, that they are led in the right way. *Let every man and woman know, by the whispering of the Spirit of God to themselves, whether their leaders are walking in the path the Lord dictates, or not.*" (*DBY, pg. 135*) Brigham Young further stated, "Now those men, or those women, who know no more about the power of God, and the influences of the Holy Spirit, than to be led entirely by another person, suspending their own understanding, and pinning their faith upon another's sleeve, will never be capable of entering into the celestial glory, to be crowned as they anticipate; they will never be capable of becoming Gods. They cannot rule themselves, to say nothing of ruling others, but they must be dictated to in every trifle, like a child. They cannot control themselves in the least, but James, Peter, or somebody else must control them. They never can become Gods, nor be crowned as rulers with glory, immortality, and eternal lives. They never can hold scepters of glory, majesty, and power in the celestial kingdom. Who will? Those who are *valiant and inspired with the true independence of heaven*, who will go forth boldly in the service of their God, leaving others to do as they please, determined to do right, though all mankind besides should take the opposite course." (*DBY, pg. 383*)

Without doing our own thinking, without having our own testimony, we can give no spiritual support to the truth. Without knowing for ourselves, we cannot glorify God. But more than that, when you stand before God at the judgment bar, you will have to stand solely on your own accomplishments, knowledge, and testimony, not anyone else's, not your mother's or father's, not your spouse's, not even the prophets'. You *must know for yourself*, independent of any other person that Christ lives, that He is your personal savior, and you must know, for yourself, what His gospel is, and by what laws you personally must live in order to qualify for a celestial glory.

We are also given to understand that in the last days, many of God's most righteous may be deceived. "For there shall arise false Christs, and false prophets, and shall shew great signs and wonders; insomuch that, if it were possible, they shall deceive the very elect." (*Matthew 24:24*) We do not believe our leaders are infallible. "When a prophet speaketh in the name of the Lord, if the thing follow not, nor come to pass, that is the thing which the Lord hath not spoken, but the prophet hath spoken it presumptuously; thou shalt not be afraid of him." (*Deuteronomy 18:22*) Is it saying here that one must wait to see if the prophecy is fulfilled in order to know if the prophet is speaking for the Lord or presumptuously? No, it is only saying that prophets aren't always speaking for the Lord when they say things and we must know when to listen to them. Said Harold B. Lee[60], "It is not to be thought that every word spoken by the General Authorities is inspired, or that they are moved upon by the Holy Ghost in everything they [speak] and write. Now you keep that in mind. I don't care what his position is, if he writes something or speaks something that goes beyond anything that you can find in the standard church works, unless that one be the prophet, seer, and revelator—please note that one exception—you may immediately say 'Well, that is his own idea.' And if he says something that contradicts what is found in the standard church works (I think that is why we call them 'standard'—it is the standard measure of all that men teach), you may know by that same token that it is false, regardless of the position of the man who says it." (*Place of the Living Prophet, Seer and Revelator, p 14, by Harold B. Lee*)

Joseph Smith also spoke to this issue when he said, "This morning I read German and visited with a brother and sister from Michigan, who thought that 'a prophet is always a prophet,' but I told them that a prophet was a prophet only when he was acting as such." (*TPJS, pg. 278*) Further the Lord has said, "And whatsoever they shall speak when moved upon by the Holy Ghost shall be scripture, shall be the will of the Lord, shall be the mind of the Lord, shall be the word of the Lord, shall be the voice of the Lord, and the power of God unto salvation." (*D&C 68:4*) Why? Because it is true and truth is things as they are, were, and will be. And how can you know whether they speak for the Lord or themselves? Indeed, you may be deceived or misled if you are unable to discern, for yourself, what is true. How do we know when they are moved upon by the Holy Ghost? Although it would be hard to go wrong when following a prophet, particularly when he states, "Thus saith the Lord," it is possible to misunderstand or receive a false perception and be misled. Also, even though what they say is truth, it *may* not be for you as you might be on a different level, in a different geometry, or have a different personal direction to go due to an individual revelation specifically for you.

So, how do we know? Well, we also must be moved upon by the Holy Ghost, for only by the power of the Holy Ghost will we know the truth of all things. "Therefore, why is it that ye cannot understand and know, that he that receiveth the word by the Spirit of truth receiveth it as it is preached by the Spirit of truth? Wherefore, he that preacheth and he that receiveth, understand one another, and both are edified and rejoice together." (*D&C 50:21-22*)

Let me again hasten to say here that it is important that we keep the commandments and stay close to the spirit or we run the risk of not being able to distinguish the whisperings of the Holy Spirit from our own inner desires or the prompting of the adversary (the Devil). If we are following our own desires instead of the Lord's spirit, we are in fact, breaking His laws and becoming a law unto ourselves. Or, in other words, we are making up our own rules. "That which breaketh a law, and abideth not by law, but seeketh to become a law unto itself, and willeth to abide in sin, and altogether abideth in sin, cannot be sanctified by law, neither by mercy, justice, nor judgment. Therefore, they must remain filthy still." (*D&C 88:35*) Again, this gives great importance to knowing the truth and we must know for ourselves. Knowing what is true for ourselves and obeying our personal revelations from the Holy Spirit is living on the edge of becoming a law unto ourselves, so we must be very careful. Even when a General Authority, or bishop, or gospel doctrine teacher, or book writer, or even your next door neighbor, or anyone at all speaks, you must discern by the power of the Holy Ghost whether what is said is, in fact, true and/or meant for you personally. Remember, you may be in a different geometry.

Clothed In Truth?

In regards to our discerning of truth, let me say that too often we place our belief of truth in physical evidences or outward appearances. When I think of this principle I can't help remembering a story that was told by a good member of my ward.[61] It seems that she and her husband decided to take a camping vacation through Canada. While there, they stopped at a campground near the small town of Cardston where there happens to be a Mormon temple which they planned to visit the following day. Late in the afternoon, a rather large group of motorcyclists came into the same camp. She described the roar of the bikes as almost deafening. They looked threatening with their black leather garb and the club insignias on their jackets. Knowing the reputation for trouble that biker clubs have, my friend and her husband nearly picked up to leave, but as they were already setup, and the motorcycle group settled down somewhat and were keeping pretty much to themselves, they decided to stay. The cyclists were up very early the next morning and no one slept past the sound of their bikes leaving the campground; however, all were relieved that they were gone. My friends packed up and went into town to visit the temple. When they pulled into the parking lot, to their surprise, they found the entire motorcycle club there at the temple. They were all members of The Church and were attending the temple, just like my friends.

We are spiritually lazy when we condescend to outward appearances as a means of judging who is righteous and who is not or whether what a person is saying is true. Like the children of Israel, we don't want to live by the Spirit of Truth; we want, as Brigham young said, to "be dictated to in every trifle." We want the Lord to give us laws that make everything black and white. And we've got them, laws a plenty. Though the laws most of us live today are a step above the Mosaic Law, they are still laws of carnal commandments and outward performances. We don't want to have to discern for ourselves who is truthful and righteous. We want visible evidences such as white shirts and ties to witness who is upright.

Truly Stunned

Not long ago I was with a business associate from the home office of a company I occasionally do work for. Just the two of us were in a restaurant for dinner when the subject of religion came up. When he learned I was Mormon he got quiet and somewhat withdrawn. I sensed there was something he didn't like about Mormons so I asked him straight out what it was. He was very reluctant but said, "There was something about Mormons that I find most disgusting. You don't want to hear about it." Thinking I had heard it all, that there was nothing he could say that would shock me, I pursued the conversation until I persuaded him to tell me what it was. He said, "It is the way you all wear white shirts."

"White shirts" I said? "What is the matter with white shirts?"

"Well," he returned, "you people wear them to show off your underwear. You know that everyone can see through white shirts so you show off your **holy** temple underwear. Then everyone can see you are one of the righteous."

As I sat stunned, he went on saying how pathetically self-righteous, pious, and sanctimonious it was and how when he was in Salt Lake City he sickened by having to see everyone's holy underwear everywhere he looked. I'm not sure how long he went on about it or exactly what all he said after that as I was in such a state of shock that I could hardly hear him. I had never in my life thought of this being the case. It wasn't until latter as I thought about it that I realized that although this man knew nothing about our "holy underwear," he made a very valid observation. I had to ask myself how often do we, how often do I, rely on such outward appearances as a means of determining a person's righteousness.

Now I wonder if this unwritten requirement and the pressure we put on the young and old male members of The Church to wear white shirts and ties could be based on our inability to spiritually determine their righteousness? It cannot be based upon a *moral issue,* as there is no inherent morality to clothes as long as they are modest and clean. What are we doing here? Are we trying to get everyone to conform to what we have determined is the look of a righteous man? Surely we are not attempting to deny the right of individual style and choice by a uniform dress code? Who is doing this? Though I am quite certain the general authorities would like us to look our very best and often encourage us to do so (particularly on the Sabbath Day or when conducting official church business), to my knowledge, there is no directive requiring members of The Church to wear any particular dress.

Of course there are some sacred ordinances such as baptism and some temple ordinances where a particular dress is required but according to the instructions given to all bishops concerning even the administration of the sacrament, all priesthood holders are required to conduct themselves with dignity and with a solemn, reverent attitude. They should *dress modestly, should be well groomed and clean*, and should wash their hands before performing the ordinance.

Too often I have seen bishops demand that their priesthood holders, particularly the Aaronic priesthood holders,[62] wear white shirts and ties when they allow the young ladies to wear dresses and other clothing that is clearly immodest (a real moral issue). I guess we think those who wear white shirts or even "holy underwear," are in keeping with the spiritual commandments as well. This is absurd. Are we so lacking in the gift of discernment? Don't we know that those who would desire to hide their personal sins can simply don the *uniform* of a righteous man (a business suit, white shirt, and tie) and assume the rhetoric in order to mask their misdeeds? It occurs to me that such a uniform tends to associate men with the Wall Street business world as much or more than anything spiritual. This uniform of the world may present an air of respectability but *proves* nothing and may be there only to cover one's *lack* of respectability. It would not be the first time the Devil has masked himself with a cloak of apparent righteousness.

It was this same principle that the Pharisees and Sadducees used to fool the masses in Christ's time. "Woe unto you, scribes and Pharisees, hypocrites! for ye are like unto whited sepulchers, which indeed appear beautiful outward, but are within full of dead men's bones, and of all uncleanness." (*Matthew 23:27*) They often wore sackcloth and ashes (I guess the white shirt and tie of the day) and prayed openly in the town squares that they might be seen of men but in their closets and their private dealings they were sinning. Yet because of their apparent righteous outward appearance they were acceptable to all but those with discernment of spirits.

I guess this issue has been with us a very long time. It should be noted that John the Baptist wore long hair and animal skins, lived in the wilderness, and ate wild honey and locust. Had he a Harley Davidson motorcycle he might have fit right in with the group my friends told us about. In any case, John's dress was not the acceptable style of the day. Because of that, The Church leaders of the time no doubt called his personal righteousness into question. Still, Christ searched him out to perform His most holy ordinance.

Too often we in The Church today condescend to judging others by their outward appearance. "He looks like a missionary, so he must be righteous," or "he can't be spiritual, he doesn't wear a dark suit, white shirt, and tie."

So here I am coming down on the white shirts and ties when, of course, **we all know, *there is absolutely nothing wrong with a white shirt and tie*** (though in the future when I purchase a white shirt it will probably be of a material thick enough you can't see through it). Should that be a man's individual choice, so be it! But we should not feel constrained, by lack of acceptance, to look like others do.

Please understand. I am not on a crusade to eradicate white shirts and ties. On the contrary, I wish I didn't have to spend any time at all talking about such mundane, temporal things. I look forward to the day when outward appearance is no issue at all. I am, however, on a crusade to promote judging by the spirit. But unfortunately, we utilize these things, everything from the length of a person's hair and the quality and style of their clothes to their occupations, cars they drive, and bank accounts. We use these things to plug them into various categories or degrees of righteousness. We have become so accustomed to judging by these outward signs that we do not appeal to the Holy Spirit to guide us.

Those who say, in accordance with Matthew 7:1, that we should "Judge not, that ye be not judged," need to read the inspired Joseph Smith Translation (JST) where he corrected the text to say, "Judge not unrighteously, that ye be not judged; but judge righteous judgment." (*JST Matthew 7:2*) The fact is that we must judge (not condemn, but judge) that is, discern, good and evil. "Wherefore, take heed, my beloved brethren, that ye do not judge that which is evil to be of God, or that which is good and of God to be of the devil. For behold, my brethren, it is given unto you to judge, that ye may know good from evil; and the way to judge is as plain, that ye may know with a perfect knowledge, as the daylight is from the dark night. For behold, the Spirit of Christ is given to every man, that he may know good from evil; wherefore, I show unto you the way to judge; for every thing which inviteth to do good, and to persuade to believe in Christ, is sent forth by the power and gift of Christ; wherefore ye may know with a perfect knowledge it is of God." (*Moroni 7:14-16*)

When we use outward appearance as the criteria, we consequently judge unrighteously and many good men and women slip into the background, while those who have the money or desire to buy the so-called proper appearance are given respectability, as well as the responsibility of leadership, credibility, and our trust. There is something very wrong with the use of these or any other outward so-called indicators of a person's individual righteousness. The white shirt and tie is my example, but the principle applies to all other things we see people do and say that make them appear to be in compliance, when in fact, it is all for show.

This is, at best, a terrestrial law. It is certainly not a celestial law. God does not place importance on such things. Why do we still insist upon doing so? How often has He cautioned us against looking to the outward appearance, but rather to look into the heart? "For the Lord seeth not as man seeth; for man looketh on the outward appearance, but the Lord looketh on the heart." (*1 Samuel 16:7*) Those who have been in The Church for some time know what is expected, what is acceptable, what things to do and say so that we may look like *good Mormons*. Of course I believe we should all look like good Mormons, whatever that "look" may be. But we should never trust such an appearance as the criteria for judging what a person may say or do to be righteous or true. "Judge not according to the appearance, but judge righteous judgment." (*John 7:24*)

It is often the *oddballs* that the Lord chooses to do His work. Enoch was classed as a "wild man". "Tarry ye here and keep the tents, while we go yonder to behold the seer, for he prophesieth, and there is a strange thing in the land: a *wild man* hath come among us." (*Moses 6:38*) Christ Himself was not accepted because He did not hold to tradition. He did not do and say (and probably did not wear) what was proper and right by religious tradition of the day and they crucified Him for it. Do not fall prey to outward appearances as a means of knowing what is true, as even the Devil can appear as an angel of light. Only by the Holy Spirit will we know the truth. Enough said on this subject of outward appearances.

I'm Waiting For Orders

Further, if we are waiting to hear *all*, that is, ***every*** truth from the mouth of the Prophet himself, we will not only be waiting for a long time, but our own testimonies and processes of knowing truth will be greatly stunted. The mysteries of heaven are revealed directly from God to righteous individuals. This is the only way you can come to know them. "For what man knoweth the things of a man, save the spirit of man which is in him? Even so the things of God knoweth no man, but the Spirit of God" (*1 Corinthians 2:11*) "Behold, great and marvelous are the works of the Lord. How unreachable are the depths of the mysteries of Him; and it is impossible that man should find out all His ways. And no man knoweth of His ways save it be revealed unto him; wherefore, brethren, despise not the revelations of God." (*Jacob 4:8*) "And to them will I reveal all mysteries, yea, all the hidden mysteries of my kingdom . . . . For by my Spirit will I enlighten them, and by my power will I make known unto them the secrets of my will—yea, even those things which eye has not seen, nor ear heard, nor yet entered into the heart of man . . . . By the power of the Spirit our eyes were opened and our understandings were enlightened, so as to see and understand the things of God . . . . Neither is man capable to make them known, for they are only to be seen and understood by the power of the Holy Spirit, which God bestows on those who love Him, and purify themselves before him." (*D&C 76:7, 10, 12* and*116*)

Not only is it the individual's responsibility to seek out and discern truth, but also if you want to know any mysteries, you must individually knock and seek in order to find. No one can do it for you. Bruce R. McConkie said (italics for emphasis), "Personal revelation is not limited to gaining a testimony and knowing thereby that Jesus, through whom the gospel came, is Lord of all, nor is it limited to receiving guidance in our personal and family affairs—although these are the most common examples of revelation among the Lord's people. In truth and in verity, there is no limit to the revelations each member of The Church may receive. It is *within the power of every person* who has received the gift of the Holy Ghost to see visions, entertain angels, learn the deep and hidden mysteries of the kingdom, and even see the face of God." (*Bruce R. McConkie, A New Witness for the Articles of Faith, pg. 489-pg. 490*)

Since The Church officially sanctions so little truth and so much is out there to be had, I submit it would be better to concern ourselves **more** with *that which is true* and not **just** *that which is sanctioned.*

So you see, my nephew's question really takes him down the wrong road. Like Euclid, he was trying to prove all things by a single geometry, when the Holy Ghost is willing, even waiting, to reveal many more geometries to us by personal revelation. We could then know for ourselves all truth, wherever it is found.

I Think, I Believe, I Know

Over the years I have developed a device that has been a great help to me in developing a solid process of discerning truth.

One of the problems in discerning truth is that, very often, the truth does not come as a great revelation, but rather like the formation of dew on the plants in the morning. This makes it hard to know, *really know*, what is true. My process is to divide things into three categories: things I *think* are true, things I *believe* are true, and things I *know* are true. That which would fall into the area of knowing are things that, over the course of my life, I have received repeated and numerous personal revelations, that is, witnesses of the Holy Ghost, as well as experienced a multitude of evidence, both temporal and spiritual, on the given matter, to the point that I know these things as surely as I am able to know anything. Examples of such things are: I *know* God lives; I *know* that Christ is my Savior; I *know The Book of Mormon* is true; I *know* that Joseph Smith is a prophet of God; and that The Church of Jesus Christ has been restored to the Earth by the hand of God. I *know* that this church has within it, the most truth, the saving ordinances, and the priesthood of God to administer those ordinances. I *know* that I love my wife and children. I *know* many earthly things, and I *know* many heavenly doctrines to be true, including many presented herein. I ***know*** these things not because of physical or temporal evidences only, but I have had a witness of the Spirit that they are true. Such spiritual witnesses carry with them *a knowledge* of truth that extends into the eternities. It is testimony that cannot be broken.

Orson Pratt[63] makes this principle clear (italics for emphasis), "Now, I want to appeal to the Latter-day Saints who occupy this room, whether this promise has been fulfilled to you, or not? I will read it again. 'But he that believeth these words which I have spoken, him will I visit with the manifestations of my Spirit, and he shall *know* and bear record.' It does not say, he shall merely have an *opinion* and bear record, but he shall *know* and bear record. Do you know that this book [*The Book of Mormon*] is true, Latter-day Saints? Do you know that what I have been reading are the words of the Lord? If you have believed these things with all of your hearts, and complied with the commands of the Most High, manifesting your faith by your works, then you have been put in possession of this knowledge, and you *know*, by the Spirit which He has poured out from heaven upon you, that they are true, and in force to all the world, and this Spirit gives you a *knowledge* concerning all truth. You are not like those who have no revelation of whom the ancient Apostle speaks, who were ever learning, and never able to come to the knowledge of the truth; but you are of those, if you keep the commandments of God, who are not only learning from the word of God, but have a knowledge of all revealed truth by the power of the Spirit, the Comforter, which is a revelator, an unction to all those who receive it; and they are able to bear record of the things which they formerly *believed* to be true." (*Journal of Discourses, [JD],*[64] *Vol.19, pg. 213-pg. 214, Orson Pratt, December 9, 1877*)

I expect others to say, "Yeah, but how will you feel when someday you find that you were wrong on at least one of these things you think you know?" In the first place, I don't "*think I know.*" I ***know***. I ***know*** these things to be true.

You see the difference? To find that they are not true *is impossible*. I can now hear you say, "Wow, how arrogant of this writer to presume always to be right and never to be wrong even on certain matters." Arrogant? No, I just *know* some things. If man is capable of knowing, really *knowing* anything, which I testify is so; then I *know* these kinds of things, by the spirit of the Holy Ghost, to be truth. Truth is eternal and I will never, not in this life or the eternal next, ever find out that that truth is *false*. John Taylor expressed these same sentiments (italics for emphasis), "Some people find fault with us about these things . . . for I have received a portion of the Spirit of the Lord and *I know it*; and if you have received a portion of that same Spirit *you know it*, and you cannot un-know it—it is impossible, you cannot un-know it, unless you sin against God and as the apostle said, grieve the Spirit by which you were sealed; then it withdraws from you, then you will not know much about it . . . ." (*JD, Vol.21, pg. 346-pg. 347, John Taylor, January 2, 1881*) If a thing is true and I know it to be so, it will remain so forever. Remember the Lord's definition of truth, "And Truth is *knowledge* of things as they are, and as they were, and as they are to come." (*D&C 93:24*) If I do indeed have that knowledge, I will always have it. Once you know a truth by the testimony of the Spirit, it is yours. You have it. You cannot lose it save through sin and your choice to deny it. Moreover, you may choose to deny it all you want, but it will not change the truth. You would simply no longer have hold of it.

In other words, I am saying that I have hold of some eternal facts; they are a part of me and will be forever.

To answer your accusation of possibly being wrong on a matter, yes, of course I may be wrong, not with the things that I *know*, but with the things I *believe* to be true or *think may* be true. Should I one day find that some of the things I *believed* to be true are not; I would be surprised but not shocked. I would not lose my testimony of the things I *know* nor would my world crumble. It would simply be a matter of not having received enough data (spiritual revelations, experience, information, and other evidences) to **know** yet whether a matter is true. Some of the concepts that I present in these writings I only *believe* to be true, I do not *know* (I try to express that distinction as I write). Should I one day discover that one or more are not true, I would still have in place many *known* truths. Also, I would still have intact my solid *process* of discernment of truth. When new data or a spiritual witness comes to my consciousness that is in opposition to what I believe, I must change my belief. Again, this will have no effect upon what I ***know***.

As far as the matters that I *think may* be true, I am not in the least surprised when I receive data that contradicts. I am often wrong in this category. It is also in this category that I do most of my reasoning and have most of my debates with people, drawing into the conversations things I know and believe as a standard against which I weigh my new thinking. However, when it comes to knowing a certain thing my mind does not argue about what I know. There is no point because I already know it, by the Spirit, to be true.

I am very careful not to move things into the "I know" category until I receive a witness of the Spirit and it comes to me as certain knowledge. I might suggest to the reader that you separate things into these three categories and when you do, don't weaken your "I know" category by putting things into it before you really know they are true. Keep them in the "I believe" or "I think" categories. Too often we testify that we *know* something when what we really mean is we *believe* or we *think* we know. That is not knowledge. As you use this process, it will help you to eliminate confusion and doubt, not only with others, but also in your own mind. As you search for the truth, you will become more confident in your ability to discern truth and know some things absolutely. Remember, it is the Spirit that enables you to *know* a thing.

Where Is Truth?

We have discussed why truth is so elusive, but where is truth found?

To answer that, I must quote a scripture that gives us perhaps the greatest truth in all of holy writ relative to the character of God and our relationship with Him. This truth, Einstein and many others paid dearly to discover. It is namely that, *"There is no such thing as immaterial matter. All spirit is matter, but it is more fine or pure, and can only be discerned by purer eyes. We cannot see it, but when our bodies are purified we shall see that it is all matter."* (*D&C 131:7-8*) If this concept does not register with you, read it again and again until you realize the import of what the Lord is saying here. I will make reference to this concept many times.

Something From Nothing?

In other words, all things are made of some kind of matter. When you think about it, it makes perfect sense. You can't have something made of nothing. If it exists, in any form, it is made of something, some form of matter. We readily accept this relevant to the elements of the earth that we can see, touch, and otherwise detect. This matter I will call *gross-matter*. What we don't so easily accept is that things that we can't see, touch, and otherwise detect are also made of matter, *spirit-matter*.

There are probably many, if not infinite kinds of *spirit-matter* and I here make no attempt to understand or explain but the few that I am familiar with. First, there are our *spirit-matter* bodies that, together with our gross-matter bodies (physical bodies), make our souls. "And the *spirit* and the *body* are the soul of man." (*D&C 88:15*) When the *spirit-matter* body leaves the gross-matter body, we call it death. "For as the *body* without the *spirit* is dead, so faith without works is dead also." (*James 2:26*) Resurrection is the reuniting of these two forms of matter. "And now I bid unto all, farewell. I soon go to rest in the paradise of God, until my *spirit and body shall again reunite*, and I am brought forth triumphant through the air, to meet you before the pleasing bar of the great Jehovah, the Eternal Judge of both quick and dead. Amen." (*Moroni 10:34*)

The Spectrum

Some other types of *spirit-matter* are obvious to us because we can see them or otherwise detect them with instruments we have developed such as radio waves, microwaves, infrared waves, light waves, ultraviolet waves, X-rays, gamma-rays, and cosmic rays. I have here only gone up the Electromagnetic Spectrum to the place where we do not yet have a means of detecting higher forms of *spirit-matter*. If you could continue up the Electromagnetic Spectrum you would find other types of *spirit-matter* that are perhaps not so obvious but nonetheless real. The spirit side of our souls is made up of unseeable, generally undetectable matter. Thoughts and emotions fall within this realm of pure *spirit-matter*. When you form a thought or feel an emotion, somehow, the brain, in combination with the spirit body, has the ability to organize *spirit-matter* into a thought. Such thoughts and emotions exist in a geometry that, like radio waves from a transmitter, can go out of the gross-matter body at great speeds to great distances, perhaps to infinity.

It's Real!

We have a tendency to think that this undetectable *spirit-matter* is somehow less real than the gross-matter that we can feel or easily discern with our physical senses. The fact is that *spirit-matter* is infinitely *more material, less confining, and more powerful*, with capabilities far beyond that of gross-matter. The problem lies in our limited perception of this *spirit-matter*. As the Lord said to Joseph Smith, when our bodies are purified, we shall see that it is matter. I submit that we will not only see it, but see how much greater and able it is, in nearly all respects, than gross-matter.

I bring this concept to our discussion here because it makes clear many heretofore, scriptural references that were confusing. The Lord has revealed a great deal, particularly to modern prophets (Joseph Smith and others), about the characteristics and properties of *spirit-matter* as it relates to religious as well as scientific themes. For instance, "God is a Spirit: and they that worship Him must worship Him in spirit and in truth." (*John 4:24*) "Even the Spirit of truth; whom the world cannot receive, because it seeth Him not, neither knoweth Him: but ye know Him; for He dwelleth with you, and shall be in you." (*John 14:17*)

Is God spirit? Yes, His spirit, like ours, is clothed in a gross-matter body (although, unlike ours, His gross-matter body is a pure, glorified physical body). Like us, He has a spirit side of His soul and according to the above scriptures, those who worship Him, or want to know Him or communicate with Him, must do so in spirit. (I will spend some time on the subject of the spirit side of the godhead in a subsequent chapter.) This is pure communication and it applies to our communications one with another as well. "Therefore, why is it that ye cannot understand and know, that he that receiveth the word by the Spirit of truth receiveth it as it is preached by the Spirit of truth? Wherefore, he that preacheth and he that receiveth, understand one another, and both are edified and rejoice together." (*D&C 50:21-22*)

These next scriptures get right to my point of all this discussion about *spirit-matter*. "For the word of the Lord is truth, and whatsoever is truth is light, and whatsoever is light is Spirit, even the Spirit of Jesus Christ. And the Spirit giveth light to every man that cometh into the world; and the Spirit enlighteneth every man through the world, that hearkeneth to the voice of the Spirit." (*D&C 84:45-46*) Truth is light. Light is spirit, and as we've already learned, spirit is matter. You see; ***truth is made of matter***, spirit-matter.

Again, since we don't know how spirit-matter works or how many types there are, we cannot say definitively which matter is which. We may assume though, that since we know there are many spheres (geometries) in which God places truth, there is a realm of spirit-matter out there that embodies all truth, and that that truth-matter emanates from Christ, the source, to fill the immensity of space. The properties of this matter are such that we, through our own spirits, can all partake of or share in it. It is called the spirit of Christ, though it is a different spirit-matter than His spirit body, that is, the other half of His soul. Apparently, it is the spirit-matter side of our souls that is capable of communion with other forms of spirit-matter, as "they that worship Him must worship Him in spirit and in truth." (*John 4:24*)

This truth-matter from Christ is further explained in this next scripture which says, "He that ascended up on high, as also He descended below all things, in that He comprehended all things, that He might be *in all* and *through all* things, the light of truth; which truth shineth. This is the light of Christ. As also He is in the sun, and the light of the sun, and the power thereof by which it was made. As also He is in the moon, and is the light of the moon, and the power thereof by which it was made; As also the light of the stars, and the power thereof by which they were made; And the earth also, and the power thereof, even the earth upon which you stand. And the light which shineth, which giveth you light, is through Him who enlighteneth your eyes, which is the same light that quickeneth your understandings; Which light proceedeth forth from the presence of God to fill the immensity of space. The light which is in all things, which giveth life to all things, which is the law by which all things are governed, even the power of God who sitteth upon His throne, who is in the bosom of eternity, who is in the midst of all things." (*D&C 88:6-13*)

Wow! Those are high concepts! Let's see if we can understand them.

Enlighten Our Understanding

How can this light of Christ or light of truth be in all things and through all things when all things are made of different elements? How can it be in the stars, sun, moon, and earth, and at the same time be the power by which they were made? How can this same light shine from the sun in our eyes and at the same time inspire our minds and give us understanding? How can this same light also be the life-giving force of all things? How can this light be in all these things and be the power of God that fills the immensity of space for eternities to come?

It would seem that this explicit and definitive scripture only adds to our confusion or lack of understanding of truth. To help us comprehend what is being said, let us take a closer look at the Electromagnetic Spectrum. Although I am no physicist, let me make an attempt to explain what the Electromagnetic Spectrum is. Simply put, all things, sun, earth, people, rocks, tables, and etc., radiate electromagnetic energy. That is, due to the interplay of the positively and negatively charged particles that make up these things, energy waves radiate from the particular thing.

An obvious example of this is the energy field created by putting the ends of two magnets near to each other or a metallic material. Although we cannot see the energy of this electromagnetic field, one can easily feel the power or force field created between the two. In the same way, all things, by their very existence, create a force field of radiating electromagnetic energy. Scientists have learned to detect this energy and measure it in terms of frequency of oscillations (how often they pulse) and length of oscillation waves (length between the crests of the waves formed by the oscillations). The frequencies of these oscillations are measured on a scale of hertz (Hz). On the very low end (slowest frequency of oscillations and greatest length or distance between waves) of detectable electromagnetic frequencies of the spectrum are electric power and audio sounds. Within this range we have all audible tones or the octaves of the piano and other instruments, each note or tone having its own unique frequency of oscillation. Think of the individual notes created by the unique vibration of the individual piano strings. We have also all other sounds with their assorted tones that fall within man's ability to hear. Of course, some people have greater hearing ranges than do others. Some animals, such as dogs, can hear much higher frequencies than people, but all of these audio tones are on the low end of the Electromagnetic Spectrum.

Also in this range is the power we use to run our electrical appliances in our homes. As you go to faster, shorter frequencies, you run into radio waves. Within this range you will find citizen band (CB), AM and FM broadcasting (your home stereo receiver), amateur, professional, and government assigned radio bands. You will also find all your TV channels on either the VHF (very high frequency) or UHF (ultra high frequency) parts of the spectrum.

Higher up the Electromagnetic Spectrum you move into microwaves, the frequencies that heat water or moisture in the food we put in our microwave ovens. Still higher on the Spectrum we have infrared light rays. This takes us to visible light from the sun. Each color of the rainbow has its own unique frequency, red being the lowest and purple being the highest. This band of visible light is a very slight part of the Spectrum. Then you move into ultraviolet rays that, although they can't be seen, will give you a sunburn. The next stop on the spectrum is X-rays, which we all know is used to detect broken bones, find cavities in your teeth, and etc. Finally, we reach gamma rays caused by atomic explosions and cosmic rays that are particles of electromagnetic energy coming from outer space and passing through the earth in great quantities at great speeds. This is as far up the Electromagnetic Spectrum as scientists have been able to detect. It is also worth noting that the higher up the Spectrum you go, the greater the power of the energy being emitted or radiated.

The Truth, The Whole Truth, And Nothing But The Truth

Now, why have I included this description of the Electromagnetic Spectrum in a discussion about the Spirit of Christ? Well, you will observe that we are running our household appliances, *hearing* radio and TV broadcasting, heating food, *seeing*, getting sun burned, and using X-rays all by means of the same substance, electromagnetic energy. Further, if we had the means to detect and continue the Electromagnetic Spectrum downward to lower frequencies, we would find that all gross-matter things (dirt, wood, flesh, and etc.) are made of this same substance. Conversely, if we could continue up the spectrum, we would find all those undetectable forms of spirit-matter including the spirit sides of our souls, thought, emotion, and, yes, truth itself, are also made of this same stuff! It is made up of matter, spirit-matter. This is how the spirit of Christ, this truth-matter is, in fact, **in all things** and **through all things** at the same time and still lights our eyes and enlightens our understanding or minds while it gives us life.

It is critical to understand that truth; a knowledge of things as they are, were, and are to come, is matter, spirit-matter. Apparently, it shines and lights the stars, moon, earth, and sun as well as increases our understanding, or in other words, inspires our thoughts.

This truth-matter is also the law that governs all things and the life-giving force in all things. It is the formative agent that, like glue, holds the spirit body in the gross body, giving it life. Further, this truth-matter lasts forever just as it is.

Speaking philosophically, *truth isn't everything, it is the* ***only*** *thing!*

This is precisely why one must never deny truth. To do so would be to separate one's self, not only from Christ, its source, but also from life-giving matter, even spiritual life. "And now behold, I say unto you then cometh a death, even a second death, which is a spiritual death; then is a time that whosoever dieth in his sins, as to a temporal[65] death, shall also die a spiritual death; yea, he shall die as to things pertaining unto righteousness." (*Alma 12:16*) Joseph Smith tells us that, "All sins shall be forgiven, except the sin against the Holy Ghost; for Jesus will save all except the sons of perdition. What must a man do to commit the unpardonable sin? He must receive the Holy Ghost, have the heavens opened unto him, and know God, and then sin against Him. After a man has sinned against the Holy Ghost, there is no repentance for him. He has got to say that the sun does not shine while he sees it; he has got to deny Jesus Christ when the heavens have been opened unto him, and to deny the plan of salvation with his eyes open to the truth of it; and from that time he begins to be an enemy. This is the case with many apostates of The Church of Jesus Christ of Latter-day Saints." (*TPJS, pg. 358*)

How do we deny the Holy Ghost? We deny truth. How do we deny truth? *We lie to ourselves.*

A Lie Is A Lie

It is probable that, at times in our lives, we will find reasons to lie to others. Whether that is a sin or not depends on the situation or the geometry within which we are operating, but there is *never*, I repeat ***never***, a proper time to lie to one's self. To lie to one's self is to deny truth. This is a simple concept that we have yet to understand or digest. When truth comes to us by the testimony of Him who testifies of *all* truth, namely the Holy Ghost, and we don't accept it, we have effectively lied to ourselves. We tell ourselves that the particular truth is *not true* and for reasons of pride, fear, jealousy, or whatever, we choose to believe ourselves. **This is an extremely dangerous place to be**! It is far more dangerous than lying to others. It does not matter the size of the truth, when you deny it, the effect is the same. You are not only searing with a hot iron that still small voice of conscience, the Holy Ghost, but you are moving away from the source of all truth, God. Yet, we lie to ourselves continually. Our psychologists today, call it *being in denial*, a nice little label that only means we are the last to know a particular truth. Let's call a spade a spade. We are lying to ourselves, period!

The more we lie to ourselves, the more we become comfortable with it until we can no longer discern truth from lies. We build scenarios or fantasies in our minds of the way we want to believe things are, were, or will be. Then we tell ourselves that these fantasies are true and because we believe what we *want or choose* to believe, we have chosen to believe our own lies. If we do it often enough, we develop a pattern. If this pattern is extended to the ultimate lie, the denial of God Himself (after we know Him), we are completely cut off from His presence and thus, die the second or spiritual death. It is as the Prophet Joseph says, a person will "say that the sun does not shine while he sees it." You may ask, "How can anyone be so stupid as to be looking at the sun and deny that it is shining?" Remember, believing what we believe is a choice and we all have reasons why we make our choices the way we do. Maybe we don't deny the shinning of the sun but we all deny some truths on some level or to some degree, because we cannot see what we refuse to see. In the words of a couple of popular songs, "There are none so blind as they who will not see."

It's funny how we all seem to have the ability to recognize this self-lying in others but cannot see it in ourselves. Don't we all know someone who is lying to himself, denying a truth that it is obvious to everyone else concerned? Do you know someone like that? Of course you do. Some people lie so much they become pathological liars, that is to say, they can no longer distinguish between truth and fantasy and they lie for no apparent reason. And haven't you asked yourself how can they believe something that is so evidently and obviously not true? They do because they choose to. We all have reasons, needs, or some other motivation that causes us to make such choices. The sad truth is that we are all the same. We all, for reasons only we can say, lie to ourselves from time to time, as if our lie will change the truth of that which we are refusing to face. It will not. Truth is things as they are, were, and are to come. No matter our attempts to change it, the truth will ultimately come forth.

Lie And Die

The key is not to lie in the least, even to others. I know a guy that I have known from my youth. For the sake of making his stories more exciting to his listeners, he *embellishes* the truth. It may make for better stories, but this guy has done it so long that when he tells a story that others or I were involved in, we can hardly recognize it. What is worse, when we call him on his *embellishments*, we find that he really believes his own version of what happened, no matter whether it makes sense or not. No amount of reason will tear him from his untruths. Like most people, when caught in a lie, he only becomes angry with us. Now, it would not be so bad if, as he tells the story, he would admit to the embellishments. We could all still enjoy the story as part fiction, without demanding absolute truth in his recall, but he tells the stories as if they were true, not *as they were*, but the way he *wishes they were*. He has done this so long that he now has great difficulty in separating truth from his false scenarios. This has permeated his life and perceptions until he can no longer discern truth. It has cost him his marriage and his standing in The Church, and unless he decides to start telling himself the truth, it will ultimately cost him much more.

When we lie to ourselves, deny the Holy Ghost, we deny the spirit-matter that gives us life, spiritual life. We separate our spirits from this life-giving spirit-matter. If you lie to yourself long enough or completely enough and against great enough truths, it takes you to that state of perdition, or eternal damnation, where, like the Devil himself, there is no truth found in you. Your denial of truth is complete and so is your separation from its source, God. "Thus saith the Lord concerning all those who know my power, and have been made partakers thereof, and suffered themselves through the power of the Devil to be overcome and to deny the truth and defy my power—They are they who are the sons of perdition, of whom I say that it had been better for them never to have been born." (*D&C 76:31-32*)

I cannot make this point too strongly. Honesty with one's self is the beginning of all personal righteousness and inevitably impacts your relationship with God.

Imagine yourself on *one* road that leads two directions, upward to the light or truth of heaven and downward to lies and outer darkness. When you deny truth, you turn your face from the light of heaven and begin to descend into darkness. The process of progress is the same on that road. The difference is what direction you are facing. Unhappily, we all spend a great deal of time looking one way then the other and back again. Our heads are spinning. Don't panic though. It is a process, and there are reasons why we must experience falseness (a subject for another chapter). I don't offer this tiny bit of consolation as an excuse but rather a fact of mortal life. So don't be too hard on yourself.

Remember The Basics

Let me take a little time out here to say in this writing I am trying to advance our understanding of certain principles; consequently, I am spending very little time on the "hows" and "ways" to come to higher truths. I am, therefore, trusting that we are all attending our organized religious meetings, studying from good books, praying, and otherwise seeking out those basic, correct principles of how to live righteous and productive lives. And of course, then living those correct principles to the best of our ability. Just because I give emphasis to understanding the particular principles I am herein attempting to advance, one should not get the idea that I mean, in any way, to devalue or relegate to unimportance those other basic principles such as integrity, wisdom, honesty, faith, patience, kindness, tolerance, mercy, temperance, humility, morality, dedication, and etc. A valiant attempt must be made to keep all the commandments of God and these as well as many more personal virtues must be brought into our individual characters or *knowledge of higher principles will do us no good whatsoever*. Hopefully, these principles of goodness and Godliness are the foundation of all organized religions and ideologies. At least, I can say this should be true of all Christian religions as Christ taught these virtues and commanded us to live them. So far as Christian sects are concerned, faith is the grand key, as you cannot be saved by the grace of a Christ you do not believe or have faith in.

As we search for truth, let Bruce R. McConkie's words guide us: "The truth seeker asks, 'Canst thou by searching find out God? Canst thou find out the Almighty unto perfection?' (*Job 11:7.*) The answer: Yes and no. Yes, if the search is in the realm of the Spirit so that the laws are learned and lived whereby revelation comes; no, if the search is in the laboratory, in the philosopher's classroom, or through the scientist's telescope. Yes, if the spiritual laws by which He may be found are obeyed; no, in all other circumstances. Truly did the Holy Ghost say, by the mouth of Paul: 'For after that in the wisdom of God the world by wisdom knew not God, it pleased God by the foolishness of preaching to save them that believe.' (*1 Cor. 1:21.*)" (*Bruce R. McConkie, The Promised Messiah, pg. 14*)

By no means do I here intend to subordinate the importance of faith and the need to live right. So that you cannot accuse me of not so stating, let me say, here and now, that we may not expect the Lord to bless us with a greater endowment of truth if we are not willing, with every fiber of our ability, to accept and live the truths He has given us and to keep His commandments. Only then are we His *disciples indeed*, and only then may we expect to *know the truth* and be set *free* thereby (see *John 8:31-32*). Joseph Smith set the example and outlined the proper course when he said, "We would say to the brethren, seek to know God in your closets, call upon Him in the fields. Follow the directions of *The Book of Mormon*, and pray over, and for your families, your cattle, your flocks, your herds, your corn, and all things that you possess; ask the blessing of God upon all your labors, and everything that you engage in. Be virtuous and pure; be men of integrity and truth; keep the commandments of God; and then you will be able, more perfectly, to understand the difference between right and wrong—between the things of God and the things of men; and your path will be like that of the just, which shineth brighter and brighter unto the perfect day." (*TPJS, pg. 247*)

Forever Truth

One of the greatest properties of truth is that it is eternal. It endures forever. Falseness and evil do not. *Untruth exists on a principle of self-destruction.* "Tolerance replies: I have the truth and know that truth will prevail. Why should I contend against others and their views? Such true principles as they possess shall prevail and all else will vanish away in due course, for truth only is eternal." (*Bruce R. McConkie, Doctrinal New Testament Commentary, pg. 63*) "We can do nothing against the truth. In the eternal sense, nothing we do to fight the truth shall prosper. However plausible and popular error may be, eventually it shall die. Truth only shall prevail." (*Bruce R. McConkie, Doctrinal New Testament Commentary, pg. 452*)

To contend against evil or untruth gives it power. "But I say unto you, that ye resist not evil; but whosoever shall smite thee on thy right cheek, turn to him the other also." (*Matthew 5:39*) That's hard to live but it is a celestial law. Please note here that this doctrine does not relieve us of our responsibility to contend with the evil within us. "For the natural man is an enemy to God, and has been from the fall of Adam, and will be, forever and ever, unless he yields to the enticings of the Holy Spirit, and putteth off the natural man and becometh a saint through the atonement of Christ the Lord . . ." (*Mosiah 3:19*) This is not a cop-out on our personal responsibility to try and make the world a better place by fighting the enemy within, but unless the Lord specifically calls us to contend against evil we should let time and the properties of evil take their natural course. It is here noted that certainly there are many that are called to be warriors and certainly there are times when we all must stand against evil, but I feel we would all be far better off if we would stop trying to fix all the perceived ills of the world. Not only may our perceptions of the wrongs be faulty, in which case we become a part of the problem; but there are also many earthly flaws that the Lord, for reasons of His own, does not want to be fixed quite yet. Further, if we would all simply concentrate on fixing ourselves, the ills of the world would consequently be fixed. My grandfather had a saying that went something like this: "Make yourself an honest man and you can be sure that there is at least one less culprit in the world." Brigham Young, concerning the Kingdom of God, gave the same good advice. "Let the Kingdom alone, the Lord steadies the ark; and if it does jostle, and appear to need steadying, if the way is a little sideling sometimes, and to all appearance threatens its overthrow, be careful how you stretch forth your hand to steady it; let us not be too officious in meddling with that which does not concern us; let it alone, it is the Lord's work." (*DBY pg. 66, see also 2 Samuel 6:6-7*)

Often the world seems upside down, but it is supposed to be (a subject for another chapter). We only need to concentrate on our own faults and let God straighten out the rest of the world how and when He chooses. Likely as not, the natural course of corruption will have saved Him the trouble. Evil will eventually turn on itself and destroy itself. Let the Devil have his own.

Where Is It Hiding?

So where is truth found? There should be no secret here. It doesn't just come from General Authorities as my nephew implied. No. It is everywhere! It is *in all things* and *through all things the light of Christ or the light of truth* (see *D&C 88:6-13, 41*).

It is hard for a person like me to expand my small mind to an understanding that there is a kind of matter that has the ability to be omnipresent throughout the expanse of space and enlighten my mind too. But if my mind can comprehend the notion that cosmic rays made of matter can speed through the earth at speeds faster than our ability to measure them, then my mind can also comprehend that a truth-matter can exist and operate in a geometry that

I am unable to see. I can hardly wait until my eyes are pure enough to see it. This I know, that truth is that spirit-matter that fills the immensity of space. It lights the heavens and the earth as well as enlightens our understanding. The most wonderful thing is that it's *up for grabs*. It is everywhere and anyone can tap into it by accepting those truths, which they have been given and by searching for more.

Brigham Young said it best when he made the following great statements about finding truth (italics for emphasis). "Our religion measures, weighs, and circumscribes all the wisdom in the world—all that God has ever revealed to man. God has revealed all the truth that is now in the possession of the world, whether it be scientific or religious. The whole world is under obligation to Him for what they know and enjoy; they are indebted to Him for it all, and I acknowledge Him in all things . . . . I want to say to my friends that we believe in all good. *If you can find a truth in heaven, earth or hell, it belongs to our doctrine*. We believe it; it is ours; we claim it . . . . *Our religion is simply the truth*. It is all said in this one expression—it embraces all truth, wherever found, in all the works of God and man that are visible or invisible to mortal eye . . . . 'Mormonism' embraces all truth that is revealed and that is unrevealed, whether religious, political, scientific, or philosophical." (*DBY, pg. 2*) "It is our duty and calling, as ministers of the same salvation and Gospel, to gather every item of truth and reject every error. Whether a truth be found with professed infidels, or with the Universalists, or the Church of Rome, or the Methodists, the Church of England, the Presbyterians, the Baptists, the Quakers, the Shakers, or any other of the various and numerous different sects and parties, all of whom have more or less truth, it is the business of the Elders of this Church (Jesus, their Elder Brother, being at their head) to gather up all the truths in the world pertaining to life and salvation, to the Gospel we preach, to mechanism of every kind, to the sciences, and to philosophy, wherever it may be found in every nation, kindred, tongue, and people and bring it to Zion." (*DBY pg. 248*) "Some who call themselves Christians are very tenacious with regard to the Universalians, yet the latter possess many excellent ideas and good truths. Have the Catholics? Yes, a great many very excellent truths. Have the Protestants? Yes, from first to last. Has the infidel? Yes, he has a good deal of truth; and truth is all over the earth. The earth could not stand but for the light and truth it contains. The people could not abide were it not that truth holds them. It is the fountain of truth that feeds, clothes, and gives light and intelligence to the inhabitants of the earth, no matter whether they are saints or sinners. Do you think there is any truth in hell? Yes, a great deal, and where truth is there we calculate the Lord has a right to be. You will not find the Lord where there is no truth . . . . If you love the truth you can remember it." (*DBY, pg. 10*) "Our doctrine and practice is, and I have made it mine through life . . . to receive truth no matter where it comes from . . . . Be willing to receive the truth, let it come from whom it may; no difference, not a particle." (*DBY, pg. 11*)

Truth is everywhere, **every-where**! It is in all things and through all things (see *D&C* 88). We must learn, by the spirit, to discern it.

The Only True Church

Relevant to our claiming all truth as ours, I must say here as a small aside, that we, as Mormons, often do not follow the counsel of our beloved Prophet, Gordon B. Hinckley,[66] "Let us banish from our lives any elements of self-righteousness." (*Semiannual General Conference, October 1997*) We are often heard to say, sometimes proudly, even arrogantly, that we belong to the ***only*** true church. I wonder what we mean when we say that? I hope we do not mean that truth is *only* found within The Church of Jesus Christ of Latter-day Saints! This is simply not true. In accordance with what was stated above by Brigham Young, truth is found within many churches and comes from many sources. Further, do we mean that everything in The Church is truth? If that were so, we would not have so many opinions on so many matters within The Church. No, Zion has not yet been established. We are not yet of one mind, though, as a church, we do a pretty good job of being one heart. However, when we state that *this is the only true church* I hope we mean that it is the only one that has been directly restored to the earth by Christ, who called prophets and transferred to those prophets (by the actual laying on of hands of heavenly beings) the priesthood or authority to act in the saving ordinances of Christ's gospel. This priesthood, of course, sets The Church in a class of its own, that may rightly be called the *only* true church of Jesus Christ and as Prophet Hinckley also says, "We should be bold in declaring this fact to the world." Still, I believe that notwithstanding our responsibility to tell the world our good news, we should never conclude that because it is the *only* true church, this is the only place truth is found. And yes, the fullness of the gospel principles have been revealed to the prophets of this latter-day church of Christ but only when we, as a people (speaking of The Church in general), recognize and live by these principles, may we declare, with a certain self-assurance (not pride, I hope), that we belong to the ***only*** true church. Until then, I fear, what we should say is, "Yes, we claim all truth, we just don't know it or live it yet. In fact, we are under condemnation, a scourging, and judgment because of our vanity and unbelief and because we have treated lightly, those prophetic truths we have received" (see *D&C 84:54-58*).

Time Is On My Side

Truth is truth, no matter what its source. If it comes from the Devil himself, it is true and will be forever. Much truth comes to us from the Devil, or should I say from his ambassadors, but it is always mingled with falsehood and is calculated to confuse us and carefully lead us astray. Once again, we must develop the power of discernment, and appeal to the Spirit for assistance, so that we can sift out that which is true and that which is not. Remember too that there is always harmony between truths, and time will prove it. The Prophet Ezra T. Benson said, "Religion and science have sometimes been in apparent conflict. Yet the conflict should only be apparent, not real, for science should seek truth, and true religion is truth. There can never be conflict between revealed religion and scientific fact. That they have often occupied different fields of truth is a mere detail. The gospel accepts and embraces all truth; science is slowly expanding her arms and reaching into the invisible domain in search of truth. The two are meeting daily: science as a child, revealed religion as the mother. Truth is truth, whether labeled science or religion. There can be no conflict. Time is on the side of truth, for truth is eternal." (*Ezra Taft Benson, Conference Report, April 1966, pg. 129*) Said Joseph Smith, "One of the grand fundamental principles of Mormonism is to receive truth, let it come from whence it may." (*TPJS, pg. 313*)

That just about says it all, and if it doesn't, I've said enough for one chapter. Just remember the words of a great poet and playwright (his name was Bill I believe), "This above all: To thine own self be true, and it must follow, as the night the day, thou canst not then be false to any man." (*Shakespeare, Hamlet*) The wonderful thing is that God has given all men the ability to recognize truth, to some degree, unless they choose to sear their conscience with a hot iron. "We are of God: Hereby know we the spirit of truth, and the spirit of error." (*1 John 4:6*)

---

[50] ***The Pearl of Great Price* (P of GP) contains the book of Moses. *The Pearl of Great Price* is a collection of works partially received by Joseph Smith as direct revelations from God and partially ancient scrolls that came into his possession, which were translated by him in 1830. These scrolls were found to be the writings of Abraham. Other writings in the collection are Joseph Smith's own story, some translations and corrections of the book of Matthew (New Testament), and a list of Articles of Faith of the LDS church. *The Pearl of Great Price*, along with *The Holy Bible*, *The Book of Mormon*, and *The Doctrine and Covenants* are considered scripture by the LDS church.**

---

[51] ***The Book of Mormon*** **gives an account of Christ appearing to the inhabitants of the Americas where he organized his church much as he did in Jerusalem by choosing apostles. Three of these apostles asked Christ to allow them to tarry in the flesh until he comes a second time that they might bring souls to him. It is believed by the LDS church that they still walk the earth today, although it is not known where.**

[52] **Mormons believe that there are three main degrees or realms of glory, Celestial, Terrestrial, and Telestial; and one realm of no glory, Outer Darkness. Each realm has different levels of spiritual laws governing them. They further believe that men will, at the resurrection of dead, be assigned to one of these four places, depending upon the respective spiritual laws they obeyed in this life. I refer to 1 Corinthians 15:40-41. "There are also celestial bodies, and bodies terrestrial; but the glory of the celestial is one, and the glory of the terrestrial is another. There is one glory of the sun, and another glory of the moon, and another glory of the stars: for one star differeth from another star in glory." A more complete description of the requirements of each realm is found in D&C 76.**

[53] **Mormons believe we are living in the "Dispensation of the Fullness of Times" as spoken of by Paul in Ephesians 1:9-10 when all things in Christ will be revealed and gathered into one.**

[54] **The Lord said unto Enoch: Behold these thy brethren; they are the workmanship of mine own hands, and I gave unto them their knowledge, in the day I created them; and in the Garden of Eden, gave I unto man his agency. (Moses 7:32)**

[55] **"Wherefore, because that Satan rebelled against me, and sought to destroy the agency of man, which I, the Lord God, had given him, and also, that I should give unto him mine own power; by the power of mine Only Begotten, I caused that he should be cast down." (*Moses 4:3*) LDS doctrine teaches of a pre-earth life (pre-existence) where the spirits of men lived with God while awaiting the time when they would come to earth to gain a body. There was a war there, which was started by the "Son of the Morning" who was cast out of heaven and became Satan. See Revelations 12, Moses 4, and D&C 29. This existence is explained fully by God to Enoch in the book of Moses in *The Pearl of Great Price*.**

[56] **Joseph Smith translated and made corrections to *The Holy Bible*, the result being called the Inspired Version or the Joseph Smith Translation (JST).**

[57] **See endnote #2.**

[58] **In the following revelation given to Joseph Smith, we learn that the Zion Society that will prepare itself for the Second Coming of Christ will be in Independence, Missouri. "Hearken, O ye elders of my church, saith the Lord your God, who have assembled yourselves together, according to my commandments, in this land, which is the land of Missouri, which is the land which I have appointed and consecrated for the gathering of the saints. Wherefore, this is the land of promise, and the place for the city of Zion.**

And thus saith the Lord your God, if you will receive wisdom here is wisdom. Behold, the place which is now called Independence is the center place; and a spot for the temple is lying westward, upon a lot which is not far from the courthouse." (*D&C 57:1-3*)

[59] **Although a Zion society could be anywhere where the saints live celestial laws, *the* Latter-day Zion Society is believed, by the Mormons, to be a place in Jackson County, Missouri, where the center of Zion will be built up in the last days to usher in the second coming of Christ. This will be a utopian society, founded only upon celestial laws, where God, Christ, and angels will visit and govern the affairs of the millennial reign.**

[60] **Harold B. Lee was the eleventh prophet of the LDS Church from 1972 to 1973.**

[61] **A *ward* is a geographical area of members, very much like a parish or diocese. There are generally from 300 to 600 saints within a ward boundary and each ward has a bishop with counselors and other administrative staff. There are generally six or more wards within a stake, which is led by a stake president with counselors and other administrative staff. There are usually several stakes in a region with a regional representative from church headquarters in Salt Lake City. All workers, on the regional level down to the wards, serve on a part-time gratis basis.**

[62] **There are two divisions to the priesthood of God in The LDS Church, the Aaronic, or lesser, and the Melchizedek, or higher.**

[63] **Orson Pratt was one of the first apostles of the restored LDS Church from 1835 to 1881.**

[64] ***The Journal of Discourses* (JD) is a compilation of discourses by latter-day prophets and apostles.**

[65] **The word temporal means temporary. It has reference to this earth life or mortality, which will one day pass away, it being a temporal existence.**

[66] **Gordon B. Hinckley is the current president, prophet, seer, and revelator of The LDS Church.**

3
Know the Only True God

The Bottom Line At The Top

With all that has been revealed to them via modern prophets, it is amazing that one of the greatest secrets that seem to elude even some Mormons is the character of the Godhead. We spend a great deal of time in our respective religion classes talking about the Godhead and yet pass over entirely some of the concepts I will put forth here in this chapter. The reason seems to be very closely related to the principles we just covered in the previous chapter on truth, so if you skipped that chapter, or didn't understand it, go back and read it again before carrying on here.

First, let us understand the importance of knowing the God we worship. Said Joseph Smith (italics for emphasis), "Let us here observe that three things are necessary for any rational and intelligent being to exercise faith in God unto life and salvation. First, the idea that He actually exists; Secondly, a *correct idea of His character, perfections, and attributes*; Thirdly, an actual knowledge that the course of life which one is pursuing is according to His will." (*Joseph Smith, Lectures On Faith, lec. 3 pg. 2-5*)[67] Of course one must believe that God actually exists. It is impossible to trust in a God you don't believe is real. Then you must understand what that God is like, His attributes, powers, etc. If you don't, you may be having faith in a false God, or trusting in the powers of something that does not exist or has no power. This is, of course, futile and vain. So, knowing God's characteristics is requisite to faith. And finally, you must know that what you are doing is what He wants, His will (we will go into this in a subsequent chapter). Joseph Smith further stated, "It is the first principle of the Gospel to know for a certainty the Character of God . . . ." (*TPJS, pg. 345*) "If any man does not know God, and inquires what kind of a being He is, if he will search diligently his own heart, if the declaration of Jesus and the apostles be true, he will realize that he has not eternal life; for there can be eternal life on no other principle." (*TPJS, pg. 344*) "And this is life eternal, that they might know thee the only true God, and Jesus Christ, whom thou has sent." (*John 17:3*) Our very eternal life depends on our *knowing* God. Let me here ask a very personal question, do you know God? I don't mean do you know about Him, I mean do you know Him? Are you personally acquainted with Him? Do you know what kind of being He is?

Plain Talk

Realize at the outset that God is a celestial being and to know and understand His character is to study celestial concepts. We must elevate our minds to a higher place where there is no room for the spirit of confusion or argumentation. I don't say that you must accept what I will say here. In fact, you may choose to discard it entirely. All I ask is that you attempt to understand what I am saying before you make that choice. I, for one, believe and do here testify that the God we worship is not *incomprehensible*, as some of our Christian friends would lead us to believe. What ***is*** incomprehensible is that God, the Father of us all, would keep His face hidden from His children who seek sincerely and diligently to know Him. Since God is the same yesterday, today, and forever, a constant God, it is more than reasonable to assume that He will communicate with His children today the same as He did to His children in days past. "For behold, I am God, and I am a God of miracles; and I will show unto the world that I am the same yesterday, today, and forever, and I work not among the children of men save it be according to their faith." (*2 Nephi 27:23*) Faith being the key, whether the communication from God is considered a miracle or not, we must expect such a communication to be entirely understandable to those to whom the communication is intended. Truth from God is what we are talking about here and as stated previously, truth is simple. It is understandable. If a truth is assigned here to this geometry or sphere where we reside, it is simple and meant for us to understand. The confusion enters when we fight the truth and believe the mystifications of the Devil who has been a liar from the beginning.

How Many?

One of the most basic subjects relative to the character of God that has been a source of much confusion and debate over the centuries is whether there is one god or many. The disputations on this subject rage on, particularly between Christian cults[68] or sects.

I will not attempt here to recite the position of any other particular religious persuasion, what they think, or believe, as I will let them speak for themselves. In fact, one of my pet peeves is that others do that to the Mormons. They take it upon themselves to know better than we what we think, feel, and believe. Talk about being presumptuous! What is worse, they broadcast to the world this assumed expertise. It is beyond me why they do not simply come to the source, a general or local authority of The Mormon Church, an ordained missionary, or at the very least, a member in good standing. Let us speak for ourselves if not for The Church. As I stated in Chapter One, the Mormons are generally not just open about what they believe, but outright eager to disclose all they know. With that said, I will speak only in generalities, making no attempt to assign a particular belief to any religious group.

A Single God?

Using good biblical references for support, there are many Christian faiths taking the stand that there is God the Father, His son Jesus Christ, and the Holy Ghost, and that these three are one in the same, a ***single*** God. Also using good biblical references, very often the very same scriptures, there are others taking the opposite stand that these three are distinctly **separate** beings. Setting aside for now the question of whether God will actually appear to men on Earth, the Mormon view on the issue of one vs. three in the Godhead, is that the entire controversy was settled once and for all in 1820 when, in answer to a 14-year-old boy's prayer (Joseph Smith), God the Father and His son Jesus Christ appeared to him as two separate beings.[69] (*Joseph Smith 2, Pearl of Great Price*)

We Mormons, I suppose in an effort to not sound like other Christian groups, spend a great deal of time trying to prove the *separateness* of the Gods. Others, in turn, spend as much time trying to prove the opposite. To affirm the Mormon side of the argument, we cite many physical evidences found in the scriptures. In the New Testament, Christ often prayed to the Father; for example, in the Lord's Prayer, at the last supper, in the garden of Gethsemane, on the cross, etc. It certainly seems incomprehensible that He would pray to Himself, does it not? And then there were those occasions when, while Christ was present on the earth, the voice of God spoke from the heavens. "And Jesus, when He was baptized, went up straightway out of the water; and, lo, the heavens were opened unto Him, and He saw the Spirit of God descending like a dove, and lighting upon Him. And lo a voice from heaven, saying, This is my beloved Son, in whom I am well pleased." (*Matthew 3:16-17*) And again while Peter, James, and John stood next to Christ on the mountain as He was transfigured, the voice of God coming from heaven declared that Christ was His son. "And there was a cloud that overshadowed them: and a voice came out of the cloud, saying, This is my beloved Son: hear Him." (*Mark 9:7*) Then when Christ appeared to the ancient people of the Americas,[70] as He was descending out of heaven, God the Father said, "Behold my Beloved Son, in whom I am well pleased, in whom I have glorified my name, hear ye Him." (*3 Nephi 11:7*)[71] How could Christ be on earth at the same time His voice is speaking from heaven? I don't think that God is trying to portray Himself as a ventriloquist.

Then there are all those references to the "Only begotten of the Father," which causes us to wonder how He, Christ, could be the ***only*** begotten of Himself. "And the Word was made flesh, and dwelt among us, and we beheld His glory, the glory as of the only begotten of the Father, full of grace and truth." (*John 1:14*) Further, when in the garden, after Christ came from the tomb, He told Mary to not touch Him, as He had not yet ascended to His Father. "Jesus saith unto her, touch me not; for I am not yet ascended to my Father: but go to my brethren, and say unto them, I ascend unto my Father, and your Father; and to my God, and your God." (*John 20:17*) One wonders how might He possibly ascend to Himself or sit or stand on His own right hand? "And said, Behold, I see the heavens opened, and the Son of man standing on the right hand of God." (*Acts 7:56*) And how can it be that He is greater than Himself. "Ye have heard how I said unto you, I go away, and come again unto you. If ye loved me, ye would rejoice, because I said, I go unto the Father: for my Father is greater than I." (*John 14:28*)

All One

The Mormons cling tightly to these physical evidences and have trouble with the multiple references to there being one God. But never mind. Others have just as much trouble with the multiple references to three separate Gods. Some of these references take both sides in the same verse. "For there are three that bear record in heaven, the Father, the Word [Christ], and the Holy Ghost; and these three are one." (*1 John 5:7*) Even for the Mormons, there is a certain difficulty and confusion resulting from some of these very good scriptures. "I and my Father are one." (*John 10:30*) "And the scribe said unto Him, Well, Master, thou hast said the truth: for there is one God; and there is none other but He." (*Mark 12:32*) The Mormons would like to say that some of these verses are mistranslations, but they cannot, as Joseph Smith, in all his corrections of *The Holy Bible's* mistranslations, made no such changes.

The situation, for the Mormons at least, worsens. Similar references to the *oneness* of the Godhead are found within *The Book of Mormon*, starting with the testimony of three witnesses found in the introduction pages. "And the honor be to the Father, and to the Son, and to the Holy Ghost, which is one God."[72] Then there are references within *The Book of Mormon* itself. "And now, behold, this is the doctrine of Christ, and the only and true doctrine of the Father, and of the Son, and of the Holy Ghost, which is one God, without end." (*2 Nephi 31:21*)[73] "And Zeezrom[74] said unto him: Thou sayest there is a true and living God? And Amulek[75] said: Yea, there is a true and living God. Now Zeezrom said: Is there more than one God? And he [Amulek] answered, no." (*Alma 11:26-29*) "And after this manner shall ye baptize in my name; for behold, verily I say unto you, that the Father, and the Son, and the Holy Ghost are one; and I am in the Father, and the Father in me, and the Father and I are one." (*3 Nephi 11:27*) "He that is found guiltless before Him at the judgment day hath it given unto him to dwell in the presence of God in His kingdom, to sing ceaseless praises with the choirs above, unto the Father, and unto the Son, and unto the Holy Ghost, which are one God, in a state of happiness which hath no end." (*Mormon 7:7*) To call such examples mistranslations would open a door to a place no Mormon wants to go.

The Mormons face even more problems in The Doctrine and Covenants with references like the following: "Which Father, Son, and Holy Ghost are one God, infinite and eternal, without end. Amen." (*D&C 20:28*) This is scripture from modern prophets! What could Joseph Smith be thinking? Didn't he know he would draw the criticism from the "single god" proponents that we don't believe in our own scriptures? And why haven't the prophets since corrected this oversight? At least Joseph Smith received a promise that there would be "a time to come in the which nothing shall be withheld, whether there be one God or many gods, they shall be manifest." (*D&C 121:28*)

The Mormon explanation to this apparent dilemma of *oneness* versus *separateness* is that the Father, Son, and Holy Ghost are "one in purpose." I cringe when I hear this from my fellow Saints; not that it is a false statement. Of course they are one in purpose, but come on! Such a weak answer to the multitude of statements made by the numerous prophets down through the ages, is to give little weight to their understanding of the character of God (or Gods as the case may be). It makes them look like fools, as if they didn't know what they were talking about. The same gospel was revealed to the Saints of old as to the Saints of today. It is my testimony that they did understand and knew very well what they were saying, that they made no mistake in their expressions of the character of the Godhead, and further, that the problem lies in our shortsighted view of what they said. If we would stop bickering over who is right, take the testimony of the prophets at face value, and then seek to know ***how*** what is said can be so, not ***whether***, I am certain we will finally come to an understanding of this issue. I will go on to clarify myself.

I understand the explanation that the Son, Jesus Christ, is sometimes referred to as the Father. This is true. It sometimes adds to the confusion of the oneness doctrine but it should not. "The Father because He gave me of His fullness, and the Son because I was in the world and made flesh my tabernacle, and dwelt among the sons of men." (*D&C 93:4*) Abinadi[76] also does as good a job as anyone in explaining this concept. "And now Abinadi said unto them: I would that ye should understand that God Himself shall come down among the children of men, and shall redeem His people. And because He dwelleth in flesh He shall be called the Son of God, and having subjected the flesh to the will of the Father, being the Father and the Son—the Father, because He was conceived by the power of God; and the Son, because of the flesh; thus becoming the Father and Son—and they are one God, yea, the very Eternal Father of heaven and of earth." (*Mosiah 15:1-4*) This, among other scriptures, explains why Christ was sometimes called the Father as well as the Son, but it does not address the question of the *oneness* or the *separateness* of the Godhead. These are not just interchangeable titles we're talking about, though the references cited make it seem so.

As we read the scriptures, it can be very confusing trying to decipher which member of the Godhead is being referred to. Some religions have founded their entire doctrinal structure on one or the other of the Godhead being the God of the Old and New Testaments. Of course, this is a moot issue if they are both one God.

The position of those who purport that all references refer to a single god seems much strengthened by some of the next scriptures I will cite, but in fact, I will show that they are only half right. "Abide in me, and I in you. As the branch cannot bear fruit of itself, except it abide in the vine; no more can ye, except ye abide in me. I am the vine, ye are the branches: He that abideth in me, and I in him, the same bringeth forth much fruit: for without me ye can do nothing . . ." (*John 15:4-8*) "I am Jesus Christ, the Son of God, who was crucified for the sins of the world, even as many as will believe on my name, that they may become the sons of God, even one in me as I am one in the Father, as the Father is one in me, that we may be one." (*D&C 35:2*) "And the Father and I are one. I am in the Father and the Father in me; and inasmuch as ye have received me, ye are in me and I in you." (*D&C 50:43*) What is all this "I in Him, he in me, I in you, one in me?" Is the Lord here just trying to be poetic? I think not.

Indwelling

To finally shed some light on this subject, let me start with the account of John, when he tells of how Christ prayed to the Father for not only His disciples, but for those who would believe what they said. "And for their sakes I sanctify myself, that they also might be sanctified through the truth. Neither pray I for these alone, but for them also which shall believe on me through their word; That they all may be one; as thou, Father, art in me, and I in thee, that they also may be one in us: that the world may believe that thou hast sent me."

(*John 17:19-21*) The key to understanding the simplicity of the *oneness* vs. *separateness* issue is held in this and similar references. Was the Lord here asking that the 12 disciples, and all others that believe their words, be made physically one? No. But He did pray for oneness, an *indwelling* relationship. Do you remember that all-important scripture I quoted in Chapter Three, "There is no such thing as immaterial matter. All spirit is matter, but it is more fine or pure, and can only be discerned by purer eyes. We cannot see it, but when our bodies are purified we shall see that it is all matter." (*D&C 131:7-8*) He was praying for oneness of *spirit-matter*, not oneness of *gross-matter*. Remember also that there are many types of *spirit-matter*, and that *spirit-matter* is no less real than gross-matter. Again, I here make no attempt to describe all the kinds of *spirit-matter* that exist, but merely say that there is a realm of *spirit-matter* that **is** Christ, God the Father, and all others who do indeed become one with them, or this *spirit-matter*. It is not just a shared *part* of that *spirit-matter*, but the *whole*. **It is had in common. It is a *singular spirit-matter*. It is the *same spirit-matter*.** "But he that is joined unto the Lord is one spirit." (*1 Cor. 6:17*) This is not just an extension of the *one in purpose* doctrine. It is far more!

Individuality?

Don't let me confuse you. We are talking here about three different kinds of matter. There is the *gross-matter* that makes up our **physical bodies**, the *spirit-matter* that makes up our **spirit bodies** (the other half of our souls), and another *spirit-matter* that **embodies all truth** or is made up of **truth-matter**. Let me here state that the latter is the *spirit-matter* that is the oneness of the Gods, and man too, when he becomes one with it. This *spirit-matter* is the Holy Ghost. "The Father has a body of flesh and bones[77] as tangible as man's; the Son also; but the Holy Ghost has not a body of flesh and bones, but is a personage of Spirit. Were it not so, the Holy Ghost could not dwell in us." (*D&C 130:22*) And why does it say that it (the Holy Ghost) is spirit? So it can dwell *in us*. "What? know ye not that your body is the temple of the Holy Ghost which is in you, which ye have of God, and ye are not your own?" (*1 Corinthians 6:19*) Paul, who knew and understood the character, perfections, and attributes of the Godhead, is explaining the Holy Ghost (that *spirit-matter*) which is in you (assuming it is in you), is of God not of you. This *spirit-matter* is God, is Christ, is the Holy Ghost, and is also your chance, your way, your opportunity to become part of, or rather, *one with*, the Godhead, not just a casual companion, not just a part, but to become the whole, to become *one in the same* with them. What a marvelous principle.

Does this mean that you lose your individual identity or personality? **No**, nor does Christ lose His own essence; singular, separate, individual intellect (own intelligence); spirit (own *spirit-matter* body); or physical body (own gross body), because He has a part of Himself that is the same matter as the Father. Separateness of all things describes the properties of this world of *gross-matter* but it does not describe the properties of *spirit-matter*. One of the greatest properties of *spirit-matter* is its ability to amalgamate or become one with other *spirit-matter*.

Remember that the Holy Ghost is a third, *different spirit-matter*, shared by all who accept the truth it embodies and reveals. Now, whether this *spirit-matter* is the Holy Ghost's spirit body, simply a body of spirit, or both, I cannot say. However, Bruce R. McConkie, along with Joseph F. Smith, seem to favor the belief that the Holy Ghost, as a spirit personage (spirit man), can be in only one place at a time and that some other *spirit-matter* associated with Him, namely the light of Christ or "*truth-matter*," makes it possible for Him to dwell in us as well as fill the vastness of the universe. President Joseph F. Smith[78] said, "The Holy Ghost as a personage of Spirit can no more be omnipresent in person than can the Father or the Son, but by His intelligence, His knowledge, His power and influence, over and through the laws of nature, He is and can be omnipresent throughout all the works of God. It is not the Holy Ghost who in person lighteth every man who is born into the world, but it is the light of Christ, the Spirit of truth, which proceeds from the source of intelligence, which permeates all nature, which lighteth every man and fills the immensity of space. You may call it the Spirit of God, you may call it the influence of God's intelligence, you may call it the substance of His power; no matter what it is called, it is the spirit of intelligence that permeates the universe and gives to the spirits of men understanding, just as Job said." (*Bruce R. McConkie, Mormon Doctrine, pg. 752*)

This truth-matter is our very real connection with God. "But there is a spirit in man: and the inspiration of the Almighty giveth them understanding." (*Job 32:8*) "And that I am the true light that lighteth every man that cometh into the world; And that I am in the Father, and the Father in me, and the Father and I are one . . . I give unto you these sayings that you may understand and know how to worship, and know what you worship, that you may come unto the Father in my name, and in due time receive of His fulness. For if you keep my commandments you shall receive of His fulness, and be glorified in me as I am in the Father; therefore, I say unto you, you shall receive grace for grace." (*D&C 93:2-3,19-20*)

The Holy Ghost

I believe I have a basic understanding of the various functions and duties of the Holy Ghost. As Brother McConkie said, "The Holy Ghost 'witnesses of the Father and the Son' (*2 Nephi 31:18*); He 'beareth record of the Father and the Son' (*Moses 1:24*); He, and He only, makes known those holy beings whom it is life eternal to know. Jesus said: 'He shall testify of me' (*John 15:26*); and He 'beareth record of the Father and me' (*3 Nephi 11:32*). And Paul said: 'No man can say [meaning know] that Jesus is the Lord, but by the Holy Ghost.' (*1 Corinthians 12:3.*) Thus the Holy Ghost is the source of saving knowledge; His mission, assigned by the Father, is to bear witness to the truth of those things, which enable men to gain eternal life. His witness is sure; it cannot be controverted; it will stand forever." (*Bruce R. McConkie, A New Witness for the Articles of Faith, pg. 267*)

My knowledge and understanding concerning ***who*** the Holy Ghost really is, his (or its) properties, or his characteristics, is **very** weak and I here make no pretense. The Holy Ghost has never been seen. Through all of holy writ, this personage of spirit (see *D&C 130:22*) has never appeared in person to anyone, although many other spirit personages have. That is to say it is not uncommon for spirit beings to appear. Examples are prevalent throughout the scriptures, yet the Holy Ghost has never been seen. We know much about his mission and purpose, but nothing about him personally. In fact, there is so little known about him personally that I for one have for years refused to teach a class or give a lecture upon the Holy Ghost. I simply know nothing about him. I have come to believe that a knowledge of this ghostly third member of the Godhead can only be received by personal revelation from God. Further, comprehending the nature of this being is key to knowing God and our relationship to Him. I believe we need to know ***who*** he really is. To find the answer to that question, I believe, is to know God.

Notwithstanding my weakness of knowledge concerning the Holy Ghost, I believe this much, that what we are pleased to call "The Spirit," the "Holy Spirit," the "Spirit of truth," the "Spirit of Christ," the "Spirit of the Lord," the "Spirit of the Son," the "Light of Christ," the "Influence of God," our "conscience," that "still small voice," the "Intelligence of God," the "Intelligence of Christ," "truth," the "Light of Truth," the "Spirit of Truth," the "Spirit of God," the "Mind of God," the "Spirit of the Father," the "Spirit of the Holy Ghost," the "Spirit of Intelligence," the "influence of God's intelligence" "God's power," the influence of God's intelligence" the "substance of God's power," and/or the many other spirit descriptions we often tend to use interchangeably or bicker about in our religion classes, are ***one in the same***: the ***Holy Ghost***!

I realize that my brothers and sisters in The Church might stone me for stating the above, but owing to the fact that truth is simple and confusion is not, I should think they would examine this belief on that reason alone. Brigham Young stated (italics for emphasis), "Our God and Father in Heaven, is a being of tabernacle . . . His Son Jesus Christ has become a personage of tabernacle, and has a body like His Father. *The Holy Ghost is the Spirit of the Lord, and issues forth from Himself*, and may properly be called God's minister to execute His will in immensity; being called to govern by His influence and power; but He is not a person of flesh as we are, and as our Father in Heaven and Jesus Christ are." (*DBY pg. 24*)

Again, I am the first to confess my lack of knowledge, not about His mission, as much has been revealed relative to that, but rather, about the personal character, makeup, or *who* the Holy Ghost is. My information on the matter is limited mostly to the above few statements and this one scripture, "The Holy Ghost has not a body of flesh and bones, but is a personage of Spirit." (*D&C 130:22*) In short, I simply do not know but tend to believe that the properties, construction, and identity of the Holy Ghost is revealed only on a personal level to those who seek earnestly to know.

What *has* been revealed is that through the Holy Ghost, the Godhead, Father Son and Holy Ghost **are** indeed ***one***. Let me state again, so I am not misunderstood, whoever the Holy Ghost is, ***he is the spirit-matter that is the oneness of the Gods***.

The Mind of God

To enhance my point and to put it in other words, let me insert the words of Joseph Smith found in the *Lectures on Faith* (italics and bold for emphasis): "There are two personages who constitute the great, matchless, governing, and supreme power over all things, by whom all things were created and made, that are created and made, whether visible or invisible, whether in heaven, on earth, or in the earth, under the earth, or throughout the immensity of space. They are the Father and the Son—the Father being a personage of spirit, glory, and power, possessing all perfection and fullness, the Son, who was in the bosom of the Father,—He is also the express image and likeness of the personage of the Father, possessing all the fullness of the Father, ***or the same fullness with the Father***; being begotten of Him,—And He being the Only Begotten of the Father, full of grace and truth, and having overcome, received a fullness of the glory of the Father, ***possessing the same mind with the Father, which mind is the Holy Spirit***, that bears record of the Father and the Son, and these three are one; or, in other words, these three constitute the great, matchless, governing and supreme power over all things; by whom all things were created and made that were created and made, and these three constitute the Godhead, and are one; the Father and the Son *possessing the same mind, the same wisdom, glory, power, and fullness*—being filled with the *fullness of the mind of the Father*; or, in other words, *the Spirit of the Father, which*

Spirit is shed forth upon all who believe on His name and keep His commandments; and all those who keep His commandments shall grow up from grace to grace, and become heirs of the heavenly kingdom, and joint heirs with Jesus Christ; ***possessing the same mind***, being transformed into the same image or likeness, even the express image of Him who fills all in all; being filled with the fullness of His glory, and become ***one in Him, even as the Father, Son and Holy Spirit are one.***" (*Lectures on Faith, Lecture 5, pg. 48-pg. 49*)

Note that it is not just the *fullness of the Father* but also the *same* fullness *with* the Father. Note also that Christ possesses the *same mind with* the Father, *which mind is the Holy Spirit* and that it is also called *the Spirit of the Father.* As expressed before, those who keep the commandments will grow grace to grace until they *become one in Him*, even as the Father, Son, and Holy Spirit are *one.* To me, the Prophet Joseph has made it very clear that the Holy Spirit-matter is the oneness of the Gods. Yet we Mormons, in our efforts to separate and define, often fuss over the definitions and meanings of the various descriptions and application of the spirits listed in the previous paragraphs and do not seem willing to let go of that confusion.

I believe even we Mormons keep this truth, this secret, because we ourselves do not understand it. Further, I believe we do not understand because we have not been seeking, knocking, or asking. It is a deep concept and takes more than a superficial study to understand it. It takes a sincere search and enormous desire to know the things of God. It takes elevating our minds from the temporal to the spiritual. Notwithstanding its abstractness, this doctrine is found throughout the scriptures and many modern prophets have attempted to expand our understanding of it. B. H. Roberts[79] put it most concisely and unequivocally when he said (italics for emphasis), "This Light then, the Light of Truth and named for us men 'the Light of Christ'—'which proceedeth forth from the presence of God to fill the immensity of space'—is also God, even *the Spirit of God, or of the Gods*, for it proceeds forth or vibrates, or radiates from all the Gods—from all who have partaken of the One Divine Nature—hence 'the God of all other Gods'—mentioned by our Prophet of the New Dispensation (*D&C 121:32*) 'the God of Gods,' 'the Lord of Lords,' proceeding from MANY yet ONE! Incarnated in all personal Deities, yet proceeding forth from them, to extend the one God into all space that He might be in and through all things; bearing all the powers in earth and sun and stars; world-sustaining power and guiding force. Bearing all the mind and spiritual attributes of God into the immensity of space, becoming God everywhere present—omni-present; and everywhere present with power—omnipotent; extending everywhere the power of God; also All-Knowing; All-Seeing; All-Hearing—Omniscient! Bearing forth in fact all the attributes of Deity: Knowledge, Wisdom, Judgment,

Truth, Holiness, Mercy—every characteristic or quality of all Divine Intelligences—since they are one; and this *Divine Essence of spirit* becoming 'the Light which is in all things, that giveth life to all things which is the law by which all things are governed, even the POWER of God, who sitteth upon His throne, who is in the bosom of eternity, who is in the midst of all things.' (*D&C 88:13*) *United in this Divine Essence, or Spirit is the mind of all Gods; and all the Gods being incarnations of this Spirit, become God in unity; and by the incarnation of this Spirit in Divine Personages, they become the Divine Brotherhood of the Universe, the ONE GOD, though made of many.*" (*Truman G. Madsen, BYU Studies, Vol. 15, No. 3, pg. 289*)

I simply don't know how it can be put plainer than this last paragraph. The Divine Essence or Spirit-matter that we call the Holy Ghost is the mind, intelligence, and essence as well as the oneness of all the Gods. Even though they are individual in their own *spirit bodies* and their glorified *gross-matter bodies*, this *divine spirit-matter*, which is the Holy Ghost, is shared in one (not part of or equal amounts, but one in the same).

Yes And Yes or Have It Both Ways

So, in answer to the question, is the Godhead separate or one? Congruent with the revelations given, the reasoning above put forth, and at the risk of sounding like I am allying with our Christian friends, let me say, **yes** and **yes**. This is a case where you have it both ways. They are both *separate* **and** *one*! Let us stop the argument!

So that no one mistake my meaning, let me state again that I agree with what Joseph Smith learned in the grove[80] that day, and let me here declare that I have no intention of rejecting the *separateness doctrine* (though, for obvious reasons, I would rather term it the *individual-ness doctrine*), as I know it to be true, but so also is the *oneness doctrine*. In the case of *spirit-matter*, oneness does not negate individual-ness. This *spirit-matter* is very real and it is in them, one and the same *spirit-matter*.

I fear that as this great secret, this *Indwelling oneness* of the Godhead doctrine, leaks out to the Latter-day Saints, it will be unpopular with many as for so long it has been our tradition to prove to the world the separateness of the Godhead. Traditions die hard, (if you don't believe it just ask the children of Israel). Why we have kept it secret from even ourselves I cannot understand, especially when it is so plainly taught in our own modern revelations, revelations Mormons alone claim to possess.

When we accept the statements of the prophets concerning this doctrine at face value, many scriptures and concepts come into focus. Also, when you realize that this Holy Ghost *spirit-matter* is shared (not a part but the whole) by all those who become one with it in the Godhead, many issues suddenly become clear and simple again.

The Gift of The Holy Ghost

By way of clarification, let me say here that the ***Gift** of the Holy Ghost*, as referred to by the Latter-day Saints, is different in that it describes a particular endowment of this Holy Ghost matter (Holy Spirit, Spirit of Truth, Spirit of Christ, etc.) of which we have been speaking. This endowment is the *power* or *right* of the constant companionship, or indwelling, of the Holy Ghost. The promise of the same is received only by the laying on of hands by an official of the Priesthood.[81] Joseph Smith tells us, "Baptism is a sign to God, to angels, and to heaven that we do the will of God, and there is no other way beneath the heavens whereby God hath ordained for man to come to Him to be saved, and enter into the Kingdom of God, except faith in Jesus Christ, repentance, and baptism for the remission of sins, and any other course is in vain; then you have *the promise* of the gift of the Holy Ghost." *(TPJS pg. 198)*

Again, this only gives you the *right* to that oneness, as actual enjoyment of this endowment is predicated on personal righteousness. Also, a man may receive the Holy Ghost without this "gift" (Mormons and non-Mormons alike) and assumedly, it will stay with him as long as he continues in righteousness, but to receive the *right*, the *gift*, one must receive the ordinance of baptism and the laying on of hands. It should also be said that those with the *right* to receive it (those who have complied with the ordinance), as a result of unrighteousness, may not actually receive it or may lose it. "The Gift of the Holy Ghost by the laying on of hands, cannot be received through the medium of any other principle than the principle of righteousness, for if the proposals are not complied with, it is of no use, but withdraws." *(TPJS, pg. 148)*

This Gift of the Holy Ghost occurs when you are Born Again or receive the Baptism of Fire. It is an event that sanctifies your *spirit-matter* body and transforms your mortal body through translation (more on this later). This does not happen by default because you are a baptized member and have received the "laying on of hands" by one having priesthood authority. That only gives you a promise of the same. As Joseph Smith said, the actual reception of this gift is received only on the principle of righteousness.

I know that many members and non-members alike think that because they have received a great witness (or even many) and revelations that they have already been *Born Again*. A careful study of this gift in the scriptures may convince them otherwise. I will discuss this subject and the evidences of being Born Again in depth in an ensuing chapter so please put off your arguments until then.

Heir-ship

You might have noticed above that Joseph Smith said we can "become *heirs* of the heavenly kingdom, and *joint heirs* with Jesus Christ." As Paul stated in Romans, "The Spirit itself beareth witness with our spirit, that we are the children of God: And if children, then heirs; *heirs of God*, and *joint-heirs with Christ*, if so be that we suffer with Him, that we may be also glorified together." (*Romans 8:17-18*) It is through this doctrine of *spiritual oneness* that we share, not just a part, not just equally, but *jointly*, a fullness. **This is how Christ can have it all, and *we can too*.** We may enjoy all power, all knowledge, all truth, all glory, all goodness, all greatness, all happiness, all mercy, all grace, all perfection, all justice, all majesty, all dominion, all principalities, all strength, all intelligence, all honors, all glory, and *all* like qualities and divine attributes when we are one with the Gods. This is the Devine *doctrine of heir-ship*.

Suffer With Him

This reference in Romans also brings up another question that is answered in the oneness doctrine. The question is that if we are ever to be like Christ, must we not do the same things that "he seeth the Father do" (*John 5:19*) namely to suffer both body and spirit as He did? As joint-heirs with Christ, we will *suffer with Him*, that we may be also glorified together (see *Romans 8:18*). You see, it is not necessary that we go through exactly the same things that Christ did because when you become one with Him, you will feel what He felt, experience what He experienced, and know what He knows. This is not just a *communication*; but, a *sharing*, a *joining*, an *indwelling*, *an experiencing of His history* (experiencing through Him what He went through), and it will be absolute with all who become one with the Father and Son. You also share everyone else's history through this *oneness doctrine*. Such a concept can blow your mind (more on this shortly).

It's Eternal

We are commanded to be one. Christ prayed that we would be. This is the central theme of the Latter-day Zion Society (*see endnote on Zion Society in*

Chapter 3) that utopian society, which will be founded in the Latter-days, built upon celestial laws only, where God, Christ, and angels will visit and govern the affairs of man just prior to and during the millennial reign.[82] "And the Lord called His people Zion, because they were of *one heart* and *one mind*, and dwelt in righteousness; and there was no poor among them." (*Moses 7:18*) This oneness is *spirit-matter*. It is real and it is eternal. It is eternal because, as said before, truth is eternal, it endures when evil and false do not. Said Brigham Young, "A perfect oneness will save a people, because intelligent beings cannot become perfectly one, only by acting upon principles that pertain to eternal life. Wicked men may be partially united in evil; but, in the very nature of things, such a union is of short duration. The very principle upon which they are partially united will itself breed contention and disunion to destroy the temporary compact. Only the line of truth and righteousness can secure to any kingdom or people, either of earthly or heavenly existence, an eternal continuation perfect union; for only truth and those who are sanctified by it can dwell in celestial glory." (*DBY pg. 282*) Again, *oneness* is an attribute of *spirit-matter*; it brings things together. Conversely, it is an attribute of gross-matter to separate.

Spiritual Death

As alluded to in the last chapter on truth, another question that is answered in this *oneness doctrine*, is why one may blaspheme or deny even the Savior of the world who died for us and still be forgiven, but in denying the Holy Ghost one may not be forgiven, in this life or the next. Why is the punishment greater for denying the Holy Ghost when He did not suffer for our sins, as did Christ? "Wherefore I say unto you, All manner of sin and blasphemy shall be forgiven unto men: but the blasphemy against the Holy Ghost shall not be forgiven unto men." (*Matthew 12:31*) It is because it is not so much a punishment but the natural consequence of the law and God cannot fix it, even by the sacrifice of His Son. He cannot help a person who refuses to accept truth, of which the Holy Ghost is the spiritual embodiment. To deny Christ is to keep oneself from a celestial glory, for that is the law of that realm; but to deny the Holy Ghost is to deny truth and to cut oneself off entirely from God, the source of that light and truth, and this is the "second death" or "spiritual death" referred to in the scriptures. (*Revelations 20:14*, *Jacob 3:11*, and *Alma 12:16*)

To the extent that we deny truth or the Holy Ghost, is to the extent we reap our damnation. If we have progressed far enough to have great truths revealed to us, even to the extent that we know God, then deny Him, we would find ourselves *sons of perdition* or cast into *outer darkness*. Again, not just because it is the law and the justice, but because we literally separate ourselves from the power and forces of life itself. That *spirit-matter* within us, that is one with the Gods, dies entirely. Our spirits become entirely separate from God's, the source of our life. That is the consequence of such an action. That is the definition of spiritual death. "Wherefore, I, the Lord God, caused that he should be cast out from the Garden of Eden, from my presence, because of his transgression, wherein, he became spiritually dead, which is the first death, even that same death which is the last death, which is spiritual, which shall be pronounced upon the wicked when I shall say: Depart ye cursed." (*D&C 29:41*)

Who's Who?

Now, relative to this *oneness doctrine*, I shall not attempt herein to wade through the many references to the Gods, or any particular God, to state definitively *which* is referred to in any particular scripture or whether they are plural or singular. I am not a scriptorian nor would I presume to know so much, but if the reader will apply the *oneness, indwelling*, concept to the relative references, I believe the meanings will become clear.

Certainly much of the confusion exists because, as a natural result of their indwelling relationship, God the Father and Jesus Christ were not slow to interchange their various names and titles when they are both referred to. In other words, there is more than one god. "A Psalm of Asaph. God standeth in the congregation of the mighty; he judgeth among the *gods*." (*Psalms 82:1*) Paul said "For though there be that are called gods, whether in heaven or in earth, (as there be *gods many* and *lords many*,) But to us there is but one God, the Father, of whom are all things, and we in him and one Lord Jesus Christ, by whom are all things, and we by him." (*1 Corinthians 8:5-6*)

It only seems logical that those gods are lords over their dominions, but to us, those who are in God the Father's dominion or a part of His creations, we are concerned only with that one god. That ***one*** is God the Father—and of course, His Son Jesus Christ, who, under the direction and authority of the Father, created us, this heaven, this earth, and all that in them are. Do you see what I just did quite naturally? Even without thinking, I referred to both of them as one. It's hard to avoid it. Perhaps this makes my point relative to that age-old argument of "who" and "how many." I know we worry about whom we are really addressing when we pray, God the Father or Christ, but relative to the big picture, it does not really matter, as they are one God. They both hear the same prayer because they share the same *spirit-matter* that you, through your prayer, are trying to connect with. It is imperative to develop a relationship with them both and, in fact, we do. When we come to know one, we come to know the other, and when we become one with either, we become one with both. "Jesus saith unto him, I am the way, the truth, and the life: no man cometh unto the Father, but by me. If ye had known me, ye should have known my Father also: and from henceforth ye know Him, and have seen Him. Philip saith unto Him, Lord, shew us the Father, and it sufficeth us. Jesus saith unto him, Have I been so long time with you, and yet hast thou not known me, Philip? he that hath seen me hath seen the Father; and how sayest thou *then*, Shew us the Father? Believest thou not that I am in the Father, and the Father in me? the words that I speak unto you I speak not of myself: but the Father that dwelleth in me, he doeth the works. Believe me that I [*am*] in the Father, and the Father in me: or else believe me for the very works' sake." (*John 14:6-11*)

We Can Be One

The great secret to which I referred in Chapter Two, that my BYU professor said we keep so well, namely, the *Gospel of Jesus Christ*, is partially expressed here in this oneness doctrine. In the interest of not only understanding the God we worship, but also learning how to become one with Him, let us come to know the truth of this *oneness doctrine.*

Why can't we see the big picture? Can we not see that there is a great design to this existence, that it had its beginnings in a far away place and that the end thereof is actually eternal? Can we not see God's plan for us? Is it so presumptuous to believe that we can be *like Him, of Him, in Him?* Is it so presumptuous to believe that we can be one in Him as He is in the Father and the Father is one in Him? Presumptuous or not, it is the plan and our hope, our only hope. Why do we not believe? Do we think it will magically happen some day when we don't believe that it can? I testify that it will **not** happen if we don't believe it can. It is no accident that even Christ's atonement spells *at-one-ment.*

---

[67] **The Lectures on Faith, *by Joseph Smith* are a series of lectures delivered by Joseph Smith during the winter of 1844-45 to a theological school in Kirtland, Ohio, called The School Of The Prophets.**

[68] **Webster's Dictionary properly defines a cult only as a system of religious worship, rites, ceremonies, doctrines, and ideologies; not the negative connotation generally attributed to the meaning of the word today.**

[69] **Joseph Smith's own account of this occurrence is recorded in *The Pearl of Great Price* (*Joseph Smith 2*).**

[70] **Shortly after Christ's death and resurrection as recorded in the New Testament, He appeared to the people living on the Central and South American Continents and taught them His gospel and also chose apostles and established His church. This occurrence is recorded within *The Book of Mormon* in a book called 3 Nephi.**

[71] **3 Nephi is a book in *The Book of Mormon* containing the account of Christ's appearance to the people in the Americas shortly after His death and resurrection.**

[72] **There were three witnesses to the gold plates from which Joseph Smith translated *The Book of Mormon.* Their names were Oliver Cowdery, David Whitmer, and Martin Harris. These men not only saw the plates, but also conversed with the angel Moroni who delivered the plates to Joseph. Their testimony is found in the front of *The Book of Mormon.* There were eight other men who saw the plates. Their testimony is written there also.**

[73] **The book of 2 Nephi is a book in *The Book of Mormon* written by the prophet Nephi, covering the history of the ancient inhabitants of the South American continent from about 570 BC to 545 BC.**

[74] **Zeezrom was a lawyer who lived on the South American continent about 80 BC. He stirred up the people to break the law and bring suit against one another that he might have more employment.**

[75] **Amulek was a contemporary of Alma, a South American prophet who lived approximately 80 BC.**

[76] **Abinadi was a prophet that lived about 140 BC on the South American Continent.**

[77] **"And he said unto them, Why are ye troubled? and why do thoughts arise in your hearts? Behold my hands and my feet, that it is I myself: handle me, and see; for a spirit hath not flesh and bones, as ye see me have." (*Luke 24:38-39*)**

[78] **Joseph F. Smith (not to be confused with Joseph Smith (Jr.), the first prophet, or Joseph Fielding Smith, the 10th prophet) was the prophet of The LDS Church from 1901 to 1918.**

[79] **B. H. Roberts lived from 1857-1933, was a president of the First Council of Seventy (of the general authorities) from 1888 to 1933, and was an assistant church historian. He is considered to be one of the most prolific writers of The Mormon Church.**

[80] **In 1820, after being moved by the fifth verse of 1 James, which says, "If any of you lack wisdom let him ask of God who giveth to all men liberally…" Joseph went into a grove of trees near his farm and prayed. The result of that prayer was Joseph Smith's "first vision," where he saw the Father and His son Jesus Christ. A complete account of this event is recorded in Joseph Smith History in *The Pearl of Great Price.***

[81] **"For as yet he was fallen upon none of them: only they were baptized in the name of the Lord Jesus. Then laid they their hands on them, and they received the Holy Ghost." (*Acts 8:16-17*)**

[82] **The millennial reign is that 1,000-year period of peace after Christ comes a second time.**

4
Other Attributes of God

He Knows All

It never ceases to amaze me how we limit God to only those powers and attributes that we can understand. It seems that God's abilities are directly proportional to our limited knowledge of Him. It is much like the child, who, in his youth, thought his father was ignorant, but when he grew up, was astonished at how much his father had suddenly learned.

Some years ago on a Sunday morning, I was talking with an old High Priest[83] in The Church foyer about the character of God, and he stated that he didn't think God concerned Himself with the little things and that He could not know what was going on without the "reporting system." I was set back. "What reporting system," I asked? I understood that God's subordinates reported their actions and the actions of those over whom they have authority, this is part of the stewardship principle of authority and accountability, but I had never imagined that such a process was for the benefit of God, and His only source of information. The notion that God might not know what was going on in the worlds of His creation were it not for some system of communication and reporting by His subordinates had never crossed my mind. I thought surely this good man had been unaware of some of the references quoted in my last chapter, about Christ being *personally in all things*. "He comprehendeth all things, and all things are before Him, and all things are round about Him; and He is above all things, and in all things, and is through all things, and is round about all things; and all things are by Him and of Him even God, forever and ever." (*D&C 88:41*) Even a sparrow falling on the ground is noticed by God, and every hair of your head is numbered to God (see *Matthew 10:29-30*).

When I referenced a few of these scriptures, he replied, "Oh, I can't understand such things." I tried to assure him that the concept is simple and not hard to understand. But he said, "This is the only thing that makes sense to me, so that's what I believe." Then he turned and walked away. I guess that was fair enough, *we all believe what we choose to believe*. Of course we are all on different levels of understanding and I am sure that, like this good man, I too often adhere to what I think I am able to understand at the expense of further light and knowledge. I feel certain that all of us appear as ignorant children to God. My intention is not to condemn the man for his beliefs but I was left stunned and wondering how many Saints, old Saints, do not understand this attribute of God, that He knows **all** things? What's worse, how could they have faith in a God that does not know all?

I have, since that time, discovered many members of the Mormon Church don't believe that God has the capacity to know all things. Such a case leaves me to wonder; what if God suddenly discovered some new truth that changes everything? This is a most disturbing thought and abhorrent to me. Do they not know that God is omnipotent, or do they not know the meaning of the word?

For those members and any others who are interested, let me make the following case: **God knows all; there is not one thought of man, one particle of truth (past, present, or future), or knowledge that God does not posses.** The events of the future are **all** known by God. "Oh how great the holiness of our God! For He knoweth all things, and there is not anything save He knows it." (*2 Nephi 9:20,* see also *1 Peter 1:2, John 16:30* and *Alma 13:3*) I am comforted that Bruce R. McConkie agrees with me on this subject. "He has all wisdom, all knowledge, and all understanding; He is the All-Wise One, the All-Knowing One. There is no truth He does not know, no wisdom hidden from His view, no laws or powers or facts for Him to discover in some distant eternity. His wisdom and knowledge are absolute and have neither bounds nor limitations. He knows all things now; He is not progressing in knowledge; He is not discovering new truths; there are no higher spheres than the one in which He now walks. His mind is infinite; His knowledge comprehends all things, and He is in fact the source and author of all truth. Were it otherwise He could not be the Creator of galaxies unnumbered; were it otherwise, He could not hold the universe in His hands and govern and control all things. Indeed, His glory and greatness and goodness exist and are because He knows all things and is the source of all truth. And if such were not the case, men could not exercise faith in Him unto life and salvation, for they would know that He might someday discover some truth that would destroy immortality, or eternal life, or the whole scheme and system of things." (*Bruce R. McConkie, A New Witness for the Articles of Faith, pg. 52-pg. 53*)

With regard to our tendency to limit God to only those powers and abilities we can understand, let me say that a good friend recently called to my remembrance a situation I faced while teaching an adult Gospel Doctrine class. We were discussing a particular miracle and one of my students was having trouble accepting how God could have worked such a miracle. At first I groped for a scientific principle that would help prove the plausibility of the miracle, but suddenly the words came to me and I said, "Try to think of God as a capable person." I am certain that much of our inability to comprehend God lies in our limited image or conception of Him. He is, indeed, a capable person!

Let me here put forth a few points in order that we might know God and His abilities, to the end that we might have full faith in Him, and also that we ***not*** limit God to our own ability, or lack thereof, to understand His mysteries.

One Eternal Now

With our finite mind, the concept of eternity is extremely difficult for us to grasp. Perhaps a few references will help (italics and bold for emphasis). "Thus saith the Lord your God, even Jesus Christ, the Great I AM, Alpha and Omega, the beginning and the end, the same which looked upon the wide expanse of eternity, and all the seraphic hosts of heaven, before the world was made; The same which knoweth all things, *for all things are present before mine eyes*." (*D&C 38:1-2*) "Now whether there is more than one time appointed for men to rise it mattereth not; for all do not die at once, and this mattereth not; *all is as one day with God, and time only is measured unto man*." (*Alma 40:8*) "The angels do not reside on a planet like this earth; But they reside in the presence of God, on a globe like a sea of glass and fire, where all things for their glory are manifest, *past, present and future, and are continually before the Lord*." (*D&C 130:6-7*) "The great Jehovah contemplated the whole of the events connected with the earth, pertaining to the plan of salvation, before it rolled into existence, or ever the morning stars sang together for joy; *the past, the present, and the future were and are with Him, one eternal Now . . . .*" (*TPJS, pg. 220*)

To help us understand eternity I like to use the analogy of the computer vs. the recording tape. On a recording tape, in order to access a specific peace of information, one must fast forward or rewind to the place where that information is recorded. This is *linear* where one thing precedes or follows another. The computer, on the other hand, is *non-linear*. The information is stored on a disc and to access any particular bit of information, the computer goes right to the place that information resides and picks it off the disc, without having to go back or forward to find it. Curiously, that's how our mind works as well. Similarly, God does not have to go back or forward in time to access a particular moment. It is **all**, past, present, and future, before His eyes.

Differences

Although the differences between God and mortal man are many, the two greatest are: First, God lives in eternity, or *a state of no time*, that is, in a place where time does not exist. Second, God has an *infinite mind*, a mind capable of infinite thoughts at any given moment. This is called *eternity*. Man, on the other hand, lives in a *linear time* where one moment must follow or precede another, and he has a *finite mind*, capable of only one thought at a time.

God's Job

God is in the business of saving souls. "For behold, this is my work and my glory—to bring to pass the immortality and eternal life of man." (*Moses 1:39*) "And this is life eternal, that they might know thee the only true God, and Jesus Christ, whom thou has sent." (*John 17:3*)

Contrary to what most of us suppose, the "*eternal life*" of man that God is bringing us to *is **not** living forever* in linear time (where one moment precedes or follows another). Everyone who is saved in the Kingdom of God, everyone who receives a state of glory as a final reward, will live forever. This is called *immortality*. *Eternal life* is more. It is living in eternity where there is no time. It is living as God lives, in the same state of being with the same powers and glory, namely, the infinite mind. It is being one with Him, through the *oneness doctrine* previously discussed, in a place where the past, present, and future are *one eternal now*. This is far more than *living forever*.

The above-mentioned differences (living in time with a finite mind) between God and man are what disable man from comprehending God fully. It is also the very thing that enables God to fully comprehend all men. Only when God has "quickened" the mind of man, has he understood this reality fully. This happened to many of the ancient prophets such as Moses, as well as, I dare say, a few modern prophets. "And it came to pass, as the voice was still speaking, Moses cast his eyes and beheld the earth, yea, even all of it; and there was not a particle of it which he did not behold, discerning it by the Spirit of God. And he beheld also the inhabitants thereof, and there was not a soul which he beheld not; and he discerned them by the Spirit of God; and their numbers were great, even numberless as the sand upon the sea shore." (*Moses 1:27-28*) For perhaps only an instant, Moses was given an infinite mind and *quickened* into eternity, where he was able to see what God sees and comprehend the same.

Eternal Punishment

This principle of the eternalness (timelessness) of God impacts the concept of punishment as well. "—they shall go away into everlasting punishment, which is endless punishment, which is eternal punishment, to reign with the devil and his angels in eternity, where their worm dieth not, and the fire is not quenched, which is their torment—And the end thereof, neither the place thereof, nor their torment, no man knows; Neither was it revealed, neither is, neither will be revealed unto man, except to them who are made partakers thereof; Nevertheless, I, the Lord, show it by vision unto many, but straightway shut it up again; Wherefore, the end, the width, the height, the depth, and the misery thereof, they understand not, neither any man except those who are ordained unto this condemnation." *(D&C 76:44-49)*

Now how can the Lord call this punishment "everlasting" and "endless" and in the same breath speak of the "*width, height, depth* and ***end***" of it? Again when we understand the *infinite vs. finite* and *time vs. eternity*: when we understand the separateness of the two realms of things; when we understand the differences of the two geometries; we begin to understand how it is possible to suffer the wrath of God in eternity and yet comprehend that such suffering will have an end.

The Lord further explained this mystery of godliness when He said (italics for emphasis), "Wherefore, I revoke not the judgments which I shall pass, but woes shall go forth, weeping, wailing and gnashing of teeth, yea, to those who are found on my left hand. Nevertheless, it is not written that there shall be no end to this torment, but it is written *endless torment*. Again, it is written *eternal damnation*; wherefore it is more express than other scriptures, that it might work upon the hearts of the children of men, altogether for my name's glory. Wherefore, I will explain unto you this mystery, for it is meet unto you to know even as mine apostles. I speak unto you that are chosen in this thing, even as one, that you may enter into my rest. For, behold, the mystery of godliness, how great is it! For, behold, I am endless, and the punishment which is given from my hand is endless punishment, for Endless is my name. Wherefore—Eternal punishment is God's punishment. Endless punishment is God's punishment." *(D&C 19:5-12)*

So how is this eternal punishment administered? The same as the great panoramic view or knowledge of the world was given to Moses in a twinkling of an eye as stated above. Even if for a moment, the woeful souls of the wicked are cast into the realm of eternity, they will suffer torment endlessly, eternally, or timelessly.

Although the Lord tells us that only those who are made partakers of this suffering will know the end thereof, presumably, after paying the uttermost farthing for their unrepentant sins, they will be taken back out of eternity and put into time and a state of glory (the only exception being those who become perdition—*for a more complete understanding of the details of this subject* see *D&C 19* and *76*). This concept adds weight to the need for repentance that our sins might be washed away by the blood or grace of our Lord Jesus Christ so that we don't have to suffer for them in eternity.

I've Been There

Do we have examples of anyone who suffered this eternal anguish and lived to tell us about it? Two come to mind, Paul (Saul of Tarsus) and Alma the younger in the Book of Mormon. Alma explains to his son that as he and his friends were traveling around persecuting the righteous saints an angel of the Lord struck them down. "And he said unto me: If thou wilt of thyself be destroyed, seek no more to destroy the church of God. And it came to pass that I fell to the earth; and it was for the space of three days and three nights that I could not open my mouth, neither had I the use of my limbs. But I was racked with *eternal torment,* for my soul was harrowed up to the greatest degree and racked with all my sins. Yea, I did remember all my sins and iniquities, for which I was tormented with the pains of hell; yea, I saw that I had rebelled against my God, and that I had not kept his holy commandments. Yea, and I had murdered many of his children, or rather led them away unto destruction; yea, and in fine so great had been my iniquities, that the very thought of coming into the presence of my God did rack my soul with inexpressible horror. Oh, thought I, that I could be banished and become extinct both soul and body, that I might not be brought to stand in the presence of my God, to be judged of my deeds. And now, for three days and for three nights was I racked, even with the pains of a damned soul. And it came to pass that as I was thus racked with torment, while I was harrowed up by the memory of my many sins, behold, I remembered also to have heard my father prophesy unto the people concerning the coming of one Jesus Christ, a Son of God, to atone for the sins of the world. Now, as my mind caught hold upon this thought, I cried within my heart: O Jesus, thou Son of God, have mercy on me, who am in the gall of bitterness, and am encircled about by the everlasting chains of death. And now, behold, when I thought this, I could remember my pains no more; yea, I was harrowed up by the memory of my sins no more. And oh, what joy, and what marvelous light I did behold; yea, my soul was filled with joy as exceeding as was my pain! Yea, I say unto you, my son, that there could be nothing so exquisite and so bitter as were my pains. Yea, and again I say unto you, my son, that on the other hand, there can be nothing so exquisite and sweet as was my joy." (*Alma 36:9-10, 12-22*)

Can we see that eternal glory and punishment is more than a linear forever, it is another whole state of being that operates under the eternal laws of God.

Back to He Knows All

When we are able to accept that God lives in this place of eternity, where *all things are continually before* His *eyes*, a place where *time does not exist*, a place where *the past, the present, and the future* are ***one eternal* NOW**, then we can begin to understand the *foreknowledge* of God. We can begin to understand that prophecy, that is, a knowledge of the future, is only *history in reverse*. Further, if we have been given "the gift of prophecy," we are only in tune with future truth as "truth is knowledge of things as they are, and as they were, and as *they are to come*." (*D&C 93:24*) Although it is certain that God knows our individual character to the extent that He can predict what we will do in any given situation, this is **absolutely not** how He knows the future of man. I often hear this as an explanation of God's foreknowledge and I cringe when I do. Again, He does not have to make a probable but uncertain guess as to what we all might do based on our predictable natures. He lives in the future! He has and *is* watching us as we do it in that future!

It is through the *spirit-matter* we have discussed in the previous chapters that God is able to know all things. As I said before, this *spirit-matter* has properties far beyond those of the gross-matter that we deal with in mortality. It is apparently infinite and timeless in its nature, as well as able to fill our own spirits or minds. God, being one with this *spirit-matter*, is *in all things and through all things*. Make no mistake. God knows all, and so will we when we achieve the same glory and power that is God's by being *quickened* by His power and becoming fully, *spiritually one with Him* in a state of eternity, Born Sons and Daughters of God. When we fully love Him (more on love coming up).

Ya Gotta Do It, Or Agency vs. Destiny?

One of the things that keep us from accepting that God knows all is the fear that because of His foreknowledge, we lose our free agency. The great argument is that if God knows we are going to do a particular thing in the future, then are we not destined to do *what He knows we will do?* **No, no, a thousand times no!** Why we cannot see that foreknowledge and free agency have nothing at all to do with each other is beyond me! He is not forcing us to do anything. He is simply in the future watching us do it! As the future is constantly before His eyes, it's not even a matter of knowing we *will* do something in the future, He is **watching us do it!** He is already in the future, in eternity. In no way does His observation of our actions force us to do anything. We act entirely upon our own accord with each choice we make. God gave us that free agency to act for ourselves. "The Lord said unto Enoch: Behold these thy brethren; they are the workmanship of mine own hands, and I gave unto them their knowledge, in the day I created them; and in the Garden of Eden, gave I unto man his agency." (*Moses 7:32*) By *knowing future truths*, by watching us, God is not acting upon us at all. Remember that truth is *a knowledge of things as they are, and as they were, and as they **are to come***. Knowing something requires no action. Forcing someone to do something is *active*. His knowing future truth is *passive*.

Let me go out on a limb here and say, *yes we are destined, to be sure*, not by God, but ***by our own will***. Our own desires determine our destiny. We are destined to become what we choose to be, that is, although we are free to choose our individual course, our own desires destine us to go a certain way. Our own natures, or more precisely put, our own inner *essence motivation*, as I am pleased to call it, will take us only the direction we ***will*** to go. In this way, we destine ourselves through the choices we make, but in no way are we destined by any outside influence (more on destiny and agency later).

Whatever the course we choose, ***we*** choose it. If it were possible to relive our lives over and over, repeating exactly the same situations, I believe we would make the same choices again and again the very same way every time. It is because our own proclivity or *essence motivation* takes us that way. I use the words *essence motivation* because it is more than desire. Desires change and can be influenced by outside forces. But there is something that is controlled by us. It originates deep within each of us and causes us to make our choices toward light or darkness. It is our *essence motivation*. That essence motivation (not God) predestines us to end up where we will.

That's What I Do

I am reminded of a story, another one of those that somehow got stuck in my memory so long ago that I have no idea of its source. If I knew I would give credit, but I don't recall. The story goes something like this: there was once a great fire in a huge forest and all the animals were running from their impending doom. A swan came to a river and as she was about to go into the water, to escape the fire, she heard a voice. "Please, don't leave me here. Take me with you or I will die by fire," the voice said. The swan turned to see a poisonous snake beside her in the grass. "Please," begged the snake, "I can't swim, but if you will let me ride on your back to the other side of the river, I will be safe." But the swan said, "If I let you on my back you will bite me and I will die." "No, no," the snake replied, "I promise I will not bite you. Don't you see? If I bite you, you will die and I will die too. I want to live so I will not bite you." This seemed logical to the swan so she let him on her back and into the river they went. Halfway across the river the snake bit the swan. "Why did you do that? Now I will die and you will too." The snake retorted, "I'm a snake. That's what snakes do."

I hope my little story illustrates that whatever we are, that is, what we were from the beginning, will ultimately emerge. No matter what changes we may go through on our own personal roads of progression, those who were snakes in embryo, *in essence*, in the beginning, will end up snakes at the end and those who are swans in embryo, *in essence*, will end up swans. It's not that we *cannot* change our essence, it's that we *will not.*

We may go through many changes in the course of our progression through this plan of life and salvation, but will finally develop out to what we *really* are, which is what we were in essence or embryo, in the beginning. The Devil was a murderer and a liar from the beginning. "Ye are of your father the devil, and the lusts of your father ye will do. He was a *murderer from the beginning*, and abode not in the truth, because there is no truth in him. When he speaketh a lie, he speaketh of his own: for he is a liar, and the father of it." (*John 8:44*) "And whatsoever is more or less than this is the spirit of that wicked one who was *a liar from the beginning*." (*D&C 93:25*). Good or bad, we are all what we were *from the beginning*. No matter what changes we go through in the median, we will eventually mature to the fullness of our basic nature. God's job is to give us that opportunity. Our essence motivation is the determining factor. Of course, right now, we don't know what end we are destined by that essence motivation to reach, so we must continue to hope and try. God, by giving us choices, helps us to eventually develop into the most we *will* to be. That's His job.

Essence Motivation

Our *essence motivation* generates entirely from us. This is, in fact, the *only* thing that initiates completely from within our self without any outside influence, even God's. It is the *only* thing that is ***not*** a gift from God. It originates exclusively from our own intelligence. If it were not so, there would be no justice in our final reward or punishment. God, or others, may give us sufficient incentives to change our desire and go in different directions, but nothing can alter our *essence motivation*. It is what we are, a devil, an angel, or somewhere in between.

Again, make no mistake; although God *may* compel us to go a certain way (more on this shortly follows), it will be for his righteous purposes and not by virtue of His *knowing* we will go that way. Why one man's essence motivation takes him a particular way while, in the same exact situation, another man's essence motivation takes him the opposite, I cannot say. If I could, I would know why the Devil chose to be an enemy of God. I would also know, relative to the choices placed before us, what makes one person choose light and truth while others continually choose to throw their lives down the dark abyss of evil thoughts and actions. What's even scarier, I would know why I make the choices I do.

Not Alone

You will note I said we make our own decisions relative to the choices placed before us. In regards to this free agency, I will say it is greatly **overrated**, that is to say, we are only as free as the choices we are given. Without choices, one has no agency. Of course God controls the choices we are given, so to that extent, He controls our agency. Said Brigham Young, "How far does our agency extend? There are certain bounds to it. What we have witnessed in thirty years experience teaches us that man can appoint, but God can disappoint. Man can load his gun to shoot his neighbor, but he cannot make the ball hit him, if the Lord Almighty sees fit to turn it away. He can draw the sword to hew down his fellow man, but instead of that, he may fall upon it himself. There are limits to agency . . . We possess no ability, only that which is given us of God . . . . Our Father controls the results of our acts at His own pleasure, and we cannot prevent it. Man can produce and control his own acts, but he has no control over their results." (*DBY pg. 62-63*)

It is not true that God leaves us alone down here to do entirely what we will; that chance or fate are the causes that affect us; nor is it true that what happens is simply a consequence of our particular choice. On the contrary, God is continually (more than we know) interfering in the affairs of each and every person. When you think about it, it not only makes sense, but good sense. I mean; to get on our knees often asking for God's intervention in our lives and various concerns, then to say that He doesn't interfere is *crazy making*. What are we praying for? Do we believe He will indeed intercede? Just because the Lord does not do things the way we expect does not mean He is not intervening. He might give us trials when we pray for faith, thus causing us to become strong and develop the faith we were praying for.

Who's In Charge Here?

We Mormons are so adamant about our God-given agency that we seem to forget He gave it to us and He can take it away or limit the same and often does. This is called *divine intervention*. It is called *divine providence*. Who told us we were the ones in control anyway? How preposterous. Don't we recognize our weaknesses and God's greater power, abilities, omnipotence? Don't we know, as King Benjamin said, "we are the dust of the earth, we are **worthless** and **nothing** before Him." (see *Mosiah 2:25, 4:5*) Do we suppose that God gave us all power and just turned us loose down here to do whatever we will? Do we think we are God? Why don't we realize that we have no powers except those he gives us? We couldn't lift our puny arm had He not given us the power to do so (many do not have even power to do that). Don't we know how desperately we need His help, in fact, that we are wholly dependent upon it? It is my testimony that He is doing all in His power to help us develop into the *most* we can, or *will to be*. He does this by carefully orchestrating our affairs, placing choices before us, or taking them away. Although we, by our own free will and propensity (essence motivation), make those choices. God controls the choices we have to make.

"For behold, by the power of His word man came upon the face of the earth, which earth was created by the power of His word. Wherefore, if God being able to speak and the world was, and to speak and man was created, O then, why not able to command the earth, or the workmanship of His hands upon the face of it, according to His will and pleasure?" (*Jacob 4:9*) "Thou wilt say then unto me, Why doth he yet find fault? For who hath resisted his [God's] will? Nay but, O man, who art thou that repliest against God? Shall the thing formed say to him that formed it, Why hast thou made me thus? Hath not the potter power over the clay, of the same lump to make one vessel unto honour, and another unto dishonour? What if God, willing to shew his wrath, and to make his power known, endured with much longsuffering the vessels of wrath fitted to destruction: And that he might make known the riches of his glory on the vessels of mercy, which he had afore prepared unto glory." (*Romans 9:19-23*) "Make a joyful noise unto the Lord, all ye lands. Serve the Lord with gladness: come before His presence with singing. Know thou that the Lord is God, it is He that hath made us, and not we ourselves." (*Psalm 100:1-3*) This is according to God's foreknowledge, plan, and His will for His children. "The great Jehovah contemplated the whole of the events connected with the earth, pertaining to the plan of salvation, before it rolled into existence, or ever "the morning stars sang together" for joy . . . *He ordered all things according to the council of His own will*; He knows the situation of both the living and the dead, and has made ample provision for their redemption, according to their several circumstances, and the laws of the Kingdom of God, whether in this world, or in the world to come." (*TPJS pg. 220*) Again, this is called divine providence. Who can claim to worship an omnipotent God and not believe in such providence?

Brigham Young said, "Be patient; do not murmur at the dealings of Providence. The Lord rules in the heavens and works His pleasure upon the earth. Can you comprehend the meaning of the Prophet Amos in the question: 'Shall there be evil in the city, and the Lord hath not done it?' His providences are constantly ruling and overruling, to a greater or less degree, in the affairs of the children of men." (*DBY pg. 266*)

Remember it was God, our Father, who took us from a place where we were raw material, which raw material, according to the scriptures, is called intelligence. "Man was also in the beginning with God. Intelligence, or the light of truth, was not created or made, neither indeed can be." (*D&C 93:29*) In this raw state we were neither able to act or be acted upon. "And if there is no God we are not, neither the earth; for there could have been no creation of things, neither to act nor to be acted upon; wherefore, all things must have vanished away. (*2 Nephi 2:1*) In other words, although God of course could act upon us, there were no interrelationships or interaction between the intelligences. Had God not changed us, there would have been absolutely no progress on our part, no options, no choices, no chance at happiness or fulfillment. Thankfully, He took this raw material and clothed it with a spirit body, then a physical body, and ultimately, hopefully, a glorified immortal body, so we could have a chance to find joy and fulfillment. "For behold, this is my work and my glory—to bring to pass the immortality and eternal life of man." (*Moses 1:39*) "And men are, that they might have joy." (*2 Nephi 2:25*) "I am come that they might have life, and that they might have it more abundantly." (*John 10:10*) He gave us our ability, our agency, by giving us choices, from our very first choice to the multitude of choices we have today. Without choice, we have no agency. Choices to make are what agency is. He gave us those choices and He controls those choices. To that extent, He controls our agency. Again, it is through our choices that He gives us agency and we freely use that agency to make these choices. But we only have agency to the extent that He gives us choices. That is the limit of our agency that Brigham Young spoke of.

We Choose

When the final curtain falls we will appreciate that God, **without forcing us**, did all in His power to help us reach that fullness of joy that is indescribable. He does this by intervening, interfering in the affairs of man. I, for one, welcome all of God's interference I can get, though admittedly, I sometimes don't like what He does in my behalf. It must be the same for others. As an example, Jonah was swallowed by a whale after he ran from what God wanted of him (see *Jonah 1:17*). He did not have much for choices there. I also remember Paul (Saul) and Alma, who were persecuting the Saints of old when the Lord stepped in with what I would call more than just a *"wake up call"*, but *a powerful incentive* to turn around. (see *Acts 22:7-10, Alma 36:6-11.*) Although, once they recovered, I guess they could have continued their wicked ways as others did who have received great manifestations of the spirit, they didn't really have a choice at the time. Certainly if God gives us a choice and we make it poorly, it is our doing, our responsibility, and we will suffer the consequence of that poor choice. But often the choices are not ours to make. These are the times that God has retained control. There are countless examples of God's interference in the lives and affairs of man, from the drowned masses of the great flood at the time of Noah (not much choice there), to the seemingly coincidental occurrences in each and every one of our individual lives. This is what the scriptures are, a history of God's relationship and dealings with man. Where did we get the idea that we are down here on our own? Are we like the prideful child that insists, "I can do it myself."? That is not the program. We have not the capability to do it ourselves. Thankfully, by His power and according to His good will and pleasure, God has been helping us *every step of the way*. It is our own pride, stubbornness, or reluctance to accept His help that stops Him from intervening to a greater extent for our good. Even when we don't know, don't believe in Him, or don't want His help, He is doing everything that he can do, short of forcing us. God does not force us to do anything. The poet William C. Gregg put it very well in the following verse:

Know this, that every soul is free

to choose his life and what he'll be;

For this eternal truth is given,

that God will force no man to heaven.

He'll call, persuade, direct aright,

and bless with wisdom, love and light,

in nameless ways be good and kind,

but never force the human mind.

God is in the business of saving souls. Though He may give us many choices and let us go our own way long enough to learn our lesson, He is only bringing us to the place we need to be. Many people will argue with this, but I submit that **God carefully orchestrates every single event of our lives, no matter how large or small**. You will notice that I said, "orchestrate," not "forced." I mean He places the choices and conditions in precisely the right place at precisely the right time so that we, all of us, might progress as far as we will to go. God relates all things, events, and people to each other in a totally beneficial way, though many of us may not feel it is so beneficial at the time. Again, **nothing** happens by *chance*. **There is no such thing as *luck***. It is not in the economy of God to do anything that is a waste of time or substance (italics for emphasis). "And in nothing doth man offend God, or against none is His wrath kindled, save those who confess not *His hand in **all** things*, and obey not His commandments." (*D&C 59:21*) "We are not, in anything, independent of God." (*DBY pg. 63*)

Let me reiterate that His guiding hand in *all* things does not relieve us of the agency He has already given us or will give us. He does not force us to go a certain way but places choices before us, and waits for us to make the choice we will. As I've said before, it doesn't matter that He knows our choices; they are still fully our choices to make. As we make them, He places more choices before us, and so on, and so on, until we, again, by our own will, rise to the very glory of God, descend to the depths of hell, or stall somewhere in between. The fact is that without God giving us options, we would have no choice and consequently, no free agency.

If we relinquish this free agency, it is by denying the truth that makes us free and, by default we give over our agency to the Devil becoming his slaves. Once agency is lost to the Devil it is difficult to regain as our own witting blindness keeps us from seeing truth. Said Brigham Young, "A man can dispose of his agency or of his birthright as did Esau of old, but when disposed of, he cannot again obtain it; consequently it behooves us to be careful, and not forfeit that agency that is given to us." (*DBY pg. 63*) Without repentance we are bound by justice of the law under which we live. We are free to make the choice but we are not free to control the consequences of that choice. Again, we are not destined by the hand of God in anything, but carefully led to the highest level we, through our own will and choice, will go.

All Things

This brings me to the next issue, a principle that I have often tried to teach but which has met with the most strenuous objection from Mormon Church members and non-members alike. You say, "I know that the scripture you just quoted said His hand in *all* things, but don't you mean God's hand is in only the *good* things that happen to us, not the bad?" No, I do not mean only the *good* things, I mean ***all*** things, and I believe that is what God meant when He gave us this scripture. "But" you argue, "surely God is the source of all good and the Devil is the source and is responsible for all the bad, the evil that happens in the world!" For support, you well may quote the following scripture. "For I say unto you that whatsoever is good cometh from God, and whatsoever is evil cometh from the Devil." (*Alma 5:40*) "Wherefore, all things which are good cometh of God; and that which is evil cometh of the devil; for the devil is an enemy unto God, and fighteth against Him continually, and inviteth and enticeth to sin, and to do that which is evil continually. But behold, that which is of God inviteth and enticeth to do good continually; *wherefore, every thing which inviteth and enticeth to do good, and to love God, and to serve Him, is inspired of God*. Wherefore, take heed, my beloved brethren, that ye do not judge that which is evil to be of God, or that which is good and of God to be of the devil. For behold, my brethren, it is given unto you to judge, that ye may know good from evil; and the way to judge is as plain, that ye may know with a perfect knowledge, as the daylight is from the dark night. For behold, the Spirit of Christ is given to every man, that he may know good from evil; wherefore, I show unto you the way to judge; for *every thing which inviteth to do good, and to persuade to believe in Christ, is sent forth by the power and gift of Christ*; wherefore ye may know with a perfect knowledge it is of God. But whatsoever thing persuadeth men to do evil, and believe not in Christ, and deny Him, and serve not God, then ye may know with a perfect knowledge it is of the devil; for after this manner doth the devil work, for he persuadeth no man to do good, no, not one; neither do His angels; neither do they who subject themselves unto him." (*Moroni 7:12-17*) The truth of this and many other scriptures like it are irrefutable. Of course it is true that God can do nothing but good for man! God cannot do anything evil or He would cease to be God. **This is true**. This I sincerely believe. But, the scripture says His *hand is in **all** things*. This I also believe to be true. I believe the Lord meant just what He said, **all things**.

If you will look a little closer at the above scripture given us of Moroni, you will note that he does not say what is of God and what is of the Devil, but rather tells us how to judge that which is of God and that which is of the Devil. He further warns us not to mistake that which is good to be evil and vice versa. What did he say is good (italics for emphasis)? "That which is of God *inviteth and enticeth to do good continually*; wherefore, *every thing which inviteth and enticeth to do good*, and *to love* God, and to *serve Him*, is **inspired of God**." Again, he told us how to judge that which is of God from that which is of the devil, "I show unto you the way to judge; for *every thing which inviteth to do good*, and *to persuade to believe in Christ*, is sent forth by the power and gift of Christ; wherefore ye may know with a perfect knowledge *it is of God*." He said it is *sent forth by the power and gift of Christ* and that ***it is of God***.

When you contemplate the events of the earth and more precisely, the events of other's lives and your own life, you will note that many of the things that seem bad, family tragedies etc., were the very things that *persuaded you to believe in Christ*. Many of these events were the humbling experiences that tuned your heart to God (if we chose to go that way). On the other hand, many of the events that seemed wonderful at the time, winning the lottery or some such thing, may lead us subtly into sin or, at best, away from God. Just because we receive a *wake-up call*, doesn't mean it came from the Devil, on the contrary, it was probably "*inspired of God*." You be the judge, but remember not to judge *that which is evil to be of God, or that which is good and of God to be of the devil*.

Without consulting the spirit of Christ, which *is given to every man* (see also: *D&C 84:46-470*), we cannot know which seemingly bad events in our lives are really good and *gifts from Christ*. In no way do I here mean to say that we should follow evil, as I believe this will make us slaves to the Devil and miserable indeed. Yet if our desire is to do good and to love God, then, having suffered evil, we will emerge with a greater resolve to be good. The challenge is to put off the evil, turn our hearts to God, and come back to a state of innocence again. This is the plan. So that which seems bad and induced by the Devil may actually be the means of bringing us closer to God. Our misperceptions cause us to think of these brushes with evil as bad. I don't believe we see things as God sees them.

The Devil Did It

The problem exists because our image of God is that of a God who does not do mean things. I would agree with that image, except that the God we worship has at times utterly destroyed His children from off the face of the earth, a seemingly very **mean** thing to do. Not only that, but it is more than obvious that He allows trouble and evil in the world. But you say, "No, that comes from the Devil." Well then, is the Devil God? Hasn't God the power to destroy the Devil and his angels with a wave of His hand? Yes, of course He has.

We sometimes think that because the Devil is opposite God in moral fiber, that he is *equal* to Him in power, only on the other end of the spectrum of good and evil. This is not true. The Devil is nothing! He has no power, even to exist, were it not for that given him by God. Even man is far more powerful than the Devil, as the Devil has power to bruise man's heel but man has power to crush his head (see *Genesis 3:15*). Joseph Smith tells us that, "All beings who have bodies have power over those who have not. The Devil has no power over us only as we permit him. The moment we revolt at anything which comes from God, the Devil takes power." (*TPJS, pg. 181*) So, since God is the *one* with the power and He still allows Satan to tempt man; since He still allows trouble and evil in the world when He could stop it; since He is indeed God; does it not naturally follow that it is His will that trouble and evil exist? Isn't God ultimately responsible for what happens? Yes, a thousand times, yes!

You may not have swallowed that. Let me try again. We have already quoted scripture that says all evil comes from the Devil. Please, please, please, don't think for a moment that this writer is saying that God does evil things. No, I say again, He will not and does not. I am not talking about *who causes evil*; I am talking about *who is responsible for it* in this world. God is indeed responsible for all that He has created, including the Devil whom He could annihilate at any time, or even refused to create in the beginning. We don't worship the Devil, that is to say, when something bad happens to us, we don't look to the Devil for relief. Such a notion is absurd (though practiced more than we want to admit, as the Devil has many faces). God is using evil; in fact, He is using the Devil to accomplish His righteous purposes. That is why He created him in the first place though He, through His eternal foreknowledge of things (which we have already discussed), knew that the Devil would be His enemy.

To make the point a little clearer, let me use an example. A general, when preparing for war, makes his plans. Those plans include sending men into battle. Though he knows that many men will die, he also knows that ultimately many more will be saved. The men go into battle and many are killed. Did the opposing force kill them or did the general? Well, of course the enemy killed them, but who is responsible for their death? The general. No one else sent them into battle knowing many would die. This is a literal example of God's dealings with His children. Perhaps you still don't see the point?

Up Without Down?

What I am saying is, God knew that to accomplish His righteous purpose, which purpose is to bring men to a state of joy, He would have to expose them to misery. Why misery? Well, there must be opposites in all things. What? Why is that necessary? "For it must needs be, that there is an opposition in all things. If not so . . . righteousness could not be brought to pass, neither wickedness, neither holiness nor misery, neither good nor bad. Wherefore, all things must needs be a compound in one; wherefore, if it should be one body it must needs remain as dead, having no life neither death, nor corruption nor incorruption, happiness nor misery, neither sense nor insensibility. Wherefore, it must needs have been created for a thing of naught: wherefore there would have been no purpose in the end of its creation. Wherefore, this thing must needs destroy the wisdom of God and His eternal purposes, and also the power, and mercy and the justice of God."(*2 Nephi 2:11-12*) You see, **opposites define each other**! You cannot have *up* without *down*. You cannot have *dark* without *light*. You cannot have *out* without *in*. You cannot have life without death. You cannot have *happy* without *sad*. You cannot have *good* without *bad*. You cannot have *joy* without *misery*. One defines the other. This being said, it is the wisdom of God that in order to bring us to a place of joy, we must have misery as a part of our experience. Hence, in its beginning, God created a world that was flawless and good. But He also set up the situation, the fall of Adam, which effectuated the fall of his posterity and all things, including the earth itself. This was done, again, not by God forcing it upon Adam and Eve, but by giving them a choice. The choice was two trees, the seemingly conflicting commandments: don't partake of the tree of *knowledge of good and evil* and to *multiply and replenish the earth*. Please note; it was God who put that forbidden tree in the garden, not the Devil, and it was God who put the Devil down here to tempt them. The Devil did not usurp God's power by coming down here on his own. He never had the power to do such a thing. He did, however, attempt to ruin God's plan for His children by drawing souls away from God but, unwittingly, played right into God's plan.

God didn't just do all this arbitrarily, without purpose. The purpose was so that Adam could, and **would**, fall, and by so doing, taste the bad that he might know the good. And yes, Adam and Eve were tempted and, by their own will and agency, broke the commandment, thereby suffering the justice of the law.

Still, you must ask yourself, who set it all up? Was it Satan? No, he was an ignorant player, a *denying player*. We wonder how stupid the Devil could be, playing into God's hands like that, but it is not a matter of stupidity; it is a matter of pride and denial of truth. He has deceived himself and actually believes he can, by drawing souls away from God, usurp God's power and glory. It seems stupid on his part to believe such a thing, but his pride and other evil intents, keep him on this course. Remember, the Devil is one who can look at the sun and say it doesn't shine.

No, our suffering and the evil that we experience is not only necessary, **it is the very reason** why God created this earth. Aside from gaining a body, suffering is the most important purpose for coming to this earth. We couldn't suffer in the pre-existence, nor will we suffer in the glorified after life. This earth is the place prepared by God for this anguish. So let us not be surprised or dismayed when we find ourselves suffering.

Who To Blame

Whose plan was this? Who set it up? Who played it out? *God*. He did it. He did it! He is the power! He is the general sending His people into battle knowing full well what **will** happen, what **must** happen, what He **wants to happen**. He is the Man. He is God. We worship no other. It was His will that all this happens in order to save our souls. For this great purpose, God allows trouble and evil in the world, and, in fact, is ultimately responsible for causing it. It is God's fault. Blame Him, as on the day we fully understand His *plan of life and salvation* we will see that He is more than willing to take that blame or responsibility, and we will praise His name for having brought these *so-called* evils upon us all.

I will suppose that by now if you still object to this doctrine, it is not because I have not made myself clear and understandable, but rather because you cannot accept it. Ok, that's all right, I guess, but think about it for a while. Pray about it. It is an important issue. It is important not only so that you know the God you worship, but also it is paramount in order to understand your relationship with Him and to exercise faith in Him.

Again, the problem we may have with this concept is our faulty *perception* of what is good and evil. Our limited mortal perspective is distorted. We are stuck in a single geometry when God works within many. Our judgment of what is good for us or bad for us is tainted by our desire to have an easy, peaceful, wonderful, good life, where no rain falls on our parades. Nevertheless, "That ye may be the children of your Father which is in heaven; for He maketh His sun to rise on the evil and on the good, and sendeth rain on the just and on the unjust." (*Matthew* 5:45) Who *maketh* and *sendeth*? Not Satan. Whose *sun* and whose *rain* is it? Not Satan's. "Shall a trumpet be blown in the city, and the people not be afraid? shall there be evil in a city, and the LORD hath not done [it]?" (*Amos 3:6*) Who done it? Not Satan. "I form the light, and create darkness: I make peace, and *create evil*: I the Lord do all these things." (*Isaiah 45:7*) Did we read that right? Did the Lord actually say that He *created evil*? Yes, we read it right. Yes, He did.

Again, I hear your voice saying that it is still the Devil that does it. To this I say yes, but God sent him and is using him as a means of bringing us to a state of sweet by having tasted the bitter. This is no fine distinction. This is a major principle, and understanding the same is profoundly necessary to our knowing God, having full faith in Him, and our ability to worship Him. You see; if we don't see Him as the responsible party, we must look to whoever ***is***. We must worship the responsible party. If that be the Devil, then perhaps we should think about changing our God?

Our Crosses

This is one of the greatest *other attributes* of God, the ability to not only stand by and allow His children to suffer, but effectively be responsible for that suffering. He not only stood by allowing His son to suffer, He actually sent Him to the cross, a seemingly very mean and evil thing to do to your own son. "For God so loved the world, that He *gave* His only begotten Son, that whosoever believeth in Him should not perish, but have everlasting life." (*John 3:16*) Note: the word gave.

We will remember that Christ in the garden of Gethsemane did not pray to the Devil asking him to remove the bitter cup. He prayed to The One in control. The Devil did not *take* Christ; God the Father *gave* Him as a ransom that we might be saved from the evil He was exposing us to. As we look at the sacrifice of our Lord, we can see the propriety of this apparently contemptible and evil thing God did to His own son. If we can see the great purpose in God's reason for sending His son to the cross, we ought also to be able to see that the reasons for *our sufferings* are equally as righteous. We should, furthermore, be able to see that it is God that is sending us to our crosses. Remember that God is in the business of saving souls—ours. He is not guaranteeing us a wonderful life here, but a wonderful eternity *there*, if we can stick it out. What we suffer is for our good. Paul said, "And we know that all things work together for good to them that love God, to them who are the called according to His purpose." (*Romans 8:28*) And the Lord said, "Therefore, He giveth this promise unto you, with an immutable covenant that they shall be fulfilled; and all things wherewith you have been afflicted shall work together for your good, and to my name's glory, saith the Lord. Therefore, let your hearts be comforted; for all things shall work together for good to them that walk uprightly, and to the sanctification of the church." (*D&C 98:3* and *D&C 100:15*, see also *D&C 105:40*) Paul didn't say just the apparent good things in your life work for your good. He said *all things*, even your *afflictions*. Nor did the Lord say only the perceived good things in your life. He said ***all things***. Of course they only help those who walk uprightly. You see, those that curse God because of their afflictions don't get it. Then all things work to their condemnation. Again, it is our limited perspective that keeps us from digesting this bit of meat.

To further illustrate my point, I will retell a story told by Deepak Chopra[84] about an old man who lived in a small village with his only son. His son was the love of his life. He was all the man really had of any worth. One day the son disappeared and after an extensive search that lasted several days, he was given up for dead. The old man cried and said, "This is bad, this is very bad. I have lost my only son." But just then the son came into the village with a beautiful white stallion. He had spent those several days stalking and capturing this beautiful horse. Now the old man laughed and said, "This is good, this is very good. My son was gone but he has returned with a prize." But the next day the son was riding the horse, fell off, and broke his leg. Now the old man cried and said, "This horse is bad, is very bad. Now my son's leg is broken and he cannot walk or work." But the next day, the leaders of the local army came into the village and took all the young men off to fight in a war, but because of the broken leg, they did not take the old man's son. Now the old man said, "This is good, this is very good. His broken leg has saved him from war and kept him by me."

Do you see what I am saying? The "bad" things that happen to us are only bad because we perceive them to be. We cannot see the big picture. We don't see that our brushes with evil, our struggles, conflict, and strife are ultimately good and necessary for us. God is using these *apparently* evil things to literally save our souls.

Often, when we get through a bad experience, we look back and recognize the hand of God in the trial and appreciate that it was good for us. This is the way it will be on judgment day. Although this is hard to believe now, we will look upon **all** our so-called *bad* experiences and praise God for each and every one. Again, we will not praise the Devil for each and every one, but God, and how can we praise God if He isn't the responsible party?

Make no mistake; it is God who is *doing it to us*. God is responsible. He has the power. He is the one we look to for relief and power. If He were not all-powerful, we could not have faith in Him.

Still you argue that God is not the one *doing it*. Well, read what king Benjamin[85] said in that great address to his people (italics for emphasis). "For the natural man is an enemy to God, and has been from the fall of Adam, and will be, forever and ever, unless he yields to the enticings of the Holy Spirit, and putteth off the natural man and becometh a saint through the atonement of Christ the Lord, and becometh as a child, submissive, meek, humble, patient, full of love, willing to submit to all things which the *Lord seeth fit to inflict upon him*, even as a child doth submit to his father." (*Mosiah 3:19*) You will observe that it is the *Lord* that is doing the *inflicting*. "Naked came I out of my mother's womb, and naked shall I return thither: the LORD gave, and the LORD hath taken away; blessed be the name of the LORD." (*Job 1:21*). The Lord giveth and the Lord taketh away. He is not, to any extent, negligent in His duty, which is to save our souls, and for that purpose, will inflict whatsoever thing He sees needful.

There are no mistakes, no happenstance, no good or bad luck, no good or bad surprises, no accidents, no fortuities, and no serendipities. All things are in order, by order of God. "The great Jehovah contemplated the whole of the events connected with the earth, pertaining to the plan of salvation, before it rolled into existence . . . *He ordered all things according to the council of His own will*; He knows the situation of both the living and the dead, and has made ample provision for their redemption, according to their several circumstances, and the laws of the kingdom of God, whether in this world, or in the world to come." (*TPJS pg. 220*) His hand is, indeed, ***in all things***. We must become as children, learn to submit, and try to understand that what the Lord is doing to us is right for whatever reason seems good to Him.

Our Own Fault

Please do not misunderstand me. Because of our own weaknesses we bring much of it on ourselves. We can leave the Devil and God out of a great deal of our suffering. It is certainly true that if God gives us a choice and we make that choice poorly, we will likely suffer the consequence of the laws governing such a choice. Poor choices are, of course, the cause of much of our own, as well as other's suffering. I am certain that much of our suffering is the consequence of our own poor choices. We could all alleviate much of that suffering by simply repenting and living by correct principles, by learning our lessons. Although not at first perhaps, eventually in the eternal outlook, correct principles and proper choices, will pay off. This is true and my firm belief. Still, in Ether 12:27, the Lord tells us that God gives man his weaknesses (more on this in a moment). So, many, if not all, of our weaknesses are God-given; then is He not responsible for the suffering caused by those weaknesses?

Poor Job

Notwithstanding the above paragraph, in this world, there is much that we suffer which is completely beyond our control. So that we might find the responsible party, it is of that suffering that I speak further. I here refer my readers not only to the above quote from Job, but the entire book of Job. Job knew this principle well, and would not curse God for what was happening to him, nor did he look to the Devil for relief. This is the entire theme of the book of Job. Many of us think that it is a story of a pact between God and the Devil, but that part is only about 16 verses out of 42 chapters. The book is really about *man's relationship with God,* and in this author's opinion, the most important book we can read on this subject. It is perhaps the most important book to understand in all of holy writ. It has all the elements of what we have been discussing in this chapter. If you want to know what God is doing with man, read the book of Job.

Therein we find that first of all, Job was a "man that was *perfect and upright,* and one that feared God, and eschewed evil." (*Job 1:1*) The script mentions his perfection several times. This eliminates the possibility of our thinking that Job *got what he deserved* or that what happened to him was justified or a result of his own misdeeds. It was not. We can also clearly see who was in charge. The Devil had to appeal to God for the opportunity and power to afflict Job. He didn't just do it on his own.

Let's read a few verses of Job so that we might have an appreciation for what he suffered. "And there came a messenger unto Job, and said, The oxen were plowing, and the asses feeding beside them: And the Sabeans fell [upon them], and took them away; yea, they have slain the servants with the edge of the sword; and I only am escaped alone to tell thee. While he [was] yet speaking, there came also another, and said, The fire of God is fallen from heaven, and hath burned up the sheep, and the servants, and consumed them; and I only am escaped alone to tell thee. While he [was] yet speaking, there came also another, and said, The Chaldeans made out three bands, and fell upon the camels, and have carried them away, yea, and slain the servants with the edge of the sword; and I only am escaped alone to tell thee. While he [was] yet speaking, there came also another, and said, Thy sons and thy daughters [were] eating and drinking wine in their eldest brother's house: And, behold, there came a great wind from the wilderness, and smote the four corners of the house, and it fell upon the young men, and they are dead; and I only am escaped alone to tell thee. Then Job arose, and rent his mantle, and shaved his head, and fell down upon the ground, and worshipped, And said, Naked came I out of my mother's womb, and naked shall I return thither: the Lord gave, and the Lord hath taken away; blessed be the name of the Lord. In all this Job sinned not, nor charged God foolishly." (*Job 1:14-22*)

You will note that Job did not say, "The Lord gave and the Devil hath taken away." No, he said, "the Lord gave, and the Lord hath taken away . . . ." he knew it was ultimately the Lord who had done these things to him. The scripture further states that Job did not sin nor charge God foolishly. In other words, Job was right to put the responsibility upon the Lord. What is more, he blessed the name of the Lord despite his sufferings, which ultimately included his health as he was covered from head to foot with boils.

Also, though it appears that the Devil did the inflicting, a closer read makes it very clear that God not only allowed it, but was effectively the cause of Job's suffering (italics for emphasis). "And the Lord said unto Satan, Hast thou considered my servant Job . . . ? It was the Lord who pointed out Job to Satan. Verse eleven of chapter one makes it apparent that it is God that is doing the inflicting. The Devil taunts God by saying "But put forth thine hand now, and touch all that he hath, he will curse thee to thy face." Then in verse three of chapter two, the Lord said to the Devil, "and still he holdeth fast his integrity, although thou movedst me against him, to destoy him without cause." You see, the Devil could do nothing to Job, it was done by the hand of God.

His wife and friends turned against him. "Then said his wife unto him, Dost thou still retain thine integrity? Curse God, and die". But he said unto her, "Thou speakest as one of the foolish women speaketh. What? *Shall we receive good at the hand of God, and shall we not receive evil?*" (*Job 2:9-10*) "Who knoweth not in all these that the hand of the Lord hath wrought this? In whose hand is the soul of every living thing, and the breath of all mankind" (*Job 12:9-10*) "And they bemoaned him and comforted him over all *the evil that the Lord had brought upon him.*" (*Job 42:11*)

As we know, Job held up, and remained true and faithful. He never cursed God, though he cried unto Him in an attempt to understand what God was doing to him and why he had lost his wealth, friends, family and health. His friends and even his wife turned on him. They tried to get him to admit some hidden fault that would explain his troubles. They even accused him of *thinking* evil. When he denied evil thoughts, they accused him of dreaming evil dreams. All this is to show us he was an innocent man. Apparently, even in his day, the popular belief required that *if you are having trouble in life, you must be wicked or doing something wrong.* Conversely *if you are apparently blessed, you must be righteous*, when in reality, it may be the other way around.

This is certainly the popular belief of our day even though the scriptures declare that, "And ye have forgotten the exhortation which speaketh unto you as unto children, My son, despise not thou the chastening of the Lord, nor faint when thou art rebuked of Him: For whom the Lord loveth He chasteneth, and scourgeth every son whom He receiveth. If ye endure chastening, God dealeth with you as with sons; for what son is he whom the father chasteneth not? But if ye be without chastisement, whereof all are partakers, then are ye bastards, and not sons." (*Hebrews 12:5-8*)

I am aware that there are those who claim that Job was not a real person, that the book of Job is not valid scripture, and should not be included in the canonized text. However, Job was apparently real enough for God to make reference to him when comforting Joseph Smith while he was suffering having been unjustly incarcerated in the Liberty Jail. "My son, peace be unto thy soul, thine adversity and thine afflictions shall be but a small moment; And then, if thou endure it well, God shall exalt thee on high; thou shalt triumph over all thy foes. Thou art not yet as Job; thy friends do not contend against thee, neither charge thee with transgression, as they did Job." (*D&C 121:7-10*)

Those who would discount this great book of Job are the same who refuse to believe in a God who inflicts His children with needed suffering. We fight these truths because we simply cannot imagine a God that has such seemingly harsh attributes. We see only a loving, benevolent, kind, merciful God. What we can't seem to accept is that this is sometimes *how* God is; loving, benevolent, kind, and merciful. This is what is needed. This is what it takes for Him to lead us to glory. I say lead because He has suffered these things, and greater, Himself.

If I still have not convinced you, or at the very least, moved you to a greater understanding, let me make this last attempt. What father does not know the propriety of having his children suffer small tragedies, that they might learn? God, the Father of us all, is doing no less, only on a larger scale.

Getting Dumped On

Not long ago I was discussing this principle with a young lady who brought to my attention a scripture that I have found myself quoting in times of trials, not only to others, but also to myself. It relates to the Lord's parable about pruning and caring for the vineyard or the house of Israel (italics for emphasis). "Wherefore, dig about them, and prune them, and *dung* them once more, for the last time, for the end draweth nigh . . . ." (*Jacob 5:64*) Untrue to the popular bumper sticker, let me say "it" doesn't just "happen." The Lord does, on more than just a few occasions, "dung" us. Sometimes it seems as though we are buried in it, but it is for our good and growth. So, when it is our turn to be the recipient of affliction, we must remember that it is a *LOVING* God who is doing it, then we will fully understand and we will look to God our Father, not the Devil, or luck, or chance, or bad karma, or any other false god. If we can remember this concept, humble ourselves, *endure it well*, and seek to know what God is doing with us, we will unavoidably draw nearer to Him and come to know the God we worship. What is life eternal, again, to know Him? "For all those who will not endure chastening, but deny me, cannot be sanctified." (*D&C 101:5*)

The Gift of Weakness

I suppose, while we are on this subject, I should bring up another secret, as it is very closely related and exposes further another great attribute of God. This concept is a truth that seems to elude even some Mormons, who, in my opinion, should know better. The essence of the issue is found in a statement by God to Moroni about our weaknesses (italics for emphasis). "Fools mock, but they shall mourn; and my grace is sufficient for the meek, that they shall take no advantage of your weakness; And if men come unto me I will show unto them their weakness, *I give unto men weakness* that they may be humble; and my grace is sufficient for all men that humble themselves before me; for if they humble themselves before me, and have faith in me, then will I make weak things become strong unto them." (*Ether 12:26-27*)

The thought that God would *give unto men weakness* is a thought to which we seem compelled violently to object. I don't know why this concept is so hard for us to accept, as we were all handed a *bundle* of weaknesses when placed in this fallen state of mortality.

Such a concept might cause us to wonder how many and which of our weaknesses were given to us by God, as if we don't have to feel responsible for, or guilty about them anymore. (I don't believe we should feel guilty about anything and I will cover this subject in another chapter.) I do contend that the above scripture is true, and that at least some, if not all, of our weaknesses are God-given. Again, in the interest of saving our souls, He has given us these weaknesses, not just to overcome, but also to keep us humble, teachable. I give as an example, the case of Paul. "And lest I should be exalted above measure through the abundance of the revelations, there was given to me a thorn in the flesh, the messenger of Satan to buffet me, lest I should be exalted above measure. For this thing I besought the Lord thrice, that it might depart from me. And He said unto me, My grace is sufficient for thee: for my strength is made perfect in weakness. Most gladly therefore will I rather glory in my infirmities, that the power of Christ may rest upon me. Therefore I take pleasure in infirmities, in reproaches, in necessities, in persecutions, in distresses for Christ's sake: for when I am weak, then am I strong." (*2 Corinthians 12:7-10*) Joseph Smith felt the same way. "And as for the perils which I am called to pass through, they seem but a small thing to me, as the envy and wrath of man have been my common lot all the days of my life . . . deep water is what I am wont to swim in. It all has become a second nature to me; and I feel, like Paul, to glory in tribulation; for to this day has the God of my fathers delivered me out of them all, and will deliver me from henceforth; for behold, and lo, I shall triumph over all my enemies, for the Lord God hath spoken it." (*D&C 127:2*)

Apparently we, as mortals, can have gigantic egos and nearly all fall victim to pride and vanity. "We have learned by sad experience that it is the nature and disposition of almost all men, as soon as they get a little authority, as they suppose, they will immediately begin to exercise unrighteous dominion." (*D&C 121:39*) My personal belief is that **pride is the worst of all faults or vices** (more on this latter). This defect alone has brought many men down to hell, including Cain and the Devil himself. In order that we may, like Paul and Joseph Smith, remain humble, we are given weaknesses. I testify that this is a true principle and one that, if accepted and studied, will also unavoidably draw us nearer to God. It turns our face to God in search of relief. Our only hope is in Christ. We must "cast thy burden upon the Lord, and He shall sustain thee: He shall never suffer the righteous to be moved." (*Psalms 55:22*)

We all carry such heavy burdens because of our weaknesses and sins. We all desperately need those burdens lifted. Yielding our wills to Christ and passing to Him the guilt for which He suffered is the only way. We must repent and give Him the sorrow of our sins. Only then will we have hope. The wonderful part is we are promised that if we will humble ourselves to a state of meekness and faith, and look to God, His "*grace is sufficient*" and He "*will make weak things strong*." What is meant by His grace is sufficient? Simply: His saving grace will justify us and remove the consequence of our sins. He *will make weak things become strong*.

Please note that **He** will make weak things strong. Like the prideful child, far too often we think we can *do it ourselves*. It is my testimony that we do not have the ability to fix ourselves, though we continue to think we do. It is a simple concept, if you could fix yourself, what need would you have for a Savior? We cannot, by ourselves, overcome the weaknesses that we have, whether of our own creation or God-given. When we try, by ourselves, to overcome them, we are denying our Savior and worshipping our own arm of flesh. We are not god. God is God. Granted, we must do our part, that is, to keep trying because we don't know when God will take the weakness from us or give us the power to overcome. Still, our **only** hope is in Christ. He gave us many of these weaknesses and He will take them away when we have learned and been sanctified by the suffering they cause. Although, like Paul, He may, at this time, choose not to take the *thorn* from our side. Still, we have the promise that His grace is sufficient and He will one day make weak things strong. Make no mistake, many of our weaknesses are God-given, but whether they are inherent in our own makeup, or God-given, we must, of course, do the right thing by these weaknesses, that is, keep trying and struggling to overcome them. We must keep trying with our most honest efforts to keep His commandments. I will not argue this doctrine further as it is plain to be understood (though hard to accept).

Why do I bring these issues to the surface? I give you these sayings that we might more fully understand and comprehend the God we worship; that we might have confidence in His greatness, power, and glory; that we might more fully understand His dealings with us; that we might have full faith in Him; and that we might know Him, the only true God. Let me finally just say, look to God. He is the responsible party. He is the power! God is God, not luck, not chance, not our own arm of flesh, nor the Devil. God is God. Look to Him.

---

[83] **A High Priest is an office in the priesthood of The LDS Church.**

[84] **Deepak Chopra is a world-renowned leader in the field of mind/body medicine and a best-selling author.**

[85] **King Benjamin was a king and prophet to the Nephite people living on the South American continent about 124 BC. The account of his great address is found in the book of Mosiah within *The Book of Mormon*.**

5
This Thing Called Love?

Confusion Reigns

"Few things in this world are as much talked about and as little understood as love, especially the love spoken of in the scriptures." (*Come Unto the Father In the Name of Jesus, The Melchizedek Priesthood Personal Study Guide #3 pg. 121*)

This above statement is one that I could not agree with more. One need only be in a Mormon group, or any other group for that matter, where this concept is being discussed to realize that there is a great secret being kept here. Satan has managed to confuse the idea of love in the world, almost beyond reparation. Still, because "God is Love," (*1 John 4:8*) and we want to know God, it behooves us to make an attempt to shed some light upon the subject.

Remember our previous discussion about three general levels of law, understanding, and glory? If we are to understand the true meaning of love, we must again elevate our minds to a celestial realm of thinking. It is my contention that most of the confusion on this subject is due to our attempt to apply the meaning of the word love in terrestrial or telestial terms. In the following discussion I will relate the subject only to celestial operations. Also, although these concepts may be new to you, remember that without *new* there is no progress. Don't discard these things just because they don't fit your traditions or a familiar geometry. Test them against the Holy Ghost who will testify of the truth of all things.

First let me ask some questions that I will, in the following discourse, attempt to answer.

1. How many kinds of love are there?

2. Is love the most important criteria for choosing a mate?

3. Does love come in degrees?

4. What obligations do we have when we find ourselves loving someone?

5. Is there a *one and only* love for everyone?

6. How do we love our enemy?

7. What controls love?

8. Is it true that when a person finds one's self in love with another person, they will do anything **for** or **with** that person?

9. Why is the greatest commandment of the law to love the Lord God with all our hearts and with all our souls and with all our minds?

10. Is the second great commandment of the law, to love our neighbor as ourselves, really possible?

In order that we might eliminate confusion on this subject of love, I will here ask you to find a definition of the word love. Remember that your definition must work in *all* applications of the word. It must fit *all* situations where the word love applies. It must work when you refer to the love between man and woman. It must work when you say you love truth. It must work when you love your neighbor. It must even work when you love your enemy. This definition must work when you refer to the love you have of the beauty of nature, trees, mountains, sea, music, and art. It must work when you are referring to the love you have for your dog or cat. It must even work when you refer to the love some of us have of money, power, cars, computers, and other worldly things. What may be even more difficult, your definition must work when you refer to the love Satan has for a lie, darkness, filth, and etc.

Love Defined

As you find your definition you can't force words like, caring, compassion, kindness, giving, understanding, empathy, intimacy, thoughtfulness, sacrifice, service, selflessness, sharing, and etc. You may try but you will find they don't fit in every situation where the word love applies. Plus, these words have definitions of their own and although they may be related to love, they do not define love.

If you are like most of us your definition quickly becomes cumbersome and complicated and the frustration is too great so you settle for something inadequate or simply surrender to the confusion. But really give it a good try. Since I have labored with this problem for so many years, I suppose that you can think about it for at least a moment or two. Stop your reading and really let yourself struggle for an adequate definition.

As you think about your definition, you are discovering that it works in some cases but not others. The answer to this dilemma seems simple and one I have heard for many years. There are *different kinds of love*, right? No, no, a thousand times no! There is only ***one definition*** and ***two kinds*** of love! I know I may have lost you at this point, but before you stone me, let me explain.

Our former discussion on the *oneness* or *indwelling* relationship of the Gods might have given you a hint.

Remember, spirit is matter. Of course we know from our discussion that God, Christ, and man have spirits. You will also remember that if anything exists it must be made of matter, gross or *spirit-matter*. We learn from Moses that *all things* have a spirit side to them. "And every plant of the field before it was in the earth, and every herb of the field before it grew. For I, the Lord God, created all things, of which I have spoken, spiritually, before they were naturally upon the face of the earth. For I, the Lord God had not caused it to rain upon the face of the earth. And I, the Lord God, had created all the children of men; and not yet a man to till the ground; for in heaven created I them; and there was not yet flesh upon the earth, neither in the water, neither in the air." (*Moses 3:5* also *Genesis 2:5*) All things were created first of *spirit-matter* and have a spirit side to them. Even things we consider to be inanimate or not alive, like the earth itself. "And again, verily I say unto you, the earth abideth the law of a celestial kingdom, for it filleth the measure of its creation, and transgresseth not the law." (*D&C 88:25*) This implies that the Earth itself has an intelligence that is capable of obeying or transgressing the law. Indeed it does. And it, as well as all things in it, has a spirit side. All things were created first of *spirit-matter* and then clothed with a *gross-matter* body or form. The very rocks and plants of the earth have a spirit side. Remember too that even our thoughts, our emotions, and other non-gross-matter things are still made of matter, *spirit-matter*. If this be true, and I testify that it is, then all things, whether temporal or spiritual, have a spirit side.

With this said, you will find that the following definition of love will work in every situation where the word applies. The definition of love is ***being***

spiritually one with whatever is the object of your love. In other words, love is ***spiritual oneness***.

I know you are quickly applying this definition to see if it works in every situation where you can use the word. Well, let us do it together. It works when you refer to the love between a man and woman. It works when you say I love truth. Remember, truth is *spirit-matter* (see *D&C 93:23*). It works when you love your neighbor. It even works when you love your enemy, though your spiritual oneness will hopefully extend only to the person and not to his evil thoughts and deeds (more on this to come). This definition also works when you refer to the love you have of the beauty of nature, trees, mountains, sea, and beautiful music and art. It works when you are referring to the love you have of your dog or cat. It even works when you refer to the love some of us have of money, power, cars, computers, and other worldly things. This definition will also work when you refer to the love Satan has for a lie, darkness, filth, and etc. He, and we, become spiritually one with the object of our love. Our *spirit-matter* reaches out to theirs and has the ability to amalgamate with theirs, becoming one.

Spiritual Oneness

Again, how *spirit-matter* works is something yet to be revealed by God and I will make no attempt to definitively say whether it is actually our spirit body or some other *spirit-matter* separate from our spirit bodies that amalgamates with the *spirit-matter* of others, other things, and God. What is certain is that, while retaining our own individuality, some part of us or rather some *spirit-matter* that is part of us, has the ability to reach out and be one with other *spirit-matter*.

Love between God the Father and Christ is just another name describing their spiritual *oneness doctrine,* that same oneness that we have already discussed in the previous chapters. You will remember that I said there is only one definition, spiritual oneness, but *two kinds* of love. I say this because there are really just two kinds of the same thing, **spiritual oneness**. I mean that there is God's kind of love and Satan's kind of love, or in other words, a *spiritual oneness God has with all that is good,* and *a spiritual oneness Satan has with all that is evil.*

God's Kind of Love

We call the oneness with God charity, which is what? "But charity is the pure love of Christ, and it endureth forever, and whoso is found possessed of it at the last day, it shall be well with Him." (*Moroni 7:47*) And how is the pure love of Christ described? "And charity [the pure love of Christ] suffereth long, and is kind, and envieth not, and is not puffed up, seeketh not her own, is not easily provoked, thinketh no evil, and rejoiceth not in iniquity but rejoiceth in truth, beareth all things, believeth all things, hopeth all things, endureth all things." (*Moroni 7:45* also *1 Corinthians 13:4*)

Charity, the pure love of Christ, is what we seek for and obtain when we are spiritually Born Again and become sons and daughters of God. "Wherefore, my beloved brethren, pray unto the Father with all the energy of heart, that ye may be filled with this love, which He hath bestowed upon all who are true followers of His Son, Jesus Christ, that ye may become the sons of God; that when He shall appear we shall be like Him, for we shall see Him as He is; that we may have this hope; that we may be purified even as He is pure. Amen." (*Moroni 7:48*) Charity, or love, describes the oneness we will have with Christ when we are one in Him and the Father. "*But he that is joined unto the Lord is one spirit.*" (*1 Corinthians 6:17*) "Whosoever shall confess that Jesus is the Son of God, God dwelleth in him, and he in God. And we have known and believed the love that God hath to us. *God is love; and he that dwelleth in love dwelleth in God, and God in him.* Herein is our love made perfect, that we may have boldness in the Day of Judgment: because as He is, so are we in this world." (*1 John 4:15-17*) Yes, it actually says, that ***he that dwelleth in love dwelleth in God*** and *he that is joined unto the Lord* ***is one spirit***.

I cannot say it any plainer. Right here in the scriptures is our definition of love, *spiritual oneness*. "And every man whose spirit receiveth not the light [Christ] is under condemnation. For man is spirit, the elements are eternal, and spirit and element, inseparably connected, receive a fulness of joy: and when separated, man cannot receive a fulness of joy. The elements are the tabernacle of God; yea, *man is the tabernacle of God*, even temples; and whatsoever temple is defiled, God shall destroy that temple." (*D&C 93:32-35*) The love of God or charity, the pure love of Christ, is the name for that *indwelling relationship*, that *spiritual oneness* upon which I spent an entire previous chapter. And how do we know if we love God, and are one in this charity? "If ye love me, keep my commandments." (*John 14:15*) If you do not keep His commandments, how can you possibly be one with Him? (We will spend more time on the meaning of charity in a subsequent chapter.)

Satan's Kind of Love

I do not have a name for the second kind of love the kind that Satan has, but be assured that such a name would represent being *spiritually one* with the *spirit-matter* that Satan loves. He is spiritually one with things like lies, deceit, confusion, selfishness, tyranny, and all the things that are dark and have no light in them as they have no truth in them (italics for emphasis). "Verily, verily, I say unto you, that Satan has great hold upon their hearts; he stirreth them up to iniquity against that which is good; And their hearts are corrupt, and full of wickedness and abominations; and they *love* darkness rather than light, because their deeds are evil; therefore they will not ask of me." (*D&C 10:20-21*) "For they cannot be redeemed from their spiritual fall, because they repent not; For they *love* darkness rather than light, and their deeds are evil, and they receive their wages of whom they list to obey." (*D&C 29:43-45*) Satan and his followers do indeed *love* evil and darkness, they *love* sin, and they are *spiritually one* with it.

Hate

It stands to reason that if love is a oneness of *spirit-matter*, and I here testify that it is, then *hate*, by definition, is a separation of *spirit-matter*. This definition works equally as well as that of love, only conversely. Those things that God hates, He is spiritually separate from. "These six things doth the Lord *hate*: yea, seven are an abomination unto Him: A proud look, a lying tongue, and hands that shed innocent blood, An heart that deviseth wicked imaginations, feet that be swift in running to mischief, A false witness that speaketh lies, and he that soweth discord among brethren." (*Proverbs 6:16-19*) And God anointed Christ "with the oil of Gladness" because "thou hast *loved* righteousness and *hated* iniquity." (*Hebrews 1:9*)

You may think I am saying it is OK to hate. I am! Of course it is right to be *spiritually separate from things evil.* That is our definition of hate. Remember? I am, however, **not** saying that revenge or returning evil for evil is the right thing to do. That is another matter (more on this to come). For further clarification, it must be said here that God, and we, can love a man but hate his actions. God loves all His children but does not love all that they do. The word hate, separation of *spirit-matter*, also works with those things the Devil hates, namely God and all the virtues related to Him.

Very Presumptuous

You may be thinking that it is presumptuous of me to put forth definitions of love and hate that the rest of the world does not even know, let alone use. No, what is presumptuous indeed is to be saddled with a multitude of definitions that are disconcerting, confusing, and non-operable. How long must we live with the perplexing concepts of love that the world has forced upon us? Perhaps it is *time* for a new definition (although it is taken from an old book, the Holy

Bible). This definition is new to us only because the Devil has confused and perverted the meaning of love for eons past. Perhaps it is time to move to a higher level of understanding and get back to the simplicity of the Gospel of Christ.

When I presented this concept in a lesson to the High Priests in my ward one Sunday, I received some opposition. One man said, and I quote, "No, no. As the world knows love, there is no way that Satan loves." I didn't want an argument, as the spirit of contention is of the Devil, but I should have said, "I'm not talking about the way the world knows love." I have, here, no interest in talking about the confusion and lesser laws of the telestial world we live in. There is a better way. *I am talking about what love really is, and how it works, and this is a celestial concept.* We have a perfect right to define our terms in celestial rhetoric. However, if I have lost any of you on this point, if you cannot accept this principle, then, stay with your old definition, whatever that is. What can I say? For the sake of my discourse though, let me continue.

As we answer the questions I asked at the front of this chapter, we will see how simple and plain this doctrine of love, *spiritual oneness*, really is. Although we have answered how many kinds of love there are, **two** (God's and Satan's), as we continue, you may assume I am talking about charity or God's kind of love.

The Real Confusion

Your major objection to this concept will probably be that you are sure there are different *kinds* of love. This is the traditional answer and we all know how hard it is to let go of tradition. But what you are really talking about is ***different kinds of relationships***, not different kinds of love. There are as many different kinds of relationships as there are people. Of course, love and relationships are connected, but ***they are not the same thing***.

If you miss this point or fail to make the distinction between spiritual oneness and relationships, you will never understand this thing called love.

Of course you have a different relationship with your wife or husband than you would have with your neighbor. Of course you have a different relationship with your in-laws than you do with your children. Of course you have a different relationship with your work, pet, art, music, or any other person or thing, but the love you have for them is the same, a spiritual indwelling, a *spiritual oneness*. Here, I promise you, is the confusion. Admittedly, because they are so closely related it is hard to do, but if you can separate the concept of love from the concept of relationships, understanding of both comes into focus.

Relationships—All Kinds

To elaborate, we have many, many kinds of relationships. We have relationships with people at work, teachers, students, bosses, co-workers, and subordinates. Some of these relationships are deep and lasting, while others are more superficial. We have family relationships that range from parent and child, husband and wife, to in-laws or distant relatives. We have casual relationships with people that we have met from time to time throughout our lives. We even have relationships with people we have never met or that we are no longer near. I give as an example, the personal relationship I have with Barbra Streisand. The spirit of her music, what she says and how she says it, reaches out to me and touches me in such a relevant way. Although it is based only on the philosophy of her music, as we have never met nor are we likely to, I have a deep and abiding relationship with her. I also have a relationship with Opra Winfrey though she may never know it (at least not in this life). Because I have been moved so many times by her great wisdom, honesty, generosity, kindness, and integrity, I have built and will always have a relationship with her and so look forward to meeting her somewhere in the future.

We also have relationships with friends and relatives who have died. Though it may be weak or strong, we certainly have a relationship with God. Further, we have relationships with *things*, living and nonliving: our pets, birds, fish, wild and farm animals, our gardens, the mountains, the sea, art work, computers, cars, houses, clothing, TV, food, books, music, and on and on the list goes. We even have relationships with non-tangible things such as sports, hobbies, concepts, ideas, poetry, stories, philosophies, character traits, politics, patriotism, and etc. Any person or thing we touch or that touches us in our existence, we have a relationship with and that relationship is unique. All these people and things we relate to in one way or another. Things and people touching each other's existence and relating to each other, in some way, is what a relationship is. The details or particulars of each relationship depend on our individual association with these people and things, as well as the timing and the surrounding situations and conditions. Many things dictate the kinds of relationships we have. What we think, feel, and experience when we touch other people or things forms the basis for these relationships.

Although most of us do, at least to some degree, become spiritually one with (love) those people and things to which we relate, it is not necessarily so. There are many relationships based on anything and everything but love. The relationship might be based upon self-gratification, power, psychological need, sexual attraction, duty or commitment, parental bond, physical security, or some other connection born out of the situation, timing, or condition. Love is an amalgamation of *spirit-matter* and may or may not be a feature of the relationship. I will say here that any and all relationships will be greatly improved by making love, spiritual oneness, the most important underlying element.

Some Side Benefits

So what part does love play in the relationship? Why love? What are the benefits? Well, there are several. Remember that we are talking about the *oneness doctrine* and some of the benefits seem obvious while others are not. Let us examine what is happening when we become spiritually one with another being. It is more than simply communicating spirit to spirit; you are ***experiencing that person***. In other words, as your spirit begins to amalgamate with theirs, you feel what they feel, you understand what they understand, you sense their needs, you discern their motivations, you see them as they really are, you comprehend them, you ***know*** them. To the degree or extent that you are **able** to *love them*, you *know them*.

What Does The Thermometer Read?

"Degree?" you may ask. "Does love come in degrees?" My answer is that for us mortals, it does. God only loves completely and unconditionally, but we mortals actually have to *learn how* to love. Very often we love what is easy to love, beautiful things and beautiful people who are nice to us; loving our enemy is something most of us have not yet touched, let alone mastered. We are fortunate, I guess, if we even "like" them. "Like" is a term I would define as a *degree* of love.

We really start to learn how to love when we are honest with and respect ourselves. If we associate ourselves with truth and virtue, we will start to be one with the virtues and truth within. We will discover our true selves and become comfortable with the good in us, or rather, we will love ourselves. That's right. We will become one with our true selves. What an accomplishment. We can then love our families, fathers, mothers, wife or husband, and children. Someone said, "Families are so we will learn to love, we are forced to live with someone long enough to love them." It is not easy to run from those with whom we have a familial bond, so we stick with them and struggle to love them.

Love Is A Choice

This brings up another question. What controls love? The fact that we must learn to love implies that it is a choice. This could not be truer. We love, or become spiritually one with things and people predicated on our desire to do so. Our own desire controls completely to what extent we will love, as surely as it controls *what* and *who* we love. What we choose to be one with is not only our choice; it is a choice for which we will be held accountable. When we internalize this fact, we understand how free we really are to love. Accordingly, if someone says that they don't love someone else, for whatever reason, they indict themselves. "But," you say, "we don't have anything in common, they are not lovable, they don't return my love, they don't even like me, they are mean to me, or whatever." It does not matter whether they are like us, whether we have anything in common, whether they love us back, nor does it matter what bad things they may have done to us. To wait until you find someone like yourself, or to wait until the other person loves you, or is nice to you, or to wait for any other circumstance is to love conditionally. This is not God's kind of love (charity). Some people will not allow you to have much of a relationship with them at all, but that should not affect your love for them. Think where we would be if the Lord said that about us, after all, His love for us is often one-sided, yet He loves us still.

One-Sided

You will note that I said God's love is often one-sided. Love is, in essence, one-sided. Your choice to be one with someone does not mean that they will make the choice to love you back. The notion that somehow love grows between two people equally is a romantic assumption. "Well," you say, "how can I be spiritually one with another person and they not be spiritually one with me?" I cannot answer that. It's just how it works. As I said before, love is one-sided. It is our choice and ability that we exhibit when we love, not anyone else's. How can the Lord be one with us and we choose not to be one with Him? I don't know, but that's the way it works. Love is dependent on each individual's desire and ability to open up to the oneness of all things.

Even Our Enemies?

Although the relationship may not be rewarding or fulfilling, we must continue to love, even those who do not love us, in return. We must even love our enemies. Not just for their sakes but for our own as well. To be God-like, we must cultivate our own ability to love, completely, without condition. We must not be afraid to love. We must accept that our love *may* be completely one-sided. We may even be repelled and rebuffed in the relationship. Regardless of the consequences, we must, like Christ, continue to love unconditionally until those we love succumb to our love or crucify us. To love like this requires only a desire to do so. It is our choice.

It is a strange thing and perhaps this is not the best way to put it, but for lack of better terminology, let me say that the person who loves another has the *advantage* over that person who does not love them back. What I mean is; the person that loves knows the other person, their feelings, their understandings, their motivations, and etc. They comprehend them. They understand what makes them tick, so to speak. It's like playing poker with a person that is showing you his hand but can't see yours. This is why a person who loves his enemy will always have the advantage. He will know what motivates him, why he makes the decisions he does, and will therefore discern his enemy's moves even before he makes them. Conversely, the enemy who does not love will not understand or comprehend what motivates his opponent or why he does what he does, therefore losing the advantage. So you see, there are benefits to the commandment to love one's enemies, though I doubt that should be our reason for loving them. If it were, I would question whether our love is true.

Can I Help You?

What is more consequential, ***unless you love someone, you are powerless to help them***. If you are not one with them, you do not know their needs. You cannot sense what is required to assist them and will therefore not know what ministration or action will benefit them most. Further, whatever action or service you render without love is liable to be wasted, as the person, sensing that you do not love them, will likely be suspicious and unreceptive to your help.

Relative to this concept, I remember how frustrated a friend was when he first started teaching high school. It seems his students would not respond to his efforts to help them. He complained that they were defensive and apathetic. I suggested that he try loving them, as he would not have the power to help them unless he did. When he began to see them as objects of his love and find ways to express and show his love for them, they turned around completely. They began to open up, trust him, and accept his help.

Remember, love is being spiritualy one. It is a spiritual thing and other people can sense, by their spirit, that you love them. When you love them, there is a better chance of a positive response. If they sense that you don't care about them, they will be suspicious and withdrawn.

Love is the first and most necessary ingredient in any positive relationship. If your motivation is to *fix* a particular person but you do not love him or her first, you are, at best, wasting your time and at worst alienating or making an enemy of that person. On the other hand, when we love someone first, we understand and comprehend them and are less likely to feel the need to *fix* them. Still, if *fixing* them is what is right for the person, at least you will know better their needs and the way to go about it. In any case, without love, we are powerless to fix or otherwise help anyone. Remember and be prepared, your love may be one-sided as the other person may choose not to return love. Still, your best—no *only*, chance to affect them positively is to love them. One-sided love in a relationship is better than a relationship with no love at all.

Unfortunately, there are far too many one-sided relationships in this world. Certainly, it is too often the case relative to our relationship with God. And what is the first and second commandment upon which hang all the law and the prophets? It is to love God and your neighbor. When you love them you *experience* them, you ***know*** them. And what is life eternal? To know God. How do you know Him? You love Him.

I Don't Have To Love You

How often have you heard divorced couples say, "Oh, we just fell out of love"? Again, this is a self-indictment. What are they really saying? They are saying that they simply chose not to love each other anymore. Ok, but that goes against not only the covenants they made with each other, but against the two great commandments. "If a man say, I love God, and hateth his brother, he is a liar; for he that loveth not his brother whom he hath seen, how can he love God whom he hath not seen?" (*1 John 4:20*) So, if we say we cannot love someone or God, if we lack love for others, we stand guilty of not keeping God's greatest commandments. Although I am certain we should concern ourselves, not so much with the penalty of a broken law as with the fact that we are no longer one with that person or God. Again, if we don't love, we must, at the very least, admit that it is our choice.

What About Feelings?

You ask, "Where do *feelings* come into this definition of love? There are always so many emotions or feelings, often unfamiliar, that are associated with love." (We will consider emotions to be synonymous with feelings.) Yes, there are, and not just with love. In fact, feelings are associated with **every** event of our lives. We have feelings of joy when an event in our lives goes in our favor. We have feelings of sadness when things go badly. We have feelings of remorse and guilt for having done something wrong. We have feelings of anger or betrayal when people wrong us. We have feelings of contempt, compassion, depression, longing, embarrassment, jealousy, resentment, inadequacy, hate, fear, and on and on goes the list of feelings that we seem to be subject to every day of our lives. Each feeling seems to be caused by an event or person who triggers that particular feeling within us. (Note that I said *seems* to be caused by events or people.)

Feelings (emotions) permeate, if not dominate, our lives to the extent that we cannot separate ourselves from them, nor should we want to, as *feelings are the language of the spirit*. Feelings are the purest form of communication and when we communicate spirit to spirit, it is through feelings. More on this in a minute, but first, let me try to correct, if I can, a misconception that has settled hard into our beliefs, so hard we have great difficulty dislodging it, though, like a rotten tooth, it needs extracting.

You Made Me Feel Bad

I know I may here make it sound like love is an absolute deliberate choice and that feelings don't play a part. Yes I am, but not exactly. Of course feelings play a part, but what part?

Relative to "feelings" let me say that we all spend a great deal of time trying to prove (mostly to ourselves) that we are not responsible for them. This is what the psychologist of the 70's and 80's told us. I often hear people say, in fact, people have often said to me, "You made me feel guilty!" or "You made me feel bad!" or "You made me feel stupid!" No! A thousand times no! No one **makes** you feel anything! Our feelings, that is, *our own* feelings, do not come from others but are generated solely within us! An event or the behavior of others may be the *catalyst*, the *action*, but you must take responsibility for how you *feel* about any given situation, just as surely as how you will *react* to any given situation. The notion that others can *cause* or *make* you feel a certain way is to give them far more power than they have a right to. It also casts you as a victim when, in fact, you are not. This is self-pity and I don't believe the Lord is going to let anyone get away with that.

My eldest daughter Letische, being a sensitive individual, very often considers herself a victim of her own feelings and when I tell her that feeling bad is her own choice she retorts with, "That may be true but it's easier said than done!" She is right. It is hard to control ones feelings but knowing it is your choice makes it a little easier. She also rightly makes the point that this concept does not excuse the offending party of their responsibility for deliberately trying to make someone feel bad. Still, how we feel is our choice, just like it is our choice to love.

So again, in the marriage relationship, when we say, we don't feel love for our spouse anymore, we are saying we choose not to love them. Don't get me wrong. I am not saying there are no reasons to divorce. I am saying those reasons should be based on the relationship or rather the whisperings of the spirit, not the lack of love. It is my belief that love is no reason to hold a relationship together that is in ruins and detrimental to all concerned. Having said that, I also believe that most marriages that break up are due to an inability or desire to love, to be one with each other, to empathize, to understand each other. When we make relationship decisions founded strictly on what is right and true for the relationship and not whether we love the other person, the relationship works better.

But It Hurts

Your painful situation, whatever that is, is real to be sure, but how you feel inside about it is entirely your choice. A poke in the eye with a sharp stick hurts. To say it does not, puts us in the category of hyping (hypnotizing) ourselves. We are then believing things that are not *as they are, were, or will be*. It hurts and there is no way around that, but how you decide to feel about it, as well as what you choose to do about it, is entirely your responsibility and your choice. You cannot pawn that responsibility off on anyone else. You must be accountable for how you feel or else submit to being entirely controlled by others, conditions, and events of your life.

Again, I am not talking here about the alleged offender's responsibility *not* to be offensive in the first place. Of course they too must take responsibility for their own actions but that's another subject. I am talking about your reaction to any given offense.

You argue that your feelings are a reaction and completely outside of your control. This is simply not true, but we continue to believe it. We choose to believe it because we do not want to be responsible for those feelings. We want to pretend that they are thrust upon us, that we have no choice in the matter. Again, whether you agree with me or not, let my testimony stand that we are not forced by others or the events of our lives to have feelings that we do not personally choose to feel.

I have spent my life working in an industry (stage and film) where it is the stock in trade of an actor to control his or her emotions to the extent that they are able to laugh, cry, or become angry according to the requirements of the script. These are real emotions or feelings that they create and the best, most talented actors are the ones that are able to make us believe the emotions they are having. Their feelings are believable because they are real yet, make no mistake, the actor is controlling those feelings. We are all actors; in our families, the work place, in fact, everywhere we happen to be. What I mean is, we all control our feelings to a greater or lesser degree, (depending upon the need of the moment, experience, practice, our degree of discipline, and/or our desire to control ourselves). If you don't believe this, remember the last time you were in an argument or angry with someone and the phone rang. I'll bet it took about three seconds for you to change your whole demeanor and answer the phone with an entirely different feeling than that which you had only moments before. Why? Because the situation called for a different feeling and you controlled or chose the appropriate one.

I Am An Island

Some people are very good at controlling their feelings, especially in extreme situations. We look to these persons as stalwart, people we can count on in a pinch. Some people, however, control their feelings to the magnitude that they no longer have them or at least they suppress their feelings to the point it appears they no longer feel at all. I don't say this is right. I'm only making the point that we are, in fact, in control of our feelings (at least to the extent that we want to be). You have the choice and can control how you feel about any given situation.

Admittedly, this doctrine is easier said than done. Too often we are unaware that we have a choice in the matter. Even when we are aware it is no easy matter to change by being proactive or choosing to feel positive about what is happening to us. It takes a conscious effort on our part. It takes practice. It takes time to learn how. Nevertheless, being responsible for how we feel can never be discharged or transferred to another, so you might as well quit trying.

I know what I have just said is new to some and a hard pill to swallow, but it is true and an immovable law that demands we take responsibility for ourselves, and the feelings we have. Unless we do, we become (or remain) subject to the events and people who would rule our lives. We will wallow in self-pity and unhappiness. **The only way to feeling happiness and joy is to choose it.** It is our choice!

Language of The Spirit

Now, I said that feelings are the language of the spirit. As support, let me quote Joseph Fielding McConkie[86] who said, "If we are to find the things of the Spirit, we must search in the realm of the Spirit. True religion can come from no other source. All true religion centers in feelings, and since feelings are not subject to a system of weights and measures, it is difficult to describe them to the unspiritual. Again our inability to describe those feelings doesn't negate their reality. An infant's ability to sense and feel the reality of parental love is not conditional on his ability to explain those feelings. To know truth by sense and feeling without being able to explain or rationally defend it is an experience common to all mankind." (*Seeking The Spirit, pg.* 8)

Let me elaborate. You will remember from our former discussion on the Electromagnetic Spectrum, how we said that all things are made of some form of matter. Even things we cannot see or otherwise detect are made of *spirit-matter* that is more pure or refined. Remember that our very thoughts are formed with or made of matter, as is truth itself. Well, feelings are the same way. Our bodies, together with our souls (spirits), have the capacity to form (create) feelings and the matter that those feelings are made of emits or goes out from us to others. In fact, this is what we are all doing to a greater or lesser degree depending upon our passion, or rather the power or intensity we put behind those feelings. We are all creating our own feelings and sending them out to everyone else in the world. Accordingly, there are a lot of feelings, or feeling-matter, floating around out there. Whenever we have (create) a feeling, good or bad, this is what is happening. Not only can we create and radiate this *spirit-matter*, but we also have the capacity to accept it from others. Of all the feeling-matter that is floating around out there, we may pick and choose what we will receive. This is, again, part of the oneness (spiritual indwelling) doctrine. This is being spiritually one with others. This is ***feeling*** what they ***feel*** or, in other words, communicating spirit to spirit.

Perhaps I can make this concept a little clearer by illustration. Suppose you enter a room and you discern bad or negative feelings emanating from those in the room. These are not your feelings but feelings coming *to* you *from* others. Once you become aware of those feelings from others, you have the choice of *what you will feel* ***about*** those feelings. You may further decide what, if any, outward action is appropriate to the situation. I am trying to draw the distinction between discerning others' feelings and generating your own. The former is an action by others, which is discerned by you and the latter is a reaction created by you.

Because our own feelings are a matter of personal choice, they will expose the level of righteousness we are on (celestial, terrestrial, or telestial). If we choose to return evil feelings for good we are probably operating on a telestial level. If we choose to return evil feelings for evil and good feelings for good we are probably operating on a terrestrial level. If we choose to return good feelings for evil we are celestial. Christ chose not to have evil feelings for those who crucified Him, "Father, forgive them; for they know not what they do." (*Luke 23:34*)

For this reason, it is paramount that we entertain and prosper only appropriate (good) feelings; not only for our sakes but also for those we love (are spiritually one with). Our love will be manifest by these feelings, so we should have feelings of compassion, feelings of service, feelings of sacrifice, feelings of forgiveness, feelings of selflessness, and many more virtuous feelings. When we truly care for a particular person, because we want the best for them, we would never have negative feelings or desires that would hurt them. If we will, by the Spirit of Truth, nurture only those feelings that exalt and uplift, we will know what our responsibility is to the relationship and what feelings or expressions of love are appropriate.

It is also important that we learn to properly discern others' feelings. The more we learn to love (become one with others) the easier it is to do this and the more we can understand others. Should others choose not to love us, they will be unable to discern our feelings. On the other hand, if we love them we can discern theirs. Like knowing the truth makes us free (see *John 8:32*), loving gives us greater freedom and capabilities.

Again, feelings are the purest form of communication. When we truly speak with the language of the spirit (feelings) there are no miscommunications or misunderstandings as there almost always is when we try to communicate with words. Feelings are the way the Gods communicate one with another. There is no need for them to use words, which must first be defined, which definitions are subject to other words, which must first be defined, and etc. No, they simply feel and because they are one (spiritually), the others have the same exact feeling. "But" you say, "Why don't we communicate this way?" Simply, because we are not one, we do not love. To the extent that we do love, is to the extent that we use this pure form of spiritual communication. We mortals must learn to develop the ability to fully communicate this way, simply by *choosing* to love. It takes oneness of *spirit-matter*. It takes an indwelling. It takes love.

And here we are back to love, back to oneness. Remember, to love is a choice and what we feel, or rather what we choose to spiritually communicate, is also a choice. Many simply choose to be on a lesser level where love and even feelings, particularly positive feelings, are wanting. If they choose not to have good feelings, good feelings cannot be communicated, or sent out to others. If they choose to have bad feelings, those are the feelings they will communicate to others. Then, those who are sensitive to spirit-matter, who don't want to be one with bad things, will shun such *spirit-matter*. They will leave those bad feelings, and consequently, those people, alone.

When we understand that feelings are the purest means of communication we can have in a relationship and that we may choose our feelings, we need no longer be subject to them. The realization of this gives us freedom; it gives us the advantage, it puts us in control, thus making us more responsible in the relationship. If we do not understand this, or perhaps refuse to accept it, we will continue to go through life reacting to people and events.

What Obligation?

Let us move on to another issue posed at the beginning of this chapter. By again, separating the concept of love from the concept of relationships, we may find an answer to the question of what obligation do we have when we find ourselves loving someone. ***We have no obligation whatsoever!***

You do not have to prove your love to anyone. You do not have to do anything with or for the person you are spiritually one with. **Loving brings with it no demands or obligations**. In fact, we have already met our obligation by loving the person in the first place. Our **only** obligation is to love. That love itself, requires of one, no other action. It is relationships that make such demands. Whether it is right or wrong, relationships have expectations and require action. Neither love nor hate require any action. To love or hate is a ***state of being. Obligations come from the relationship, not from love***.

You see, the obligations of the marriage relationship come from the covenants and vows you make during the marriage ceremony, not the love that you should already be sharing. No matter what the relationship—friend, family, business, or whatever; whether chosen or imposed; whether casual or deep; obligations come from the properties of that relationship, **not love**. It does not matter whether they are; written, spoken, or implied, obligations come from covenants and commitments which are inherent in relationships, **not from loving, not from being one with a person spiritually**. I cannot make this point strong enough!

So, when you meet someone and perhaps choose to love him or her, how do you know whether or to what degree you should commit or obligate yourself to that person? The Spirit of Truth, the Holy Ghost, should dictate the parameters of each and every relationship we develop. You must be open and in tune with that spirit and you must be willing to submit your own will and desires to the direction of that Spirit of Truth. It may direct you to go ahead and express your love in one way or another or it may direct you to *not express* that love. It may direct you to only serve a particular person in some way. Despite your mutual love, the spirit may direct you to *get away from them*, as they may not be good for you (or you for them). I can most certainly guarantee that the spirit will ***not*** direct you to commit adultery or fornication with that person because you find yourself loving them.

The Curse of Eve

Here is where the young go astray, particularly our young women. They are more vulnerable than the men as they have the "curse of Eve." The "curse of Adam" was that he would have to earn his bread by the sweat of his face and thorns and briers would beset his path to torment him. This curse has, indeed, been a torment to man down through the ages, just as the curse of Eve has been equally troublesome to the woman. The curse is that they are drawn to the man (italics for emphasis). "Unto the woman He said, I will greatly multiply thy sorrow and thy conception; in sorrow thou shalt bring forth children; and *thy desire shall be to thy husband*, and he shall rule over thee." (*Genesis 3:16*)

Please do not misunderstand my meaning. I do not mean by this statement that women are more sexually attracted to men than men are to women. In fact, it is obvious that, sexually speaking, the opposite is probably the case. No, I mean that the woman's ability to love is greater. As a consequence of her naturally greater maternal tendencies, a woman thinks more about the man and is more concerned with his welfare than is the man of hers; apparently her dedication to the relationship is far greater than is that of the man. This is generally speaking of course. I believe this is why, in most cases, the Lord will hold the male more responsible for the breakdown of the marriage relationship than He will the woman. Although it is most certainly a virtue, the woman is more willing to give, to compromise, sacrifice, and do for the man, which puts her, at a disadvantage in the relationship. Brigham Young put it this way. "I do not know what the Lord could have put upon women worse than He did upon Mother Eve, where He told her: 'Thy desire shall be to thy husband.' Continually wanting the husband. 'If you go to work, my eyes follow you; if you go away in the carriage, my eyes follow you, and I like you and love you; I delight in you, and I desire you should have nobody else.' I do not know that the Lord could have put upon women anything worse than this, I do not blame them for having these feelings. I would be glad if it were otherwise." (*JD page 167*) This is the *curse of Eve*, to be so compassionate, caring, and willing when the man is not. This is the source of much pain for women, but in the long run it will be in their favor. I suppose that the curse will be lifted someday, perhaps when the man has learned that same dedication to the relationship.

In any case, when our young find themselves deeply one spiritually with another (in love), they feel obligated; especially the woman, and they allow themselves to do things that are not appropriate outside the marriage covenant. Again, for emphasis, love and relationships are two different things. *The obligation comes from the marriage covenant not from love*. Keeping your covenants and commitments to others, to yourself, and to God is a matter of integrity. "But whoso keepeth His word, in him verily is the love of God perfected: hereby know we that we are in Him." (*1 John 2:5*) If the young could internalize this, it would help them to understand their feelings and what to do about them. It would also help empower them to resist temptations and even help them find the mate the Lord wants them to be eternally with.

I Can't Love You—I'm Married

It is also at this point where married persons, when drawn spiritually to another (in love) who is not his or her mate, become confused and often make mistakes that cost dearly. I am talking about infidelity. So you love someone. You find yourself spiritually one with them; no you have chosen to be spiritually one with them. That is good and no guilt should be associated with such an event. You are not being unfaithful to your covenants or with your spouse because you share a spiritual oneness with another, nor are you cheating on them in your heart. In fact, you are obeying the Lord's commandment to love everyone. This is the only way you may obey this commandment. On the other hand, if you begin to fantasize sexual intimacy with that person you are crossing the line and committing adultery in your heart. That is lust, not love. "But I say unto you, that whosoever looketh on a woman, to lust after her, hath committed adultery already in his heart. Behold, I give unto you a commandment, that ye suffer none of these things to enter into your heart." (*Matthew 5:28,* and *3 Nephi 12:28-29*)

I believe that if the relationship is truly based upon love, a spiritual oneness, and not lust, the spirit will not allow you to think such irreverent thoughts about the other person. True love would not allow you to do harmful things to the person you love, even in your mind. "Love worketh no ill to his neighbour . . . ." (*Romans 13:10*) In fact, this is how you can tell if it is love and not lust. In other words, if you are having lustful thoughts about that other person, you are not "loving" them. "And he that looketh upon a woman to lust after her shall deny the faith, and shall not have the spirit, and if he repents not he shall be cast out." (*D&C 42:23*) And why shall those who lust *not have the spirit* and *deny the faith*? Because to love is to tap into the oneness of God and if lust is allowed in, out goes the spirit of God and the oneness, the love is gone.

So you find yourself loving another person but you are already married, so what? You are, in fact, living God's Celestial law upon which hang all the law and the prophets, to love God and your neighbor, to love everyone. The fact is that sometimes other people can fulfill our spiritual needs better than our own spouses. To my mind, it is presumptuous and not right to expect our spouses to have the capacity to fulfill us in every way. This is a heavy burden to put on another person. I don't believe it is wrong to have other loving relationships that are fulfilling to us, so long as those relationships are appropriate and kept within the bounds the Lord has established. Just because you find yourself loving (spiritually one with) another person, does that mean you should throw away all you have or divorce your wife or husband so you can marry them? No, of course not. Just accept that you share a spiritual oneness that is good, even wonderful, and leave it at that. Further, love, that spiritual oneness, will render the relationship infinitely more fulfilling than any physical intimacy can ever do. As the relationship develops, let the Holy Ghost dictate what is proper and remember that keeping your covenants and commitments to your spouse and to God is the ***right*** thing to do. We must be strong and keep the spirit with us by keeping our thoughts and actions pure and above reproach. If you can't, or don't feel strong enough to do this, my advice is to stick to the lesser law and end the relationship quickly or you may fall, losing your self-respect, causing great sorrow and pain to all concerned. Though a sad commentary, in this fallen state of mortality, this is a course most of us may be forced by duty and integrity to take. In any case, **never use love as an excuse to throw over your integrity** by breaking your holy covenants and promises or going against the spirit of truth.

Love Is Forever

As an aside, I must here add this note to all those whose spouses have died and feel that they are being unfaithful or untrue to the love of the departed when they choose to love someone else. It is easy for me to say, but I know they would feel differently if they could again separate the love from the relationship. One cannot be untrue or unfaithful to love, only relationships. To love is divine and no one will ever replace the relationship you had (and will continue to have in the life hereafter) with a former mate. The oneness of love will last through the eternities and the relationship of a couple will also continue and be unique.

Homosexuality

As another aside, this spiritual oneness concept of love also has a direct bearing on how men and women feel about the same sex. I am talking about homosexuality now. When a person finds him or herself deeply loving (being spiritually one with) someone of the same sex, they are confused and again, they misconstrue those feelings, which they recognize to be good, and mistake their obligation to the relationship, which then can become homosexual. There are no barriers, whatsoever, to loving, but there are barriers to improper relationships. It is true that God loves (is spiritually one with) those of the same sex, but He is not homosexual. To indulge in homosexual practices is a perversion of the principle of physical oneness, is against eternal celestial law, and is strictly forbidden.

I know that the common explanation of homosexuality by those who claim to be is: "I have no choice. I have these feelings and I must be true to them." Remember that feelings are a choice. "But" they say, "these are my physical traits." What they fail to recognize is that God also has all virtuous traits. He has not just those virtues that we commonly associate with a male person, but those we associate with a female person as well. That is to say, He has all kindness, all gentleness, all grace, and etc. Virtue knows no gender. We are the ones that arbitrarily assign such traits to one gender or the other. Still, God is a man. Though her being may be womanly, our heavenly mother[87] no doubt, has all the virtuous traits we would commonly associate with the male gender: strength, robustness, courage, power, leadership, and etc. When we find the stereotypical traits of the opposite sex within us, we assume there is something wrong with us. It is a time to rejoice, not change our gender. Further, we are not to act upon all the urges and feelings we might have. Not all feelings come from God. If they don't *"entice us to do good"*, they are of the Devil. I for one, being a *natural man*, am often attracted sexually to many women, but I know I cannot give in to those impulses just because *they are my physical traits*. Those sexually drawn to someone of their own gender should not give in to such impulses either. Remember, "The natural man is an enemy to God, and has been from the fall of Adam, and will be, forever and ever, unless he yields to the enticings of the Holy Spirit, and putteth off the natural man and becometh a saint through the atonement of Christ the Lord." (*Mosiah 3:19*) This is no secret kept by the Mormon Church and I will devote no more time to the subject.

Free To Love

With all this being said, if we could understand this concept, this celestial concept of love being spiritual oneness, and comprehend that love is one thing and relationships are another, we would know that it is OK to love. Love is wonderful and good. It is divine. It is *not just OK* to love, it is the first and second, the greatest commandments of God. Love, that is charity, is not just good, *it is celestial.* It is the essence of celestial. It is being one with the Gods. It is being one of heart as Zion is expected to be. We are *free to love*, that is, be spiritually one, in fact, we are commanded to love, but we are not free to pursue whatever kind of relationship we may desire.

Let me quickly and emphatically emphasize that when I said, *we are free to love*, I don't mean we are free to fantasize, make sexual innuendoes, voice sexual insinuations, or play any other sexual mind games with ourselves or with others. This is dangerous and not sanctioned by God. "For as he thinketh in his heart so is he . . . ." (*Proverbs 23:7*) Any person participating in such forbidden activities will sooner or later be brought down by them. Again let me quote, "And he that looketh upon a woman to lust after her shall deny the faith, and shall not have the Spirit, and if he repents not he shall be cast out." (*D&C 42:23*) "Let thy bowels also be full of charity towards all men, and to the household of faith, and let virtue garnish thy thoughts unceasingly; then shall thy confidence wax strong in the presence of God; and the doctrine of the priesthood shall distill upon thy soul as the dews from heaven." (*D&C 121:45*) There is no fine line here, because when our true motivations are examined, it becomes obvious (if not to the particular individual, at least to those around him) whether we are loving or lusting and exploiting. The Holy Spirit directs when and how a relationship should be and to what extent love may be expressed.

This principle of universal love is difficult to live, even precarious. So, if one is not strong in testimony and character, he or she has no business trying to live it. For it is better to live a lesser law than to be condemned by a higher one. Nevertheless, if we could visualize the celestial kingdom, we would see everyone loving deeply, completely, without restraint. We would also see that all occupants would be expressing love to one another, and this freely, as they will have put off the natural man and the carnal mind. We will be in a state of innocence, like children. If we are to be celestial, we must practice this oneness of spirit, love, with each other.

The Greatest Criterion For Marriage

Should the advent of love be the greatest criteria for marriage? No!

I catch a lot of flack on this one. Everyone knows that you don't get married unless you are "*in love.*" Unfortunately, you probably will not have developed the ability to love, learn to love, or expand your capacity to love until you have lived with someone for a very long time. Ask any old married couple if this is not true. On the other hand, the ability to love knows no age limits. Very often we have a greater loving capacity in our youth and suppress it as we experience the harsh realities of unkind, untrue, relationships. Such relationships take their toll on us and we learn to protect our sensitive feelings from rejection by not loving in the first place or loving but holding back our expressions of the same. Young or old, we need to learn, or relearn, not only to love but how to express our love, not just to our spouses, family, and friends, but everyone. I speak to myself on this matter. Expressing my inner feelings, exposing myself, is one of the most difficult things I can do. But let us continue.

Choosing a mate is perhaps one of the most important decisions we are likely to make in our lifetimes. It will have a major impact on our lives, as well as effect our eternal progression. After all, it is with the commitment of marriage and family that the Lord teaches us how to love, to be one with another person. This is the reason the family is the most important social structure of our existence. It is, in fact, the very organization of the heavens themselves and why the Lord expects our every effort to preserve it. The order of heaven is family. It is into this order that we are spiritually reborn (*Born Again*) into the family of God and the powers of God are transferred to us. The true, celestial, order of the priesthood of God is patriarchal. This is also why it is so heartbreaking for the Lord to see couples give up on relationships. One or both of them are, in effect, saying, "I do not want to love, I don't want to be a part of your family."

I submit that if you have learned how to love, that is, increased your capacity to love to a place where you can, in fact, be one with everyone in the heavenly family; then love becomes a moot issue in your decision to choose a mate. In the long run, in the eternal perspective, you will be able to love and live eternally with anyone who is celestial! You will love everyone. Like God, you will be one with everyone—that is our definition of Christ's love, charity, remember?

One and Only; Soul Mates

Well then, you say you don't believe in a "one and only" love for everyone! I do believe in a "one and only," but not based on love. What then is the proper criterion for choosing a mate? It is not personalities, or common values, or common interests, though certainly these and many like factors should be considered in such an important decision. But people change, and only God knows what you need now as well as in the future. I find it unthinkable to choose an eternal mate based upon what I think I know today, let alone what I think I will know tomorrow. Who even knows themselves, let alone a prospective mate, and worse, who knows the future of the relationship?

So the most important criterion is ***truth***. Is it the right thing to do? If a particular person is the one you think you should make eternal covenants with, you should *know* this is the one with which the Lord wants you to form such a relationship. Such a decision should never be made without the approval of the spirit. Don't let love get in the way of that decision (what a strange thing for me to say). Let truth dictate. Let the Holy Spirit dictate.

The Lord may have a *one* for each of us, and personally I believe that there is, a *one and only*. To me, it is inconceivable that God, who loves so personally, would have no opinion or will on a matter of such far-reaching consequences. But that one and only relationship is based on what is right for us, not on love. A decision of this magnitude requires all the inspiration you can get. The Holy Ghost is there to witness of the truth of it, and you have a right to know.

Someone Got The Wrong Message

On occasion I have had people ask me something like the following: "Well I prayed and got the revelation from God that she was the "One and Only" but apparently she did not get the message because she refused my proposal of marriage. How can this be? How can I get one revelation and she get the opposite?" Well, the Lord may have many reasons why this could be so. It might be a test of faith, one or the other of the two may not truly be in tune with the spirit, it might be a matter of agency, the Lord may want a testimony against an offending party, or the Lord may have something for you to suffer relative to the relationship. I certainly cannot say nor is it my place to give reasons to such personal questions. This is not just a "copout" on my part. There is a very great principle involved here. Remember the Lord is in the business of saving souls and he may want you to struggle with the choice of a mate for some reason or other. It is up to each individual to go to the Lord and reconcile these kinds of questions.

Did I Blow It?

Furthermore, on the down side, you may have put your best spiritual effort in to the choice of a mate, prayed for and got the revelation to marry someone but the whole thing ends in misery and divorce. Relative to divorce, ill health, death, bankruptcy, or any other calamity that may come upon us, we must realize that the Lord, in order to save our souls, may want us to go through some hell (and to me there is no greater hell on earth than a bad marriage or family relationship). This may seem harsh but we must trust in the will of God and have faith in His wisdom. It may be that we are to experience certain things in this life so that we can have compassion for others and be more able to relieve their sufferings. This is part of the reason for Christ's suffering in the garden and on the cross. He had to descend below all things. He had to innocently suffer greater suffering than anyone else would ever suffer in this world so that He might be our savior. You too may be innocent but need to have the experience as part of your history.

I give as an example Joseph Smith's suffering in the Liberty jail in 1839, where he was incarcerated unjustly for six months. He and some of his close friends were put in a small dungeon where they were unable to even stand upright. They suffered horribly at the hands of their captors. The Prophet Joseph cried out to God to give reason to their afflictions and received the following revelation: "And if thou shouldest be cast into the pit, or into the hands of murderers, and the sentence of death passed upon thee; if thou be cast into the deep; if the billowing surge conspire against thee; if fierce winds become thine enemy; if the heavens gather blackness, and all the elements combine to hedge up the way; and above all, if the very jaws of hell shall gape open the mouth wide after thee, know thou, my son, that all these things shall give thee experience, and shall be for thy good. The Son of Man hath descended below them all. Art thou greater than he?" (D&C 122:7-8)

Though it may be a hard pill to swallow, if the Lord wants you to suffer divorce or any other adversity relative to our relationships (or anything else for that matter), you must yield your desires to Him and follow His will. Without the spirit, who can tell what is the mind and will of God? Remember that He is in the business of saving souls and there may be some advantage to your suffering. Although this is not a very pleasant thought, it could be true in some cases. We will discuss this concept at a greater depth in an ensuing chapter. But remember, we must "becometh as a child, submissive, meek, humble, patient, full of love, willing to submit to all things which the Lord seeth fit to inflict upon him [us], even as a child doth submit to his father." (*Mosiah 3:19*)

The important thing is that you live by the spirit in your relationships and your decision-making processes. It is also important that you hold fast to your testimony, even if the relationship ends up on the rocks. You must not undermine your decision-making process by thinking that you made the wrong decision, when that decision was made "by the spirit" at the time. Of course, if you were not in the spirit at the time you made the decision, then you may certainly have cause to doubt or consider that you may have made a mistake.

The Greatest Benefit of Love

Now let me say a little more about love, this feeling of oneness with someone else.

Speaking very personally, even though I understand the necessity, the propriety of it, I sometimes hate mortality. What I mean is, there are things about this world that seem so unreal, so uncomfortable, and so *not right*. I hate how hard it is to understand and to communicate. I hate how difficult it is to discern truth. I hate the frailties of the body and how subject we all are to the hazards of life and suffering. It makes me feel so helpless at times. I hate the evil in the world, the fear and guilt I feel as I look around me and witness the inhumanity and cruelty of mankind. I hate being inadequate and unable to protect. I hate my own vulnerability. I hate the uncertainty of not knowing. I hate my own weaknesses and inability to overcome those weaknesses. I hate the feelings of impotence and incompetence I all too often have. I hate being wrong (my pride is showing, I know) and I hate my insecurities.

I know that I expose myself here. I know that I am showing my lack of faith (another fault I hate). But, of all of life, the thing I hate the most is the *loneliness*. Being alone. I mean; we all live so much within ourselves, so alone. No matter what numbers of people surround us, people that care for us and we for them, it seems that we are still so alone in the inner thoughts of our heart, the deepest feelings of our soul. Because we know ourselves better than anyone else, we feel shame and unworthiness. We feel the pain of disappointment, depression, fear, weakness, and uncertainty. We feel these things somewhere deep in us, so deep that others cannot get there. No one else can reach that far down into our profoundest thoughts and inner desires to see our abysmal contemplations. The irony is that we *all* feel these same things, we are all so alike; yet do not share with others our most sacred musings.

Whether forced upon us or self-inflicted, this loneliness, I feel, is the most awful perdition that we could experience in mortality or eternity. Our *only* saving grace is love, that spiritual oneness with another being that we may experience if we can only get outside of ourselves and spiritually into another person. Those who are most miserable are those who have not yet chosen to love. They are *spiritually small*. Sharing of love is an expansion process. It brings to us understanding, compassion, tolerance, and many other virtues. To be spiritually joined with another enlarges us. This *spirit-matter* has the capacity to transfer to others without diminishing in amount. It gets bigger until it fills all the immensity of space and eternity as well as the dark places in our hearts. As I said before, to love is a choice. We are the only ones who can let our spirits out to connect with others. Since it is our choice, we don't have to wait until someone loves us. We can love the stranger on the street as deeply as we are capable of loving.

The Stranger

Some people seem to choose or have a greater capacity to love than do others. Sadly, you could be near a person all your life and if you do not love them, you do not know them. You are not one with them and do not *experience* them. Also, depending upon *your* ability to return love, you may not be aware, sense, or recognize that someone loves you. It is said (though I am not sure, I believe it was Joseph Smith) that two strangers having the Holy Ghost can know each other better in five minutes than two brothers who have lived together all their lives. Why is this so? Remember, the Holy Ghost is the oneness of the Gods. When the Holy Ghost intervenes in a relationship, that *truth-matter* unites to a oneness the parties involved. Both spirits who have chosen to love each other are "*quickened*" and can know each other instantly.

Loving a stranger may seem strange or uncomfortable at first, as we are too accustomed to thinking that the relationship must come first and be right, but it is not so. I repeat; **this is not true**. It is *our* capacity; *our* ***ability to love*** that is paramount. The mysterious thing is that the more we love, the greater becomes our capacity to love.

I remember when I embarked on my quest to understand this *thing called love*. I had enrolled in a family relations class at BYU just to fill a requirement. I was just arrogant enough to think there was little I could learn in this particular class. It was a large class in a long room that slanted down to where the instructor stood. On my first day in the class, I found a position on the very last row so I could lean my head against the wall and catch a few winks. The professor was an old man (or I thought at the time he was old, though now I am fast approaching his age, so I guess he wasn't so old after all) named Reed Bradford. The first day of class he started right out on the subject of love and I was only half alert when I heard him say, "I love you all as much as I do my own children." This statement grabbed my attention and unable to stop myself, I raised my hand and said, "That can't be true." I was so far back he had me stand and repeat myself. I said, "You can't love me. You don't know me. How can you say you love me as much as you love your own child?" He looked across the sea of students' heads with eyes that focused on me alone, somehow separating the two of us from the rest of the world, then started to cry. He said, "I don't even know your name but I want you to know that I love you as much as I am capable of loving anyone, and if life will be obliging, I will show you that I love you to the depth of my capacity to love." At that moment I was absolutely overwhelmed with a flood of warmth that filled me to my very core. I could feel this man's spirit literally pour into me and I was so overcome, so deeply touched by the force of this man's love reaching out to me so completely, so unconditionally, that I was moved to tears and could not speak another word. I sat down in my seat, consumed with a joy that I am still not able to describe. I knew then that this man knew something about love that I did not. I never sat on the back row again. I have, since that time, made this principle of love the central theme of my studies.

Although, at that time, I had little understanding of how love works. I did not even know the definition of love as I now do, but I began to experiment with it. Some days later, I was driving down the highway in deep thought on this concept of love, when I saw a young man hitch-hiking. I stopped to give him a ride and as he got in my car I said to myself, "I am going to love this person. I am going to reach out to him and fill his needs in any and every way I possibly can. I will try to love him." I asked if there was anything I could do for him. Was he hungry? Did he need a place to stay for the night? As we talked, I felt an immediate closeness. We talked about things that were important to each of us and we shared deep feelings on subjects more intimate than I had ever shared with a stranger. I found myself taking him several miles out of my way and as he got out of the car, it was as if we did not want the conversation, indeed, the relationship, to end. We shook hands for a long time and I knew he felt my sincere love for him. God was showing me that loving others is my choice and how sweet it is to love.

Expanding Love

As another aside, let me make a point that will help us understand a subject we seldom like to discuss. Without any great explanation (it would take volumes to cover the subject), I will say that I believe we need to understand that this principle of love, *spiritual oneness*, will make it possible to live the celestial law of polygamy. Yes, this is a celestial law and we will see it again, probably in the Zion Society. Although the *relationship* with each person is different, in fact, it will be forever unique; *the oneness is the same* and will be greater than can be imagined, much greater. It is a synergistic situation where the whole is greater than the sum of its parts. Remember, the more you love, the more your capacity to love increases.

The laws and level of laws governing such relationships, the intensity, and greatness of love required to live such an order are celestial and demanding. One must rid him/herself of all jealousy, envy, strife, pride, selfishness, and etc. The quantities and depth of personal virtues required to live this law are the same that make someone celestial in the first place. Although this high order was restored to the earth in the latter-days to Joseph Smith, most of the Saints were not prepared to live it. Also, because of the persecution, heaped upon The Church from non-members and the US government, the prophet Wilford Woodruff[88] petitioned the Lord as to what should be done. The result was a revelation that was presented to The Church on October 6, 1890 forbidding the Saints, from that time forward, to enter into the practice of polygamy. Since then, under penalty of excommunication, the practice has been strictly forbidden in The Church. This is now the law of the Lord, through his prophet, to his people and I do here go on record as supporting, sustaining, and obeying the same. Still, the law of polygamy is celestial and it is my *personal* belief that when we are more celestial in our obedience, when we have increased our personal righteousness and our ability to love, and the Lord is ready, we will see it again. Apparently I am not alone in this belief as Bruce R. McConkie said, "Obviously the holy practice will commence after the second coming . . ." (see *Mormon Doctrine* page 578). But, for those who do not understand or might choose to set themselves up as my enemy to take advantage, enough said.

My One And Only

Speaking very personally, I must say that I have been blessed in my life to have loved much and deeply. I remember when I first met my wonderful wife of thirty-eight years. It was on a blind date and somehow I was forced into another date with her later that same week or I surely would never have asked her out again. I had seen her before and my impression of her was that she was spoiled and immature. In fairness, I will also say here that her impression of me was not much better. She thought I was a know-it-all return missionary. On the evening of the second date, I felt strangely compelled to ask her out the following night. This I did and although my opinion of her hadn't really changed much, that night I felt impressed to ask her to marry me. I fought off the impulse as reason told me that I did not want to marry a spoiled, immature girl. But I did ask her for another date the next (fourth) night. This night, the feeling was stronger to the extent that as the evening wore on, I felt that she might be "the one and only" that the Lord wanted me to marry. We were in my car after a dance, and I felt such an attraction to her that I thought my hormones must surely be working overtime and I had to get away from her. I excused myself, telling her I had to go to the men's room. When I got out of the car, I began to pray. I told the Lord that I had never felt so strong about anything in my life and that if, when I got back in the car, I felt the same way, I was going to ask her to marry me, and it would be His fault. No sooner did I get back in the car than I had the feeling twice as strong. I asked her, she accepted, and we both felt so comfortable about it, we laughed all the way home.

Now, we had been together a total of about twelve hours over a one-week period. I did not know her. I certainly did not love her. There was no great spiritual oneness there. I didn't really know much about her at all. All I knew was that she was spoiled and immature and that I didn't like her very much. I did not know at the time that this spoiled, immature girl would be a truly wonderful wife and mother to our five children. I did not know at the time how hard she would work to make a home. I did not know at the time the many sacrifices she would make for me. I did not know what a wonderful wife and lover she would be. I did not know at the time how much she would love the Lord and I had no idea how much she would come to love me. But I did have a testimony that this was the right thing to do and that testimony has carried us through some very difficult times. You see; the Lord knew the future and what I needed. She is now my best friend. She has taught me much about love and now when we look into each other's eyes and touch hands, I feel that oneness and it is so good, so comfortable, so miraculous, and so un-lonely. I only hope all can know such joy. (By the way, it has lasted 38 years so far and every day is sweeter.)

Tapping Into The Spirit of God

How wonderful it is when we make that connection with another person. We want that association to last forever and in fact, it will. Love only goes away if we choose it to. How sweet is the feeling when our spirit amalgamates with another. When it happens, it is not just for the moment. Though the association or relationship may be only a moment long, the oneness will last forever. Even though you may be separated, just the recollection of that oneness shared brings a rushing back of a fullness of the sweetness, and you are blessed by it. If this life is not accommodating enough for us to be together, the next will be, and when we come together again, it will be as if we had never parted.

This is the way of the Zion Society of the latter-days, the heaven-on-earth society. When we choose to be spiritually one with another person, we begin to see what they see, understand what they understand, and feel what they feel. We begin to communicate precisely and completely, often without words. We are exhilarated by the energy of another life force flowing within ours and it fills us in ways that we can't even comprehend. I am not referring only to an oneness with our spouses, or even just the opposite sex. I mean all people, all things beautiful, and God. When we love good things we tap into the spirit of God for all good things are of Him. Gone is the uncertainty, the hopelessness, the helplessness, the fear, the pain, as is the loneliness. In short, *love is the cure for loneliness*. The *loneliness* is consumed by joy, true joy, full joy, that wondrous joy of being, not alone, but one with God.

Since I have internalized this concept, I have felt *free to love*. I have been fortunate to love many persons and many beautiful things. I recognize that to love is good and to develop the ability to love is only to partake of the spirit of He who is Love. Although I still have difficulty reaching out spiritually to express my love, my capacity to love has increased and my life has been far richer and not so lonely. Let me say to you, the reader, that like my old BYU professor, I love you, and if life will be obliging enough for us to one day meet and perhaps build a relationship, I will try to show you my love.

How wonderful it is when we live this second great commandment, to love our neighbor, for this is the way to love God. "Inasmuch as ye have done it unto one of the least of these my brethren, ye have done it unto me." (*Matthew 25:40*)

"Jesus said unto him, Thou shalt love the Lord thy God with all thy heart, and with all thy soul, and with all thy mind. This is the first and great commandment. And the second is like unto it, Thou shalt love thy neighbour as thyself. On these two commandments hang all the law and the prophets." (*Matthew 22:38-40*) "Beloved, let us love one another: for love is of God; and every one that loveth is born of God, and knoweth God. He that loveth not knoweth not God; for God is love . . . . If we love one another, God dwelleth in us, and His love is perfected in us. And we have known and believed the love that God hath to us. God is love; and he that dwelleth in love dwelleth in God, and God in him." (*1 John 4:7,8,12, 16*)

God bless you that you may love, love deeply, love often, love without fear or constraint, love completely, that we may be not only one with each other but one with God. Love.

---

[86] **Joseph Fielding McConkie is the son of Bruce R. McConkie.**

[87] **Mormons commonly believe in a mother in heaven, and that our spirit bodies are the offspring of the union of Heavenly Father and Heavenly Mother. "In the heavens are parents single? No, the thought makes reason stare! Truth is reason, truth eternal, tells me I've a Mother there." (*From a hymn by Eliza R. Snow, quoted by Bruce R. McConkie, Mormon Doctrine, pg. 517*)**

[88] **Wilford Woodruff was the prophet of The Church from 7 April 1889, to 2 September 1898.**

6
Life, What Meanest Thou?

The Big Deception

"Oh no. Now this author is going to presume to tell me the meaning of life. Yeah, sure," you say. "Who are you to tell me what is most important in life or what it means?" O course you are right. As stated at the beginning of this document, I am but a common man, but beware as I may be speaking the truth for which you will be held responsible, regardless its source. Perhaps I am jumping over the edge here, still, I made a promise to myself when I undertook this project to not pull punches, so here goes.

I am not sure why, but the concept I am about to present seems to be kept secret from the best of us. I guess because the truth is so hard to take in this case. It is not milk and bread, but strong meat. I think for this reason, we keep the meaning of life secret, not only from others, but even from ourselves.

We have, to this point, spent a great deal of time talking about spirit, *spirit-matter*, and eternal, celestial concepts. It seems the more you talk and think of spiritual things, the less interest you take in this mortal earthly existence. This is good. It shows that your heart is coming off the things of this world and turning heavenward. This is, in fact, essential to our reaching for and understanding the mysteries of heaven. The Devil's intent is to distract us with worldly things and take our minds off what is not only more important but **more real** in the eternal sense. This world is a deception; it's artificial. Think of it. If this mortal existence were the real McCoy, the most real, the best place to be, don't you think we would spend more of our time here? Eternally speaking, our 70- to 80-year life span is but a blink of the eternal eye. We have already spent a very long time (though we don't know how long) in the pre-earth life, and our life after will reach into the eternities. Does it not stand to reason that if this life were the best place to be, we would spend a larger portion, if not the end of our existence in it? In the words of Bob Dylan, "This is just a *phase* you're *going through*, not a *place* you're *going to*." Since it is such a slight time that we spend here, we must give our attentions to the place where we will spend the greatest amount of time: heaven. I fear that if this life were our only hope, we would be in deep "do-do" (trouble). "If in this life only we have hope in Christ, we are of all men most miserable. But now is Christ risen from the dead, and become the first fruits of them that slept. For since by man came death, by man came also the resurrection of the dead. For as in Adam all die, even so in Christ shall all be made alive." (*1 Corinthians 15:19-22*)

We Need A Body

Notwithstanding the short time spent here, this wide spot on our eternal road to glory is very important. Mormon doctrine tells us that the first and perhaps most important reason for coming to this life is to gain a body. Why is it that we must have a body? "For man is spirit. The elements are eternal and spirit and element, inseparably connected, receive a fulness of joy; and when separated, man cannot receive a fulness of joy." (*D&C 93:33-34*) Apparently, only through the uniting of gross-matter (physical body) with *spirit-matter* (spirit body) may we have the greatest joy. This is a primary purpose for our coming to this degradation.

The Test

The second purpose, for many, is also a very important reason for being here. The Lord opened a vision to Father Abraham wherein he was shown the pre-mortal existence of man (italics for emphasis). "Now the Lord had shown unto me, Abraham, the intelligences that were organized before the world was; and among all these there were many of the noble and great ones; And God saw these souls that they were good, and He stood in the midst of them, and He said: These I will make my rulers; for He stood among those that were spirits, and He saw that they were good; and He said unto me: Abraham, thou art one of them; thou wast chosen before thou wast born. And there stood one among them that was like unto God, and He said unto those who were with him: We will go down, for there is space there, and we will take of these materials, and we will make an earth whereon these may dwell; And we will *prove them* herewith, to see if they will do all things whatsoever the Lord their God shall command them; And they who keep their first estate shall be added upon; and they who keep not their first estate shall not have glory in the same kingdom with those who keep their first estate; and they who keep their second estate shall have glory added upon their heads for ever and ever." (*Abraham 3:22-26*)[89] It is clear that we are to be tested. Although this second reason is no secret to the Mormon community, as we are often found proclaiming its propriety, we still do not seem to comprehend what it means in our everyday lives.

In the previous chapter on the other attributes of God, we discussed the need to have opposition in all things. We also talked about how God set up that opposition and is helping us through it. When you think about it, this life is the only place where trouble and evil are meant to be, can be, or will be. We did not come to earth to find heaven (we were there already), but to find hell.

In our pre-mortal existence, pre-earth life, we lived in the presence of God. Aside from the war that was started by Satan (our spirit brother) where he took a third of the spirits with him as he was cast out,[90] we apparently lived in peace in the presence and light of God. After this life we will again live in the peace, light, and presence of God or in the peace and light of a lesser glory. There will be no evil or trouble in these places. So, in order that we may experience the opposition necessary to having joy, we must come to this earth the Lord has prepared and ordained for peace and light to co-exist with trouble and evil. "And it must needs be that the Devil should tempt the children of men, or they could not be agents unto themselves; for if they never should have bitter they could not know the sweet . . . ." (*D&C 29:39*) Notwithstanding the good we experience here, this is the place set apart by God for us to experience trouble and evil. There is sufficient trouble and evil that few, if any, can escape its result: suffering. Brigham Young said, "You cannot give any persons their exaltation unless they know what evil is, what sin, sorrow, and misery are, for no person could comprehend, appreciate and enjoy an exaltation upon any other principle. (*DBY pg.* 55) It makes you glad that this life *is* only a blink of the eternal eye and not longer.

The problem we have is that we grow up thinking in terms of gross-matter and worldly events. We become so accustomed to this mortal existence that we forget we are spiritual beings having a physical experience, not physical beings trying to have a spiritual experience. I might add, at this point, that if you love this world, if you are really comfortable here, you may be in trouble; this is a telestial or terrestrial world at best. That is to say, we are most comfortable with the law we choose to live. Like I said before, if we were thrust into the presence of God but were not living the celestial law, we would be very uncomfortable, or if we were put in a lesser environment with liars, cheaters, and murderers, but were living a celestial law, we would, again, be very uncomfortable. Probably most of us are most comfortable being in the terrestrial realm with the honorable, independent men of the earth. This is all right, I guess, but it is not where God dwells in the oneness of truth and light.

We would do well to ask ourselves where, and with what people, are we most comfortable? Of course, each person will have to answer that question for himself. Think about it. If we are living celestial laws, we will be comfortable in that realm and with that kind of people. If we are not, but want to change (and that is the hardest part, *wanting* to change), we must get out of our comfort zone and get comfortable with the higher laws and people.

Temporary

Because we are so involved in this temporal existence, we suppose that God thinks in terms of temporal things also. This is not true. "Wherefore, verily I say unto you that all things unto me are spiritual, and not at any time have I given unto you a law which was temporal; neither any man, nor the children of men; neither Adam, your father, whom I created. Behold, I gave unto him that he should be an agent unto himself; and I gave unto him commandment, but no temporal commandment gave I unto him, for my commandments are spiritual; they are not natural nor temporal, neither carnal nor sensual." (*D&C 29:34-35*) All things, to the Lord, are spiritual.

Thankfully, this mortal life is not the only act in town. As stated before and often in the scriptures, we must think spiritually, but if we could tally our thoughts and put temporal thoughts in one column and spiritual thoughts in another, how would our totals compare? I submit that, for most of us, the temporal column would far outweigh the spirit column. Here we are, living in a temporal world, thinking mostly temporal thoughts, and doing mostly temporal things, as if we don't know that the very word "temporal" means "temporary." So, we are spending most of our time on temporary things. Well, you say, "I have to! I live in this temporal world. I've got to go to work every day and deal with such things. What do you expect?" It really doesn't matter in the least what I expect, and I sympathize with you as I am in the same boat. However, the question should be, "What does God expect?" I suppose the answer to that will be that we must separate ourselves, especially our thoughts, from this world, to learn to be *in* the world but not *of* the world.

Where Is Our Treasure?

You may think I am departing from the meaning of life, but I am actually getting to it. This next scripture reference is one that would help us lift our thoughts if we could keep it in mind (italics for emphasis). "Behold, there are many called, but few are chosen. And why are they not chosen? Because *their hearts are set so much upon the things of this world*, and *aspire to the honors of men*, that they do not learn this one lesson . . . that the rights of the priesthood are inseparably connected with the powers of heaven, and that the powers of heaven cannot be controlled nor handled only upon the principles of righteousness." (*D&C 121:34-36*) Here is the test, the second reason for being here: to see if we will **or** will not *set our hearts too much upon the things of this world*.

Most people spend their energy and means trying to build a successful career, obtain a beautiful home, a nice car, a good retirement, build a thriving business, have an easy or fun life, travel, be successful in something, and etc. The list of things goes on and on. But are these goals eternal or temporary? What is it you work for? What do you want, what do you expect out of life? Mark what column it is in, "for where your treasure is, there will your heart be also." (*Matthew 6:21*) And you don't have to be rich to set your heart upon the things of this world. "Wo unto you poor men, whose hearts are not broken, whose spirits are not contrite . . . whose eyes are full of greediness, and who will not labor with your own hands!" (*D&C 56:17*) That is called coveting and laziness.

Shame On Us

You might ask, "How do I know if my heart is set too much upon this world?" I will answer that by telling you about a couple of people I know. The first is a woman that kept a very neat and clean house. She was not rich but she had some very nice things. She would not allow her children to mess up her things. There were a lot of rules like they could only play in their rooms, they had to take their shoes off when they came in, they couldn't eat anywhere but the kitchen, and etc. Her home was so rigid and uncomfortable that her children's friends would not come over to play with them. As a result, they were always away at friends' houses. When her grandchildren came along, they wanted to go see Grandma, but since there were no rooms for kids in her house anymore, she would not let them play in the house at all. They were to stay outside where they couldn't make a mess or break things. Even in the winter months the grandchildren were not allowed to play in the house. Well, it wasn't long before the grandchildren stopped asking to go to see Grandma. It was no fun. Now, I ask you, was her heart set too much upon the things of this world? That woman died never really knowing her grandchildren or they her. A very great price to pay for *things* she ultimately left behind.

To more fully illustrate the point, I will tell on myself as I tell you about this second person. This friend of mine takes very good care of the things with which the Lord has blessed him. He's the type that will not let people eat in his car, no matter how long the trip, and he almost never loans things to people because they don't take as good of care of them as he does. One day he bought a new car and was quite pleased with it. He brought it over to show me. My teenage son happened to be there at the time and the two of us went out to "ooh" and "ah" over his new car. It was very nice, to say the least, and my son was very excited about it. That smell that only comes with new cars reached out and teased our senses as soon as I opened the door. It had been raining that day and my friend had put plastic mats down to keep the mud and water from his new carpet. This only made sense, and when he asked me if I wanted to take a ride, of course I accepted. As my son and I started to get in the car, he turned to my son and told him he didn't want to get any more dirt in the car than he had to and that he could not come along. It didn't really register to me what I had done until after we pulled away. I shall never forget the look on my son's face, as he stood there alone, watching us pull away. What message had I inadvertently sent to my son? That he was somehow not good enough to ride in a new car? I should have told my friend that if his car was too good for my son, it was too good for me. This incident may not seem like much to others, and perhaps my son has forgotten all about it, but it is these kinds of things that I most deeply regret in life. I would climb the highest mountain to take them back if I could. Anyway, my friend eventually found the car to be a lemon. He ended up hating it, and sold it at a loss. Once again I ask; was his heart set too much upon the things of this world? Yes, and I let him get away with it. Shame on us both.

We've all done these kinds of things. When choosing people for the team, we let our desire to win be the basis for our choice of players, leaving someone to always be chosen last or not at all. Isn't winning a thing of this world? Yes, competition is a terrestrial law and foreign to the spirit of Christ (more discussion on this later). And haven't we all, from time to time, been guilty of, for the sake of appearances, only inviting a select group of people to ride with us somewhere or come to our parties or ball game or something else? Isn't this *aspiring to the honors of men*? Are we so desperate for success that we make compromises relative to the moral choices we make? I've known people in the filmmaking industry that will do anything, and I mean **anything**, if they thought it would make them a star or get them down the road to their career goal. It is hard for Mormon people, other Christians, and moral people everywhere to compete with that.

There are times when we all put things before people. I am not talking about the wise use of and taking care of the worldly possessions the Lord has entrusted into our care. The Lord expects this of us. No, I am talking about **setting our hearts upon those things**. Even in The Church, we sometimes put programs before the very people those programs are meant to serve. If these things are prevalent in our lives, I submit that perhaps our hearts are *too much upon the things of this world.* Am I making my point?

It has been my experience that as soon as my heart is set upon something in this world, the Lord uses it as a test to see if it is more important to me than He is. Does He come down and stand before us and ask us to make a choice between the worldly thing and Him? No, instead He gives us an opportunity to choose between *our things* and serving others or making them feel good. "Inasmuch as ye have done it unto one of the least of these my brethren, ye have done it unto me." (*Matthew 25:40*) You see, unfortunately for most of us, God is not that real, but our friends, neighbors, and even an occasional stranger, is. "Oh no," you say. "Making us choose between worldly things and people sounds like God is playing a game with us." Yes, well, he's doing something with us, but it is not a game.

Sacrifice = Faith

It is all about yielding our will to God. Again, remember, we are not alone down here. The Lord is doing all He can to bring us to a higher place and, as we discussed in the previous chapters, He is using whatever means, including some things that we may perceive to be evil, to lift or challenge us to the maximum level we will go. He knows what is best for us and is testing to see if we will yield our own will to that of His. If we will not, we struggle and suffer. He keeps trying and we keep struggling and suffering. He can't force us, although sometimes we feel the lack of choices He gives us is a form of coercion. Perhaps it is, as we know that the Lord's hand or divine providence is in all things and we further know that He chastens those He loves (this we learned from Job). Still, I suspect our **un**willingness to surrender our will to the Lord, or poor choices on our part cause much of our own suffering. The key to relief is **sacrifice**. "Sacrifice?" you ask. "What sacrifice?" You must sacrifice your will, your desire, your wants, and your appetites to do and have what you want. You must bring your heart to a place where you can say to God, "I no longer want to do what *I want* to do, but I want to do what *you want* me to do." Ours is the responsibility to make the sacrifice and prepare our self to receive the gifts. What sacrifice? "Thou shalt offer a sacrifice unto the Lord thy God in righteousness, even that of *a broken heart and a contrite spirit.*" (*D&C 59:8*)

Our willingness to sacrifice must extend to everything we have and are. Everything! Said Joseph Smith (italics and bold for emphasis), "For a man to lay down his all, his character and reputation, his honor, and applause, his good name among men, his houses, his lands, his brothers and sisters, his wife and children and even his own life also . . . requires more than mere belief or supposition that he is doing the will of God; but actual knowledge, realizing that, when these sufferings are ended, he will enter into eternal rest, and be a partaker of the glory of God . . . . Let us here observe, that *a religion that does not require the sacrifice* ***of all things*** *never has power sufficient to produce the faith necessary unto life and salvation*; for, from the first existence of man, the faith necessary unto the enjoyment of life and salvation never could be obtained without **the sacrifice of all earthly things**. It was through this sacrifice, and this only, that God has ordained that men should enjoy eternal life; and it is through the medium of the sacrifice of all earthly things that men do actually know that they are doing the things that are well pleasing in the sight of God. When a man has offered in sacrifice all that he has for truth's sake, not even withholding his life, and believing before God that he has been called to make this sacrifice because he seeks to do his will, he does know, most assuredly, that God does and will accept his sacrifice and offering, and that he has not, nor will not seek His face in vain. Under these circumstances, then, he can obtain the faith necessary for him to lay hold on eternal life." (*Joseph Smith, Lectures On Faith, lec.* 6:5 and 7)

Why must we sacrifice all? So that we may know that we are doing the Father's will and not our own. Does this mean that we just quit everything, give everything we own away, and go to the mountains to become a monk or something? No, although this is similar to what Christ asked of the twelve disciples. Remember; be **in** the world and not **of** the world. The Lord may not literally require the sacrifice of all things, but you can be certain that He expects us to be *willing* and *ready* to sacrifice ***all*** things. You will know through the spirit what the Lord requires as a sacrifice from you and it will no doubt be something of utmost importance to you. This is how we gain the conviction that we are doing what the Lord wants us to do instead of being driven by our own desires. You may recall the Prophet Joseph's words quoted in an earlier chapter (italics for emphasis), "Let us here observe that three things are necessary for any rational and intelligent being to exercise faith in God unto life and salvation. First, the idea that He actually exists; Secondly, a correct idea of His character, perfections, and attributes; Thirdly, *an actual knowledge that the course of life which one is pursuing is according to His will.*" (*Joseph Smith, Lectures On Faith, lec.* 2:5) It is very important to know that we are pleasing God in everything that we are doing in our lives. Pleasing Him is our worship of Him. Further, Joseph Smith said, "*An actual knowledge to any person, that the course of life which he pursues is according to the will of God, is essentially necessary to enable him to have that confidence in God without which no person can obtain eternal life*. It was this that enabled the ancient Saints to endure all their afflictions and persecutions, and to take joyfully the spoiling of their goods, knowing (not believing merely) that they had a more enduring substance."

(*Joseph Smith, Lectures On Faith, lec.* 6:2) And take "joyfully the spoiling of your goods, knowing in yourselves that ye have in heaven a better and an enduring substance. Cast not away therefore your confidence, which hath great recompense of reward. For ye have need of patience, that, after ye have done the will of God, ye might receive the promise." (*Hebrews 10:34-36*)

The Apostle Paul and the Prophet Joseph Smith knew that sacrifice is the process, the way you gain the faith in Christ to endure your afflictions. That is the method. We must be willing to *sacrifice everything worldly and especially our will.* Said Joseph Smith, "Those, then, who make the sacrifice, will have the testimony that their course is pleasing in the sight of God; and those who have this testimony will have faith to lay hold on eternal life, and will be enabled, through faith, to endure unto the end, and receive the crown that is laid up for them that love the appearing of our Lord Jesus Christ. But those who have not made this sacrifice to God do not know that the course which they pursue is well pleasing in His sight; for whatever may be their belief or their opinion, it is a matter of doubt and uncertainty in their mind; and where doubt and uncertainty are, there faith is not, nor can it be. For doubt and faith do not exist in the same person at the same time; so that persons whose minds are under doubts and fears cannot have unshaken confidence; and where unshaken confidence is not, there faith is weak; and where faith is weak the persons will not be able to contend against all the opposition, tribulations, and afflictions which they will have to encounter in order to be heirs of God, and joint heirs with Christ Jesus; and they will grow weary in their minds, and the adversary will have power over them and destroy them." (*Joseph Smith, Lectures On Faith, lec.* 6:*10* and *12*)

Remember, *sacrifice is not just doing without but also a demonstration of our faith. It is a test of our trust in the divine. It is symbolic of our willingness to give up our will to God.*

Do we get the principle, the law Joseph Smith is teaching here? Do we understand how it works? The only way we know that we are pleasing God is to sacrifice all, including our own will, to Him. Once we do, we have the testimony that we are doing what He *wants* us to do, not what *we want* to do. That testimony will carry us. Then we *will* have the faith to endure. **This is the process of receiving faith in Christ. There is no other way!**

Belief Or Faith?

Now, although we often interchange the words belief and faith as they are often interchanged in the scriptures, they are not the same. Belief is before faith, is requisite to the obtaining of faith, and faith is before knowledge.

Belief is a choice but faith is a gift from God and a principal of great power, not as much as knowledge, but great power nonetheless. Said Brigham Young, "Faith is an eternal principle; belief is an admission of the fact. Faith, to us, is the gift of God; belief is inherent in the children of men, and is the foundation for the reception of faith. Belief and unbelief are independent in men, the same as other attributes. Men can acknowledge or reject, turn to the right or to the left, rise up or remain seated, you can say that the Lord and his Gospel are not worthy of notice, or you can bow to them . . . If we speak of faith in the abstract, it is the power of God by which the worlds are and were made, and is a gift of God to those who believe and obey his commandments. On the other hand, no living, intelligent being, whether serving God or not, acts without belief. He might as well undertake to live without breathing as to live without the principle of belief. But he must believe the truth, obey the truth, and practice the truth, to obtain the power of God called faith." (*DBY pg. 153*)

One might ask, "If faith is a gift, why are we commanded to have it?" It is so we will seek, strive, and struggle for it because God cannot give a gift if you don't *want* it. "For what doth it profit a man if a gift is bestowed upon him and he receive not the gift? Behold, he rejoices not in that which is given unto him, neither rejoices in him who is the giver of the gift." (*D&C 88:33*) Since belief is before faith and it is a choice, we can desire to have faith and choose to believe.

I love a scripture that I have only recently found in the ninth chapter of Mark. Here Mark was telling about a time when a father brought his son, who was possessed by an evil spirit, to Christ to be healed. The boy was so afflicted that he was apparently out of control. The apostles had already tried to cast the evil spirit out of the boy, but in vain. They afterwards asked Christ why they could not cast out the spirit, and we will discuss that point in a moment, but the wonderful thing that I found in this story is in verses 23 and 24 where it says (italics for emphasis), "Jesus said unto him, If thou canst believe, all things are possible to him that believeth. And straightway the father of the child cried out, and said with tears, *Lord, I believe; help thou mine unbelief*." (*Mark 9:23-24*) This sounds like a contradiction but it is not. I can't say how many times I have felt like that father. *Yes Lord I believe, help thou mine unbelief*. What did he mean? He meant, yes Lord, I believe because I choose to believe, but my faith is weak. Please help me with my faith. God has promised us that if we will believe, He will bless us with faith and great power.

A False Future

There is another point made by Alma that needs stating. Even when God blesses you with faith, you still do not *know*. "Faith is not to have a perfect knowledge of things; therefore if ye have faith ye hope for things which are not seen, which are true." (*Alma 32:21*) This faith is not "knowing something"; it is having the courage or ability to act on your belief. In other words, with this courage or ability, given you of God, you act upon that which you believe to be true. It is then that you have *faith* that this particular thing is true and will actually transpire.

What is also paramount to understand are the three little words on the end of that verse, "*which are true.*" You see; *it is of no use to have a hope or believe in a future event, which is not true*. What do I mean by that? I mean that you can't just hope or believe that something in the future will happen, it must *actually* ***be true***. Again, what do I mean by that? Remember that truth is things as they *are, were, and* ***will be***. Take, for example, it is obvious that if you are hoping and believing in a past event, but that event did, in fact, not happen, then your hope and belief is in vain. No faith or power will be forthcoming based upon such a belief. We all know you cannot change past events, so your hope and belief will not change the event, no matter how hard you hope or how deeply you believe. Should you act on such misinformation, you will be wrong, and the consequences of that action will naturally follow. If it is not true, it is not true, and nothing can make it true. The same is so of future events. You cannot change the truth of future events either. You see, a false belief in the future is the same as a false belief in the past. If you are wishing, hoping, and believing that a future event will happen (perhaps the healing of the sick or some other miracle) but it is not supposed to happen, it is *not true*, then your hope and belief is in vain. Again, should you act on such misinformation, you will be wrong, and the consequences of that action will naturally follow.

"But," you say, "can't my faith change the future event?" No, no more than your so-called faith can change past events. I say, so-called faith because God will not give you the gift of faith or power in a future event, or anything else that is not true. I give as an example the great prophet Mormon who had, many times, lead his Nephite people to victory in battle against their enemies but because they would not repent and turn back to God, he refused to continue (italics for emphasis). "And it came to pass that I, Mormon, did utterly refuse from this time forth to be a commander and a leader of this people, because of their wickedness and abomination. Behold, I had led them, notwithstanding their wickedness I had led them many times to battle, and had loved them, according to the love of God which was in me, with all may heart; and my soul had been poured out in prayer unto my God all the day long for them; nevertheless, *it was without faith*, because of the hardness of their hearts." (*Mormon 3:11-12*) Why could he not pray with faith? Because he knew, by the spirit, that what he was praying for was not a true future event. He knew that they were to be destroyed from off the face of the earth (see *verse 15*). He could not have faith in a false future and neither can we. We cannot heal the sick if it is not the *true future*, the will of God. We cannot raise the dead, or move mountains, or anything else that is not the will of God or truth (things that will be). If your belief is false you may be listening to your own will or desire instead of God's.

I will hasten here to say that the Lord may have reasons to bless you with great faith and power to act upon a certain belief in a future event; yet the event does not come to pass, as you *believed* it would. I take as an example, the Saints in Nauvoo,[91] Illinois. They were commanded to build their city and a temple to their God. I feel certain that when they embarked upon that venture, they believed they would finally have a beautiful city of peace and prosperity which would be the center of God's latter-day church and kingdom, yet it ended by their being driven out by mob persecution. Their dream and belief in that dream ended in tragedy. Does this mean that their faith was weak? Not necessarily. In fact, God gave them great faith and power and they accomplished wonderful things because of that faith. He also blessed them with great faith and power in their pioneer trek westward, as well as giving them power to make the desert blossom as a rose once they got there. These things they accomplished by faith because they believed. God's will, relative to many of these accomplishments, was not manifest until after the trial of their faith. Did the Saints at the time of Nauvoo believe in a false future? Some of them did and when it did not come to pass, their testimonies were shattered. They would have been right to believe that the process of building their temple and city was right, no matter how it ended. God has often kept us in the dark but required of us a belief that He is wiser and knows, better than we, what is good for us.

"Well," you ask, "how do I know what future events are true?" By appealing to the spirit of truth, the Holy Ghost, who knows and testifies of the truth of all things, past, present, and future. This is the only way. This is why you must be strictly in tune with the will of God so that you know what He wants and what is truth, even future truth. Sacrificing your own will and desire is the only way you can know that what you are doing is what God wants you to do. Accordingly, you may have faith and power in events and things, *which are true*. But remember, God may not tell you how the event will end, leaving you inspired to go ahead trusting in His mercies and not the end result. To God, the journey and how it is traveled is often more important than the destination.

Crossing The Bridge

Let me illustrate the points I have made in these last paragraphs by building a scenario. A man is walking along and he comes to a large canyon. There is a footbridge across the canyon but it is old and does not look safe. There is no way to know whether the bridge is safe without trying it. He has no means of trying the bridge without walking out on it. This could be fatal. The man looks the bridge over and decides to *believe* that it is safe. But how does he know? Of course he does not know. What does the man do? If he is a man who does not believe in God or is not in tune with spiritual inspiration, he has no way of knowing if it is safe to cross. He has two choices. He may, at his peril, blindly proceed (blind faith) or he must stay off the bridge. It does not matter what he chooses to believe. Remember, we all believe what we choose to believe and that belief may not resemble things as they really were, are, or will be. If he walks across the bridge with nothing but his belief, he is, in effect, *taking his chances*. Even if this bridge does not fail, some future bridge will. On the other hand, the man who believes in God can appeal to Him for the truth concerning the bridge. He may expect, through the whisperings of the still small voice (the Holy Ghost), to receive inspiration on the condition of the bridge and instructions as to whether or not he should proceed. Say that the spirit tells the man that the bridge is safe. He still does not have *a knowledge,* but, because of the promptings of the spirit, has something *(faith)* upon which to apply his *belief* that it is safe. That faith gives him the courage and power to act on his belief. With confidence and surety he walks with faith across the bridge. Now he has *a knowledge* that the bridge is, in fact, safe.

A man's faith gives him powers that the man without faith does not have. That power is a tap on truth, things as they really were, are, and will be. Of course, one must exercise his spiritual communication process enough to recognize the spirit when it speaks; if he does not recognize the voice, the spiritual whisperings do no good at all. Also, as stated before, part of that process of receiving communication or revelation from God is sacrificing one's own will. If you don't, you will hear your own voice of desire and not the whisperings of the Holy Spirit. Sacrificing our own will to do God's makes us righteous individuals. Remember, (italics for emphasis) "that *the rights of the priesthood are inseparably connected with the powers of heaven*, and that the powers of heaven cannot be controlled nor handled only upon the principles of righteousness." (*D&C 121:34-36*)

Now you say, "What if, in accordance with your above scenario, the man looks the bridge over and comes to a *belief* that it is *not safe*, yet the spirit tells him to cross anyway. Is that possible?" Yes, in which case the man may expect the miraculous intervention of the Lord to somehow support his safe crossing. But what if the spirit reveals to him that the bridge will collapse under his weight yet compels him to cross anyway. What good does his faith do him then? Well, it will still give him the confidence, courage, and power to do what he knows he should or must do. Didn't Joseph Smith tell us that we must be ready and willing to sacrifice even our own lives, if necessary, to gain the faith that what we are doing is pleasing to God. That would be the ultimate sacrifice of our will and many men have gone to their death knowing, by the spirit, that it was the right thing to do. The ancient martyrs, the apostles, Joseph Smith, and Christ Himself I give as examples, though there are many more.

There is great power in our faith, born of a willingness to submit our will to God, even when we know, by the spirit, that the end will bring personal tragedy, even death. I testify, that the worth of our lives will be used by God for a good purpose. Perhaps like the ancient martyrs, many souls will be saved as a result. On the other hand, it might be for the benefit of saving only one soul, our own. Can we live with this principle? If not, perhaps, at the very least, we must admit we are not yet willing to submit our will to God's.

Further, like Abraham of old, who was commanded to offer his only son as a sacrifice, we do not know at what point the Lord will say it is enough and provide a ram in the thicket instead (see *Genesis 22:1-13*). But again, like Abraham, our willingness to make the sacrifice will please God and we have His promised faith, no matter what the outcome!

In any case, a man with faith has powers that a man without faith has not. So can we see why faith is so important? Why must we have it? It is through faith that we are able to use the powers of heaven to accomplish difficult, even impossible tasks, or what we call miracles. This is the power of God's priesthood. We must have belief to begin the transfer of this faith or power from heaven, from God to man. The Prophet Joseph tells us that to enjoy miracles or any other of the gifts of God, we must have faith first. "Because faith is wanting, the fruits are. No man since the world was had faith without having something along with it. The ancients quenched the violence of fire, escaped the edge of the sword, women received their dead, etc. By faith the worlds were made. A man who has none of the gifts has no faith; and he deceives himself, if he supposes he has. Faith has been wanting, not only among the heathen, but in professed Christendom also, so that tongues, healings, prophecy, and prophets and apostles, and all the gifts and blessings have been wanting." (*TPJS, pg. 270*) "The gospel must be preached unto every creature, with signs following them that believe." (*D&C 58:64*, see also *Mark 16:16-18*, *Ether 4:18*, *Mormon 9:24* and *D&C 84:65*.) Do we have gifts? Do we have faith? Do we have belief? Again allow me to quote, "And your minds in times past have been darkened because of unbelief, and because you have treated lightly the things you have received—Which vanity and unbelief have brought the whole church under condemnation. And this condemnation resteth upon the children of Zion, even all. And they shall remain under this condemnation until they repent and remember the new covenant . . ." (*D&C 84:54-58*)

Moving Mountains or Unloading Trucks

Not long ago I was helping a friend unload a large truck. It was a hot day and we were both sweating. As we were struggling with the heavier items, my friend casually said, "It's too bad we can't use our minds and levitate these things so we wouldn't have to work so hard." I thought for a moment and realized that my friend was far closer to truth than he knew. The words of Christ, spoken to His apostles who were unable to cast out a devil from a young man, came to me, "And Jesus said unto them, because of your unbelief: for verily I say unto you, if ye have faith as a grain of mustard seed, ye shall say unto this mountain, Remove hence to yonder place; and it shall remove; and nothing shall be impossible unto you." (*Matthew 17:20*) This was no idle statement. This is a celestial concept. This is the place we are trying to go. This is what faith is about! There is an easier way, by faith. If God had been unloading that truck He would likely not have done it by physically hefting its contents. God did not physically go out and gather the materials for this earth in the course of creating it. The arm of flesh is not the only alternative. There is a better way. There are higher powers, celestial powers of the priesthood, powers that a Zion Society or a Zion *person* would use to solve his problems and accomplish his righteous purposes. We mortals call examples of these priesthood powers, miracles. Celestial beings, I am certain, call it simply getting the job done.

Miracles or Tapping Into The Power

I have found that the word *miracle* means different things to different people. It might, therefore, be appropriate here to give some definitive meaning to the word so that we may be of one mind. A common definition of a miracle is an unexplainable occurrence. This implies that if an event can be explained, it is not a miracle at all. Take, for example, the parting of the Red Sea by Moses. Scientists have attempted to explain this event in terms of natural phenomenon. They say the Red Sea is extraordinarily shallow in that place and that with tides, earthquake, or strong winds, such an event could have been a natural occurrence. They make the same case concerning the plagues of Egypt, that some chemical got into the water turning it a blood red color, killing the fish, and driving the frogs out of the water onto the land. This upset the ecological balance and there began to be an abundance of fly larva, which resulted in swarms of flies infecting the cattle with diseases and causing boils on the people. Then, a natural hailstorm upset the camp fires, causing things to burn, and this storm caused a strong wind which naturally brought with it locusts, and so on. Since all these things can be explained by natural causes, there were no miracles involved. There are those who say that since there are logical explanations to every occurrence, even though we do not know what the explanations might be, these things cannot be considered true miracles. Such a definition leaves us with no miracles whatsoever, as there are indeed explanations to everything and, it is supposed, God works from natural laws and means (at least it is natural to him). To God, who knows all the geometries and laws, there certainly are no miracles. He fully understands the laws with which He works His wonders and I feel certain that when our thoughts and ways are as high as His, nothing will seem miraculous to us either. Still, to man, there are occurrences that are completely unexplainable. Not only that, but we must take into account the timing of the event. Though it is true that the plagues of Egypt and the parting of the Red Sea may have been done by what we consider natural laws, still, *God did it* and did it *at **precisely the time** it was needed* by His people. We therefore must include in our definition of a miracle not only the extraordinary circumstance itself, but the timing, the need prompting a greater power to initiate the event at a time, in a place, and in a manner that solves a problem that otherwise had no apparent solution, regardless of any natural means of that solution.

This puts God and His powers in the event and requires some sort of relationship between Him and the benefactors of the miracle. As the relationship between God and man gets closer, His powers begin to transfer to man. It is God's will that we receive increasingly greater endowments of power as we learn to use such powers for God's good and righteous purposes. Those who want to explain away the miracles of God deny His will and gifts of power, and will never gain such power. Belief and then faith is the beginning of the transfer of power. How can they have faith in a God they deny? How can they have faith if they don't believe in miracles? They are, by default, stuck with their own weak arm of flesh and will never empty the contents of a truck with *real power*.

Why do we not believe? Why do we limit or reject God's offer of power to us by unbelief? "But," you say, "I believe in miracles." Yes, and so did the apostles who were unable to work the miracles. Why? It is because they lacked faith. Deep down inside, they really didn't believe. Had they, or we, the faith of a mustard seed, we too might cast out devils, turn water to wine, multiply loaves and fishes, heal the sick, raise the dead, move mountains, part the seas, or unload trucks effortlessly.

We Better Get It, And Soon

This is the great secret of why faith is so very important. Belief and faith are the process of tapping into those powers. That is what is important about belief and faith! Why do we not believe that we can tap into those powers, when doing so is the very thing God is trying to teach us? *Please know that it is the desire of God that we receive these powers in the priesthood, this endowment.* It is only through such an endowment that we can have a fullness of joy or become like God. It is the primary element of the Gospel of Jesus Christ.

With all that the Saints (I might add, *all people*) now suffer, as well as what they will be called upon by God to soon suffer; we need His gifts, we need to feel His constant presence, we need His powers, we desperately need the miracles. We must not deny them. This principle is too important. We are in the latter-days. We will shortly face days of extreme chaos and suffering. We will soon be thrust into a state of disquietude, fear, and foreboding, where our true colors will become evident to others, God, and ourselves. Will we have learned, by belief and faith, to call down these powers of heaven to solve our problems, accomplish our purposes, and administer to the needs of our people? The prophecies will unfold into the now as the Kingdom of God rolls forth to cover the earth. The anguish, torment, and misery will be indescribable. If we are to survive, and I don't mean just physically or literally, I mean if we are to not lose our hope, if we are to have the strength of spirit, to carry on, as our goods and our very lives are spoiled, we must have faith, we must have power. We must have the kind of faith and power that Job and the Brother of Jared[92] enjoyed. "For if there be no faith among the children of men God can do no miracle among them; wherefore, He showed not Himself until after their faith. Behold, it was the faith of Alma and Amulek that caused the prison to tumble to the earth. Behold, it was the faith of Nephi and Lehi that wrought the change upon the Lamanites,[93] that they were baptized with fire and with the Holy Ghost. Behold, it was the faith of Ammon and his brethren which wrought so great a miracle among the Lamanites. Yea, and even all they who wrought miracles wrought them by faith, even those who were before Christ and also those who were after. And it was by faith that the three disciples obtained a promise that they should not taste of death; and they obtained not the promise until after their faith. And neither at any time hath any wrought miracles until after their faith; wherefore they first believed in the Son of God. And there were many whose faith was so exceedingly strong, even before Christ came, who could not be kept from within the veil, but truly saw with their eyes the things which they had beheld with an eye of faith, and they were glad. And behold, we have seen in this record that one of these was the brother of Jared; for so great was his faith in God, that when God put forth His finger He could not hide it from the sight of the brother of Jared, because of His word which He had spoken unto him, which word he had obtained by faith. And after the brother of Jared had beheld the finger of the Lord, because of the promise which the brother of Jared had obtained by faith, the Lord could not withhold anything from his sight; wherefore He showed him all things, for He could no longer be kept without the veil." (*Ether 12:12-21*) It is our time and we must learn this principle quickly, this celestial law of sacrifice, so we can have faith, so we can have the gifts and powers of God. This is how it happens. Can we not see that this is the foundation of the Gospel of Christ here on earth?

The Real Purpose

We need God's priesthood powers because this life is not easy. It was not meant to be. Where did we get the notion that our purpose down here was to have a wonderful, peaceful life? Who told us that the course would be easy and fun—the Devil, no doubt? Who told us that, even if we live the commandments, our lives would be *hunky dory* (as we used to say way back in the '60s)? Life is not meant to be accommodating. It is a place to hurt, a place to sin, a place to fall down, and a place to suffer the consequence of ours and others' sins. It is the purpose of this earth life. Yes, man is that he might have joy, but *joy is not fun*. Fun and joy are not the same. True joy is "*knowing*" God, having that *fullness of love* with the Father and His Son, Jesus Christ. It is having the fullness of His power and glory revealed to us. We can have that joy ***in our sufferings*** if we have made our sacrifice to Him. Paul rejoiced in his afflictions (italics for emphasis). "Therefore being justified by faith, we have peace with God through our Lord Jesus Christ: By whom also we have access by faith into this grace wherein we stand, and rejoice in hope of the glory of God. And not only so, but *we glory in tribulations* also: knowing that tribulation worketh patience; And patience, experience; and experience, hope." (*Romans 5:1-5*) Hope? Hope in what; our insurance policy, in our company retirement program, in our government welfare program, in the food storage we put up, or that gun and ammunition we keep handy, in our own arm of flesh? No, no, never! In Christ is our faith and hope, our **only** hope.

Too often we lose sight of why we are here, or perhaps we never understood. You are not here to necessarily *have fun, a good time*. In fact, speaking on an individual basis, you might be here to suffer. Your sacrifice may require you to fail in business, suffer terrible health, feel pain over the death of a loved one, a broken marriage, boredom, loneliness, or experience some other tragedy of life. Without the bad things happening in our lives to turn us around and keep us humble, we would go our own way without God. Without His help we would make no progress, at best, or destroy ourselves, at worst.

We must get back to the counsel of King Benjamin to "becometh as a child, submissive, meek, humble, patient, full of love, willing to submit to all things which the Lord seeth fit to inflict upon him, even as a child doth submit to his father." (*Mosiah 3:19*) Remember the Lord requires the sacrifice of all things, the submitting of our will to God. Then we will know that we are pleasing Him. Then, despite our suffering, if that is what we are called to do, we will have faith and hope. Somehow we will know that to God, all things are possible, and we find ourselves never, never, never giving up. When we are encircled round about in the arms of His eternal love, we lose all fear; we will have peace and joy. "There is no fear in love; but perfect love casteth out fear; because fear hath torment. He that feareth is not made perfect in love." (*1 John 4:18*) You cannot have love and fear at the same time. It is impossible.

Unhappy Endings

When you give your own will over to the Lord, He may lead you one direction and then another. As I said before, you may correctly act upon inspiration from God to do something that ends in a dismal failure. *This does not mean that your inspiration was bad*. Inspiration from God is truth, is knowledge, or rather, a knowledge of things as they were, are, and will be. That truth will stand forever. Don't undermine your inspiration, your testimony, and decision-making ability that way. If you brought your best thinking, logic, and inspiration to the choice, hold tight to your testimony. You will be able to do that if, in the process of the decision, you sacrifice your own will in the matter. Then, and only then, will you, as the Prophet Joseph said, have the *confidence*, the *faith*, even a *knowledge* that you are pleasing God. If you do that, you will be able to endure the suffering with joy in your heart. Don't ever think that you did the wrong thing just because it brought scorn upon you, caused you suffering, you met with failure, or it otherwise had a less than happy ending. Reconcile yourself and your situation to God, as did Job, and try to find out what it is He is doing with you. In so doing, you will inevitably draw nearer to Him and even come to know Him.

You Must Have Done Something Wrong

With regard to this principle, we tend to look at people, and if their lives are going well, we make the judgment that God has blessed them because they are righteous. Conversely, if someone is having a hard time, we judge them to be doing something wrong and worthy of their punishment. Remember that Job's friends and wife made that same judgment about his predicament, but they were mistaken. His suffering was not because he did anything wrong. To make such judgments is likely just the opposite of the truth. It is a way the

Devil confuses us. "Woe unto them that call evil good, and good evil, that put darkness for light, and light for darkness; that put bitter for sweet, and sweet for bitter!" (*Isaiah 5:20*) The Devil would like us to think we are righteous because our lives are flowing without problems. At such times, we often lose our humility. However, he will help us succeed if we do it his way. His support, however, is for the short term.

Although we feel at times because of our suffering or failure that the Lord has forsaken us, in the long term, He will bless us with a far greater weight of glory. "For our light affliction, which is but for a moment, worketh for us a far more exceeding and eternal weight of glory." (*2 Corinthians 4:17*) It may not be in this world, as Paul said, "knowing in yourselves that ye have in heaven a better and an enduring substance." If the knowledge of future glory is not good enough for us now, we may be trading an eternity of joy for a few years of fun here on earth. Remember, "And ye have forgotten the exhortation which speaketh unto you as unto children, My son, despise not thou the chastening of the Lord, nor faint when thou art rebuked of Him: For whom the Lord loveth He chasteneth, and scourgeth every son whom He receiveth. If ye endure chastening, God dealeth with you as with sons; for what son is he whom the father chasteneth not? But if ye be without chastisement, whereof all are partakers, then are ye bastards, and not sons." (*Hebrews 12:5-8*) Said Brigham Young, "All intelligent beings who are crowned with crowns of glory, immortality, and eternal lives must pass through every ordeal appointed for intelligent beings to pass through, to gain their glory and exaltation. Every calamity that can come upon mortal beings will be suffered to come upon the righteous few, to prepare them to enjoy the presence of the Lord. If we obtain the glory that Abraham obtained, we must do so by the same means that he did. If we are ever prepared to enjoy the society of Enoch, Noah, Melchizedek, Abraham, Isaac, and Jacob, or of their faithful children, and of the faithful prophets and apostles, we must pass through the same experience, and gain the knowledge, intelligence, and endowments that will prepare us to enter into the celestial kingdom of our Father and God. How many of the Latter-day Saints will endure all these things, and be prepared to enjoy the presence of the Father and the Son? You can answer that question at your leisure. Every trial and experience you have passed through is necessary for your salvation." (*DBY pg. 345*)

More Sacrifice?

I once knew a professor at BYU who told me, "I don't eat breakfast in the morning without knowing it is in accordance with the will of God." I thought at the time that such a position was extreme, to say the least, but now I am not so sure. You see; the Lord might want you to fast that day so you might be more spiritually in tune to receive a revelation, administer to the sick, suffer a trial, or do some other thing that would require a greater endowment of faith. The only way to receive such a spiritual endowment is to be willing to sacrifice all things. That would certainly include sacrificing our desire to own more and bigger toys, but it may include our desire to eat breakfast as well, as food is one of the basic earthly needs and for most of us, a deep-rooted desire. Fasting is a sacrifice, and sacrifice brings forth the blessings of heaven. Again, sacrifice is the only way to gain the confidence that we are pleasing God, then we are prepared to receive His gift of faith and power. Even the apostles could not receive faith or power enough to work miracles without fasting and praying first. After failing to cast that evil spirit out the Savior told them, "Howbeit this kind goeth not out but by prayer and fasting." (*Matthew 17:21*) Fasting and prayer are fundamental ways to show God that you are, indeed, interested in pleasing Him. I know we don't want to hear that, but it is true. "They did fast and pray oft, and did wax stronger and stronger in their humility, and firmer and firmer in the faith of Christ, unto the filling their souls with joy and consolation, yea, even to the purifying and the sanctification of their hearts, which sanctification cometh because of their yielding their hearts unto God." (*Helaman 3:35*) You will also note that, along with their fasting and prayer, they *yielded their hearts to God* or sacrificed their will to His.

You might here voice the complaint that, "I *have* fasted. I have tried to give up my will, but when I prayed, I didn't receive any answer. The Lord did not bless me with the power to overcome the problem or the opportunity to achieve the goal!" What do I do now? My answer is, first, don't despair or give up; second, try to reconcile yourself with God and figure out what is His will on the matter (remember, God is trying to save souls and that our thoughts are not His); and third, to carry on as best you can with what you feel is the best course. Brigham Young condensed this principle when he told us, "My religion is to know the will of God and do it." (*DBY, pg. 8*)

This idea was well put by Johnny Cash on a TV talk show I once saw where they talked about his success in the music business. When they opened it up to the audience to ask questions, a young man, seeking a formula to success, asked Mr. Cash what he must do to make it in the business. The answer that came was not one the young man relished hearing. Mr. Cash said, "You do what you do best, the best way you know how to do it. If you make it, God has blessed you. If you don't make it, God has blessed you." You see; he knew that the key was to do your best and leave the outcome up to God. The only other way is to sell your soul to the Devil and believe in his false promise of success. For impression's sake, I know I am repeating myself here. But this process seems to have been a secret too long.

God may indeed have a great scientific, philosophical, political, social, or religious work for you to do. If He has ordained that you achieve something in this life, nothing, save your own lack of faith, will stop you from doing so. I refer you to Alma's words: "And thus they have been called to this holy calling on account of their faith, while others would reject the Spirit of God on account of the hardness of their hearts and blindness of their minds, while, if it had not been for this they might have had as great privilege as their brethren. Or in fine, in the first place they were on the same standing with their brethren; thus this holy calling being prepared from the foundation of the world for such as would not harden their hearts, being in and through the atonement of the Only Begotten Son, who was prepared." (*Alma 13:4-5*)

On the other hand, God may have ordained that you suffer some great tragedy here, for whatever reason He might have. In either case, the principle is the same. Sacrifice your will in order to have the faith to make it through.

Wait, They Got A Penny Too!

Another mistake we make in our judgments of people is in believing that there is a sort of imaginary scale, and all our good deeds go on one side and all our bad deeds go on the other. Then, at the judgment day, whichever is the heavier side wins out. This could not be further from the truth. Although we don't give credence to deathbed repentance, in reality, it is possible. Of course it is a fool who thinks he can wait to the last moment to repent, as one never knows when the last moment will be, nor can one be certain he will have time to make the change. Still, the analogy of the balancing scale is not correct. A better analogy would be a Geiger counter that passes over us at the pearly gates. Notwithstanding the fact that we may have committed many sins, if we have repented, if we learned from those sins, if we are righteous enough, then we will rate high enough and we're in. "But," you say, "if I have lived all my life a good person and the other guy didn't turn good until near the end of his life, won't I be better off than he?" Well, no, you will not. This is the whole point of Christ's parable of the laborers. "For the kingdom of heaven is like unto a man that is an householder, which went out early in the morning to hire labourers into his vineyard. And when he had agreed with the labourers for a penny a day, he sent them into his vineyard. And he went out about the third hour, and saw others standing idle in the marketplace, And said unto them; Go ye also into the vineyard, and whatsoever is right I will give you. Again he went out about the sixth and ninth hour, and did likewise. And about the eleventh hour he went out, and found others standing idle, and saith unto them, Why stand ye here all the day idle? They say unto him,

Because no man hath hired us. He saith unto them, Go ye also into the vineyard; and whatsoever is right, that shall ye receive. So when even was come, the lord of the vineyard saith unto his steward, Call the labourers, and give them their hire, beginning from the last unto the first. And when they came that were hired about the eleventh hour, they received every man a penny. But when the first came, they supposed that they should have received more; and they likewise received every man a penny. And when they had received it, they murmured against the goodman of the house, saying, These last have wrought but one hour, and thou hast made them equal unto us, which have borne the burden and heat of the day. But he answered one of them, and said, Friend, I do thee no wrong: didst not thou agree with me for a penny? . . . . Is it not lawful for me to do what I will with mine own? Is thine eye evil, because I am good?" (*Matthew 20:1-15*) You see, the first laborers were thinking in terms of terrestrial law, quantifying everyone's contributions. The Lord's law is celestial. Those who live the law of the celestial glory will inherit that glory, no matter when or where along the road of eternal progression they finally choose to live it. Though it is true that "if a person gains more knowledge and intelligence in this life through his diligence and obedience than another, he will have so much the advantage in the world to come" (*D&C 130:19*), such an advantage would be in abilities developed, not end rewards. I promise you that **if** you are indeed a celestial being, you will be glad for anyone else that receives the same reward. If you are not glad for others who received the same reward though they didn't work as hard as you, as long as you, or suffered what you had to suffer, you will not **be** a celestial being. We will go deeper into celestial law in the chapter on The Zion Life.

In A Nutshell

The meaning of life and our purpose for being here should be no secret to Mormons or anyone else. Preeminent to our understanding of what is going on in our daily lives is knowing that it is **not meant to be a picnic**, that we are **not meant to be comfortable with this life**. We must understand that this world is upside down and that it is *meant* to be that way. It is *right* for it to be that way. This is not only a place to gain a body, but also **a place to sin, a place to suffer, to be tested, and a place to gain faith through sacrifice**.

We will suffer the wrath of God for our sins. But if we are righteous we will perhaps suffer because of the sins of others. Or, if we are righteous we will be chastened and scourged so we can taste the bitter and know the sweet (see *Hebrews 12:5-8*). Either way, we suffer. There is no escape. It's what we are here to do. We're in a hell of a situation (pun intended).

A Little Hope Here, Huh?

Now that I've painted such a black picture, let me say that although I am quite certain that suffering is inescapable, I am also equally certain that by turning to God, cheerfully accepting His will, becoming "as a child, *submissive, meek, humble, patient, full of love, willing to submit to all things which the Lord seeth fit to inflict upon him*, even as a child doth submit to his father . . ." (see *Mosiah 4:2-6*) we may find peace. It is entirely possible to create a heaven in our hearts if we yield our own will to God and follow a few simple steps. These steps are amply expressed in a small book written by Don Miguel Ruiz called The Four Agreements. Therein Ruiz talks about the multitude of agreements we make with others and ourselves that keep us in a state of suffering and how to replace those agreements with four simple agreements that will alleviate ninety percent of our suffering. In short these agreements are: 1—Be impeccable with your word or in other words, speak with integrity, say only that which is true and avoid using our words against ourselves or others. 2—Don't take anything that others say or do personally, realizing that all things they do and say are a reflection of their own perception of reality, not yours. 3—Don't make assumptions or rather communicate clearly and concisely with others. 4—Always do your best in any and all situations. This will eliminate any sense of guilt.

My point is that much of our suffering is because of our own weaknesses and it is not only possible, it should be our aim, our goal to rise above such self inflicted suffering. Ruiz's book can change your life if you will follow his four simple agreements. They are correct principles and I can testify they will take you to higher ground. I highly recommend you obtain a copy and discover some uncomplicated solutions to finding peace and creating a heaven in the midst of this mortal hell in which we find ourselves.

Notwithstanding any and all attempts at avoiding suffering in this life, I still maintain that to absolutely do so would thwart the plan of ultimate joy God has for us. Suffering is not only right, it is vital to our comprehension of and our relationship with God and how to come to know Him, to be one with Him, to love Him, to love His laws, to love His truths, and to love His operations upon us. Understanding that **suffering and pain are an inherent part of life** forces us to look to God in faith, to try to know His will, to give up our own will, and to appeal to Him for the power to do His. If we resolve to do this, it will give meaning to our sacrifices and our suffering. It will insure that our sufferings have not been wasted. Greatest of all, it will enable us to have faith in the God that created us which will make possible our return to a higher state where our powers will be great and our delight will be in truth and a **fullness** of joy.

---

[89] **The book of Abraham is found in *The Pearl of Great Price* (P of G P). See footnote on *The Pearl of Great Price.***

[90] **Mormons believe that Satan was in the preexistence with all the rest of the spirits God created. Satan rebelled and was cast down. See endnote about Moses 4 under chapter 3. Also see Revelations 12:3-9, D&C 29:26-39, Moses 4:3 in the P of G P.**

[91] **The Mormons between 1839 and 1846 built Nauvoo on the banks of the Mississippi River. As the headquarters of The Church, it was a city of considerable size for its day (15,000 at its peak). Its economy was agriculture, manufacturing, and shipping. In the winter of 1846, approximately two years after the martyrdom of Joseph Smith, the Mormons were driven out by mob persecution.**

[92] **The Brother of Jared, whose name was Mahonri Moriancumer, was a prophet who lived about 2200 BC. His people, the Jaredites, came from the great tower of Babel, in Mesopotamia, to the Western Hemisphere. Their record or history was found by the Nephite people and is contained in *The Book of Mormon* (see the book of Ether). He is best remembered for his great faith.**

[93] **Laman was the brother of Nephi. He rebelled against his family and the teachings of God. The Lamanites were called after him and were, generally, the more unrighteous people of *The Book of Mormon.***

7
Who's The Boss?

The Agreement

One of the greatest secrets kept by The Mormon Church is the kind of relationship the Gods have with each other. Understanding more about this would help us understand ourselves, and our relationship with God. We have already talked about the oneness of the Gods which enables each to have all power, all knowledge, all glory, and etc., but if they are one, who's the boss?

When I first opened a business some years ago, I went into partnership with a friend I knew through a company for which we had both worked. I guess we figured if we could make money for the company, we could make more money for ourselves. He and I sat down to outline the parameters of our partnership; who would do what and who would get what. We had both been warned about partnerships, how they didn't work without having everything in writing. So we attempted to put it all in writing. After several hours, flared tempers, and hurt feelings, we were no further along than at the first, and this was at the start of the partnership. We were very much concerned with protecting ourselves, deciding who had what authority, quantifying contributions, and keeping score. We nearly turned ourselves into lawyers by the time we finished drafting the multiple page document laying down what we thought was every possible future eventuality of our partnership. We even covered what our families would get in case of our deaths or the dissolution of our partnership. The document was, from the beginning, a source of consternation and it remained so throughout the life of our relationship. We were constantly changing the wording to cover a situation we failed to think of beforehand. Neither he nor I were at all content that this document would protect our individual interests, nor did it satisfy the needs of the partnership, as invariably something would come up that we had not foreseen.

I was convinced it was the document itself that made the whole thing so difficult, so I abandoned the writing of an agreement in the next partnership I entered. I have been in partnerships of one kind or another at least a dozen times since, some of them good experiences and others not so good. Whether the particulars were in writing done by us or by an attorney, or there was no formal document at all, there have been problems with authority, protection, and distribution of assets. For a long time I held to the belief that such issues were unavoidable and unsolvable.

Being a "good" Mormon, I determined that bringing celestial principles into the partnership would surely eliminate the problems. As I contemplated the various principles I thought to be celestial and how to bring them into the partnership, I made an interesting discovery. I found there is no such thing as a partnership in a celestial environment.

The Proclamation

"Oh," you say, "that can't be true. Partnerships have been prevalent down through time. They are a way of life." Yes, but not a celestial way of life. If you say that a partnership means only an association with one or more persons, I might make a concession to the above statement. But you will not find the word partnership in the scriptures, as this is a relatively modern term. You will find the word used in our most recent modern scripture, *A Family Proclamation To The World.*[94] Some will argue that this is not scripture because it is not included in the Mormon *sanctioned* scriptures: *The Holy Bible*, *The Book of Mormon*, *The Doctrine and Covenants*, or *The Pearl of Great Price*. Let me refer you to our former discussion on truth and where it is found. "And whatsoever they shall speak when moved upon by the Holy Ghost *shall be scripture*, shall be the will of the Lord, shall be the mind of the Lord, shall be the word of the Lord, shall be the voice of the Lord, and the power of God unto salvation." (*D&C 68:4*) There is so much powerful doctrine in *A Family Proclamation To The World* concerning the sanctity of marriage and the role of the family in the eternal scheme of God's plan, that you should laminate it and put it with your other scriptures as the revealed word of God through His prophets. When the word partner is used in the scriptures, it is in reference to or means an *association* only. This quote in *A Family Proclamation To The World* is no different. "By divine design, fathers are to preside over their families in love and righteousness and are responsible to provide the necessities of life and protection for their families. Mothers are primarily responsible for the nurture of their children. In these sacred responsibilities, fathers and mothers are obligated to help one another *as equal partners*." (*A Proclamation To The World by The First Presidency and Council of the Twelve Apostles, in General Relief Society Meeting, Sept. 23, 1995*) The brethren here are not addressing the properties of partnerships but are trying to make the point that the role of the woman is equally as important as the man's. "Nevertheless neither is the man without the woman, neither the woman without the man, in the Lord." (*1 Corinthians 11:11*) Though their roles are different, one cannot do without the other. One is no more important than the other. They are equal in the sight of the Lord and any attempt to make the man more significant than the woman because he is appointed to preside over her is a violation of the will and law of God.

I Did My Part

Still, I cringe when I hear people say that marriage is a 50/50 partnership. Even as an *association* it is a 100/100. Each must do **all** within his or her power to make it work, not do 50 percent and sit back waiting for the other to do his/her 50 percent. That is *quantifying contributions* and *keeping score*. This is not done in a celestial environment. Again, *there is no such thing as a partnership in heaven!*

Typically, in our understanding today, a partnership describes fixed personal interests in a business, usually equal interest. By definition, like my first partner and I tried to do, a partnership defines the *separateness* of the interests each has in the joint venture. The participants don't own one thing in common, but own different parts, rights to separate portions, or assets of the one thing. These rights are limited and bound by the partnership agreement. Who owns what? Who owes what? Who pays what? Who gets what? Who must do what? Who cannot do what? This separateness of a partnership renders it a lesser law and not applicable or viable in a Zion Society or heaven. "But," you say, "isn't God in partnership with Christ?" No, a thousand times no! Nor is God in partnership with anyone else, including our mother in heaven. This secret has somehow been kept even from most Mormons, as they always seem surprised to discover this bit of information. Partnerships are, at best, a terrestrial law. Again for emphasis, ***there is no such thing as a partnership in heaven!***

The Corporation

I have come to believe that corporations are a terrestrial law also. When you think about it, to create a corporation is to create an entity, in fact, an unreal person or being, which is not responsible for its acts. That is the whole purpose of a corporation, to protect the individuals making the decisions from being sued for making those decisions. That's what is called the "corporate veil" and it means that those with a fiduciary responsibility to run the company may do as they choose while only the corporation, not they individually, may be held responsible or sued. This is how the officers of a corporation can bleed a company dry with huge salaries to themselves and when the company is no longer solvent, unable to operate, they declare bankruptcy, leaving all creditors and stockholders high and dry, with no recourse. If that's not immoral, I don't know what is; yet it is legal and considered an acceptable way of doing business. It is another means of giving big business the advantage over the small business. Further, the greatest tax advantage is given the corporation by the government of this country by permitting different fiscal tax years. This allows big business to create several different corporations with different tax years and by means of shuffling assets and liabilities around on paper, no company shows a profit at their tax deadline. The profits grow and keep circling between companies, never being taxed. Again, though legal, if it is not immoral, I don't know what is. To my mind, it is white-collar crime sanctioned by the government. But enough on corporations, let's get back to partnerships.

Who Was Supposed To Do It?

As I said, partnerships are a terrestrial law. So, "What is wrong with partnerships?" you ask. Nothing, if you want to live a terrestrial law. One problem lies in *authority* and *accountability*. In other words, who has the ultimate authority, and who is finally accountable? Having two or more persons at the same level of responsibility and authority complicates and hinders the progress of any given situation. Can you imagine standing before God on the judgment day, in a partnership, trying to sort out who was responsible for what? It's like trying to get something done in a committee situation where the task is not specifically assigned to an individual. When it is time to report, just try to find who is responsible for the task not being accomplished. You see the difficulty? Remember, *where authority is shared equally, no one has any authority*. But you say, "This could be averted in a partnership situation by simply dividing duties and assigning responsibilities to individuals." But who has the authority to make such assignments, and authority of recourse if the job is left undone, or to settle disputes? "Well," you say, "you simply divide the authority too." Well enough, but you then end up in a situation like my first partnership, with an inadequate document that grows in size as the partnership keeps facing situations that have not already been considered. This is the very reason we have courts and immense law libraries with shelves filled with cases and documents trying to settle disputes between those who allege to be partners. I believe the only way partnerships work (and statistically most do not) is that those involved settle in to either dominant or recessive, predictable roles.

What Then?

Well, if there are no partnerships in heaven, what is there? There are *stewardships*. "It is wisdom in me; therefore, a commandment I give unto you, that ye shall organize yourselves and appoint every man his stewardship. That every man may give an *account unto me* of the stewardship which is appointed unto him. For it is expedient that I, the Lord, should make every man *accountable*, as a steward over earthly blessings, which I have made and prepared for my creatures." (*D&C 104:11-13*) What's the difference? Well, let's see. "And verily in this thing ye have done wisely, for it is required of the Lord, at the hand of every steward, to render an account of his stewardship, both in time and in eternity. For he who is faithful and wise in time is accounted worthy to inherit the mansions prepared for him of my Father." (*D&C 72:3-4*) Stewardships are the celestial means of controlling activities, at the core of which is the doctrine of *oneness*. In other words, of what God *has*, He *assigns* (not gives) a portion to us, making us stewards. This is not God hiring us to do something. **There are no hirelings in heaven either**. No. In a stewardship situation the steward holds their particular stewardship in common with those who are stewards over and under them. Each possesses the stewardship *in common, together*, not each having a part. As we improve upon our stewardships we are assigned more, until we have in common with God (the highest steward with which we have to deal) all that He has. Let me elaborate.

In my own case, I have been in a business "partnership" with a man for over 20 years. His name is Bruce Inglis. Other partners have come and gone in quite a number of enterprises, yet Bruce and I are still together. In reality though, it is not a *partnership*. We both have determined to make it a *stewardship* and bring as many celestial principles to our alliance as we can. At the outset, it was decided that in the film production company we own, I would be the head steward. We have had two other business ventures where it was decided that Bruce would be the head steward. These were the first decisions made and all others came from them. When there was disagreement, and there was ample, the head steward made the final decision as the ultimate authority rested with him. Whether it was Bruce or me who had the ultimate say, when the discussion was over and the decision was final, the other got behind that decision 100 percent. There was no further argument, dragging of feet, "I told you so's," or blaming if the decision didn't quite work out. Bruce and I have, with this philosophy, accomplished a great deal over the years.

The Circles

So, how do stewardships work? Well, make a circle and put within all the people and things over which you have authority and are responsible. Looking beyond that circle you would find you are engulfed in others' circles or stewardships. It might look a little like this.

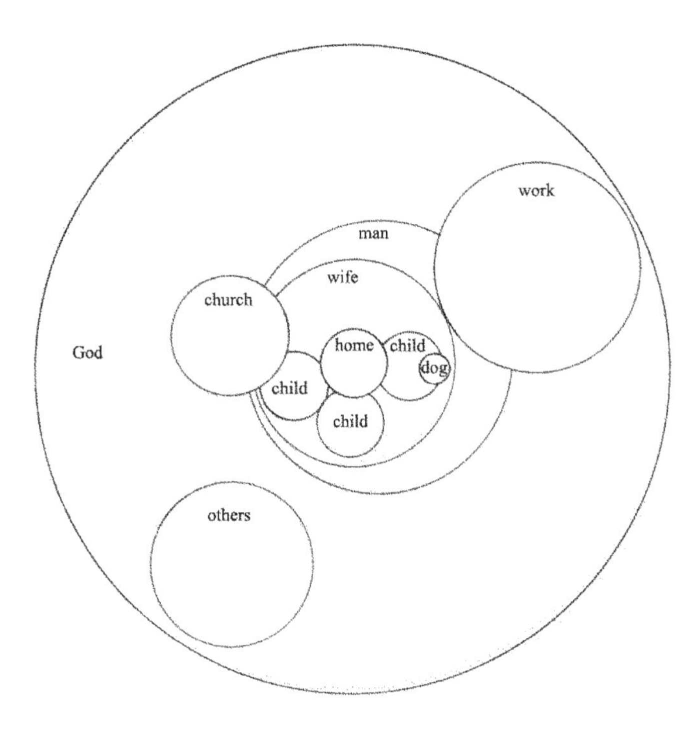

In the above over-simplified illustration, you will note that the man's stewardship encompasses the wife, home, children, and dog. The dog is first the duty and responsibility of the child steward, then the mother steward, then the father steward. Though the man may not be directly responsible for taking care of the dog, as this is an assigned duty or stewardship to the child, the father is responsible for what the child does or fails to do, as the dog falls within the wife's stewardship which, in turn, falls within his stewardship as well. Ultimately, God is responsible as all things and people fall within His stewardship, His scope of responsibility. You will also note that each child does not have stewardship responsibility over the other children, the man's work falls within his stewardship but not his wife's (more on this shortly), and church may fall within the scope of several of the household.

By Assignment

Which stewardship is whose, and what each will encompass, is a matter of ***assignment by those in the stewardships over them***. Note also that we do not outright individually or personally own our stewardships. There is a *singular* ownership by all. As expressed by the circles above, possession of the same falls within the greater stewardship, and so on, back to the grand steward over us all, God. Such a system is certainly not a democracy, and you may say that such a system seems more like a theocracy, monarchy, or a dictatorship; not exactly. Notwithstanding the supreme power and authority being vested in one individual (God, the King) who is the highest steward in a stewardship, each person has his or her own power and authority and, like God, governs his or her own stewardship according to his or her own will and pleasure. Of course they must be responsible for, report to, and be obedient to their higher stewards. Nevertheless, God, who created us, appointed each of us our stewardships. He gave us the authority, power, and responsibility of that stewardship. The authority of each steward does not rest with a committee or even a partnership, nor are the decisions of that stewardship made by a democratic vote. It rests solely with the steward, who is answerable to the steward above him/her. They can handle their stewardship according to their own good will and pleasure (as God Himself does) as long as it does not conflict with the mandates of the stewards above them.

The Church today nearly follows the pattern of the stewardship system in that we do not vote on matters but rather sustain the decision of those in authority over us. Our Bishops do not make decisions by committee. Although they may delegate power and authority to others, although they may take counsel from any number of people (including their counselors), they make the final decision and must stand accountable for it.

Church AND Kingdom

I feel obliged here to make the distinction between *The Church* of God and *The Kingdom* of God. I have discovered that many Mormons see them as the same thing, but they are two separate entities. The first (The Church) is with us, well organized, in full function, but will eventually pass away. The second (The Kingdom) has hardly begun to be established but when it is, will consume the entire earth and will never pass away. I mention this here because we need to understand that the order and government of each is a little different in that when it is fully established, the Kingdom of God, being a celestial order, will be patriarchal stewardships. The Church, with its order and government, will continue very much as it is until it has fulfilled its purpose and passes away (more on this later).

How Come He's Over Me?

Now you may be asking why the wife's stewardship is included in the man's but not all the man's is encompassed in the wife's? That's because it is not a partnership. The husband-wife relationship is **not** a partnership. There, I said it! *Marriage is not a partnership it is a* ***stewardship*** or should be.

As stated above, I realize that many General Authorities have said that marriage is a partnership but, for the reasons herein established, I can only hope they meant that it is an *association*. As an association, I can readily see where one might say we are in partnership with the Lord but it should more properly be described as our stewardship within the Lord's stewardship. Whether the relationship is with the Lord, a business associate, or a husband or wife, someone must ultimately be in charge. Someone must be The Boss. This is the celestial order. This is celestial law.

I know this goes against the grain of many women who are, without a doubt, smarter and more capable than the men within whose stewardship they find themselves. Well, the fact is, it is not based upon strength, intelligence, know-how, or any other ability of either person. Again, **it is *based on the assignments made by the higher authority or steward*.** These assignments are made upon whatever basis the higher steward chooses, for whatever reason he/she might have. Why God has put the woman and man in their respective places and whether that will ever change, I cannot say, nor would I venture to try. To me it is a little like asking why I am the son of my father, subordinate to him, and must respect his position, or why my boss at work, my bishop at church, or a prophet, or Christ is in a higher position of authority than I, when they are only my brothers?[95] I would not presume to ask. I feel certain that God, the highest steward of all, has His reasons and they, no doubt, relate to need and the saving of souls (among them mine).

I would also say that, in God's eyes, being in a lesser stewardship (a position of lesser authority) does not mean that one is consigned to an inferior place, joy, glory, or happiness. Though this is hard for men and women alike to accept, being a woman encompassed in a man's stewardship ***does not make them inferior to the men in any way.*** Joseph Fielding Smith made it clear when he said, "There is nothing in the teachings of the gospel which declares that men are superior to women. The Lord has given unto men the power of priesthood and sent them forth to labor in His service. A woman's calling is in a different direction. The most noble, exalting calling of all is that which has been given to women as the mothers of men. Women do not hold the priesthood, but if they are faithful and true, they will become priestesses and queens in the kingdom of God, and that implies that they will be given authority. The women do not hold the priesthood with their husbands, but they do reap the benefits coming from that priesthood." (*Joseph Fielding Smith Jr. Doctrines of Salvation,*

Vol.3, p 178) I will say, relative to the above quote, that you need not concern yourself should you be single or a woman unable to have children. It does not negate the promise of being a priestess and queen in the Kingdom of God. They will have the opportunity to be mothers. In the words of Brigham Young, "Many of the sisters grieve because they are not blessed with offspring. You will see the time when you will have millions of children around you. If you are faithful to your covenants, you will be mothers of nations." (*DBY pg. 200*) The point is that these and many other anomalies will be taken care of by the Lord in His own time. The most important thing is that all faithful stewards, male and female, will be joint-heirs with Christ entitled to inherit all that the Father has. If they do their duty, there will be no less joy or glory given to those who were assigned positions of lesser authority or to a woman who is in the man's stewardship.

Further, having the feeling of being lesser seems to me a moot issue, since everyone has many stewards over them: fathers, mothers, several bosses at the office, bishops, prophets, and even Christ. To be unhappy or unsatisfied with God's assignment is nothing less than prideful. Of course, that is easy for me to say as I am a man and have things in my stewardship that are not included in my wife's. Let me reiterate. Just because she is not running the show, a woman is no less entitled to the Gift of The Holy Ghost or any and all other gifts of the spirit the Lord may deem proper to give her. This includes gifts of power, great power, that are presently only associated with priesthood callings. God's gifts know no gender.

Personally speaking, I often think I would rather not have so much of the responsibility assigned to me. I sometimes hate the responsibilities and the expectations others have of me just because I happen to be a man. I would sooner hand them off to anyone willing to take them. On the other hand, my heart goes out to single mothers, struggling to take up the slack, having the weight of responsibility heaped upon them, not only of their stewardship, but that of the absent steward. I can't help but want to reach out to them and try to lift some of their burden. Not that they can't handle it, but who wants to walk alone? Life is hard enough; we need allies in our struggles. God bless them.

I also must say on this subject that many of the duties stereotypically assigned to one gender or the other are simply that, assignments. Such assignments are often social tradition and have nothing at all to do with what is proper, moral, right, or true. I *believe* we would all do well to quit playing the gender game. I *know* we would be better off if we would treat each other according to performance and ability rather than gender, and seek equal treatment and fair consideration of each.

Part of Each Other

I will say; it is a fool who doesn't counsel with, take advice from, and support those who are within his or her stewardship. Though I've seen it happen more times than I care to count, it is counter-productive to not assist our subordinate stewards with their stewardships as they are within and part of our own. What is theirs is ours. It would be like shooting ourselves in the foot, or cutting off our nose to spite our face. It is administering poison to our self not to give every aid in our power to those who are part of us, that is, those who are within our stewardship. Though they have the power to do so by virtue of their position as stewards, mistreatment of subordinates by their stewards, **for any reason**, is particularly reprehensible. "We have learned by sad experience that it is the nature and disposition of almost all men, as soon as they get a little authority, as they suppose, they will immediately begin to exercise unrighteous dominion. Hence many are called, but few are chosen. No power or influence can or ought to be maintained by virtue of the priesthood, only by persuasion, by long-suffering, by gentleness and meekness, and by love unfeigned." (*D&C 121:39-41*) Abuse, of any kind, of anyone within our stewardship will condemn us to lose that stewardship. Also, please know that the more righteous we all become, the more *one of mind and heart* we will be, and the less controlling there will be in stewardships, until we reach a point where we all simply grow, create, and report our improvements without restraint.

One Without The Other?

The responsibility without authority and power impedes the ability of the steward to do his or her job. This is a major mistake I often see in management. Many people are willing to give another person the responsibility of a task but will not relinquish the power or authority of that position. Of course, to give someone the authority and power without the responsibility is a waste, as the job will likely not get done. I have made it a habit of *demanding* the authority and power whenever someone gives me a responsibility.

Creativity, Agency, And Individuality Preserved

That doesn't mean I go my way and do anything I want. I expect to have limits and parameters as well as receive advice, particularly on things I have never done before. It does mean, however, that those in authority over me must let me do it the best way I can. If it must be done *their way only*, then I give them back the responsibility. It can't work any other way. This freedom within our appointed stewardships allows for personal expression, thereby preserving our creativity and individuality. Our individuality, creativity, and agency are not taken from us, as they would be, say, in a dictatorial, a communistic, or even a democratic system. This is no small distinction as commitment is far greater when a person has an involvement in the processes of a particular program. We may develop, within the parameters of our assigned authority, our own style and methods; what remains constant is the accountability for our actions.

As I have often been found in a position of authority, I recognize that when giving a person an assignment, I must pass on a certain amount of power and authority, then cut that person enough slack to allow them to get the job done. A steward must accept the honest attempt of his or her subordinates. Like God, we must be patient with those who are growing, as long as they are trying. To God, it is the growth of the apprentice that is important, not the success of the program in which they may be involved. Short of no effort on the part of the lower steward, the higher steward must not take back the duty and authority of that duty, but must help them understand their duty and assist them to accomplish it. This is the obligation of each steward. As simple as this law is, I see it violated constantly by those who *can't let go*, those who must have it done *their way*. I also see people demanding power and authority they don't need. Then we wonder why we have relationship and management problems.

The Promise

I must say here, that whatever our stewardships, it is a matter of personal integrity to do our level best to faithfully discharge our duties, relative to them. There is a saying that I love dearly and have placed its meaning securely at the foundation of my scaffolding to heaven. I cannot remember its source, so I will put it in quotes, as it is not mine. It goes like this, "Good relationships are based upon two principles, wisdom and integrity. Integrity is making good your promises and wisdom is knowing when not to promise." I believe that one of the most shameful things a person can do is not keep his or her word or commitments. "But whoso keepeth His word, in him verily is the love of God perfected: hereby know we that we are in Him." (*1 John 2:5*)

To me, it is particularly appalling whenever a proclaimed Christian is found so lacking. Said Christ to the scribes, "But what think ye? A certain man had two sons; and came to the first and said, Son, go work today in my vineyard. He answered and said, I will not; but afterward he repented, and went. And he came to the second, and said likewise. And he answered and said, I go, sir. And went not. Whether of them twain did the will of his father? They say unto Him, the first. Jesus saith unto them, Verily I say unto you, That the publicans and the harlots go into the kingdom of God before you." (*Matthew 21:28-32*) I know we all fall down in our responsibilities at times and no one is perfect, but a pattern of unfulfilled promises is disgraceful. As the above saying goes, it shows a lack of integrity or wisdom. Notwithstanding the fact that I have found more dedicated people within the organization of The Mormon Church than I have ever found in any other fraternity, too often I see members casually making promises that they fail to keep. I guess that since it is a church with unpaid lay ministers and volunteers, some think that they are somehow not obligated to keep their commitments. Too often, when the call is issued to help at the cannery,[96] go to the temple, be on a dinner committee, get involved in a road show or ward play, teach a class, or work on a project, we casually sign our names to the roster without due consideration to the commitment we are making. Then, when we find ourselves over-committed, something better comes up, or whatever, instead of salvaging some integrity by finding someone to take our place or, in the very least, giving proper notice to the person that is counting on us, we forget about it. Again, I personally find this disgraceful and I am quite certain the Lord does too.

Of course this problem is not limited to The Mormon Church. In fact, it permeates every industry and walk of life. I see husbands and wives failing to keep their marriage covenants. I see children failing to fulfill their assignments to take out the garbage, mow the lawn, or do the dishes, even after they have agreed to do it. I see employers, laborers, businessmen, and politicians going back on their word, not keeping their promises. What happens to the relationships with those to whom we have made those promises? Perhaps we would all do well to not give our word so quickly. We need to consider whether we really want to or are even able to keep our commitments before we make them. It is often greater wisdom to say no. Should we decide it is right to commit, then we should break our backs making good those promises.

Sometimes we find ourselves with stewardship commitments requiring far more than we bargained for. The Lord Himself often puts us in situations and calls us to tasks that require sacrifices or dedication we had no idea they would involve. I am thinking of life itself. In fact, most of life's endeavors are that way: Marriage, careers, having children. Who knows what is involved until going through it? Still, does that absolve us of our responsibility to do our very best? No, it does not. Whatever our stewardships or however we came by them, the Lord expects us to do our best, and I don't mean to **just try**, but actually **do our best**. "I'll try" is *noncommittal*. It is a cop out, a door left open to failure. To fulfill our stewardship is a matter of personal integrity. To break our promises is to bring ruin to our relationship with those within our stewardship and those within whose stewardship we find ourselves. Remember, God is the great steward and our relationship with Him depends upon our honest, best effort to keep our promises to Him and His children.

United We Stand

There is also a continuity of purpose in stewardships. All persons concerned have the same objectives, personal motivations, and general commitment to any given goal. What helps one helps all. Of course, when all involved in any particular resolution are righteous, they all receive the same inspiration from the same source of truth and are thereby united in mind having no dissension. This is one of the greatest characteristics of stewardships, that they do not *separate* as partnerships do, they *unite*. Stewardships do not *subject*, as other forms of ventures, they *include*. Are you aware that when the twelve apostles[97] meet in counsel on any given issue, they come to unanimity of what is the proper course to take? That isn't to say they do not have differing opinions going in but not withstanding their differences and respective stewardships, when a vote is taken it is not a majority vote, or even a two-thirds majority, but a unanimous *sustaining* vote. They are all motivated by the same inspiration, spirit of truth. This is not difficult when all concerned are actually in search of truth and rid themselves of pride, personal ambition, jealousy, envy, and etc. "Only by pride cometh contention." (*Proverbs 13:10*) "One mind, one heart." This is the description of a Zion Society.

You may say that the twelve apostles live in a more perfect environment and that their situation does not apply to us; but isn't this what we should all be working to achieve in our own associations and stewardships? Oneness of mind and heart is possible in this life. Really, it is.

Even Steven or Consecration

There is another aspect of the relationship between the Gods that needs stating. My business associate, Bruce, and I have found this concept very important to our success. That is the celestial *law of consecration*. The word consecration means to sanctify, canonize, or to give a hallowed gift. You may have noticed that the two words, consecration and stewardship, in the Mormon

Church, are often used in conjunction. Relative to our business relationship, we have tried to live this law of consecration and stewardship. What I mean by that is that both of us, so far as it is possible, owing first to our other obligations (wives, families, and etc.), consecrate or commit all we have to the stewardship. There is not ever, I repeat, **not ever** any *scorekeeping* or *quantifying* and valuing of our individual contributions. We always try to be fair *with* the other but never demand fairness *from* the other. You can't even think about what is fair or equal as evaluating contributions in that way is not celestial. You simply have to accept that things are rarely fair or equal in this mortal world. Justice is even wanting here.

I presume this lack of justice and equality in the world does not come as a shock to anyone. I remember the very day when this realization came to me. It is sad but true, those who have an acute sense of fairness and equality are some of the most frustrated people I know. You are stuck in this telestial world that doesn't care for these principles, so all I can say is, *get over it*. I know it is easier said than done, especially for those who try to be fair, equitable, and just themselves. Also, this bad news is no excuse to give up and not to work for fairness, justice, and equality. I believe that a full measure of these things will be found in a Zion Society[98] (more on the Zion Society later).

Giving no thought to what is fair, Bruce has worked hard to financially keep my family and me going. He has sacrificed much in my behalf, and I in his. When it comes to distributing the money or assets, they go to he who *needs them most*. The checkbook requires either my name ***or*** his, not both. He could wipe me out at any given time and I him. But this is a relationship built on trust. It is a relationship of care, love, and devotion. So far as is possible in this lesser environment, we live the Law of Consecration and Stewardship,[99] at least with each other. This relationship was not easy to achieve, but it has given us much hope in the future of humanity. Not unlike those men who face death together in the heat of battle, we have shared much, faced much, have overcome much, and have enjoyed much. We are often so one in mind and heart that, without a word, we know what the other is thinking. I don't know anyone, save my wife, who knows me so well and still loves me.

How To Live It

To live this law means to rid oneself of some **not so virtuous** personal character traits such as jealousy, personal ambition, selfishness, faultfinding, egotism, insecurity, distrust, envy, rivalry, spite, contention, competition, and coveting. These personal traits must be replaced with compassion, selflessness, and love.

There is an excellent musical play written by Carol Lynn Pearson with music by Lex De Azevedo called *The Order is Love*. The story is historically based on a small town in Southern Utah called Orderville where a group of Saints, under the direction of Brigham Young, for nearly ten years, lived what was called the United Order[100] (I will comment further on the United Order in a subsequent chapter). This United Order was a giant step toward the Law of Consecration and Stewardship, the celestial way God lives. The play is not only well done, having all the elements of superb writing, characterizations, situation comedy, music, plot, and etc. (as a filmmaker, these things are important to me), but it shows the kind of love and personal virtues as well as the dedication necessary to live such a high law. Sadly, despite a valiant attempt, it also shows the failure of Orderville. It graphically shows that without these virtues in each and every person participating, it will fail. Having come to know the play well, I have concluded that not only is this, by far, the greatest musical ever written by Mormon people about Mormon people, but it is profound in its message, a message we would all do well to devour and keep close to our hearts. This play should be a required event for every stake[101] in The Church.

The Joy of It

I want to say here that the relationship Bruce and I have developed over the years is wonderful, to say the least. We often joke about our determination to save each other's souls and how great will be our joy for so doing after laboring what seems a whole life with each other. "And if it so be that you should labor all your days in crying repentance unto this people, and bring, save it be one soul unto me, how great shall be your joy with him in the kingdom of my Father!" (*D&C 18:15*) We still don't know, however, who is saving whose soul, but we do know our joy is already great.

The Eye of A Needle

Before I end this chapter on stewardships let me make an observation that may certainly be classed as judgmental on my part. As I have had occasion to drive through this beautiful state of Utah, in which I live, I am sometimes stunned at how many huge mansions I see dotting the hills. I wonder if these people really need such large homes (many of them in excess of 5 or 6 thousand square feet)? I also see an abundance of boats, jet skis, campers, motor homes, quad runners, and other expensive toys. My observations are not just limited to Utahans as this is probably typical everywhere I travel. I wonder if this is a very wise disposition of what the Lord has blessed us with in our stewardships. I wonder how many of these people need or can really afford such things or have we become slaves to them, requiring both parents to hold jobs in order to keep up payments on the debt? Even if we are blessed with a great income should we spend it all on bigger, better, and more expensive things just because we can? Is there not a better use of surplus and abundance? Of course it is easy for me to pass this judgment as I have never been blessed with great wealth and perhaps there is something about it that I don't understand. Still, "Jesus said unto him, If thou wilt be perfect, go and sell that thou hast, and give to the poor, and thou shalt have treasure in heaven; and come and follow me. But when the young man heard that saying, he went away sorrowful; for he had great possessions. Then said Jesus unto his disciples, Verily I say unto you, that a rich man shall hardly enter into the kingdom of heaven. And again I say unto you, It is easier for camel to go through the eye of a needle, than for a rich man to enter into the kingdom of God." *(Matthew 19: 21-24)*

I have a good friend that has made a really wonderful living for some twenty years now and has always spent that and more thinking that the river would always run to his door. Now he is experiencing difficulty in his career and stands a very good chance of losing it all.

When I see such opulence it causes me to take a closer look at myself to see if my heart is not set too much upon the things of this world. "Behold, there are many called, but few are chosen. And why are they not chosen? Because *their hearts are set so much upon the things of this world . . . .*" *(D&C 121:34)*

Let us be found wise and profitable stewards, having improved upon that which, belonging to the Lord, has been entrusted to our care and keeping, that we may assimilate glory to ourselves as we bring glory to Him.

---

[94] ***A Family Proclamation to the World*** **is a statement by the prophet Gordon B. Hinckley, his counselors, and the Council of the Twelve Apostles. The proclamation was given to The Church as part of Elder Hinckley's message at General Relief Society Meeting on September 23, 1995. It contains doctrine and revelation on the sanctity of the family and its place in the eternal plan of God. A copy of this proclamation may be obtained from any Church library.**

[95] **Mormons believe that as spirit children in our pre-mortal state, we were all brothers and sisters, including Christ and Lucifer (Satan).**

[96] **For the assistance of the poor, The LDS Church has welfare farms and food canneries that administer to the physical, temporal needs of its members.**

[97] **Along with the Prophet and his counselors, there are twelve apostles administering the affairs of The LDS Church. See endnote #2.**

[98] **See endnote #50 on Zion Society.**

---

[99] **The Law of Consecration and Stewardship is the economic system of the Zion Society.**

[100] **The saints, under Brigham Young, as a deterrent to economic dependency on outside sources, instituted the United Order, a derivative of the Law of Consecration and Stewardship. It was also a kind of experiment to see if the saints could live a communal order. There were over 200 United Orders formed between 1874 and 1893. They took many forms in their operations, the most famous and most successful of which was the wholly independent town of Orderville in Southern Utah, which lasted for nearly 10 years. The main difference between the United Order and the Law of Consecration and Stewardship is that the United Order strips the person of their individualism whereas the Law of Consecration and Stewardship does not. (For a complete treatise, see *Encyclopedia of Mormonism*, Vol. 4: United Orders.)**

[101] **A Stake is a geographical area like a parish or diocese, overseen by a Stake President and High Council. It usually has several wards within its boundaries which are smaller areas overseen by bishops and their counselors. The Stake gets its name from the Children of Israel who, in their travels, would set up camps by driving a stake into the ground, which designated the center of each tribe's area of jurisdiction.**

8
Prophecy
or
The Future Is Now

A Very Great Undertaking

When I set sail upon this journey to bring into the open some of the secrets we of The Mormon Church unwittingly keep, not only from the world but ourselves as well, I recognized that some of our greatest secrets are the prophecies of the latter-days. Because of the abundance of holy writ that has, through modern prophets, been given to the Mormons, we, of all the people on the face of the earth, should have a greater cognizance of the future events affecting it. Unfortunately, and I cannot say why, we do not take them seriously. We do not comprehend the big picture. We accept that the second coming of Christ in His glory is inherent in the great last purpose of this earth, but somehow miss the purpose itself. Consequently, although we may look forward to the unfolding of these latter-day events, it is not with understanding and peace of mind. Certainly, we talk of the storms that are on the horizon and recognize the importance, even the necessity of preparing for them, but we do not seem to perceive the relationship of these latter-day events to our personal lives.

This phenomenon may be due to our reluctance to believe that life, as we know it, will not go on forever. It may be due to our not understanding that the Kingdom of God on earth is the purpose and end of such events. It may be due to our fear of whether we will be worthy when Christ comes again. Or, it may also be due, partially at least, to our inability to put the prophecies into a form we can easily understand and visualize. I would in this chapter make the attempt to do so, but recognize that the subject itself demands a greater treatment than is possible to present here in one chapter. It would require an entire book. It also would require of me a presentation of things that I am not, as yet, prepared sufficiently to submit. So, I will postpone such an attempt and refer you to my next book.

Sorry!

9
The Zion Life, A Picture of Paradise

A Zion Society

Please observe that I have made a quantum leap by passing up the subject aroused in the previous chapter. There is much we know about the chaos that will engulf those who live through the wars and rumors of wars, famines and pestilence, earthquakes, volcanoes, seas heaving themselves beyond their bounds, and etc. These events will indeed be wonderful (wondrous), amazing, and magnificent as they transpire. To skip the ushering in of the Millennium and all the scenes leading up to and the event of the second coming of Christ in His glory is indeed a huge jump into the future. Still, for the reasons given in the previous chapter, I will move right on to one of the greatest secrets unwittingly kept by The Mormon Church. The secret is what it will be like to live in a Zion Society under celestial law.

I will here define Zion as not only two places, Jerusalem (old Zion) in Israel and the New Jerusalem (a city to be built in Missouri), but also as a state of mind describing the Saints of God, those who are *pure in heart* and of *one mind and one heart*, no matter where they might be. In other words, Zion can be anywhere a righteous individual or group of righteous Saints dwell. For the purposes of our discussion, I will herein refer mostly to the New Jerusalem, the city to be built on the American continent where the Saints will gather in the Zion Society that will be prepared to receive Christ at His second coming.

What will it be like, to live in a Zion Society? This is a subject almost never discussed in our religion classes. As often as we talk about latter-day prophecies and how we are looking, with professed anticipation, for the day we will return to Independence[102] in Jackson County, Missouri, to establish the New Jerusalem, we almost never talk about how that will occur or what it will be like to live in such a society. I can only surmise why this is so. I believe it is because the concept is nebulous and vague. Since we have no real experience with an actual Zion Society (I will later qualify this statement), we find it difficult to visualize. We don't really know the kind of life we will live, should we be chosen to do so. Again, this is a shame, as much has been revealed on the subject. You might note that I said we would be "chosen" to live in the Zion Society, because not just anyone will be accepted into this society. "There has been a day of calling, but the time has come for a day of choosing; and let those be chosen that are worthy. And it shall be manifest unto my servant, by the voice of the Spirit, those that are chosen; and they shall be sanctified; And inasmuch as they follow the counsel which they receive, they shall have power after many days to accomplish all things pertaining to Zion." (*D&C 105:35-37*)

Wait, I Thought I Had A Ticket In

The Lord here refers to a group that will be "chosen" and "sanctified" and they will be given power to establish Zion. Not all Mormons will be automatically chosen (probably relatively few). In fact not even all the active members will be chosen, as our activity in The Church does not necessarily equate to personal righteousness. Remember, the wheat and tares are growing together now. They have not yet been separated. The sad truth is that the members have embraced the world so completely that unfortunately The Church in general now resembles Babylon far more than a Zion Society. Again, in general, we are further from the Zion Society than we were when Joseph Smith first established The Church. I am not pointing fingers or assigning blame, only stating the obvious. Further, because of their personal righteousness, some out of The Church will be "chosen and sanctified" and will assist in establishing Zion (more on this group in a subsequent chapter). Only those who have developed a personal relationship with the Savior will be "chosen, sanctified, and given power" to establish the City of The Living God in Jackson County, Missouri. Only those who have been born of fire and the Holy Ghost will be candidates for such a calling. These men and women will become members of the General Assembly and The Church of The Firstborn (I will expand on The Church of the Firstborn and what it really means to be Born Again in a later chapter). Those chosen will already be living the celestial law or they will not be invited to become a part of the Zion Society.

After the western boundaries of the state of Missouri are swept clean[103] and a mountain is cast up in the center thereof,[104] the righteous of the earth will be called to go back and in the midst of general world chaos, build a city that will be called the New Jerusalem.

What Mountain?

As an aside, it was amazing to me, only more recently to discover, that Mormons generally do not believe there will be a mountain in the middle of Missouri when the city of New Jerusalem is built. Yet the prophecy is clear (italics for emphasis), "And it shall come to pass in the last days, that the *mountain* of the Lord's house shall be established in the *top of the mountains*, and shall be *exalted above the hills*; and all nations shall flow unto it. And many people shall go and say, Come ye, and let us *go up to the mountain* of the Lord, to the house of the God of Jacob; and He will teach us of His ways, and we will walk in His paths: for out of Zion shall go forth the law, and the word of the Lord from Jerusalem." (*Isaiah 2:2-3* see also *2 Nephi 12:2-3*) When I quote this scripture to my fellow Mormons I get, "Oh, but the Lord is speaking figuratively." It always amazes me how when we don't want to believe a prophesied miracle, we say that the prophet or the Lord is *speaking figuratively*. I guess people don't believe it can happen because Missouri is now very much a flat land, as if God cannot make the low places high and the high places low. How can one *go up to the mountain of the Lord,* without there being a mountain? Perhaps ones belief would be strengthened by knowing there is a fault line dissecting the state of Missouri. This fault line is over twenty times larger than the San Andreas Fault in California. I, for one, believe that this is a prophecy and that it will be literally fulfilled. Time will prove.

The Zion City

Anyway, twenty-four temples will be built in the New Jerusalem that will not be used for the ordinance work for which temples today are commonly used. "At the time when Joseph Smith was planning the temple in Kirtland,[105] he was also giving attention to developments in Missouri. In 1831 he had placed a cornerstone for a future temple at Independence in Jackson County, which had been designated as the 'center place' of Zion. In June 1833 he drew up a plat plan for the city of Zion, specifying that twenty-four temples or sacred buildings would be built in the heart of the city to serve a variety of priesthood functions. When the Latter-day Saints were forced to flee from Jackson County that fall, plans to build the city of Zion and its temples were postponed." (*Encyclopedia of Mormonism, Vol.4, TEMPLES*)[106]

It will be from this center stake that all the affairs of the ushering in of the second coming will be administered, as well as the government of the earth after His coming, "for out of Zion shall go forth the law." (*Isaiah 2:3*) These twenty-four temples will not be used for the work we Mormons now associate with temples. They will be administration buildings where Christ Himself will walk the halls and personally attend to not only the affairs of *The Church* of God, but *The Kingdom* of God as well. They are two different entities (more on this later). "We believe in the literal gathering of Israel and in the restoration of the Ten Tribes, that Zion (the New Jerusalem) will be built upon the American continent, that Christ will reign personally upon the earth; and, that the earth will be renewed and receive its paradisiacal glory." (*Articles of Faith #10, Pearl of Great Price*) "For the LORD hath chosen Zion; He hath desired it for His habitation." (*Psalms 132:13*) There is much to be said relative to this wondrous subject of the gathering and building up of the Zion City, the Zion Society, but it belongs in the previous chapter (the book I have yet to write); so let it here suffice to say that this city of the New Jerusalem, this Zion Society, will indeed be built as above stated.

Understanding The Zion Society

In my attempt to describe such a celestial society, let me start with a fundamental scripture in which is embedded the key to understanding and visualizing the Zion Society (italics for emphasis). "And Zion cannot be built up unless it is by the *principles of the law of the celestial kingdom*; otherwise I cannot receive her unto myself." (*D&C 105:5*) Read that quote again. It is a most important concept that we must keep in mind as we contemplate the Zion life. Only the celestial law will be lived there.

If that scripture is true, and I testify that it is, to understand what it will be like to reside in a celestial society, one need only know what is celestial law and what is not. (We will discuss more about ***the** Celestial Law, New Law*, or the *New and Everlasting Law or Covenant.*) It is not that difficult to determine what celestial law is. One need only imagine what it would be like to live in heaven with our Heavenly Father. You see; the laws are the same, in fact, **exactly** the same. According to that scripture we just read (*D&C 105:5*), the Zion Society will be, in fact, can *only* be built upon the *law of the celestial kingdom*.

Obedience: A Ticket In

Let me again here make it clear that not all the world will live the celestial law. There will be no telestial people remaining upon the earth after the consuming fire and other deadly events at the coming of Christ in His glory. Those that remain will be terrestrial and celestial. The terrestrial will be scattered over the whole world. ***Only those who are sanctified Born***

Again saints, living the celestial law will be invited to join with those in the New Jerusalem, the Zion Society, the utopian society about which prophets have prophesied, philosophers have dreamed, and poets have written for millennia past.

You may notice I ***emphasized*** only those who ***are living*** *the celestial law* will come to Zion. It is important to note here, that the requirements of the celestial kingdom or the celestial Zion Society must be complied with *prior* to entering. An example used by Joseph Smith on this subject I will relate here (italics for emphasis). "It is necessary for men to receive an understanding concerning the laws of the heavenly kingdom, *before* they are permitted to enter it: we mean the celestial glory. So dissimilar are the governments of men, and so diverse are their laws, from the government and laws of heaven, that a man, for instance, hearing that there was a country on this globe called the United States of North America, could take his journey to this place without first learning the laws of governments; but the conditions of God's kingdom are such, that all who are made partakers of that glory, are under the necessity of learning something respecting it *previous* to their entering into it. But the foreigner can come to this country without knowing a syllable of its laws, or even subscribing to obey them after he arrives. Why? Because the government of the United States does not require it: it only requires an obedience to its laws *after* the individual has arrived within its jurisdiction." (*TPJS, pg. 51*) Whether the kingdom of heaven or the kingdom of heaven on earth, the necessity to not only know the laws, but to be *living them*, is requisite.

Who Will Remain?

I said that there would be no telestial people upon the earth after the Millennium starts. This is because Babylon will be destroyed at Christ's coming. "And He cried mightily with a strong voice, saying, Babylon the great is fallen, is fallen, and is become the habitation of devils, and the hold of every foul spirit, and a cage of every unclean and hateful bird." (*Revelation 18:2*) You see, in these last days, two words will soon become paramount: Babylon and Zion. The word Babylon represents and describes all that is evil in the world. The word Zion represents and describes all that is good, pure, and true. These words not only characterize two opposing specific places (the city of Babylon and the city of the New Jerusalem), but a state of mind, or state of being, as well as a general description of the condition of the world in the last days. Babylon represents all the liars, murderers, thieves, adulterers, and otherwise evil persons, or in short, the telestial people of the world. These telestial people will all be destroyed at Christ's coming, leaving only terrestrial (honorable persons) and celestial (valiant persons) on the earth for the duration of the one thousand years. For support on this, let me refer you to Joseph Fielding Smith, Jr., who said, "When Christ comes, the earth will be changed and so will all upon its face. It will become a terrestrial world then and will so remain for 1,000 years; and all those who have lived a telestial law will be eliminated. They will be as stubble and be consumed. The earth will be cleansed from its wickedness and pass into the terrestrial order. This will necessitate a change in the very elements of the earth, and also of its inhabitants; yet they will still be mortal. Those who belong to the terrestrial order will dwell upon the earth during this period.

"Some members of The Church have an erroneous idea that when the Millennium comes all of the people are going to be swept off the earth except righteous members of The Church. That is not so. There will be millions of people, Catholics, Protestants, agnostics, Mohammedans, people of all classes, and of all beliefs, still permitted to remain upon the face of the earth, but they will be those who have lived clean lives, those who have been free from wickedness and corruption. All who belong, by virtue of their good lives, to the terrestrial order, as well as those few who will have kept the celestial law will remain upon the face of the earth during the Millennium.

"Eventually, however, the knowledge of the Lord will cover the earth as the waters do the sea. But there will be need for the preaching of the gospel, after the Millennium is brought in, until all men are either converted or pass away. In the course of the thousand years all men will either come into The Church, or kingdom of God, or they will die and pass away." (*Joseph Fielding Smith Jr., Doctrines of Salvation, Vol.1, pg. 85-pg. 86*)

When all telestial people and telestial things are destroyed from off the face of the earth, the earth itself will become terrestrial (the middle of the three kingdoms of law and glory). Initially (at the start of the Millennium), the terrestrial people will be scattered throughout the entire world while the celestial people will be gathered to the Zions, the *Old* Zion in Jerusalem and the *new* Zion or the New Jerusalem, where Christ will personally govern the affairs of the world. These relatively few celestial people will still be mortal but will have undergone a physical and spiritual change and will live by celestial law and power. Eventually (as the Millennium progresses), the terrestrial people, including the newborns, will either be converted and live celestial laws, becoming a part of the expanded Zion Society, or die off. This will leave only celestial people on the earth by the end of the Millennium.

Now, in the following discussion I will refer only to that Zion Society of the New Jerusalem, the City (or Society) that will be located on the American continent and which will, during the Millennium, spread throughout and consume the world. I will not be referring to the terrestrial law or people that will also be living upon the earth at that time. Since the law of that Zion Society is the same as the law being lived in heaven, I will be comparing that celestial law to the laws we now live. Remember, to discover what it will be like to live in such a Zion Society, one need only imagine what it will be like to live in heaven, as the laws and conditions are, again, the same.

We're Not There Yet

As I said before, I can only surmise the reasons why we don't talk about what it will be like to dwell in such a wonderful society, but deep down, I am afraid it's because we have settled. We have *bought* into a lesser law. I know we are not telestial. We are not liars, sorcerers, adulterers, and whoremongers. Surely we are above that, but we are not celestial either, nor do we live by celestial laws. That leaves us somewhere in the terrestrial realm. We think we are living celestial laws, but most of the time we are not. When I make this statement, I catch a lot of flack from my fellow Saints who want to consider themselves celestial quality. They are simply not willing to admit that **we are not living celestial laws**. It is time now to qualify this statement, as I promised. Qualify, yes, explain, yes, but I will not back off of this statement. You will remember that we, the so-called Saints of the Latter-days, because of our vanity and unbelief, because we treat lightly the things we have been given, namely the mysteries of God or the priesthood keys to discover the same, are under condemnation, a scourge, and judgment (see *D&C 88:54*).

Please note, I am not saying we do not have celestial potential, or that we cannot or even that we *will* not live celestial law (though, frankly speaking, I am afraid that many will not). I am saying that **we are not presently doing so**. I am also sure that many members and non-members alike *would* live celestial laws if they knew them and were given an opportunity or be required to live them.

We all like to classify ourselves among those willing, but I sometimes wonder. According to the parable of the ten virgins, a parable that refers specifically to the members of The Church (the so-called Saints of the Latter-days), fifty percent will be found without sufficient oil in their lamps when the bridegroom comes. Five out of ten were not spiritually prepared. Those who were wise could not share of their oil, as it had to be obtained personally (see *Matthew*

25:1-13, and *D&C 45:56-59*). This is prophecy, truth of things as they are to come.

Concerning we so-called Saints of the Latter-day, let me again repeat what the Lord said to Nephi (italics for emphasis), "For behold, at that day shall he [the Devil] rage in the hearts of the children of men, and stir them up to anger against that which is good. And others will he *pacify, and lull them away into carnal security*, that they will say: *All is well in Zion*; yea, Zion prospereth, all is well—and thus the devil cheateth their souls, and leadeth them away carefully down to hell. Therefore, *wo be unto him that is at ease in Zion!* Wo be unto him that crieth: All is well! Yea, wo be unto him that hearkeneth unto the precepts of men, and *denieth the power of God, and the gift of the Holy Ghost!* Yea, wo be unto him that saith: *We have received, and we need no more!* And in fine, wo unto all those who tremble, and are angry because of the truth of God! For behold, he that is built upon the rock receiveth it with gladness; and he that is built upon a sandy foundation trembleth lest he shall fall. Wo be unto him that shall say: *We have received the word of God, and we need no more of the word of God, for we have enough!* For behold, thus saith the Lord God: I will give unto the children of men line upon line, precept upon precept, here a little and there a little; and blessed are those who hearken unto my precepts, and lend an ear unto my counsel, for they shall learn wisdom; for unto him that receiveth I will give more; and from them that shall say, We have enough, from them shall be taken away even that which they have." (*2 Nephi 28:20-22, 24-30*)

These words by the Prophet Nephi are very frightening to me, perhaps more than any other latter-day prophecy. This isn't referring to the wicked of the earth, or the gentiles who will refuse to accept *The Book of Mormon* when they say, "A bible! A Bible! We have got a Bible, and there cannot be any more Bible." (*2 Nephi 29:3*) No, these are the so-called Latter-day Saints of today who are *thinking* and *saying* that all is well in Zion. These Latter-day Saints will refuse further light and knowledge, claiming that they have enough of the word of God and need no more. These Latter-day Saints as members of The Church are at ease, confident in the false belief that they are living celestially. They have been *pacified and lulled by the Devil into a carnal security*. Remember, the saints in the latter-days are not walking in darkness at noon-day because of sin, that ***is*** the very grievous sin, to be walking in darkness at noon-day. (see *D&C 95:5-6*) Though these Latter-day Saints will preach Christ and the Holy Ghost, they will deny the power and gifts thereof. They will buy into the precepts of man, or should I say Babylon? These Latter-day Saints will even become angry with those who want to learn more. The Lord warns such, with a *wo be* *unto them,* for what they have will be taken from them. Only those who hearken and continue to humble themselves will be given more.

These are powerful words given by a prophet who said, "Thus sayeth the Lord God." Can we disregard or take them lightly? Do we dare? **We** are the Latter-Day Saints that he was talking about. ***We, you and I***! "Wherefore the Lord said, Forasmuch as this people draw near me with their mouth, and with their lips do honour me, but have removed their heart far from me, and their fear toward me is taught by the precept of men: Therefore, behold, I will proceed to do a marvelous work among this people, even a marvelous work and a wonder: for the wisdom of their wise men shall perish, and the understanding of their prudent men shall be hid." (*Isaiah 29:13-14*) I know that the popular Mormon interpretation of this scripture is that they "this people," who are the subject of the scripture, refers to those who are not members of His church and that the "marvelous work and wonder" is *that* church restored to the earth through Joseph Smith. To this I would take issue. We already read from Nephi's prophecy that it is the Latter-day Saints "that hearkeneth unto the precepts of men, and *denieth the power of God, and the gift of the Holy Ghost!*" I submit that *the marvelous work and wonder* is not **just** the restoration of The Church but an event that will be brought about ***within that restored church*** and/or among those who do **indeed** draw near to God with their mouths and their hearts. This marvelous work will be done among those who seek God diligently. It will be among those who will **not** say *we have received the word of God, and we need no more of the word of God, for we have enough!* It will be among those who do not *denieth the power of God, and the gift of the Holy Ghost* (*2 Nephi 28:20-29*). I will say more in the next chapter upon this subject of this marvelous work and wonder that God will proceed to do. The point I make now is that *we are walking in darkness at noon-day* and by so doing have sinned, not just a grievous sin, but a *very* grievous sin (see *D&C 95:5-6*). Again, the light is there, we just choose to walk in the shadows. No wonder we stumble and fall.

Who Me?

Ah but you say, "Surely I am not one of those. I am not walking in darkness. I do not deny the power of God or the gift of the Holy Ghost." Well, it is not my place to point the finger but is it possible, is it just possible, that we have been *pacified and lulled by the Devil into a carnal security*? Is it possible that we are asleep.

At the risk of being stoned, may I not so subtly ask, do the above prophetic statements relating to the Latter-day Saints strike home to anyone? To you?

Are hemlock knots and flying pieces of glass becoming more than familiar to us? (*TPJS pg. 331*) Do the same-old; same-old discussions in gospel doctrine or bible study classes resemble this prophecy? When will we wake up? When will we step out into the light of noon-day? When will we ask, knock, and seek after more of the word of God, take hold of that iron rod. When will we take hold of the powers of God and be Born Again? I am aware that most active Mormons as well as the "Born Again" Christians of the world believe that they are already Born Again and perhaps we can take a closer look at that later, but for now let me testify the Lord has more to tell us! Let us give ear!

The Church Is Still Here

But oh no, we think because we attend our meetings, pay our tithes, or otherwise obey the carnal commandments and outward performances, that we are safe and living the required celestial law. No, a thousand times, no! We are not living the law of the celestial kingdom, and bear in mind that "Zion cannot be built up unless it is by the principles of the law of the celestial kingdom." (*D&C 105:5*) Though there are certainly Zion individuals, the Zion Society is not yet established! We think we are civilized, we think that this capitalistic, democratic system is the only act in town. It is the **main** act in town, but the town is Babylon, not Zion. As Joseph Smith said, the governments of men and their laws are "dissimilar" and "diverse" from the government and laws of heaven. **Zion is not yet established!**

How do we know that we are not yet in Zion? How do we know that we are still in Babylon? We know because we are not of *one heart or one mind*, as Zion people must be. "I say unto you, be one; and if ye are not one ye are not mine." (*D&C 38:27*) We still have not *come to a unity of the faith* or *a knowledge of Christ* nor are we *perfected in Him* having received His *fullness*. "And He gave some, apostles; and some, prophets; and some, evangelists; and some, pastors and teachers; For the perfecting of the saints, for the work of the ministry, for the edifying of the body of Christ: *Till* we all come in the unity of the faith, and of the knowledge of the Son of God, unto a perfect man, unto the measure of the stature of the fulness of Christ: That we henceforth be no more children, tossed to and fro, and carried about with every wind of doctrine, by the sleight of men, and cunning craftiness, whereby they lie in wait to deceive." (*Ephesians 4:11-14*)

Our missionaries often quote this verse to show that the Lord has called apostles and prophets in these latter-days but we don't seem to comprehend *why* or for *how long*. Why? Why, for the *perfecting of the Saints*, *work of the ministry*, and the *edifying of the body of Christ*. Until when? **Until**, we come to a *unity of the faith* and a *knowledge of the Son of God*. When we do come to a unity of the faith, when we know the Son of God, and we measure up to the stature of the fullness of Christ, **The Church will pass away**! Only The Kingdom of God will endure forever.

Well folks, The Church is still here! We are still in need of a church organization to minister and teach us. Sadley, we are not yet united in mind and heart. But worst of all, we do not yet *know* the Son of God. We are yet in need of teachers, prophets, and etc., to guide us. We are still tossed to and fro by false or incomplete doctrines. Within The Church we too often sit in our meetings and argue about doctrines, requirements, laws, and church policy.

With all sorrow and remorse of heart, let me say again, Zion is not yet established. We are still in Babylon and how do we know that? Because we live in a state of confusion, discord, corruption, contention, strife, folly, and fashion. It is sold to us on every street corner, even in our own homes, **and we have bought into it**.

I say we have *bought* into Babylon, these lesser laws, because that's what I mean. **Bought**! You see, when the Lord placed Adam and Eve on the earth, He *gave* them not just what they needed, but everything! Even after they were cast out of the garden, the world and everything in it was theirs, *free* for the taking. But the Devil swindled, robbed, usurped, and stole. He *scarfed* it all up and has, ever since, been selling it back to us at a very high price: OUR SOULS!

Not Living Celestial Laws

Very few of the laws we live are celestial. Again, I quote Joseph Smith (italics for emphasis), "I have tried for a number of years to get the minds of the Saints prepared to receive the things of God; but we frequently see some of them, after suffering all they have for the work of God, will fly to pieces like glass as soon as anything comes that is contrary to their traditions, they cannot stand the fire at all. **How many will be able to abide a celestial law**, and go through and receive their exaltation, I am unable to say, as many are called, but few are chosen." (*TPJS, pg. 331*) No, we do not know what it will be like to live in a Zion Society under celestial law because we have no real experience doing so. We do not even *know* the celestial laws required to live such an order, let alone *live* them.

So what will it be like to live in a Zion Society with Christ, under celestial law? Again, if you want to understand the systems, procedures, science, art, philosophy, government, and economy of a celestial environment, you need only imagine what it will be like to live in heaven with God. The heaven on earth (Zion) and heaven itself, operate under the same systems, same principles, same laws, and same conditions. They are quite different from the terrestrial and telestial ways and laws we now live. Even within the Mormon Church we will find many and striking differences. Try not to be shocked as we make the comparison between the "heaven on earth society" and how we now live. Also, let us try once again to elevate our minds to a level of celestial thinking. Bear in mind that when I speak of a Zion Society, I am speaking of a celestial order, not terrestrial or telestial. Also, even though it may take some time for even those in Zion to learn how to operate with the celestial powers that will be bestowed upon them, it will not be long before Zion itself will be functioning according to the powers and laws of heaven that will soon spread through the whole world.

Full Power, Scotty!

What are the differences between how we live now and a Zion Society? Here we go! Well, realize that there will be an outpouring, an endowment of the spirit and priesthood powers of God greater than we can now conceive. "For behold, I have prepared a great endowment and blessing to be poured out upon them, inasmuch as they are faithful and continue in humility before me." (*D&C 105:12*) "For since the beginning of the world have not men heard nor perceived by the ear, neither hath any eye seen, O God, besides thee, how great things thou hast prepared for him that waiteth for thee." (*D&C 133:45*) The same miraculous powers we have referred to before such as turning water to wine, parting seas, moving mountains; unloading trucks; healing the sick; resurrecting the dead (we will not raise the dead as there will be no death); controlling the elements; communicating with life in other realms (spirit world and etc.); solving transportation, communication, and construction problems; as well as gaining knowledge and working with God in His creative purposes will be the powers used during the Millennium in the Zion Society. I repeat, again, to jog our consciousness, *we will finally be using our full priesthood powers (God's power) to do the things we do*, just as God uses His full powers to do what He does. I'm talking freedom and power beyond our wildest dreams. Let me here testify that through Christ all things are possible. "And Christ hath said; If ye will have faith in me ye shall have power to do whatsoever thing is expedient in me." (*Moroni 7:33*)

This is not a new program. Not only are we familiar with the powers given Moses to call down plagues on the Egyptians, but in *The Book of Mormon*, Jacob tells us that they obtained "a hope, and our faith becometh unshaken, insomuch that we truly can command in the name of Jesus and the very trees obey us, or the mountains, or the waves of the sea." (*Jacob 4:6*) Also, "the brother of Jared said unto the mountain Zerin, remove—and it was removed." (*Ether 12:30*) These men were not just prophets, they were men who finally began to use the full priesthood powers of God. Unlike most of us Saints who haven't yet thrown off the vanity and unbelief curse (see *D&C 84:54-58*), they believed and God gave them the power. When we finally do give up our vanity and unbelief, Zion will, by the power of the priesthood, be established and maintained.

What About Women?

At the risk of overstepping my bounds, I might add here that women are included in the use of priesthood powers to accomplish their respective duties and callings. I say this because there is a discernible, ongoing controversy as to whether women should or will ever hold the priesthood. To me it is not a question of whether but **when**. Brother McConkie seems to feel the same way. "Women do not have the priesthood conferred upon them and are not ordained to offices therein, but they are entitled to all priesthood blessings. Those women, who go on to their exaltation, ruling and reigning with husbands who are kings and priests, will themselves be queens and priestesses. They will hold positions of power, authority, and preferment in eternity." (*MD pg. 594, Priestesses*) Of course it is God's power, it is His priesthood and, as in the past, He will impart the same to whomever He will, whenever He will. Said John Taylor, "You have been ordained kings and queens, and priests and priestesses to your Lord; you have been put in possession of principles that all the kings, potentates, and power upon the earth are entirely ignorant of; they do not understand it; but you have received this from the hands of God." (*John Taylor, The Gospel Kingdom, pg. 221-222*) Since we (the Saints) have been ordained to become kings and queens, priests and *priestesses*, in this author's opinion, it follows that the Millennial Zion Society is where woman will begin to hold and exercise keys of their full priesthood powers. Does this mean that they will assume the role of the patriarch and become the head or ruling king? I do not believe it. Woman will exercise their priesthood powers within the roles of queens and priestesses, within the domain or stewardship wherein God has placed them. As stated in the previous chapter on stewardships, neither the woman nor the man will ever, worlds without end, usurp the stewardship of any steward to which they are subordinate. It should be noted that it will also be in the Millennial Zion Society that men will need to learn to use their full priesthood powers as they, for the most part, are not yet doing so to any great degree. Though the callings and duties of men and women will no doubt be different from each other and will likely resemble the duties and callings they now have, this endowment of priesthood power will be available to all those who choose to take advantage of it by preparing themselves for such gifts, by giving up their vanity and unbelief, and by living the laws that govern them.

The Heavenly Economy

Getting back to the concept of Zion, God's kingdom on earth, remember it will be built only upon celestial principles and laws. Remember, too, these are the same laws that govern heaven. To begin to understand the greatness, the eminence and the glory of such laws and powers and how they will be used, one must again expand one's narrow mind nearly to the boundlessness of God's. In the Millennium, the endowment of priesthood power to be experienced, even by the least Saint, will be awesome. Those who do not wish to accept this endowment will simply reject it, very much like we reject and deny the gifts of God today. Such will be sanctified, by the terrestrial law they will accept. However, those who will acquire this endowment will soon discover that the methods and economy of The Celestial Society are vastly different from what we now know.

Imagine what kind of economy exists in the heavens with God. Are there hungry? Are there poor? Would you have a greenback dollar with Christ's picture on the front? Whoa! Such a thought seems blasphemous and well it should. Are there banks or savings and loan companies in heaven? Do we don the Wall Street uniform, a dark suit, white shirt, and silk tie, grab our briefcases, and go out to do business with our fellow angels? I don't think so. No, such things are ridiculous in a heavenly environment. In the heaven on earth Zion Society, as in heaven, there *will not be money or any other medium of exchange.* It will not be *business as usual.*

Can you imagine real estate companies in heaven? Which planet or stars will you own? If you want to move up, can you sell or trade yours for bigger ones? No again. In Zion, as in heaven, there will be no ownership of anything at all. I know this is a new concept to many but believe me—there will be **no private ownership! None!** There will only be *stewardships.*

I know *ownership* is the prevailing Mormon belief, but the notion that in Zion there will be deeds, bills of sale, or titles is completely erroneous. The very concept of ownership will not exist. It is not a celestial law. There is no such thing as The Law of Consecration And *Ownership*. It is The Law of Consecration And *Stewardship*. As discussed in a previous chapter, stewardships are states of co-ownership through the oneness doctrine, not individual ownership of a part of the whole. The celestial law is *to have all things in common.*

When you think about it, it makes perfect sense. As a Saint in Zion, you promise to consecrate all that God has blessed you with, as well as all He may bless you with, to the Lord, for the building of His Church and Kingdom. Through His servants, you are given a stewardship of which you wisely take good care. But what if some new people move in and they don't have anything, so the Lord's servant comes back to you and says, "Brother, we need some of your stewardship to give to these poor people." What are you going to say? "No, you can't have it back. You gave it to me. It's mine." How preposterous! Of course you will give whatever is needed for the good of the whole. Who owns it anyway? Is it not all God's? Again you are only taking care of that which the steward above you has *appointed* you to govern, not *given* you to own. This may not be an easy doctrine to accept as we have lived for so long in the present system of *mine*, or private ownership. I'm afraid some of our hemlock knots have become quite hard or perhaps our selfishness preempts our ability to accept. Well, all I can say is, try to assimilate, as this is the celestial economy.

United Order

Before I leave this and move on, let me say that the *United Order* is not the same as The Law of Consecration and Stewardship. The United Order, as mentioned in a previous chapter, was only a mildly successful attempt by some of the early Saints to live the personal principles inherent in the higher law of stewardships. Had the Saints been able to live the United Order, they may well have moved on to the Law of Consecration and Stewardship. Like the Saints in Missouri, at the time Joseph Smith introduced the Law of Consecration and Stewardship, their personal inability and unrighteousness held them to a lesser law. "Verily I say unto you, concerning your brethren who have been afflicted, and persecuted, and cast out from the land of their inheritance—I, the Lord, have suffered the affliction to come upon them, wherewith they have been afflicted, in consequence of their transgressions; Behold, I say unto you, there were jarrings, and contentions, and envyings, and strifes, and lustful and covetous desires among them; therefore by these things they polluted their inheritances. Verily I say unto you, notwithstanding their sins, my bowels are filled with compassion towards them. I will not utterly cast them off; and in the day of wrath I will remember mercy." (*D&C 101:1-2,* 6, 9) "Behold, I say unto you, were it not for the transgressions of my people, speaking concerning The Church and not individuals, they might have been redeemed even now. But behold, they have not learned to be obedient to the things which I required at their hands, but are full of all manner of evil, and do not impart of their substance, as becometh saints, to the poor and afflicted among them; And are not united according to the union required by the law of the celestial kingdom; Therefore, in consequence of the transgressions of my people, it is expedient in me that mine elders should wait for a little season for the redemption of Zion . . . ." (*D&C 105:2-4,* 9)

As before, when we talked about the play *The Order Is Love*, the success of such a society, or any social order for that matter, hangs on personal righteousness. Each individual must rid themselves of jealousy, coveting, envying, and the multitude of sins that we go over and over in our Sunday school classes each week. So, when is it going to be established, this Zion Society (defined above, as individuals that become pure of heart)? When will this, the utopian society happen? Well, when the Saints, in fact, rid themselves of these ungodly traits. The curse will not be lifted until we give up our vanity, unbelief, and stop treating the revelations and powers of God lightly (see *D&C 88:54*). These sins must be replaced with the virtues of Godliness. Further, it will be in the Lord's own time and cannot happen until He sees fit to pour out a much greater endowment of His spirit. "That they themselves may be prepared, and that my people may be taught more perfectly, and have experience, and know more perfectly concerning their duty, and the things which I require at their hands. And this cannot be brought to pass until mine elders are endowed with power from on high. For behold, I have prepared a great endowment and blessing to be poured out upon them, inasmuch as they are faithful and continue in humility before me." (*D&C 105:10-12*) "For the preparation wherewith I design to prepare mine apostles to prune my vineyard for the last time, that I may bring to pass my strange act, that I may pour out my Spirit upon all flesh." (*D&C 95:4*) Like all the gifts of God, we can only prepare ourselves to receive these great endowments of the Zion Society. We cannot force it to happen. I will expand upon this concept shortly, but keep in mind that one of the greatest preparations is to learn and live the economy of God, that is, the Law of Consecration and Stewardship.

Rich At Last

You must also realize that this Law of Consecration and Stewardship is **not welfare or a poverty program**. "For the earth is full, and there is enough and to spare; yea, I prepared all things and have given unto the children of men to be agents unto themselves. Therefore, if any man shall take of the abundance which I have made, and impart not his portion, according to the law of my gospel, unto the poor and the needy, he shall, with the wicked, lift up his eyes in hell, being in torment." (*D&C 104:17-18*) As is also stated in this reference, it is not for us to withhold from the poor that with which the Lord has blessed us. "And also, ye yourselves will succor those that stand in need of your succor; ye will administer of your substance unto him that standeth in need; and ye will not suffer that the beggar putteth up his petition to you in vain, and turn him out to perish. Perhaps thou shalt say: The man has brought upon himself his misery; therefore I will stay my hand, and will not give unto him of my food, nor impart unto him of my substance that he may not suffer, for his punishments are just—But I say unto you, O man, whosoever doeth this the same hath great cause to repent; and except he repenteth of that which he hath done he perisheth forever, and hath no interest in the kingdom of God." (*Mosiah 4:16-18*) This is not a law or program for the Zion Society as there will be no poor then. It is a law and program to *get us to* the Zion Society. The Law of Consecration and Stewardship will preempt or make such laws obsolete. "The fact is this, a man is bound by the law of The Church, to consecrate to the Bishop, before he can be considered a legal heir to the kingdom of Zion; and this, too, without constraint; and unless he does this, he cannot be acknowledged before the Lord on The Church Book . . . ." (*TPJS, pg. 22*) The law requires a consecration of not just our surplus, but all we have. In a Zion Society, it will not just be a matter of not withholding our bounty from those who have less, but we will have all things in common and no one will be in want for anything. We will be given a stewardship over things and people and, as a part of that stewardship; all our needs will be taken care of. It will be up to the individual to decide what his needs are. In a Zion Society there will be no *greed* or *scarcity mentality*. Remember, although our basic needs are food, raiment (clothing), and lodgings, all things will be available to us. There will be no lack of majesty, beauty, premium quality, and grandeur. I cannot say that the streets of the earthly Zion City will be paved with gold, but if they are, the difference will be that no one will have their heart set upon those things, none will be barred from the enjoyment of them, nor will there be wonderful adornments for some while even one man sits in the gutter of such gold paved streets, hungry or in want of anything. Also, in all my imaginings, I cannot see God dressed in second rate or substandard clothing or living in a house that does not exemplify the beauty and majesty He deserves. Such will be our inheritance as well, to the extent that fine things will be so commonplace that no value will be placed upon them. When we become joint heirs with Christ, all God has will be ours as well. This is no poverty program!

Cover Thy Self

There will also be no fear that we may lose such riches. Again, there will be no need for a scarcity mentality. I might add here that there will be no trusting in insurance policies. There will not be *insurance* in a Zion Society. When you think about it, insurance is, at best, a terrestrial law. It attempts to eliminate the need for faith, that is, our trust is transferred from God to our own arm of flesh or, rather, our insurance agent's arm. Further, it eliminates the need of others to help. In the old days, before insurance, when a man's house burned down, his neighbors came together to help him, resulting in strong relationships founded upon trust, mutual giving, and love. Insurance fosters separateness and independence from each other rather than the *oneness* for which Zion will be known. I hear the argument that The Mormon Church believes in insurance, even owns an insurance company. Well, all I can say is that it is just one more evidence that Zion is not yet established and The Church, like we individuals, must attempt to somehow operate in a telestial world while looking forward to the day we can live the higher law. At any rate, there will be no insurance or even a need to build barns to store the harvest (a form of insurance against spoilage), as nothing will spoil our goods and effects. There will be no thieves or destroyers from which to protect, and nothing will decay (in the Zion City). The weather will be controlled by the powers of the priesthood to the extent that there will be no extraneous or unwanted rain or hail on our crops. In fact the weather patterns, as well as the geography, will be vastly different than we are accustomed to today. The earth will be watered by a mist (no rain at all), as it was before the flood. (see *Moses 3:6 & Abraham 5:6*)

They Did It

Having such an endowment of priesthood powers will be all but unprecedented in the history of the earth. I know of only three cases in our scriptures when God's people were righteous enough to live such powerful laws: the people of Enoch, the city of Salem, and to a lesser degree, the people on the South American continent after the visitation of Christ. "And the Lord called His people Zion, because they were of one heart and one mind, and dwelt in righteousness; and there was no poor among them." (*Moses 7:18*) "And they had all things common among them; therefore there were not rich and poor, bond and free, but they were all made free, and partakers of the heavenly gift. And it came to pass that there was no contention among all the people, in all the land; but there were mighty miracles wrought among the disciples of Jesus. And it came to pass that there was no contention in the land, because of the love of God which did dwell in the hearts of the people. There were no robbers, nor murderers, neither were there Lamanites, nor any manner ofites; but they were in one, the children of Christ, and heirs to the kingdom of God. And there were no envyings, nor strifes, nor tumults, nor whoredoms, nor lyings, nor murders, nor any manner of lasciviousness; and surely there could not be a happier people among all the people who had been created by the hand of God." (*4 Nephi 1:3, 13, 15-17*) These examples of righteousness should give us hope and a greater desire to work for such a utopian society. It should help us to see that there is a better way. Why do we cling to this capitalistic system as if it is the ultimate? Do we not know that its accompanying greed, selfishness, and separateness are the cause of most of the suffering in the world? "But it is not given that one man should possess that which is above another, wherefore the world lieth in sin." (D&C 49:20) In the Zion Society there will be no inner societies, class distinctions, or racial categories that will separate one from another. There will be a oneness and an acceptance of each other for who we are.

Imagine

Let us go on comparing the laws, powers, and conditions of heaven with that of the heaven on earth (the Zion Society), for remember, such laws, powers, and conditions are the same. Again, though we will still be mortal, we will live by celestial principles, laws and powers. So, if you can imagine it in heaven, then you must imagine it in the Zion Society as well.

Can you imagine suffering in heaven? No, of course not, and since the conditions are the same you must not imagine suffering in Zion. Can you imagine hospitals, doctors, and mental institutions in heaven? Will we have to go to medical school so we may relieve suffering and heal the sick? I don't think so. (All though at first infantile in execution, we will use priesthood powers to save others, the world in general, and ourselves from suffering.) No, we cannot imagine such things in heaven and they will not be in Zion either. No suffering of any kind, mental or physical, will exist in the Zion Society. There will be no blind, no deaf, no cancer, no heart disease, no palsy, no lame, no insanity, nor any other such diseased condition of the physical body or mental capacity. I will probably make a few friends when I say here that no one will be overweight either. There will be no addictions of any kind. There will be no afflictions or maladies whatsoever in the Zion Society. It should be noted, particularly at the beginning of the Millennium, that the terrestrial people living upon the earth will not enjoy these priesthood blessings until the celestial missionaries take those endowments to them.

No Death Or Taxes

What about death? Can you imagine death, funerals, and graveyards in heaven? Unthinkable! If you cannot imagine these things in heaven, they will not be in the Zion Society either. "And there shall be no sorrow because there is no death." (*D&C 101:29*) In a celestial Zion Society (not the rest of the terrestrial world) we will not die, that is, we will not taste death. "In that day an infant shall not die until he is old; and his life shall be as the age of a tree; And when he dies he shall not sleep, that is to say in the earth, but shall be changed in the twinkling of an eye, and shall be caught up, and his rest shall be glorious." (*D&C 101:30-31*) Further on this subject, there will be no death or killing of any kind. We will not eat meat. The lion will lie down with the lamb, and all carnivorous animals will become herbivores. "The wolf also shall dwell with the lamb, and the leopard shall lie down with the kid; and the calf and the young lion and the fatling together; and a little child shall lead them. And the cow and the bear shall feed; their young ones shall lie down together: and the lion shall eat straw like the ox. And the sucking child shall play on the hole of the asp, and the weaned child shall put his hand on the cockatrice' den. They shall not hurt nor destroy in all my holy mountain: for the earth shall be full of the knowledge of the Lord, as the waters cover the sea." (*Isaiah 11:6-9*) Did you note? There is that mountain again. Also, not unlike Dr. Doolittle, we will communicate with the animals in ways we now cannot comprehend. Oh, by the way, there will be no taxes either.

What? No NBA Or NFL?

There is another major difference between the Zion Society and our present way of life. Can you imagine competition in heaven? You know, people trying to be the fastest, biggest, brightest, and best cosmos builder? In heaven there will eventually be no time; how can one be the fastest? Size is relative, so how can one be the biggest? We will all be filled with the glory of God, so how can one be the brightest? When we are one with the Gods, how can we be the best? This is, of course, an over-simplification and perhaps does not quite fit with an earthly Zion, but I think it makes the point nonetheless. There is **no competition** in a Zion Society. Sorry sports fans, but competition is foreign to the spirit of Christ, which is to reach down and lift others up to your level, not *beat them*.

Ahh—I Can Breath Again

Are there weeds in heaven? It is said that "*a weed is only a flower out of place,*" but in any case, there will be no weeds in Zion. All plants and fruits will grow spontaneously, without the impediment of noxious weeds. There will be a temperate climate. You will be neither too hot nor too cold. There will be no need to pollute the air or earth with methods of staying warm or cool. "And the Lord will create upon every dwelling place of mount Zion, and upon her assemblies, a cloud and smoke by day, and the shining of a flaming fire by night: for upon all the glory shall be a defense. And there shall be a tabernacle for a shadow in the daytime from the heat, and for a place of refuge, and for a covert from storm and from rain." (*Isaiah 4:5-6*) Your house will be illuminated, heated, and protected from the elements by the power of God. We will be working with the priesthood powers of heaven to solve such problems and to build our cities. No pollution! Ah, breathe deep!

Travel And Communication

That brings up another issue. Can you imagine cars in heaven? I know there are a lot of guys that are not interested in going there without their cars, but I promise you, there will be other machines and technologies to tinker with that will be far more interesting and exciting than cars. If that will not do, perhaps they can sneak out of the back gate of Zion and visit some terrestrial garage, huh? But remember, don't set your heart too much upon such things of this world or you may not get back in. I guess I didn't have to say that. In any case, as the Millennium moves on, modes of transportation will become spiritual in nature. Really, can you imagine God going out to His garage and getting in His car whenever He wants to go somewhere? Does He have to get into a space ship to cross the universe? I don't think so. This, as well as other tasks, we will accomplish by means of the priesthood powers we have already been given. "And in that day whatsoever any man shall ask, it shall be given unto him." (*D&C 101:27*) This is no idle promise or prophecy. We will have power in the priesthood to work whatever "miracles" we need.

Will we have to talk over a phone, read books, watch TV, listen to tapes, or play with computers to communicate with or learn from each other? No, the methods of communicating and learning will be beyond our ability to now comprehend. Your communications will be direct through feelings. Being one with whomever you are communicating, you will experience their exact feelings and thoughts and there will be no misunderstandings whatsoever. You will share your deepest thoughts and emotions freely with everyone without fear or inhibitions. You will share your love (be spiritually one with) every other person without restraint or fear. Such love and communication will be infinitely fulfilling to the relationship.

Finally, A Free Lunch

Perhaps the greatest difference we will encounter in Zion will be realized when we try to imagine *working for a living.* Can you imagine working for a living in heaven? You know, your wife fills your lunch box and sends you off to a heavenly job you hate but must do in order to provide the necessities of life for you and your family? And if you fail to complete your angelic duties properly that day, say, if you don't create your allotted quota of stars, will they fire you or make you live in a smaller mansion or something? Will you have to work hard for five days a week at something you don't really enjoy, so you can have the weekend off, to do what you want? Or, perhaps you will earn that two weeks vacation a year for that purpose? No, no, a thousand times no! If I had to *work for a living* in heaven I'm afraid I would consider it hell. You will note I said, "work for a living" not just "work." Yes, of course we can imagine work in heaven, and plenty of it, but not as we define work here and certainly ***not for a living!*** I believe it was best put by Hugh Nibley[107] in his treatise *Work We Must, But the Lunch Is Free.*[108] This composition should be required reading for anyone looking to live in a Zion Society. I must say I personally have never had so much trouble accepting a principle in my life. For some reason (pride probably), we will not accept a gift from God. As I said before, when Adam and Eve were put on this earth, all things were free. The Devil commandeered these things, convinced us all that *there is no free lunch*, and has been selling God's free gifts back to us for the price of our souls. To illustrate my point, ask yourself, what is **not** a gift from God? As you consider this question, you will find that from your talents and abilities, your temporal blessings, and on to your spiritual blessings, *all things* are a gift from God to you. Without His blessings, you would have nothing and you would be nothing. "For behold, are we not all beggars? Do we not all depend upon the same Being, even God, for all the substance which we have, for both food and raiment, and for gold, and for silver, and for all the riches which we have of every kind?" (*Mosiah 4:19*) Even your very life is a gift from God. Now think about it and remember that by definition, **a gift cannot be earned**. You cannot work for a gift or it becomes a wage.

The Work Ethic

The Devil has taken the *work ethic* and convinced us that it means we must work for the *lunch*, for the gifts of God. Then, as Nibley expresses, the Devil convinces us that we need a bigger lunch, and that others aren't worthy of the same lunch as ours. He scares us out of faith in God by telling us that we may lose our job security and therefore must trust in our insurance policies, meaning him. The Devil has manipulated this *work ethic* to the point that we worship it (and him) even until it controls our very lives, from birth to the grave. I am not saying that work is not a virtue; on the contrary, in a celestial environment we will work *because it is a virtue* and not *because we are compelled* in order to obtain the lunch.

The celestial *work ethic* means that we *will* to work, we *want* to work, because it is a virtue in itself. We will work not to receive something, but because it is the right thing to do. And the work in which we will be engaged is building up of The Kingdom of God, not something to make money to *buy the lunch*. God has promised us that if we will look to Him in faith, we need not worry about the necessities of life. "Give us this day our daily bread." (*Matthew 6:11*) "Therefore I say unto you, Take no thought for your life, what ye shall eat, or what ye shall drink; nor yet for your body, what ye shall put on. Is not the life more than meat, and the body than raiment? Behold the fowls of the air: for they sow not, neither do they reap, nor gather into barns; yet your heavenly Father feedeth them. Are ye not much better than they? Which of you by taking thought can add one cubit unto his stature? And why take ye thought for raiment? Consider the lilies of the field, how they grow; they toil not, neither do they spin: And yet I say unto you, that even Solomon in all his glory was not arrayed like one of these. Wherefore, if God so clothe the grass of the field, which to day is, and to morrow is cast into the oven, shall He not much more clothe you, O ye of little faith? Therefore take no thought, saying, What shall we eat? or, What shall we drink? or, Wherewithal shall we be clothed? For after all these things do the Gentiles seek: for your heavenly Father knoweth that ye have need of all these things. But seek ye first the kingdom of God, and His righteousness; and all these things shall be added unto you. Take therefore no thought for the morrow: for the morrow shall take thought for the things of itself. Sufficient unto the day is the evil thereof." (*Matthew 6:25-34*) I recognize that many people think Christ was talking only to the apostles, but this is not so. I repeat, this is not so. There was nothing given to the apostles of old or to the contemporary apostles that is not promised to all if we will exercise a little faith. This is *The Sermon On The Mount*, given to all the world. This is Christ revealing the celestial law that the children of Israel were unable to live when Moses first brought it down from the mountain, after which they had to settle for a lesser law. Let me here add my testimony to that of Hugh Nibley's that our Lord was talking to everyone. He was here admonishing us all to have faith enough to believe that the Lord will indeed take care of the lunch that our *needs* **will be met**. Remember too, that our needs are food, raiment (clothing), and lodgings, any more than that is a *want* not a *need*. This is a celestial law and requires a celestial faith to live it. Be careful that you don't discard this concept with the excuse that it does not apply because we are living in a telestial or terrestrial world. Perhaps you would like me to say that it is impossible to live such a law in our present day. I cannot, as I believe that, with enough faith, it is possible to live the spirit of the law, if not literally. The essence of it is giving up our will to God. We must also give up our will to beat the Joneses to the nearest shopping mall. We must be wise and prudent with the temporal things with which God has blessed us. Most of all, we must not worry, we must *take no thought for our lives, what we shall eat, or what we shall drink or what we shall put on* (see *Matthew 6:25-34*). It is my testimony that with only a little faith, we can live it, even today. Please read Hugh Nibley's exhortation on this subject.

Gifts

To further press my point let me refer to Moroni, who, on the last pages of his mortal writings, implored us to have faith and not deny the gifts of God. "And again, I exhort you, my brethren, that ye deny not the gifts of God, for they are many; and they come from the same God. And there are different ways that these gifts are administered; but it is the same God who worketh all in all; and they are given by the manifestations of the Spirit of God unto men, to profit them. And Christ truly said unto our fathers: If ye have faith ye can do all things, which are expedient unto me. And now I speak unto all the ends of the earth—that if the day cometh that the power and gifts of God shall be done away among you, it shall be because of unbelief. And wo be unto the children of men if this be the case; for there shall be none that doeth good among you, no not one. For if there be one among you that doeth good, he shall work by the power and gifts of God. And again I would exhort you that ye would come unto Christ, and lay hold upon every good gift, and touch not the evil gift, nor the unclean thing." (*Moroni 10:8, 23-25, 30*) You will note that Moroni did not say to work for the gifts. He simply said to lay hold upon them. Do we believe what the Lord promised? If so; then *give no thought*, no ***worry***, to life. That's a tough one. We are all so used to worrying about just about everything. This only shows our lack of faith and our reluctance to turn our will, our desires over to Christ. But believe me, your life will change dramatically if you can assimilate this concept, this celestial concept.

Further, Paul referred to sin as having a wage. "For the wages of sin is death; but the gift of God is eternal life through Jesus Christ our Lord." (*Romans 6:23*) Apparently we can work for the Devil and obtain our *wage of death*, but eternal life is a *gift of God*. All things from God are gifts, only the Devil makes us work for things. Still, referring to the Latter-day Saints at least, it is so ingrained in us that we are *working out our salvation* (see *Philippians 2:12, Alma 34:37*, and *Mormon 9:27*), we cannot accept that all things are gifts of God, the greatest of them being eternal life. "And, if you keep my commandments and endure to the end you shall have eternal life, which gift is the greatest of all the gifts of God." (*D&C 20:26*) "Wherefore, beware lest ye are deceived; and that ye may not be deceived seek ye earnestly the best gifts, always remembering for what they are given. For verily I say unto you, they are given for the benefit of those who love me and keep all my commandments, and him that seeketh so to do; that all may be benefited that seek or that ask of me . . . ." (*D&C 46:8-9*) Can you imagine someone giving you a gift, perhaps a birthday gift, but when they offer it to you, you refuse to take it until you come over to their house to *work it off*, maybe by mowing their lawn, washing their car, or some other labor? What an insult to the giver! How would you feel if people refused to take gifts that you offered until they worked off the value of the gift? I am certain the Lord feels the same way. You've read my quote of this scripture before, but it really fits here also. "For what doth it profit a man if a gift is bestowed upon him and he receive not the gift? Behold, he rejoices not in that which is given unto him, neither rejoices in him who is the giver of the gift." (*D&C 88:33*) He is offering us the best gifts. All He asks us is that we prepare ourselves to receive them, and not to deny them when they are offered.

Slackers

I am not talking here about the sluggard, slacker, or otherwise slothful person who, because of laziness, refuses to do his or her duty. There are scriptures a plenty that state that the laborer is worthy of his hire and the idler shall not eat the bread nor wear the garment of the laborer (see *Proverbs 20:4* and *D&C 42:42*). We are talking, however, of a condition that affects only the lower kingdoms of law. There will be no idlers in a Zion Society as there are none in heaven. Remember that one must prove himself before being chosen to enter.

Sweat of Thy Face

I know you are still saying that we must do something of ourselves; after all, we must work out our salvation with fear and trembling, right? (see *Philippians 2:12*, *Alma 34:37*, and *Mormon 9:27*.) This we will discuss on a deeper level in an ensuing chapter where we will discover what it really means, but for now, let me get back to the gift of the *free lunch*, which I testify is, indeed, a **free gift**. "But," you say, God told Adam the ground was cursed for his sake. It would bring forth thorns and thistles and by the sweat of his face he would eat his bread all the days of his life. (see *Genesis 3:17-19*) Yes, that is the curse of Adam all right. But friends, curses can be lifted. Must we settle? When will the curse be lifted if we will not prepare for it? With just a little faith we might get back to the garden. The garden will be called Zion.

Can you see how in a Zion Society, the principle of the *free lunch* alone will free us to live for what is important? This is the economy of Zion, to receive of the common goods, our substance and support, a free gift. When this principle is properly lived, public servants don't have to protect their "sacred cows," budgets don't have to be wastefully expended for fear of not getting a similar budget the following year, and individuals don't have to worry about losing their jobs, for when the job is done, they move on to the next without a break in their support. There would be no temptation to hoard goods; all that is needed is there for the asking. Of course, all will pull their share of the load.

Downsizing

Think of the professions that will be done away with in a Zion Society. There will be no police, as there will be no crime. There will be no attorneys or judges, as no laws will be broken, no laws will need interpretation, in fact, there will be no laws. That's right. We will all live without law, or rather, with only one law, the law of God, love. Remember our discussion on truth and law and how God, knowing all law, is effectively *without law* (more on this later)? We will live entirely by the spirit of truth in love so there will be no need for written laws. No one will be inconsiderate or selfish in any way. No neighbor will play his stereo too loud. No one will throw gum wrappers on the ground instead of in the trashcan. Whatever will be the form of transportation, no one will take your parking spot or *cut you off* on the freeway. No one will, in any way, infringe upon your rights. This lack of needed attention to law will allow us to focus completely on what is important.

As before mentioned, there will be no doctors or morticians. There will be no optometrists, as all will have perfect vision (in fact they will see into the eternities). There will be no magicians or the like to entertain us, as magic is a deception, and no one will want to deceive nor will anyone be able to be deceived. There will be no factories for slave-like workers to produce the latest fashions or modes of transportation. There will be no huge corporate conglomerates; in fact, there will be no corporations at all. There will be no fast food chains or processed foods full of preservatives and other chemicals or any other unnatural ingredients. Without constraint, we will all live the Word of Wisdom fully, not just the part that says to abstain from tobacco, alcohol, tea, and coffee. There will be no janitors, only beautifiers, as no one will spoil or defile. There will be no graffiti and no trash on the streets. In fact, there will be no waste and, therefore, no city garbage dumps or waste disposal plants. There will be no locksmiths, as there will be no need for locks. There will be no soldiers or arms makers. Even before the second coming, in the midst of world chaos, lawlessness, confusion, anarchy, and terrorism, Zion will be a refuge. "And it shall be called the New Jerusalem, a land of peace, a city of refuge, a place of safety for the saints of the Most High God; And the glory of the Lord shall be there, and the terror of the Lord also shall be there, insomuch that the wicked will not come unto it, and it shall be called Zion. And it shall come to pass among the wicked, that every man that will not take his sword against his neighbor must needs flee unto Zion for safety. And it shall be said among the wicked: Let us not go up to battle against Zion, for the inhabitants of Zion are terrible; wherefore we cannot stand . . . And that the gathering together upon the land of Zion, and upon her stakes, may be for a defense, and for a refuge from the storm, and from wrath when it shall be poured out without mixture upon the whole earth." (*D&C 45:66-70, 115:6*) Zion will not be "terrible" because of her weapons or munitions; they will simply destroy their enemies by a wave of their hand. Of course, after the wicked are destroyed, Zion will have no need to be a refuge.

New Careers

One can only begin to imagine the impact celestial law will have on the society that will live it. What occupations *will* there be? What work *will* we do? There will be educators and resource people or missionaries for those who have not yet received of the *heavenly gift* (fullness of His glory). In fact, we will all be educators, as once we learn something we will want to share our knowledge with others. There will be scientists because the mysteries of the universe, from the smallest particle of the atom to the greatest structures of the cosmos, will be ours to have. "Yea, verily I say unto you, in that day when the Lord shall come, He shall reveal all things—Things which have passed, and hidden things which no man knew, things of the earth, by which it was made, and the purpose and the end thereof—Things most precious, things that are above, and things that are beneath, things that are in the earth, and upon the earth, and in heaven." (*D&C 101:32-34*) We will all be writers, as we will seek to document our findings, whatever our area of study. We will be poets, musicians, and artists. Even the scientists will recognize the art contained in the structures and subjects they study. We will all be farmers, although it will take very little of our time and attention, as the earth will plentifully bring forth its fruits and they will be free to all. Some will be public servants in administering the affairs of the kingdom of God for the good of the people on the earth. In fact, we will all have ample time and opportunity to study and pursue whatever activity we choose. Eventually, like God, the master scientist and artist, we will all be everything, scientists, artists, and so on,. We will inevitably get around to doing everything, including our genealogy[109] (a little Mormon humor there). There will be no opposition to our progress in any field. Truth will be easily attainable and discernible. In fact, truth will be so easily attainable, it will be difficult to have surprise parties; the intended recipient will no doubt know, from the spirit, what is about to take place. There will be no debating of true principles because only the truth will be taught. There will be no dissensions or differing opinions. No one will feel the need to be right. No one will, out of tradition or pride, argue points, but rather receive them with gladness. In other words, we will be of ***one mind***. Hallelujah!

Only Truth

On truth, let me further say, we will not perpetuate untruths of any kind. Now days we tell many half-truths and justify ourselves because we think they are cute or we somehow feel they are necessary traditions. Take as a case in point, the Tooth Fairy and Santa Claus. In a Zion Society these symbols will be reduced to the cartoon characters, the fantasies that they are. I catch a lot of flack when I suggest in my classes that now might be a good time to start living this higher law (Higher law?—Like we've never heard that we should not lie!). Then I quote from that great discourse on truth delivered by God to Joseph Smith, Frederick Williams, and other early brethren of The Church (italics for emphasis). "Ye were also in the beginning with the Father; that which is Spirit, even the Spirit of truth; And truth is knowledge of things as they are, and as they were, and as they are to come; And *whatsoever is more or less than this is the spirit of that wicked one who was a liar from the beginning*." (*D&C 93:23-25*) "Every spirit of man was innocent in the beginning; and God having redeemed man from the fall, men became again, in their infant state, innocent before God. And that wicked one cometh and taketh away light and truth, through disobedience, from the children of men, and because of the *tradition* of their fathers. But I have commanded you to bring up your children in light and truth. But verily I say unto you, my servant Frederick G. Williams, you have continued under this condemnation; You have not taught your children light and truth, according to the commandments; and that wicked one hath power, as yet, over you, and this is the cause of your affliction." (*D&C 93:38-42*) Tradition dies hard, but a lie is a lie, and these and all other *traditional lies* we tell our children, as well as each other, will be done away with in the Zion Society. Also, while on the subject, I must say that the celebration of pagan holidays, rooted in superstition and fear, such as Halloween and Valentines Day, will no longer be observed. We will, no doubt, have new dates and events to remember and celebrate. I suspect they will be religious events like Christ's birth, which, by the way, we will celebrate on the correct date, April 6th, instead of December 25th.[110]

The Greatest Difference

But by far, the greatest distinction of this Zion Society from the way we live now will be our spirituality. Remember the endowment I spoke of? For the

Zion City of the New Jerusalem, the veil between the earth and unseen worlds will cease to exist. There will be little need for a veil or barrier between two societies that are living the same celestial laws. This will happen even before the coming of Christ in His glory and will continue right through the Millennium. We will all, individually, walk and talk with and be taught by heavenly beings. Think of what will be learned and accomplished over a one thousand year period with direct communication with the angels of heaven as well as other of God's creations on other planets. All studies will be advanced to the endless heavens, from technologies to philosophies. Further, we will no longer be torn between Babylon and Zion. We will no longer have the carnal mind. "And in that day Satan shall not have power to tempt any man." (*D&C 101:28*) We will have no desire to sin. There will be no pride, no vanity, no hatred or bigotry, no anger, no malice, no selfishness, no envying, no coveting, and no jealousy. Lack of jealousy alone will enable us to live the law of polygamy (which by the way is a celestial law) in the Zion Society. "And in that day seven women shall take hold of one man, saying, We will eat our own bread, and wear our own apparel; only let us be called by thy name, to take away our reproach." (*Isaiah 4:1*) There will be no cheating of our fellow man or desire to take advantage of him in any way. We will be completely honest, not only with our fellow man, but with ourselves (a giant leap). No one will have their hearts set too much upon the things of this world or aspire to the honors of men. There will be no false gods, including our own weak arm of flesh. There will be no fear of any kind, but complete peace of mind. And again, we will communicate with each other spirit to spirit, in complete honesty and openness, with no confusion or misunderstanding.

No Keeping Score

The order of stewardships will be based upon the family structure. Irregularities or breaks in the family line will eventually be remedied or restored and all will be one family. Unlike many of the family relationships we now know, which are filled with contention, backbiting, or superficial associations, it will be one *big happy family*. This great family will be void of sibling rivalries born out of jealousy, envy, competition, or any other ignoble character trait. There will be no keeping score or valuing contributions to the whole. Without judging and with no expectations of others, all will give all and do all that is within their capability to give and do. Blessed are those who are able to accomplish this celestial order even now, in this telestial or terrestrial world as there is no greater joy than a celestial family association. Conversely, there is no greater hell than that of a dysfunctional family. There will be no such dysfunctional families in the Zion Society.

No Loneliness

There will be no loneliness of any kind. We will have wonderful relationships with each other, having the desire and ability to know and understand each other's deepest thoughts, without the desire for sexual oneness, as we will no longer have the carnal mind which is subject to such temptations. There will be no individualism or detachments, that is to say, notwithstanding the retaining of our individual personalities and the celebration of the differences in those personalities, we will no longer seek to be self-reliant. We will have no desire to be separate or self-sustaining as the desire to be self-sufficient is a terrestrial law. Rather, we will desire to be one with everything and everybody. As stated in the chapter on love, all will love all. Further, we will be permitted and able to express our love, and, as we understand love to be spiritual oneness, we will truly be of ***one heart***. Hallelujah again!

I have just described Zion: a people who are of **one heart and one mind**, one heart in love and one mind in truth.

A New Teacher

When we come to a unity of the faith, when we are no more tossed to and fro by every wind of doctrine, when we are no more deceived by other men, when we all come to a knowledge of the Son of God, and are perfected in Christ, we will have no more need for a church and as stated before, it will pass away. As the Millennium progresses and even the terrestrial people are converted, there will be no more need for a work of the ministry either. We will not need to haggle in our religion classes over which doctrines are true and which are not. We will all know the truth of all things. "And they shall not teach every man his neighbour, and every man his brother, saying, Know the Lord: for all shall know me, from the least to the greatest." (*Hebrews 8:11*) You see; we will have a better teacher, Christ. This is most profound to contemplate. The fulfillment of our deep desire to learn, to be taught, these and many other things by the **resurrected Savior, Jesus Christ** Himself, will come to fruition. Yes, we *all* will have a deep and personal relationship with our Savior. We will be face to face for as long as it takes to know Him (actually, that will probably happen in a moment of eternity, not time). "For the day must come when no man need say to his neighbor, Know ye the Lord; for all shall know Him—from the least to the greatest." (*TPJS pg. 149*) Is it possible? Is it really possible? Not only is it possible or even probable, it *must* be. It is future truth. It will happen.

Living Zion Laws Now

"But," you say, "we can't live it today. Zion has not yet been established." Brother McConkie and I do not agree with you. "What, then, will be the nature of worship during the Millennium? It will be pure and perfect, and through it men will become inheritors of eternal life. And in this connection, be it known that it is the privilege of the Saints today to separate themselves from the world and to receive millennial blessings in their lives. And any person who today abides the laws that will be kept during the Millennium will receive, here and now, the spirit and blessings of the Millennium in his life, even though he is surrounded by a world of sin and evil." (*Bruce R. McConkie, The Millennial Messiah, pg. 682-pg. 683*)

How? How can we live it now? Well, you can start with your family—your spouse. Whether written (prenuptial agreement) or assumed, how many of you have, with your spouses, a *what's yours is yours and what's mine is mine* arrangement? How many of you separate your time, your interests, and your goods (separate income, separate check books, separate hobbies or interests, jealously guarding your own time, and etc.)? How can you expect to have all things in common with an entire society when you can't even have a few things in common with your wife or husband? It is amazing to me that we teach our children to be unselfish, to share, to give to the poor, while we, by example, set our hearts too much upon this world. Do we hoard our goods, means, and time, not loaning or sharing with others, even our families? This is not love. This is not oneness of heart.

Zion—One Mind, One Heart

If you want to become one of mind and heart with your family and extend your oneness to others, you must make truth paramount in your life. You can only be one in truth. Falseness does not foster oneness but separateness. You must especially be honest with yourself. Then you must communicate your knowledge of truth and your feelings of love to others. Bear your testimony and express your love for them. To do so expands the soul and the recipient has something upon which to base his or her judgment. The Holy Ghost then has a truth of which to testify. Of course, you cannot say one thing then do another. That is hypocritical at best, betrayal at worst. The point is that in order to become one with someone in heart and mind, you must share yourself, your soul, with them. Your spirits must amalgamate, becoming one.

Too often fear stands in the way; fear of rejection. We are all so afraid to open up, afraid to love, afraid to spiritually give ourselves to others, afraid to express our love, afraid to be vulnerable. We live with these fears because we have been hurt so many times by those to whom we gave our love and our trust. We have been betrayed. We have been burned too many times. We judge that this is reason enough to hold back, yet the challenge is to continue to love in the face of the consequences. Remembering that the Holy Spirit must dictate the parameters of the relationship but we must, like Christ, continue to love others unconditionally until those we love succumb to our love or crucify us. In either case we will have done all that was within our power to do for them.

Fear, Is There No End?

Let me take a moment to say that I sometimes think the only subject that should constantly occupy our minds, our hearts, and our attention, is the subject of fear. What we don't realize is that it *already does* constantly occupy our minds and our hearts. Although most of us are unaware, fear, a byproduct or consequence of pride, is the root of most of our misdeeds. It is the most basic of human experiences. It permeates or at the very least affects nearly every choice we make. Fear manifests itself as pride, anger, jealousy, impatience, insecurities of all kinds, confusion, carnal desires, addictions of all kinds, compulsive behavior, the need to accumulate wealth, and influence or notoriety, violence of all kinds, macho behavior, self righteousness, bigotry, greed, prejudice, depression, revenge, regret, and feelings of superiority or inferiority. There are many other manifestations of fear but one of the most common is the need to judge others. Remember, whenever a person judges another as being wrong in their choices they are overstepping their rights. We have the right to judge if a person's actions are right or wrong for us but not whether they are right or wrong for them. Whatever level of law, truth, and glory (celestial, terrestrial, or telestial) a person chooses, they are not wrong. They are simply exercising their God-given right to choose from the choices God has placed before them. Again, it is not a matter of right or wrong but a matter of choice and we do not have the right to pass judgment on others' choices.

All the above manifestations have their root in fear. The fear of rejection; fear of failure; fear of loneliness; fear of pain (physical or psychological); fear of not getting enough or what we want; fear of being wrong; fear of embarrassment or humiliation; fear of being powerless; fear of being hated or at least unloved; fear of being inferior; fear of not measuring up to others as well as our own expectations; as well as many other fears cause us to act or react in a multitude of negative ways.

This subject could, itself, occupy an entire book but let me just say before I go on with our discussion of Zion that when we find ourselves acting or reacting in a negative way, we need to ask ourselves *what am I afraid of?* If we search our own souls, if we are really honest with ourselves, we will find that the problem lies within us and it has as its root, **pride**. It is not about what someone else or the world is doing to you. It is about the fear within you. Becoming aware of your feelings of fear will then give you choices as to how you can face that fear. And what is the answer? Love. Remember that love casts out fear. "There is no fear in love; but perfect love casteth out fear; because fear hath torment. He that feareth is not made perfect in love." (*1 John 4:18*) The key that opens the door to a Zion Society is to love and to feel God's love for you. If you really knew how much He loves you, nothing else would matter. When you finally feel His love deep in your soul, you will fear nothing! You begin to feel His love **when you love others**. Others will lose their fears when they feel your love for them. Do not be afraid to love or be loved.

Let Us Come To Mount Zion

Our time here is short, and our time there will be eternal. Why are we not living these celestial laws? What are we waiting for, a signal from the Prophet? We have signals aplenty. If we wait, it may be too late, for we will not have cultivated within us the personal traits it will take to do it. I cannot help but quote the powerful words of John Taylor to the Saints in April of 1854, "Have you forgotten who you are, and what your object is? Have you forgotten that you profess to be Saints of the Most High God, clothed upon with the holy priesthood? Have you forgotten that you are aiming to become kings and priests to the Lord, and queens and priestesses to Him? Have you forgotten that you are associated with the Saints of God in Zion, where the oracles of truth are revealed, and the truths of God are made manifest, and clearly developed; where you and your posterity after you can learn the ways of life and salvation; where you are placed in a position that you can obtain blessings from the great Elohim, that will rest upon you and your posterity worlds without end? Have you forgotten these things, and begun to turn again to the beggarly elements of the world, and become blind, like others we have spoken of, turning like the sow that was washed to her wallowing in the mire? We ought to reflect sometimes upon these things, and understand our true position." (*John Taylor, JD, 1:372*)

I recognize that in this telestial world we are constantly forced to condescend, to accept, or at least, to work with lesser terrestrial and even telestial principles. Though this is no excuse for not trying, it is part of God's eternal plan of life and salvation. Still, in our hearts, if not in actuality, we can, indeed, live celestial principles. We should all be practicing the same, giving no thought to the consequences, whatever they may be. Then we should be looking forward to the time when we can live in a society where all live by celestial laws, where all love, where all are one. We should talk about how it will be to live in the utopian Zion Society of one heart and one mind. We should study it. We should have uppermost in our minds, a clear vision of these celestial systems, sciences, and economies, else how can it come to pass? It is, after all, what we are hoping and working for, is it not? It can only come about by each individual living celestial laws; how shall we live them if we don't know them? Will we settle, through apathy, fear, or laziness, for lesser laws? Do we *fly to pieces like glass as soon as anything comes that is contrary to our traditions?* Why can we not *stand the fire*? How many of us *will be able to abide a celestial law, and go through and receive our exaltation*? Why are we asleep?

It is true that we, along with our father, Adam, were cast out of the Garden of Eden, from the presence of God, to work by the sweat of our faces. How long must we live in this "*lone and dreary world*" before we turn our faces back to Eden and the Tree of Life? How long must we live by the Devil's rules instead of by faith? Will we stay with the loneliness, confusion, suspicion, sadness, fear, strife, and fashion of Babylon ***or*** will we, at the very least, strive to understand what is expected of us and desire to live the same, even when this telestial world makes it seem impossible? In the words of the songwriters Leigh & Rosenthal (*Man of La Mancha*) and Rogers & Hammerstein (*South Pacific*), can we not dream the *impossible dream*? Without a dream, how can you have a dream come true? At least in our hearts can we not begin to "*get thee out of Babylon*" to Zion? Can we not rid ourselves of vanity and unbelief and come out from under the curse? Then we must wait, looking forward with anticipation and readiness, for the day the Lord will pour out His endowment upon us. Then the Lord's own prayer will be answered. Then His *kingdom will come, on earth as it is in heaven* (see *Matthew 6:9-13*).

"These are they who are come unto Mount Zion, and unto the city of the living God, the heavenly place, the holiest of all. These are they who are just men made perfect through Jesus the mediator of the new covenant, who wrought out this perfect atonement through the shedding of His own blood. These are they whose bodies are celestial, whose glory is that of the sun, even the glory of God, the highest of all." (*D&C 76:66, 69 and 70*)

---

[102] See endnote on location of Zion, chapter 3.

[103] The following prophecy was given by Brigham Young and retold by J. Golden Kimball in a conference in 1930. "The western boundaries of the State of Missouri will be swept so clean of its inhabitants that as President Young tells us, when we return to that place there will not be as much as a yellow dog to wag his tail." (*J. Golden Kimball, Conference Report, October 1930, pg. 59*)

[104] "But in the last days it shall come to pass, that the mountain of the house of the Lord shall be established in the top of the mountains, and it shall be exalted above the hills; and people shall flow unto it. And many nations shall come, and say, Come, and let us go up to the mountain of the LORD, and to the house of the God of Jacob; and he will teach us of his ways, and we will walk in his paths: for the law shall go forth of Zion, and the word of the LORD from Jerusalem." (*Micah 4:1-2 and Isaiah 2:2-3*)

[105] Kirtland, Ohio, was where the Saints built the first latter-day temple in the 1830's.

[106] See also *Times and Seasons*, Vol. 6, pg. 786, an explanation of the plot of the city of Zion, sent to the brethren in Zion, the 25th of June 1833.

[107] Hugh Nibley has been a renowned author and religious professor at BYU for many years.

[108] It is found in the *Collected Works of Hugh Nibley*, Vol. 9, Ch. 8, pg. 209. The meat of it is also found in one of his latest works, *Approaching Zion*.

[109] Genealogy is a fundamental work done by members of The Church in an effort to connect with their forefathers as well as for the purpose of doing ordinance work (such as baptism and eternal marriage) for them in temples so that they, with us, may be saved in the kingdom of God.

[110] *The Doctrine and Covenants*, the first sentence of section 20, indicates that Christ was born on April 6th.

10
Grace and Letting Go

Search Our Souls

I recognize that many of the concepts within this offering are controversial and I suspect some may dismiss them as folly. I fear many may use my alleged impertinence as an excuse to cast this text away, not having even reached this page. Of course that is their choice, but I worry about those whose minds are closed or their own foundation of truth is so insecure that they are afraid to test ideas and concepts that may be new to them. I question whether their testimony will stand the refiner's fire. I also worry about those who become angry with or persecute those who do seek, ask, and knock. If I am mistaken or misguided in what I have said herein, a compassionate person would try to help me find the error of my ways, not become angry. What if what I have said is true? Then "wo unto all those who tremble, and are angry because of the truth of God! For behold, he that is built upon the rock receiveth it with gladness; and he that is built upon a sandy foundation trembleth lest he shall fall." (*2 Nephi 28:28*) Also, "when a corrupt man is chastised he gets angry and will not endure it." (*TPJS pg. 194*) I rush to say that these writings are not meant to be a chastening or a reprimand, though some may receive them that way. Search your soul. I have and feel a need to repent.

Still, I do not condemn anyone for what they choose to believe, as they must make their choices and it is not my place to condemn. As far as their weaknesses, I hasten to repeat Joseph Smith's words, "If you will not accuse me, I will not accuse you. If you will throw a cloak of charity over my sins, I will over yours—for charity covereth a multitude of sins." (*TPJS pg. 193*)

Work vs. Grace?

"What?" you ask, "Can we be saved in our sins?" No and yes. *No* we cannot be saved in the Kingdom of God as sinners, so we are all lost, *but yes*, that is, if we comply with the ordinances of faith, repentance, and baptism of water, then we may expect, at some point in time, the grace of our Savior to intervene and wash our sins away, in which case we would no longer be sinners. This is done through the Baptism of Fire and the sanctification of our bodies and souls.

It is very important to continue to seek, to pray, and to think or meditate upon the doctrines and the mysteries of heaven. We must continue in humility, with our minds open and our hearts not set upon the things of this world. We must not be asleep (as most of us are) or dead to spiritual things. We must obey the commandments, all of them, that in our weakness, we can obey. I cannot stress enough that it is a case of *thinking* **and** *doing*. To those guilty of thinking only, I say, "Start doing!" And to those guilty of only doing I say, "Start thinking!" It is not *either or.* Just one or the other will not prepare us. We must both **think and do**. Still, it is by the grace of our Savior that our sins are forgiven, no matter what we think or what we do.

Why do we insist upon keeping the grace of our Lord a secret and continue to trust in our own arm of flesh? Is it because we are afraid we might begin to sound like the so-called Born-again Christians? Perhaps we should take a lesson from them. How often have our missionaries argued with them that it is our **works** that save us, not grace? "For as the body without the spirit is dead, so faith without works is dead also." (*James 2:26, 17, 20, Hebrews 6:1*) It seems these Born-agains have received a personal witness that being *saved by grace* is true, and since it is, to give that up would be to ask them to deny truth, give up their integrity, and renounce their testimony. They rightly counter with, "For by grace are ye saved through faith; and that not of yourselves: it is the gift of God." (*Ephesians 2:8*) "Who hath saved us, and called us with an holy calling, not according to our works, but according to His own purpose and grace, which was given us in Christ Jesus before the world began." (*2 Timothy 1:9*) And if they were believers in *The Book of Mormon*, they could also quote Nephi who said, "Wherefore, my beloved brethren, reconcile yourselves to the will of God, and not to the will of the devil and the flesh; and remember, after ye are reconciled unto God, that it is only in and through the grace of God that ye are saved." (*2 Nephi 10:24*)

One would have as much chance of drawing the Born-again Christians away from the *saved by grace doctrine* as one would have of convincing a Mormon that *The Book of Mormon* is false. This is as it should be. Both *should* hold fast to the truths that God has given them. But let us get together, which could be done if we would quit trying to prove each other wrong.

We Mormons should have taken the clue given by Nephi in this next passage. "For we labor diligently to write, to persuade our children, and also our brethren, to believe in Christ, and to be reconciled to God; for we know that it is by grace that we are saved, after all we can do." (*2 Nephi 25:23*) We Mormons, for the sake of our argument, like to put the emphasis on those last five words, "*after all we can do*," but I believe Nephi really meant, "*no matter what we do*." Why is it that the Mormons only pick up on the "*after all we can do*" at the exclusion of "*for we know that it is by grace that we are saved*"? And to our Born-again brothers, I ask why you refuse to recognize not only the part of the scripture that states the *need* for works, but the simplicity of the logic that dictates if we have commandments there is some *need* to obey them (or at least try)? What could that need, be? Could obeying the commandments or good works be requisite to receiving grace?

To my Mormon friends I again ask, "What doth it profit a man if a gift is bestowed upon him and he receive not the gift? Behold, he rejoices not in that which is given unto him, neither rejoices in him who is the giver of the gift." (*D&C 88:34*) Christ is offering us His **gift** of grace. Are we refusing it? The hard line taken by Mormons that you must "work out your own salvation with fear and trembling," (see *Philippians 2:12, Mormon 9:27*) has caused us to erroneously think it is by our own doing we are saved. Working out your own salvation only refers to your responsibility to keep working and trying. It does not address the need for the grace of Christ in order to be finally saved. It is **not possible** for us to save ourselves. **It is not**! We simply do not have the power.

Salvation is a *gift* from God. The more we think we can save ourselves through our good works, the more Christ gets left out of the picture. Conversely, the more we think it is all up to Christ, the less we are prepared to receive His gift of eternal life when He is ready to bestow it, thereby wasting His sacrifice.

It is only through our attempts, weak though they may be, to keep the commandments that we learn our lowly place, our nothingness, and put our hope and faith in Christ. It is through our struggles to keep the laws that we learn we ***cannot***. It is through our attempts to keep the commandments that our hearts become broken and contrite. This is our part to do. Then, and only then, are we candidates for His grace, the grace that He promises us if we will come to Him. Awake all you Mormons and other Christians! You are both right! It is a case of ***BOTH*** not *either or*.

The Irrevocable Decree

My good Mormon brothers and sisters say, "Oh yeah, we know that! Sure, it is Christ that saves us." But then we go right back to acting like our good works can somehow give us the power to reach our puny arms of flesh up into heavens and pull the gift of salvation down upon our own heads. No, no, a thousand times no! All we can do is *prepare* ourselves to receive the gift. "Well, isn't that the same?" you ask. No, it is not, nor is it even a fine line of distinction. It is the difference between worshipping God and worshipping our own arm of flesh. That is no small difference. *Winning* or *earning* is not the same as receiving a *gift*.

Perhaps this aspect of Christ's grace we Mormons either don't quite understand or refuse to accept. I can't really say which it is.

The Chicken And The Egg

Again it relates to our previous discussion about God giving men weaknesses (italics for emphasis). "Fools mock, but they shall mourn; and my grace is sufficient for the meek, that they shall take no advantage of your weakness; And if men come unto me I will show unto them their weakness, *I give unto men weakness* that they may be humble; and *my grace is sufficient for all men that humble themselves before me*; for if they humble themselves before me, and have faith in me, then will I make weak things become strong unto them." (*Ether 12:26-27*) There is an apparent contradiction here because we are expected to overcome our sins and keep the commandments, but all our sincere struggles prove we are too weak to do it. It becomes a "chicken before the egg" circumstance. We can't overcome our weakness and keep the commandments without the help of Christ, but we can't get the help of Christ without obedience to the commandments. Which comes first?

Paul did more than just comment on this. "For the good that I would I do not: but the evil which I would not, that I do. Now if I do that I would not, it is no more I that do it, but sin that dwelleth in me. I find then a law, that, when I would do good, evil is present with me. For I delight in the law of God after the inward man: But I see another law in my members, warring against the law of my mind, and bringing me into captivity to the law of sin which is in my members. O wretched man that I am! Who shall deliver me from the body of this death? I thank God through Jesus Christ our Lord. So then with the mind I myself serve the law of God; but with the flesh the law of sin." (*Romans 7:19-25*) He is saying that he *wants* to do good, but *doesn't* and he *doesn't want* to do evil, but *does*. Finally, he thanks God that at least in his mind and heart he desires to do good even if, because of weaknesses of the flesh, he sins. His frustration is the same that is felt by many as the war between the flesh and the spirit wages within each of us. Thus, "watch and pray, that ye enter not into temptation; the spirit indeed is willing but the flesh is weak." (*Matthew 26:41*) I know that I am making it sound like the road to heaven, not hell, is paved with good intentions. This is exactly what I am saying. If our sincere desires are righteous, Christ will eventually step in and give us power to overcome.

Still, many of us Mormons get it backwards. We struggle alone to perfect ourselves so that we may present ourselves to Christ, complete and whole, without sin, when in fact it is impossible to become perfect without Him. We must first come to Him *because* of our sins, in our sins and weakness. We must come to Him *in* our sins and plead for mercy and his saving grace.

The Right Direction

So until Christ steps in and gives us power to fully overcome, how do we get a stronger spirit that we might put the flesh in subjection to the spirit? We must do what we have been given power to do. It is like the alcoholic or drug addict who, *incrementally*, over a period of time, has given his power to a drug that now controls him. On his own, the addict is not strong enough to just quit. He, and we, must sacrifice what we have the strength to sacrifice. Then we will grow in power to overcome, *incrementally*, over a period of time, until we prove ourselves worthy of God's grace. The addict is strong enough to at least *desire* to quit, or maybe to humble himself and ask for help from others, or be in places and with people who can inspire him, or do other things that will postpone or distract him from acting on his impulse, or do other little things that he has power to do that will strengthen him in general. Of course, accomplishing the task is a struggle, but understanding the concept makes it a lot easier. Some of the power comes in a progression, that is, God gives us a little power and as we act on that power, He gives us a little more and so on and so on. It is almost always a *way of life*, not *a single act*. We don't build our scaffolding to heaven all at once, but plank by plank. A single act, change of heart, change of attitude, commitment, or covenant, can change our direction on the road, at either end of which is heaven or hell, but rarely does a single act take us very far down or up that road. Still, it is our responsibility to make the right choices even with the small decisions. This will keep us going the right direction on that road.

More Power

There is not a man that God has not given some power or gift to do something. "The Spirit of the Lord enlightens every man that comes into the world. There is no one that lives upon the earth but what is, more or less, enlightened by the Spirit of the Lord Jesus. It is said of Him, that He is the light of the world. He lighteth every man that comes into the world and every person, at times, has the light of the spirit of truth upon Him." (*DBY, pg. 32*) If we expect more light and power, we must obey the commandments the Lord has already given us the power to obey. Joseph Smith said, "But we cannot keep all the commandments without first knowing them, and we cannot expect to know all, or more than we now know unless we comply with or keep those we have already received." (*TPJS, pg. 255*) Further, I cannot make this next point strong enough. We **should not ever quit praying and trying** to overcome our sins; we never know when the Lord will answer our prayers and give us the power to do so. Again I say for emphasis, **it is our duty, our sacred duty, to keep trying!**

Since I have used the alcoholic as an example, it might be appropriate here to quote the prayer of Alcoholics Anonymous: "God grant me the serenity to accept the things I cannot change, the power to change the things I can, and the wisdom to know the difference." (*Alcoholics Anonymous Prayer*) Herein are embedded all the principles of this doctrine. We must accept that we have weaknesses beyond our ability to change. The knowledge of this will break our hearts; if we turn to Christ in this condition, our spirits will be contrite. We must appeal to God, the source of power, for the endowment of power to overcome. Then we must keep trying so that when He gives us the power, which He has promised to do, though it may be in His own time (not ours), we can, indeed, overcome. This is repentance, and if we will confess our sins, not just to the world, but to ourselves, and do all we can, He has promised us "my grace is sufficient for all men that humble themselves before me; for if they humble themselves before me, and have faith in me, then will I make weak things become strong unto them." (*Ether 12:27*)

Laws And Blessings

To strengthen their argument that we must work our way to heaven, my brothers will often quote, "There is a law, irrevocably decreed in heaven before the foundations of this world, upon which all blessings are predicated—And when we obtain any blessing from God, it is by obedience to that law upon which it is predicated." (*D&C 130:20-21*) "For all who will have a blessing at my hands shall abide the law which was appointed for that blessing, and the conditions thereof, as were instituted from before the foundation of the world." (*D&C 132:5*) Doesn't that put the ball in our court? Well, yes, and it has always been in our court. I here make no attempt to relieve us all of our responsibility to keep the law, to prepare, to do good works.

I do not believe by saying that it requires both *works* **and** *grace* that I have, in any way, eliminated either.

Although the scripture does say, if we are to *obtain any blessing from God*, we must obey the *law upon which it is predicated*; it does not say that *if we obey a law we will receive the blessing we expected to receive*. Also, as discussed in the chapter on the meaning of life, our perception of what is a blessing or curse may not coincide with what the Lord's deems a blessing or curse. Further, the problem is, we think spiritual laws (celestial laws, the Law of Christ) are the same as the temporal laws (telestial and terrestrial laws), like *if you obey the laws of business or industry, you* ***will*** *get rich*. Or, *if you are prospering, then you* ***must have been keeping*** *some law of business or industry*. It does not work quite that way. Remember, "Verily I say unto you that all things unto me are spiritual, and not at any time have I given unto you a law which was temporal; neither any man, nor the children of men, neither Adam, your father, whom I created." (*D&C 29:34*) When the Lord gave Adam the commandment in the garden concerning the two trees, was it a temporal commandment? No. Although it had temporal repercussions, to be sure, the spiritual repercussions were by far the greatest. Take the Word of Wisdom. Since it is a law of health one would expect the blessings to be mostly physical, or temporal. It is the other way around. Though it does have physical blessings attached to it, the superlative benefits are spiritual. "And all saints who remember to keep and do these sayings, walking in obedience to the commandments, shall receive health in their navel and marrow to their bones; And shall *find wisdom and great treasures of knowledge, even hidden treasures*; And shall run and not be weary, and shall walk and not faint. And I, the Lord, give unto them a promise, that *the destroying angel shall pass by them*, as the children of Israel, and not slay them. Amen." (*D&C 89:18-21*) Finding *wisdom and great treasures of knowledge, even hidden treasures*, and a promise *that the destroying angel shall pass us by*, has nothing to do with temporal blessings. "I the Lord am bound when ye do what I say, but when ye do not what I say, ye have no promise." (*D&C 82:10*) The Lord is bound to keep the promises He makes to us when we do what He says, but you will note here that He did **not** say, "I the Lord am bound to give you whatever you want, when you want it, if ye do what I say." No, they are *His promises*, not *our wants and wishes*. When His promises are fulfilled, we will see they are far greater than anything we could have supposed or imagined, and they will be eternal blessings, not temporal. Further, they are yet to be had, that is, they are *promises*. They are yet to be fulfilled. Even though we do what He says now, we may still have, as yet, only His promises. Of course, whether *in this life or the next*, He will indeed make good His promises. But again, the blessings will likely not be as we expect, for **too often we are expecting temporal blessings for our obedience, when His blessings are spiritual and eternal**.

What I am trying to say here is that we do not know what the spiritual laws *are* that blessings are *predicated upon*, nor do we know what the spiritual blessings *are* that are attached to those laws. To think if you strictly obey the Word of Wisdom you will never become ill or die is obviously not so. To think if you work hard all your life you will get rich is obviously not so. To think if you always tell the truth you will be respected, believed, and admired, is obviously not so, as there have been many righteous martyrs. To think if you keep any celestial laws you will inevitably prosper in this telestial world is, again, obviously not so. Celestial laws do not work in telestial or terrestrial environments.

Celestial Law In A Telestial World

This is one reason so much confusion and doubt exists. We don't seem to comprehend the fact that we are living in a telestial world, terrestrial at best, and only the laws of those realms work here. You can lie and cheat your way to the top while the honest, fair person is left in the dust. When you go into Babylon to compete, you will be called upon to compromise your celestial principles, as celestial principles are not recognized in lesser environments. If you will not stoop to terrestrial or telestial laws, you will not achieve. My advice, *get thee out of Babylon* to Zion, where your principles will be recognized and appreciated. Still, the counsel from the prophets is to stay where we are and build Zion in our respective geographical areas, and since I believe in obeying the prophets, I will go and stay where I am commanded. Where we are physically or geographically is of little consequence. What matters is that we literally, in our hearts, families, and churches, build Zion (italics for emphasis). "Go ye out from among the nations, even from Babylon, from the midst of wickedness, which is *spiritual* Babylon." (*D&C 133:14*) Then we can look forward to the day when the wheat and the tares must be separated in preparation for the harvest of the wheat and the destruction of the tares (see *Matt 13:25-30*). Then the word will be to literally, physically, get thee out of Babylon. Then "wherefore, prepare ye, prepare ye, O my people; sanctify yourselves; gather ye together, O ye people of my church, upon the land of Zion, all you that have not been commanded to tarry. Go ye out from Babylon. Be ye clean that bear the vessels of the Lord." (*D&C 133:5-6*) So until this becomes Church policy, until Zion is gathered into a Society, we must continue to struggle to live celestial laws in a place and circumstance that will not prosper our efforts.

It is amazing to me that more people don't understand this concept! It should be no great secret, yet it is. We keep expecting to succeed in Babylon and live celestial law at the same time. It cannot be done! If you are committed to living God's law, only He can make you prosperous, which, hopefully He will do, *despite* your environment. But let me here testify and warn you (if you haven't already figured it out) that the laws and principles we have discussed in this book will not insure you success in this telestial world. Do not expect them to pay off temporally here. Celestial laws do not apply here. They are ***Celestial Concepts in a Telestial World***. Accordingly, obedience to temporal laws will not yield celestial blessings. The sad part is we think we are obeying celestial laws when most of the time those laws are in fact terrestrial if not telestial. Even the laws given through The Church are temporal carnal commandments and performances. They are not the celestial *law of Christ*. They are not the laws God lives by. Our challenge is to discover the higher celestial *law of Christ* and live by that law (more later on the "Law of Christ"). Most of us, even good members of The Church, do not know the celestial laws. We keep living the lesser laws of carnal commandments and performances thinking that will do. It will not. There is a higher, better way.

Nevertheless, let no reader here assume that I am saying we need not obey the lesser laws of carnal commandments and performances. It is only in doing so that we progress to the higher celestial law.

Because celestial laws do not work in this telestial world it requires faith to live them down here. Except for the whisperings of the spirit, we have little immediate temporal or tangible evidence that what we are doing is right. As we attempt to live celestially, we will continue to face overwhelming opposition in this world. Even many of our own, who should know better, will scoff, betray, and fight against those who attempt to tell the great secret, the Gospel of Christ. Notwithstanding this fact, my testimony and admonishment is to keep obeying celestial laws, whether or not they pay off in this life. This telestial life is short, 70, 80, 100 years at the most. Our next life will be eternal, without end! The Lord will keep His promises. Though we may not receive our temporal wishes, we ***will*** obtain the blessings upon which these celestial laws are predicated. God will vanquish our enemies. We will obtain the power of God to know the mysteries, work miracles, and control the elements, though it may not be now, it *could* be now, or *soon*.

It is my testimony also that the blessings and laws referred to in the above quoted D&C 130:20-21 are mostly spiritual and eternal in nature. In some cases, if not most, we cannot even imagine, let alone comprehend, what those blessings will be, nor the greatness and glory attached to them. If my testimony is true and these blessings are eternal, then they are not temporal (temporary) and may not be evident while you are in a temporal environment. Our blessings are spiritual and eternal. They are in store, that is, *in storage*, up in heaven. I pray our warehouse is large and full.

Perfection, Is It Possible?

I cannot say how it is in other churches, but there has been an ongoing debate within the Mormon Church about whether it is possible to become perfect in this life. We completely miss the mark by even asking that question in the first place. The question should be, is it possible *to make* ***ourselves*** *perfect* (in this life or any other life, for that matter)? The answer: **it is impossible**. Only Christ can perfect us. We are mortal and subject to the weaknesses of the flesh. Once we break even one law of God we come under the condemnation of that law and are no longer justified by the law.

Like Paul, who appealed to God to remove the thorn from his side, we cannot do it ourselves. To pretend we can is to deny the atonement of Christ. He is the only one who has overcome all things and He will *help us* overcome all things. It may not be today, or tomorrow, or next week, or even in this life. Like Paul, He may keep that thorn in our side. He may want to keep us humble, or want us to suffer that we may know the joy. We cannot pull down the gifts from heaven but only prepare ourselves, and wait with a *broken heart and a contrite spirit* to receive the blessings when He, in His own time, chooses to grant them. The power is God's, not ours.

Even that great Prophet Nephi, after experiencing many great spiritual blessings, ministering of angels, revelations, and great visions, lamented that he was unable to live the law perfectly. "Nevertheless, notwithstanding the great goodness of the Lord, in showing me His great and marvelous works, my heart exclaimeth: O wretched man that I am! Yea, my heart sorroweth because of my flesh; my soul grieveth because of mine iniquities. I am encompassed about, because of the temptations and the sins which do so easily beset me. And when I desire to rejoice, my heart groaneth because of my sins . . . O then, if I have seen so great things, if the Lord in His condescension unto the children of men hath visited men in so much mercy, why should my heart weep and my soul linger in the valley of sorrow, and my flesh waste away, and my strength slacken, because of mine afflictions? . . . And why should I yield to sin, because of my flesh? Yea, why should I give way to temptations, that the evil one have place in my heart to destroy my peace and afflict my soul? Why am I angry because of mine enemy?" (*2 Nephi 4:17-19, 26-27*) Does Nephi's brutally honest lamentation sound familiar to you? I hope so. If so, you may be closer than you know to that necessary broken heart and contrite spirit.

The Demands of Justice

A couple of paragraphs back I said, "Once we break even one law of God we come under the condemnation of that law and are no longer justified by the law." Justification is a legal term meaning the justice according to the law or in other words, the law demands justice. There are only three ways to be justified by the law. First, don't break the law, and then that law justifies you. No one, save Christ, has ever managed to do this. James tells us that we are incapable of keeping the whole law. "For whosoever shall keep the whole law, and yet offend in one point, he is guilty of all." (*James 2:10*) Since none of us is perfect, since we have all sinned, either in the past, now, or in the future, we will all be found guilty by the law. Second, you may pay the penalty or take the punishment demanded by the law and be thereby justified. Those who don't repent will do exactly that. "Therefore I command you to repent—repent, lest I smite you by the rod of my mouth, and by my wrath, and by my anger, and your sufferings be sore—how sore you know not, how exquisite you know not, yea, how hard to bear you know not . . . . But if they would not repent they must suffer even as I; Which suffering caused myself, even God, the greatest of all, to tremble because of the pain, and to bleed at every pore, and to suffer both body and spirit . . . ." (*D&C 19:15, 17-18*) Third, someone else may pay the penalty so that the demands of justice are filled. This is Where Christ comes in. "For behold, I, God, have suffered these things for all, that they might not suffer if they would repent." (*D&C 19:16*) We will inevitably fall short. "For it is expedient that an atonement should be made; for according to the great plan of the Eternal God there must be an atonement made, or else all mankind must unavoidably perish; yea, all are hardened; yea, all are fallen and are lost, and must perish except it be through the atonement which it is expedient should be made." (*Alma 34:9*) "We are all as an unclean thing, and all our *righteousness* is as filthy rags; and we all do fade as a leaf; and our iniquities, like the wind, have taken us away." (*Isaiah 64:6*)

It is impossible to keep all the laws perfectly through our own efforts in this mortal life. All our struggles to keep the laws will ultimately lead us back to this conclusion. The irony is that **this conclusion is the *right* place to be**, the very place we *must* be. Let me add my testimony to that of the prophets by saying it is impossible to be saved by keeping the law or by trying to, but only through Christ's gift of grace may we be saved. I read on in Nephi's lamentation (italics for emphasis). "Awake, my soul! No longer droop in sin. Rejoice, O my heart, and give place no more for the enemy of my soul. Do not anger again because of mine enemies. Do not slacken my strength because of mine afflictions. Rejoice, O my heart, and cry unto the Lord, and say: O Lord, I will praise thee forever; yea, my soul will rejoice in thee, my God, and the rock of my salvation. O Lord, *wilt thou* redeem my soul? *Wilt thou* deliver me out of the hands of mine enemies? *Wilt thou* make me that I may shake at the appearance of sin? May the gates of hell be shut continually before me, *because that my heart is broken and my spirit is contrite*! O Lord, *wilt thou* not shut the gates of thy righteousness before me, that I may walk in the path of the low valley, that I may be strict in the plain road! Lord, *wilt thou* encircle me around in the robe of thy righteousness! O Lord, wilt thou make a way for mine escape before mine enemies! *Wilt thou* make my path straight before me! *Wilt thou* not place a stumbling block in my way—but that thou wouldst clear my way before me, and hedge not up my way, but the ways of mine enemy. O Lord, I have trusted in thee, and I will trust in thee forever. I will not put my trust in the arm of flesh; for I know that cursed is he that putteth his trust in the arm of flesh. Yea, cursed is he that putteth his trust in man or maketh flesh his arm. Yea, I know that God will give liberally to him that asketh. Yea, my God will give me, if I ask not amiss; therefore I will lift up my voice unto thee; yea, I will cry unto thee, my God, the rock of my righteousness. Behold, my voice shall forever ascend up unto thee, my rock and mine everlasting God. Amen." (*2 Nephi 4:28-35*) Did Nephi say, "I can do this, just give me another chance, a little more time and I can do it?" No, his plea was, "*Wilt thou.*" He trusted **not** in his own arm of flesh, but appealed to God to make him righteous, to encircle him in the robe of God's righteousness, to cause him to shake at the appearance of sin. And did he receive the fulfillment of the promise? Yes. "But behold, the Lord hath redeemed my soul from hell; I have *beheld His glory*, and I am *encircled about eternally in the arms of His love*." (*2 Nephi 1:15*)

The Requirements

I can still hear you say, "It can't be true that we sit back and do nothing! We must not give up trying." I didn't say that, nor did the prophets. Like Nephi we must realize our *wretchedness*, our *nothingness* before God. As King Benjamin said, we must yield "to the enticings of the Holy Spirit, and putteth off the natural man and becometh a saint through the atonement of Christ the Lord, and becometh as a child, *submissive, meek, humble, patient, full of love, willing to submit to all things which the Lord seeth fit to inflict upon him*, even as a child doth submit to his father . . . The knowledge of the goodness of God at this time has awakened you to a sense of your *nothingness*, and your *worthless* and fallen state . . . And they had viewed themselves in their own carnal state, even less than the dust of the earth. And they all cried aloud with one voice, saying: O have mercy, and apply the atoning blood of Christ that we may receive forgiveness of our sins, and our hearts may be purified; for we believe in Jesus Christ, the Son of God, who created heaven and earth, and all things; who shall come down among the children of men." (*Mosiah 3:19, 4:2-6*) After teaching this to his people in that great spiritual address, the "Spirit of the Lord came upon them, and they were filled with joy, having received a remission of their sins, and having peace of conscience, because of the exceeding faith which they had in Jesus Christ . . . ." (*Mosiah 4:3*) These people were awakened to a sense of their *nothingness, worthlessness,* and fallen state (see *Mosiah 4:5-11*). They let go! "And they all cried with one voice, saying: Yea, we believe all the words which thou hast spoken unto us; and also, we know of their surety and truth, because of the Spirit of the Lord Omnipotent, which has wrought a mighty change in us, or in our hearts, that we have no more disposition to do evil, but to do good continually." (*Mosiah 5:2*) Did *they* make the change in their own hearts? No. Was this a self-help seminar where they hyped themselves into finally deciding to not sin anymore, and then didn't? Not hardly. It was not within the power of their own weak arm of flesh to make such a change. It was through the grace of Christ that the change came about in their hearts. They humbled themselves, they believed, and the Lord did the rest. This is *the* law that was irrevocably decreed before the foundations of the world, upon which all blessings are predicated. What is this law? It is the *Law of Christ*. It is the *New Law*, the *New Covenant* (more on this soon). Unlike we so-called Saints of the Latter-days, *they* came out from under the condemnation, scourge and judgment of their *vanity and unbelief* (see *D&C 84:54-58*), and were Born Again of the spirit. Let me again add my testimony to that of the prophets: *it is impossible* by trying to keep the commandments and laws to be justified thereby.

"But," you say, "do we not covenant at the time of our baptism to keep the commandments and do we not renew that covenant each Sunday when we partake of the sacrament?" No, not exactly. When we read carefully the sacramental prayer, we discover that the Lord's requirement is not quite so harsh (italics added). "O God, the Eternal Father, we ask thee in the name of thy Son, Jesus Christ, to bless and sanctify this bread to the souls of all those who partake of it, that they may eat in remembrance of the body of thy Son, and witness unto thee, O God, the Eternal Father, that they are *willing* to take upon them the name of thy Son, and always remember him and keep his commandments which he has given them; that they may always have his Spirit to be with them. Amen." (*D&C 20:77*) You will notice that the Lord requires that we be *willing* to take upon us the name of the Son, *willing* to remember Him, *willing* to keep His commandments. This is a declaration of *what we want* not *what we are capable of* (or rather *not* capable of). We are contracting that we are *willing* to accept the gift of God's grace, otherwise, it is a gift offered but not accepted, and "what doth it profit a man if a gift is bestowed upon him and he receive not the gift?" (*D&C 88:34*)

Is this a loophole in the Lord's legal contract letting us off the hook? No, in fact, we are only "on the hook" if we choose to be, if we are *willing* to be. Does this mean we need only *profess* a willingness to obey but not try? Not hardly. There is a requirement requisite to receiving God's gift of grace. There is a *sacrifice* you must make. Remember that Joseph Smith told us the only way to know we are pleasing God is by sacrifice. Then, and only then, may you have the confidence that you are doing His will. Again what is that sacrifice (italics for emphasis)? "Thou shalt offer a *sacrifice* unto the Lord thy God in righteousness, even that of *a broken heart and a contrite spirit*." (*D&C 59:8*) Like Nephi and King Benjamin's people you must come to that point where your heart is broken and your spirit is contrite, for "redemption cometh in and through the Holy Messiah; for He is full of grace and truth. Behold, He offereth himself a sacrifice for sin, to answer the ends of the law, unto all those who have a *broken heart and a contrite spirit*; and ***unto none else can the ends of the law be answered.***" (*2 Nephi 2:6-7*) **A broken heart and contrite spirit *is the only* prerequisite to receiving His greatest gift of grace, *of Charity, yet paradoxically, it is our vain attempt to keep the commandments that brings us to that place where our hearts are broken and our spirits are contrite, so that we are ready to receive the gift*.**

Remember, a gift, by definition, cannot be earned or it becomes a wage. In other words, the *only way* to keep the commandments is to lose the desire to commit sin, and that only happens when you are born of God, encircled in Christ's love. Then, like the rest who are Born Again, you continue to keep the commandments out of expediency, not fear. Then and only then may you be, made perfect by Christ, in Christ, and of Christ. "These are they who are just men made perfect through Jesus the mediator of the new covenant, who wrought out this perfect atonement through the shedding of His own blood." (*D&C 76:69*)

Pride

What stops us, what gets in the way of this broken heart and contrite spirit? Pride. Yes, pride.

Let me here express a few of my own observations relative to this thing we call pride. I consider it to be the root of all evil. It is the rot from which all fruit is spoiled. It is the bacteria from which all things decay. It is the core from which all other character flaws issue forth. It has brought down many great men, including Cain of old and even the Devil himself. (see *Moses 4:1-4* and *D&C 29:36*)

Yes, a sacrifice is required. You must let go! Let go? Let go of what? Your pride! *Your pride!* ***Your Pride!*** "Behold, are ye stripped of pride? I say unto you, if ye are not ye are not prepared to *meet* God." (*Alma 5:28*) You must let go of your need to be right. You must let go of your need to fix everyone and everything that is wrong (or what you perceive to be wrong). You must let go of your rebellious nature and become humble and submissive. You must let go of the burden you carry as a result of your weakness. You must let go of your guilt. You must let go of your sense of responsibility to achieve. You must let go of your worry. You must let go of your goals, plans, and schemes. You must let go of all your concerns, past, present, and future. You must let go of every other evidence of your vanity. Said Brigham Young, "If I were to ask you individually, if you wished to be sanctified throughout, and become as pure and holy as you possibly could live, every person would say yes; yet if the Lord Almighty should give a revelation instructing you to be given wholly up to Him, and to His cause, you would shrink, saying, 'I am afraid he will take away some of my darlings.' That is the difficulty with the majority of this people. *(JD 2:134)* Brigham here calls our desires "darlings" and we would be hard pressed to give **any**, let alone **all** of them up.

Yes, you must let go of your expectations. But most of all you must let go of ***all your desires*** (that's a hard one) because your desires are driven by pride.

I know what I will say next will sound wrong but it is not. You must let go of your vision of how things *should* be; what is *right*, what you *want* to happen, what you *think* ***should*** happen, your plans to ***make*** things happen, and even your ***desire*** for things to happen according to your perception of how they ought to happen. If you don't, you are forced to live in the world judgmentally. You are constantly judging others and yourself. The problem with that is, you see; we don't know enough to know what *is* right or what *should* happen in this world. Only God knows so much. Remember, it is His world after all.

I know this is difficult, as we have grown up in a world that judges and condemns. We are constantly taught that not only do we have the right, but it is an absolute necessity to judge everything and everybody, including ourselves, and even God. Further, we are taught that we can do anything if we just make our plan and think positively as we work that plan. Well, my testimony is that such an attitude is far from *yielding our will to God* and *becoming as a child, submissive, meek, humble, patient, and full of love, willing to submit to all things which the Lord seeth fit to inflict upon us.* (see *Mosiah 3:19*) Such an attitude is not just holding tight to our pride and vanity, it is self-worship (wrong god folks).

By saying the above, one **must not** think that this author is in any way telling you that you need not struggle honestly to keep the commandments or achieve good things. **I am not!** That is not what I am trying to say here. You **must** do **all** in your power, or rather in the power given you of God, to keep all the dictates of the Holy Spirit that is directing you. This you must do as completely as you, in your weakness, are able. I did not say *quit* or *give up*. I said ***let go***. Let go of your expectation of the outcome of your good efforts. Let go of your desire for a certain end. Leave the results or success up to God (it is anyway). You must let go to capture, you must lose to win, you must die to live, or, in other words, you must give your very will to God, that is, *let go of your own desire and will,* even your vain desire to be righteous as such desires are born of pride. Again, our righteousness is like filthy rags.

So you want to be perfect? "Be ye therefore perfect, even as your Father which is in heaven is perfect." (*Matthew 5:48*) This commandment, without understanding, is the source of much frustration. As I said earlier, ***it is impossible to perfect ourselves* but it *is possible to be perfected*.** There is only one way. As Moroni said, "Yea, come unto Christ, and be perfected in Him, and deny yourselves of all ungodliness; and if ye shall deny yourselves of all ungodliness and love God with all your might, mind and strength, then is His grace sufficient for you, that by His grace ye may be perfected in Christ; and if by the grace of God ye are perfect in Christ, ye can in nowise deny the power of God." (*Moroni 10:32*)

Notwithstanding the need for man to do his part, let us not make the mistake of believing that it is we that do the perfecting and not God. Such a mistake will cause us to deny the power of God and end up worshipping a false God, ourselves. Like the determined child, we cannot continue to insist *we can do it ourselves*. Although you must receive the gift, God only can make you perfect. It is by God's grace that we are made perfect, if we are but *willing* to accept it. Giving up our own will to God, what we really want deep down in our souls, is the determining factor (italics added). "And in that day the Holy Ghost fell upon Adam, which beareth record of the Father and the Son, saying: I am the Only Begotten of the Father from the beginning, henceforth and forever, that as thou hast fallen thou mayest be redeemed, and all mankind, even as many as *will*. (*Moses 5:10*)

My Attitude Is Gratitude

What does it mean to have a broken heart and a contrite spirit? Well, it means to be humble, lowly, and meek. It also means to *be grateful*. Grateful for not only our perceived blessings but for the hand of God in *all things*, in our lives, even our trials, like Paul who gloried in his tribulations. Said Brigham Young, "I do not know of any, excepting the unpardonable sin, that is greater than the sin of ingratitude." (*DBY pg. 228*) He further said, "We rejoice because the Lord is ours, because we are sown in weakness for the express purpose of attaining to greater power and perfection. In everything the Saints may rejoice—in persecution, because it is necessary to purge them, and prepare the wicked for their doom; in sickness and in pain, though they are hard to bear, because we are thereby made acquainted with pain, with sorrow, and with every affliction that mortals can endure, for by contact all things are demonstrated to our senses. We have reason to rejoice exceedingly that faith is in the world, that the Lord reigns, and does His pleasure among the inhabitants of the earth. Do you ask if I rejoice because the Devil has the advantage over the inhabitants of the earth, and has afflicted mankind? I most assuredly answer in the affirmative; I rejoice in this as much as in anything else. I rejoice because I am afflicted. I rejoice because I am poor. I rejoice because I am cast down. Why? Because I shall be lifted up again. I rejoice that I am poor because I shall be made rich; that I am afflicted, because I shall be comforted, and prepared to enjoy the felicity of perfect happiness, for it is impossible to properly appreciate happiness except by enduring the opposite." (*DBY pg. 228*)

The need for opposition and the person responsible for that opposition, I believe I have discussed amply in former chapters. What I have not given adequate attention is this need to appreciate or be grateful for that opposition and our afflictions. When we recognize the hand of God is in our afflictions, we will, as Brigham said above, rejoice in them. If you cannot recognize His hand in *all things*, you cannot have gratitude for what He is affecting in your life, not the good nor the bad. "And in nothing doth man offend God, or against none is His wrath kindled, save those who confess not His hand in **all** things . . . ." (*D&C 59:21*) God does not only expect this gratitude, *it is an unequivocal prerequisite to our preparation to receive His great gift of grace, of love.* It is not that God's love is conditional; it is that we cannot receive His love without a broken heart and contrite spirit. Humility and gratitude to the Lord in *all things* is key and absolutely necessary to receiving His grace. Let me say again for emphasis, *humility and gratitude to the Lord in* ***all things, good and bad****, is key and absolutely necessary to receiving His grace*. How can I say it stronger? Do not keep this *key* a secret!

Pride Again

Let me comment further on this thing called pride. I consider it to be the greatest downfall, not only of many within our Mormon community, but of all people everywhere. Let me explain by telling you about a man I have known since my youth. He has a painful collection of personal character traits. He is passionate and romantic but, unfortunately, he is weak as well. These, with other lesser traits, have given rise to his committing infractions against many spiritual laws. As a result, he (as well as those close to him) suffers great pain. However, I deem his worst fault to be pride. He is filled with pride. He cannot accept criticism. He cannot accept help from anyone. He keeps trying, by himself, to overcome his weaknesses. The more he tries, the more he fails. The more he fails, the more he justifies his failure, then runs from the situation, and accordingly, from all those who have watched him fail. To stay around them, with his pride, would be far too painful. In consequence of this, he has moved far away from all those who love him and could help him, if he would let them. His life has become a string of mistakes, failures, and unfinished projects. His pride and all the rest of his weaknesses and mistakes have caused him to sin the great sin of *idolatry*. Although he tries hard to be religious, he worships a false God, namely, his own weak arm of flesh. He has not found his Savior Jesus Christ. To find Christ would require humility I can't imagine him having. "Be thou humble, and the Lord thy God shall lead thee by the hand, and give thee answer to thy prayers." (*D&C 112:10*) As his friend and one who still cares and loves him, I would try, though I don't know how, to convey to him that he needs to understand the above principles; that, like the alcoholic, he hasn't the power to overcome by himself; that he must come unto Christ, whose *grace is sufficient* and who will *make weak things strong*; and that he must not deny the gifts of God, no matter from what source they come.

If he, and we, will rid our self of *pride, vanity,* and *unbelief* then we have God's promise. "I, the Lord, am bound when ye do what I say; but when ye do not what I say, ye have no promise." (*D&C 82:10*) Remember, God can fix our weaknesses but He cannot fix our rebellion, our *unwillingness*. He would be tampering with our agency should He change our unwilling hearts. Still, the Lord's gifts are not only for those who keep all His commandments but also those who "*seeketh*" to keep them. "For verily I say unto you, they [God's gifts] are given for the benefit of those who love me and keep all my commandments, and him that seeketh so to do—. (*D&C 46:9*)

Guilt

But there is another dominant trait in this man's life. He has, what I call, an *overdeveloped sense of guilt*. Let me here state that I DO NOT BELIEVE IN

GUILT! Guilt is anti-Christ. Excepting discouragement, guilt is perhaps the greatest tool of the Devil and is well worn. The wicked do not have to worry about guilt as they have seared their conscience with a hot iron, but the Devil will stick it to anyone who is trying to be righteous. As soon as we sin, he is right there with a *guilt complex*. This makes us feel bad, weakens our spirits, and takes power from us. He would like us to condemn ourselves because such thoughts are immobilizing and damning in themselves. We stop our spiritual progress and disassociate ourselves from the spirit of God. When we feel guilty, we feel unworthy to be in places and with people that are righteous; consequently we stay away from them. The same principle causes us to stop praying when we sin, even though praying is precisely what we should be doing, that we might appeal to God for strength to overcome the weakness. Instead, we go off, on our own as this man has done, and try to do what our own arm of flesh is not capable of doing. When we do this, we please the Devil. This is not what God wants.

"But," you say: "If we don't feel guilty, we will not know right from wrong." Not so! God wants us, by means of the Holy Ghost, to know what is true or false, right or wrong, **before the fact**. Hopefully **before** we make the choice. That is why He has given us the Holy Ghost, to teach us truth, not to make us feel guilty. Making us feel guilty is not the job of the Holy Ghost. God wants you to know the proper course before you act, but whether you listen to the spirit before or after, the Holy Ghost does ***not*** proffer *guilt trips*, he is only witnessing to that which is true and right. If we choose wisely, there is no guilt. If we choose poorly, the Devil jumps in and lowers the guilt boom. This is the way he, and, unfortunately, some parents, spouses, friends, bishops, and etc., wittingly or unwittingly manipulate people. They take advantage of a "good person's" sense of conscience.

All those who have experienced guilt (and I think that includes everyone) knows the devastating effect it can have on the soul. "Oh, but," you argue, A conscience is good. We are cautioned not to sear our conscience with a hot iron yet it sounds like you are telling us to do just that." No, I am not. I am talking about two different things: conscience (that inner voice or whisperings of the Holy Spirit) or godly sorrow for sin *vs.* guilt. "For godly sorrow worketh repentance to salvation not to be repented of; but the sorrow of the world worketh death." (*2 Corinthians 7:10*) And what is that *sorrow of the world?* It is guilt that worketh death.

Once again, so you don't misunderstand me, our conscience or sense of right and wrong is the Holy Ghost bearing testimony to us of the truth of something, either before the act or godly sorrow after the act. This is right and good. To deny these promptings of the Holy Ghost *is to sear our conscience with a hot iron* and soon we will cease to receive such witness. That's when we are in real trouble.

No, what I am really talking about is **self-condemnation** and I would rather refer to it as such but unfortunately, by tradition, it has already been labeled "guilt." The proper meaning of the word guilt relates to the legal expression of blame, fault, or responsibly for a particular act and, when used properly, does not evoke a specific feeling at all. I would usually demand that we stick to proper definitions and use the word *self-condemnation*, but I know you will know what I'm talking about when I say *guilt*. So, I will continue using the word guilt, though it is of self-condemnation that I really speak. It is that feeling of guilt that immobilizes our spirits.

Perhaps, with that said, you can now agree with me that guilt (self-condemnation) is anti-Christ. "Happy is he that condemneth not himself in that thing which he alloweth." (*Romans 14:22*) And what do we allow? Those things we do wrong, our weaknesses. Yet we all condemn ourselves, if not continually, at least on occasion. Like my friend, we usurp the authority and place of God, presuming to self-judge, then self-condemn. Because we think we know ourselves, our hidden sins and the unrighteous thoughts of our hearts, we think we deserve to be condemned. Perhaps we do, but it is not our place to do it. God knows us even better than we know ourselves. "For if our heart condemn us, God is greater than our heart, and knoweth all things." (*1 John 3:20*) He sees the big picture and knows the whole story. I don't believe God is as anxious to condemn us, as we are to condemn ourselves. He is trying to get us as far down the path of eternal progression as He can, as far as we will go. He does not jump on our every mistake saying, "Ah ha! You messed up, now I get to damn you!" No, why would He make the ultimate sacrifice for us if He did not want to help us, if He did not want to relieve us of the pain and suffering required by the justice of the law? He made that ultimate sacrifice so that we could be the most we will be. He loves us. He is not eager to convict us. Why should we be?

There is another logic here that you may rightly question for soundness. When you think about it, if you do something wrong but didn't mean to, that is, you didn't consciously choose to, then what you did is merely a mistake. In this case, you have no business feeling guilty, you wouldn't have done it had you known better and you certainly won't do it again. On the other hand, even if you know something is wrong and you choose to do it anyway, **where's the sense in feeling guilty about it**? Of course, this last sentence is more a joke than sound doctrine, but it makes a point.

Guilt, Load Me Up Please

Too often we attend our church meetings to be fed spiritually but go home with a huge fresh load of guilt. Does this sound familiar? The Gospel of Christ is not intended to do that. On the contrary, it is meant to give us peace of mind and comfort in Christ. Also too often, people use guilt to control others. I hope this is not the case in our church environment. In any case, be aware. Don't let anyone heap guilt upon you. More importantly, don't do it to your self.

Another of the major pitfalls relative to self-condemnation is our comparing ourselves to others. We go to church or generally look around us and see others who we presume to be more righteous, and upon comparison we come up short. The irony is that those same people are probably comparing themselves to us, and thinking the same thing. We are all in the same boat, to a greater or lesser degree, whether we confess it or not. Whether great or small, we all sin and fall short. "*For all have sinned, and come short of the glory of God.*" (*Romans 3:23*) We know our own sins and although we struggle to keep up appearances, we feel compelled to secretly punish ourselves and do so with a daily dose of grief and anguish brought on by self-condemnation (guilt). Again, leave the punishing to Christ. I suspect he will be more merciful to us than we are to ourselves.

Guilt, self-condemnation, is counter-productive. It is against reason. It is Satan-induced. It is foreign to the spirit of Christ. It is downright wrong! We would all be better off not to waste our time feeling guilty. We need to stop nailing ourselves to the cross; Christ has already been there for us.

Another Poor Excuse

Relative to the above statements on feeling guilty, you will remember our discussion back in the chapter on love where we said that no one **makes** us feel anything! The behavior of others or an event in our lives (even our own mistake) may be the *catalyst*, the *action*, but we must take responsibility for how we *feel* about any given situation. Your feelings should not be subject to even your own faults. Your sins are real to be sure, and it hurts to be weak and stupid but how you feel about it and further, what you do about it is entirely your choice. You may also feel sorry for yourself or use your plight as an excuse for not doing your best, but such excuses will not hold at the judgment day. The Lord inflicted you by giving you a weakness, or weaknesses, (see *Ether 12:27*) so you would turn to Him, have faith in Him, and come under His grace, which He promises to all who prepare themselves.

Guilt is a feeling, a feeling you may or may not choose to have. You must take the responsibility for how you feel or submit to being controlled by the guilt in your life. Admittedly, this doctrine is easier said than done, but wallowing in guilt or self-pity is harsher than taking advantage of the grace of our Savior.

Climb Out of It—Get Off It—Get Over It

Confession and repentance are the means of climbing out of the *guilt rut* or off the *pity pot*. When we sincerely confess and repent, the Lord's spirit can and will take the feelings of guilt and despair from us. He is there to fill our souls with joy and positive things, not guilt. Christ will justify the broken law, which He *can* do as a result of His sacrifice for that law. To continue in feelings of guilt or despair is to **turn your back on God and deny His atonement and His saving grace.** Forget self-pity, despair, and guilt!

If I haven't convinced you that self-condemnation (guilt) is not right, if you think guilt is a positive influence in your life, what can I say? Carry on, but please consider this concept. Letting go of self-judgment and self-condemnation can make an enormous change your life.

In all your "letting go:" let go of self-condemnation (guilt); let go of your need to be right; let go of your need to fix everyone and everything you perceive to be wrong in the world; let go of your rebellious nature and become humble and submissive; let go of all the burdens you carry as a result of your weaknesses; let go of your sense of responsibility to achieve anything; let go of your worry; let go of all your concerns, past, present, and future; let go of your plans and goals; let go of your pride and vanity; let go of your expectations; in short, let go of *all your desires*. Make a sacrifice of these things to the Lord by giving your life and future over to Him and live as the wind letting God blow you where He will. "The wind bloweth where it listeth, and thou hearest the sound thereof, but canst not tell whence it cometh, and whither it goeth: *so is every one that is born of the Spirit.*" (*John 3:7-8*)

His gift of grace is the great blessing of the Gospel of Christ, but again, what does it profit the giver *or* the receiver if the gift is not accepted? What good does it do us to know the principles and yet *not* let the gospel bless our lives?

11
The Great Secret

Snooze And Lose

My old BYU religion professor's riddle, "What is the best kept secret of The Mormon Church?" and its answer, "The Gospel of Jesus Christ," has had a great impact upon my life. So often over the years, in the course of teaching one religion class or another, I have marveled at the truth of it. Are any of the concepts I have set forth in this composition *new* to us? If so, perhaps my professor was right, *we do* keep The Gospel of Christ a secret.

Because of the multitude of revelations given through latter-day prophets, we Mormons, of all the peoples of the earth, should know *The Gospel of Jesus Christ*, yet we stall in our progression along that road to eternal glory. I worry about those of us who slumber. I fear we are asleep in a comfortable place at a time when we should be on the watchtower.

Greater Yet

Although the above concepts are relevant and need stating, I have departed somewhat from exposing that simple secret about the Gospel of Christ, that key that we must all comprehend in order to become true Saints, sons and daughters of God. We have been discussing some very important concepts. We have talked about the need to seek and knock in order to receive and the fact that it is not only possible to know the mysteries, but an outright commandment to do so. We have talked about truth, where it is found and how to know it. We talked about the necessity of knowing God with all His attributes and what His purpose is for creating us and putting us here on this earth. We have also talked about what may be expected should we be one of those who are not just *called*, but *chosen* to live as God lives in a Zion heaven on earth. We spent a great deal of time on the doctrine of oneness, or love. Knowledge of these concepts is important and necessary to knowing God and preparing ourselves to receive His grace, His greatest of all gifts, eternal life, but, I will here state that understanding or knowing *about* these concepts, though essential, will not get us there. That is, knowing about these things is not the *knowledge of God* or to *know Him*. This may seem very strange to say, but all the concepts we have discussed so far *pale in importance* when compared to the concept I will now put forth.

The New And Everlasting Covenant

Notwithstanding our reach to the heavens to try to understand some of the celestial principles of the mysteries of the Kingdom of Heaven, we have still not fully answered my old professor's second question: "What is the Gospel of Jesus Christ?" Oh, we said it is faith, repentance, and baptism of water and fire (receiving the Holy Ghost), but embedded deep within those ordinances is the secret, not only to salvation, but to exaltation as well. Let me carefully, if I can, uncover this great secret. This secret is charity. According to the scriptures, Charity is the pure love of Christ.

"Oh but," you say, "I've known about charity all my life. Where is the secret?" Well, let's see. On my way to an explanation, let me lay some foundation planks to our scaffolding.

You will remember that the Lord said He has given us a *New Law*, a *New And Everlasting Covenant*. "Behold, I say unto you that all old covenants have I caused to be done away in this thing; and this is a new and everlasting covenant, even that which was from the beginning." (*D&C 22:1*, see also *Jeremiah 31:31*, *Hebrews 8:8* and *13*, *12:24* and *D&C 132*) You will also remember that we, as Latter-day Saints, are under condemnation because of our vanity and unbelief (even all) because we have treated lightly the things we have been given. Let me quote again, "And your minds in times past have been darkened because of unbelief, and because you have treated lightly the things you have received—Which vanity and unbelief have brought the whole church under condemnation. And this condemnation resteth upon the children of Zion, even all. And they shall remain under this condemnation until they repent and remember the new covenant, even *The Book of Mormon* and the former commandments which I have given them, not only to say, but to do according to that which I have written—That they may bring forth fruit meet for their Father's kingdom; otherwise there remaineth a scourge and judgment to be poured out upon the children of Zion." (*D&C 84:54-58*) What have we treated lightly? Why, the new covenant! What is the new covenant? It is not just *The Book of Mormon* as one might surmise from the above scripture, nor is it just eternal marriage, as one might assume from reading section 132 of the D&C which talks about that part of the new and everlasting covenant. No, it is much more than that.

The Teacher?

Let me go back to that same eighty fourth section of the D&C (italics for emphasis). "Yea, the word of the Lord concerning His church, established in the last days for the restoration of His people, as He has spoken by the mouth of His prophets, and for the gathering of His saints to stand upon Mount Zion, which shall be the city of New Jerusalem. *And this greater priesthood administereth the gospel and holdeth the key of the mysteries of the kingdom, even the key of the knowledge of God.* Therefore, *in the ordinances thereof, the power of godliness is manifest.*" (*D&C 84:2, 19-20*) You will note that it is the greater priesthood that "administereth the gospel", not the lesser. Remember, we talked about the two gospels before; the *lesser gospel* of repentance, baptism of water and obedience to the carnal commandments and performances; and the *greater gospel* of Christ, knowing the mysteries of the kingdom and knowledge of God. And what are the mysteries of the kingdom and knowledge of God? Just that, knowing what God knows, understanding how God lives and works, and *knowing* God, not just about Him but ***knowing Him, literally, personally***. It is in knowing Him that we experience, not only the love of God but the powers of God as well.

And how do you discover these great secrets? Not from your study. Not from this book. Not from others. **You must learn them from God Himself.** Joseph Smith said, "Reading the experience of others, or the revelation given to them, can never give us a comprehensive view of our condition and true relation to God. *Knowledge of these things can only be obtained by experience through the ordinances of God set forth for that purpose.* Could you *gaze into heaven* five minutes, you would know more than you would by reading all that ever was written on the subject." (*TPJS pg. 324*) *All that ever was written* includes even the standard works[111] and the sealed portion[112] of *The Book of Mormon*, among all other writings in the world. *Gazing into heaven is the key.* I repeat; ***Gazing into heaven is the key.*** You must *personally* receive from God an endowment of His knowledge (the knowledge of God including all truth), His love, charity (that oneness in him), and His glory.

God must teach you of this new covenant. "And every one that hearkeneth to the voice of the Spirit cometh unto God, even the Father. And ***the Father teacheth him of the covenant*** which He has renewed and confirmed upon you . . . ." (*D&C 84:47-48*) "For *by my Spirit will I enlighten them*, and by my power will I make known unto them the secrets of my will—yea, even those things which eye has not seen, nor ear heard, nor yet entered into the heart of man." (*D&C 76:5-10*) "Jesus therefore answered and said unto them, Murmur not among yourselves. No man can come to me, except the Father which hath sent me draw him: and I will raise him up at the last day. It is written in the prophets, *And they shall be all taught of God . . . .*" (*John 6:43-45*) Who does the *teaching*; your gospel doctrine teacher, your bishop, the Prophet? No. *God the Father must teach you the new covenant*. This is the only way.

I know it sounds like I am saying that each of us not only can but also *must* meet God and His Son, face to face. ***That is exactly what I am saying!*** Not only that, but it is possible to do so while in this life (italics and bold for emphasis). "But great and marvelous are the works of the Lord, and the mysteries of His kingdom which He showed unto us, which surpass all understanding in glory, and in might, and in dominion . . . . *Neither is man capable to make them known, for they are only to be seen and understood by the power of the Holy Spirit*, which God bestows on those who love Him, and purify themselves before Him; To whom He grants this privilege of seeing and knowing for themselves; that through the power and manifestation of the Spirit, ***while in the flesh***, *they may be able to bear His presence in the world of glory*." (*D&C 76:114, 116-118*)

(Taking A Small Side Trip) But No Man Has Seen God

The notion that we may *have the privilege of receiving the mysteries of the kingdom* and *be in the presence of the Father and Son* **while in this life** seems incredible. To imagine being in the presence of Christ right now would cause us to shrink dead away (I speak for myself). We somehow accept that such a thing could happen after we die but not in this life. Where is the consistency in such an idea? We saw Him before we came to this life and we will see Him after we leave this life. Why not in this life? I know that Adam and Eve were cast out of the garden, out of God's presence, but the whole object is to get back into His presence; the sooner we can do that, the better.

I know I may lose many of my readers at this point resulting from my audacity to suggest that seeing God face to face should be our aim in life. I guess it is inevitable as this is a hard doctrine for the unbeliever to swallow. Christ Himself lost quite a number of his followers when He preached this doctrine (italics for emphasis). "Not that any man hath seen the Father, save he which is of God, *he hath seen the Father*. I am that bread of life. This is that bread which came down from heaven: not as your fathers did eat manna, and are dead: he that eateth of this bread shall live for ever. *Many therefore of his disciples, when they had heard this, said, This is an hard saying; who can hear it?* When Jesus knew in himself that his disciples murmured at it, he said unto them, Doth this offend you? It is the spirit that quickeneth; the flesh profiteth nothing: the words that I speak unto you, they are spirit, and they are life. And he said, Therefore said I unto you, that no man can come unto me, except it were given unto him of my Father. *From that time many of his disciples went back, and walked no more with him.* Then said Jesus unto the twelve, Will ye also go away? Then Simon Peter answered him, Lord, to whom shall we go? Thou hast the words of eternal life." (*John 6:45, 48, 58, 60-61, 63, 65-66, 68*)

You will remember Moses also had great difficulty getting the children of Israel to accept this great blessing from God while in this life (italics for emphasis). "And this greater priesthood administereth the gospel and holdeth the key of the mysteries of the kingdom, even the key of the knowledge of God. And without the ordinances thereof, and the authority of the priesthood, the power of godliness is not manifest unto men in the flesh; For without this *no man can see the face of God, even the Father*, and live. Now this Moses plainly taught to the children of Israel in the wilderness, and sought diligently to sanctify his people *that they might behold the face of God*; But they hardened their hearts and could not *endure His presence*; therefore, the Lord in His wrath, for His anger was kindled against them, swore that they should not enter into His *rest* while in the wilderness, *which rest is the fulness of His glory*. Therefore, He took Moses out of their midst, and the Holy Priesthood also . . . ." (*D&C 84:19-25*)

The Lord Himself argued with those who professed to know the scriptures, yet denied what they said, "And the Father Himself which hath sent me, hath borne witness of me. Ye have neither *heard His voice at any time, nor seen His shape*. And ye have not His word abiding in you: for whom He hath sent, him ye believe not. Search the scriptures; for in them ye think ye have eternal life: and they are they which testify of me. And ye will not come to me, that ye might have life." (*John 5:37-40*) Here the Lord was telling them that despite their reading and study of the scriptures, they denied the very God of which their scriptures abundantly testified, and would not *hear His voice nor see Him*. Even though they thought they had eternal life, "*for in them ye* ***think*** *ye have eternal life*," He said they did not. Why? Well, because you don't get eternal life just from reading the scriptures. You get eternal life from receiving the new covenant directly from Him. You see, they had neither heard Him nor seen Him. In other words, they did not know Him. And what is eternal life? **To know God**.

Are we not doing the same thing today? We spend our efforts studying, testifying, and teaching about Christ from a multitude of revealed scripture, but refuse to believe we can actually see His face and hear His voice. We deny the gift. Remember the curse we are under because of our vanity and *unbelief*. (see *D&C 84:54-57*)

How Can This Be?

I recognize the idea of meeting God face to face while in this life has been rejected by many on the basis of the several scriptures that say, "No man hath seen God at any time; the only begotten Son, which is in the bosom of the Father, He hath declared Him." (*John 1:18*) "No man hath seen God at any time. If we love one another, God dwelleth in us, and His love is perfected in us." (*1 John 4:12*) I can't say these and other like scriptures are mistranslations but I do believe something is missing. The correct interpretation of those scriptures should be, "For no man has seen God at any time in the flesh, except quickened by the Spirit of God. Neither can any natural man abide the presence of God, neither after the carnal mind." (*D&C 67:11-12*) "And without the ordinances thereof, and the authority of the priesthood, the power of godliness is not manifest unto men in the flesh; For without this no man can see the face of God, even the Father, and live." (*D&C 84:21-22*)

These scriptures make it apparent that, technically speaking, in order to see God or Christ face to face, in order for us to stand their glorious presence, a change must be made, either in God or in us. If we are the ones that change, what is that change? "Wherefore, He is possessor of all things; for all things are subject unto Him, both in heaven and on the earth, the life and the light, the Spirit and the power, sent forth by the will of the Father through Jesus Christ, His Son. But no man is possessor of all things except he be purified and cleansed from all sin. And if ye are purified and cleansed from all sin, ye shall ask whatsoever you will in the name of Jesus and it shall be done." (*D&C 50:27-29*) We must be purified and cleansed from all sin. Who does that? Well, as already discussed, we prepare ourselves and our Savior does the rest through the redemption and sanctification of the birth of fire. And, *if you are* purified and cleansed, whatever you ask in His name, you will get. "But know this, it shall be given you what you shall ask . . . ." (*D&C 50:30*) Of course, you will be one with truth so you will ask for only that which is right.

"And again, verily I say unto you that it is your privilege, and a promise I give unto you that have been ordained unto this ministry, that inasmuch as you strip yourselves from jealousies and fears, and humble yourselves before me, for ye are not sufficiently humble, *the veil shall be rent and you shall see me and know that I am*—not with the carnal neither natural mind, but with the spiritual." (*D&C 67:10-11*) No matter who is changed, God or us, it is clear that we may see the face of God.

Some Have Seen Him

We have more than sufficient evidence that down through time men have, indeed, seen God. Stephen, as he was being stoned, saw God. "But he, being full of the Holy Ghost, looked up stedfastly into heaven, and saw the glory of God, and Jesus standing on the right hand of God. And said, Behold, I see the heavens opened, and the Son of man standing on the right hand of God." (*Acts 7:55-56*) Jacob apparently saw God. "And Jacob called the name of the place Peniel: for I have seen God face to face, and my life is preserved." (*Genesis 32:30*) Moses, Aaron, and over 70 elders of Israel saw God. "Then went up Moses, and Aaron, Nadab, and Abihu, and seventy of the elders of Israel: And they saw the God of Israel: and there was under His feet as it were a paved work of a sapphire stone, and as it were the body of heaven in His clearness." (*Exodus 24:9-10*) "And he saw God face to face, and he talked with Him, and the glory of God was upon Moses; therefore Moses could endure His presence." (*Moses 1:2,* see also *Moses 1:31*) Many in the latter-days have seen God and we have some of the records. Joseph Smith and Oliver Cowdery give us this testimony, "The veil was taken from our minds, and the eyes of our understanding were opened. We saw the Lord standing upon the breastwork of the pulpit, before us; and under His feet was a paved work of pure gold, in color like amber." (*D&C 110:1-2*) Sidney Rigdon and Joseph Smith give us this testimony, "And now, after the many testimonies which have been given of Him, this is the testimony, last of all which we give of Him: That He lives! For we saw Him, even on the right hand of God; and we heard the voice bearing record that He is the Only Begotten of the Father." (*D&C 76:22-23*)

Now I know that many churches teach and many people believe that it is not possible to see God while in this life. While I disagree, I will not further argue this point with them. To me, the evidence and gospel doctrines are overwhelming. If they choose not to believe it, so be it. They have the right and agency to believe what they choose to believe, and as we know, we will all believe what we choose to believe regardless of what is truth. Notwithstanding, I testify they are denying not just the power of the Holy Ghost and the greatest gift of God (knowing God or eternal life), but the gospel itself.

Through The Priesthood Ordinances

This is the promise given us of God. "Blessed are the pure in heart: for they shall see God." (*Matthew 5:8*) Do you think our Lord meant after you die? Of course all of us will see him after we die. Why bless the pure in heart with a blessing everyone will enjoy after death? It is my testimony that you do not have to wait until you die. "Verily, thus saith the Lord: It shall come to pass that *every soul* who forsaketh his sins and cometh unto me, and calleth on my name, and obeyeth my voice, and keepeth my commandments, shall see my face and know that I am." (*D&C 93:1*) This is the very reason God has given His priesthood to us (italics for emphasis), because "the power and authority of the higher, or Melchizedek Priesthood, is to hold the keys of all the spiritual blessings of The Church. *To have the privilege of receiving the mysteries of the kingdom of heaven, to have the heavens opened unto them, to commune with the general assembly and church of the Firstborn,* ***and to enjoy the communion and presence of God the Father, and Jesus the mediator of the new covenant.***" (*D&C 107:19-20*) "Therefore, *in the ordinances thereof, the power of godliness is manifested.* And without the ordinances thereof, and the authority of the priesthood, the power of godliness is not manifest unto men in the flesh." (*D&C 84:20-21*) Is this priesthood available to man? Yes it is! Has God tried to transfer His power to man down through the history of this earth? Yes He has! Where is this priesthood today? It is in The Church of Jesus Christ of Latter-day Saints, having been restored to the earth by the laying on of hands by angels of God who held that power and authority in life, namely Peter, James, and John. It has been given to the Prophet Joseph Smith, not just as a part of the restoration of His Church but also as the actual restoration of *the Gospel of Jesus Christ.*

Remember, "that the rights of the priesthood are inseparably connected with the powers of heaven . . . ." (*D&C 121:36*) But what has man done with this priesthood, not only down through time, but today? Unfortunately, at worst, we have defiled it or completely cast it aside. At best, we have *treated it lightly* (see *D&C 84:54-55*). So, since we have not taken advantage of this great power, God has left us, like the children of Israel, with the lesser law, *lesser gospel.* "And the lesser priesthood continued, which priesthood holdeth the key of the ministering of angels and the preparatory gospel; Which gospel is the gospel of repentance and of baptism, and the remission of sins, and the law of carnal commandments, which the Lord in His wrath caused to continue with the house of Aaron . . . ." (*D&C 84:26-27*)

You will note the Lord states that this preparatory gospel of carnal commandments includes repentance and baptism for the remission of sins. This is all very preparatory, necessary to the reception of the Holy Ghost or Baptism of Fire. The Lord does not include the reception of the Holy Ghost (the Baptism of Fire) in this lesser priesthood of outward performances and carnal commandments. This lesser priesthood or preparatory gospel receives only *the ministering of angels* (see *D&C 84:26* and *107:20*). It does not include seeing the face of God and receiving the mysteries of the kingdom. The higher Melchizedek priesthood holds the keys of the mysteries. Only the lesser priesthood was had at the time of John the Baptist. Let us read again (parenthesis and italics added), "Which gospel is the *gospel of repentance and of baptism, and the remission of sins, and the law of carnal commandments,* which the Lord in His wrath caused to continue with the house of Aaron among the children of Israel until John, whom God raised up, being filled with the Holy Ghost from his mother's womb. For he was baptized while he was yet in his childhood, and was ordained by the angel of God at the time he was eight days old unto this power, to overthrow the kingdom of the Jews, and to make straight the way of the Lord before the face of His people, to prepare them for the coming of the Lord, (through Christ himself was the higher priesthood, the priesthood of all power given) in whose hand is given all power. And the sons of Moses and of Aaron shall be filled with the glory of the Lord, upon Mount Zion in the Lord's house, *whose sons are ye*; and also many whom I have called and sent forth to build up my church." (*D&C 84:27-32*) Referring to us Latter-day Saints as the sons of Moses and Aaron, He says we will be sanctified and *filled with the glory of the Lord* and will receive great blessings and power. Continuing, "For whoso is faithful unto the obtaining these two priesthoods of which I have spoken, and the magnifying their calling, are sanctified by the Spirit unto the renewing of their bodies." (*D&C 84:33*)

(Back On Track) The Process

There is a process that we are all hopefully going through which process will bring us back into the presence of God, face to face. This process is the same for everyone, no matter what our station in life, our Church calling, our Church membership, or any other unique difference there may be about us. This process is the Gospel of Jesus Christ, namely; faith in Jesus Christ, repentance, baptism of water, and Baptism of Fire and the Holy Ghost.

The first three steps, the preparatory gospel of carnal commandments and performances, we have just discussed. That last step, Baptism of Fire and the Holy Ghost, is to receive the Second Comforter, either through the Baptism of Fire and Translation, or having our Calling and Election Made Sure (though technically different, the level of endowment is the same—more on Calling and Election and translation later). This process is how we are sanctified of spirit and translated of body, which we must be in order to survive in the presence of God when we see Him. We have often confused ourselves thinking there is more to it than that. There is not. But the secret kept, seems to be what it means to go through that process.

You will remember that when Nicodemus, a ruler of the Jews, came to Jesus by night and asked him what must a man do to enter the kingdom of God, "Jesus answered, Verily, verily, I say unto thee, Except a man be born of water and of the Spirit, he cannot enter into the kingdom of God." (*John 3:5*) You will note that he did not say, "Unless you are a full tithe payer, you cannot enter the kingdom of God." He did not say, "Unless you do not smoke or drink, you cannot enter the kingdom of God." He did not say, "Unless you wear a white shirt and tie, you cannot enter the kingdom of God." He did not say, "Unless you attend church regularly, you cannot enter the kingdom of God." Nor did he say, "Unless you keep the Ten Commandments, you cannot enter the kingdom of God." No, He did not mention these or any other carnal commandments and performances. Remember, these are the preparatory gospel. He didn't even qualify or quantify our state or level of righteousness. He simply said that a man must be born of water (baptized) and born of the Spirit (receive the Baptism of Fire and the Holy Ghost). We all know what it means to be baptized of water, though we might argue as to the necessity of having it done by the proper authority, but at least we know what it is and means. Do we know what it means to be born of Fire and the Holy Ghost? Let's see if we can shed some light on the subject.

Why Born Again?

Christ said, "That which is born of the flesh is flesh; and that which is born of the Spirit is Spirit." (*John 3:6*) Yes, you were born into this mortal world in the flesh, but because it is a mortal fallen state, you have sinned and are spiritually dead or dead to things spiritual. We have all suffered the second death. "And now behold, I say unto you then cometh a death, even a second death, which is a spiritual death; then is a time that whosoever dieth in his sins, as to a temporal death, shall also die a spiritual death; yea, he shall die as to things pertaining unto righteousness." (*Alma 12:16*) Because of the fall of Adam we are all in this sinful state. We are dead spiritually. We must, therefore, be spiritually Born Again, sons and daughters of God. This is done through Christ. "For as in Adam all die, even so in Christ shall all be made alive." (*1 Corinthians 15:22*)

A friend I have more recently come to know, M. James Custer, calls us the "living dead" or the "walking dead," an interesting way to put it. (Incidentally, I can highly recommend his series of books, *The Unspeakable Gift*. The depth of doctrine within makes it a slightly difficult read but it also makes it a book one should put on one's **must read** list.) If not the walking dead, at the very least, we must classify ourselves as sleepwalkers. "And the Lord said unto me: marvel not that all mankind, yea men and women, all nations, kindreds, tongues and people, must be Born Again; yea, born of God, changed from their carnal and fallen state, to a state of righteousness, being redeemed of God, becoming his sons and daughters: And thus they become new creatures; and unless they do this, they can in nowise inherit the kingdom of God." (*Mosiah 27:25-26*)

Some Examples

Down through history there are many personal and group examples of people being Born Again. Adam himself was born of the spirit and quickened in the inner man (*Moses 6:64*). In the Book of Mormon, Mosiah 27:8-32, Alma the son of Alma and the sons of Mosiah experienced the Baptism of Fire as they were going about persecuting the church of God. An angel appeared to them and they were converted. Said Alma, "—I have repented of my sins, and have been redeemed of the Lord; behold I am born of the Spirit. (*Mosiah 27:24*) Chapters 18 and 19 of Alma tell the story of King Lamoni, his wife, and many others who received the Baptism of Fire. Helaman 5:18-50 gives us an account of the rebirth of Nephi and Lehi, sons of Helaman, as well as many others. In Mosiah the fifth chapter we see the conversion of many people after King Benjamin's great speech. Many people received the Baptism of Fire at the time of Christ's visit to the Americas as recorded in III Nephi 19:6-14, and 26:17-18. Of course on the day of Pentecost many received the Baptism of Fire and spoke in tongues and etc (see *Acts 2:*). In Acts 8:9-21 we read about Peter and John's ministry to many who received the Baptism of Fire. In chapter 9 of Acts we read about Paul's (Saul's) conversion and Baptism of Fire. In fact, the entire book of Acts is one incident after another of people receiving the Baptism of Fire and the Holy Ghost. The scriptures hold so many examples of Baptism of Fire that it would be impossible to list them all here.

Evidences of Being Born Again Or Having Received The Baptism of Fire

I recognize that many people, in and out of the church, believe they have already been Born Again of the spirit. Perhaps they have. (We're all "Born Again" Christians right?) Who am I to pass judgment on such a personal event? But let's look at the evidence.

It is noted that we know little about what actually happens at the time of Baptism of Fire and the Holy Ghost, as it is entirely a personal event and the endowment of power and glory is beyond human tongue to describe. Further, it is an "*unspeakable event*"; that is for the most part those who experience this great happening are forbidden to write or speak of it. Not withstanding this being the case, the following events and many more that could be sighted, give some understanding of the great changes and powers given those who have been Born Again. Let's make a list and see how many (if any) of these powers we possess.

Power To Spare

"Therefore it is given to abide in you; the record of heaven; the comforter; the peaceable things of immortal glory; the truth of all things; that which quickeneth all things, which maketh alive all things; that which knoweth all things, and hath all power . . ." (*Moses 6:61* see also *D&C 76:50-70, D&C 93:26-28* and *92-95*) Here is quite a list to start with. What is the *record of heaven?* It is the history of how all things came to be, a knowledge of the processes and history of all heavenly things, of all of God's creations and this will be in you, a part of your memory.

The comforter (the Holy Ghost) must be in you as well. What does it mean to have the *peaceable things* of immortal glory in you? It means you know and understand the propriety of all things, the balance, the peace, and beauty of God's plan or, in other words, you see the big picture, the purpose, how all things are good, and how all things work together for the benefit of God's creations (man). You finally see as God sees and you think as He thinks.

The *truth of all things* will abide in you as well. You will know all things as they were, are, and are to come. You are now a prophet. "God shall give unto you knowledge by his Holy Spirit, yea, by the unspeakable gift of the Holy Ghost, which has not been revealed since the world was until now;" (*D&C 121:26*)

Further, the life-giving spirit-matter will renew you so that you are no longer subject to death, neither of the spirit nor of the body. "For whoso is faithful unto the obtaining these two priesthoods of which I have spoken, and the magnifying their calling, are sanctified by the Spirit unto the *renewing of their bodies*." (*D&C 84:33*) What does it mean to have a renewed body? It means your body is changed, purified, sanctified, made perfect, capable of withstanding a state of celestial glory, not subject to sin or death. In our case, since we are still in this mortal existence, we are translated giving us power over life and death (more on translation in a moment). This is how the ancient patriarchs such as Adam and Methuselah lived to be so old, in the case of Methuselah 969 years. It wasn't because they had that much better bodies or that they didn't eat any junk food or live in a polluted environment; they were Born Again with renewed translated bodies having power over death. They, like Christ Himself, did not "give up the ghost" until they chose to, until the appropriate time.

You shall have *all power*, over what? All things! You'll have power over your enemies, sin, elements, sickness, and ignorance, to name a few. To do what? Why to do **anything** that you need to do and is right for you to do, from changing water to wine, to healing the sick, to feeding the masses, to moving mountains, to raising the dead, to traveling through space and solid objects, to seeing spirit-matter the way we see and perceive solid matter now (see *D&C 131:6-8*), and many, in fact infinite other things we will be able to do.

These are heavenly gifts and powers just waiting to be given to us here in a telestial world. Joseph Smith tells us that, "If the Latter-day Saints will walk up to their privileges, and exercise faith in the name of Jesus Christ, and live in the enjoyment of the fullness of the Holy Ghost constantly day by day, *there is nothing on the face of the earth that they could ask for, that would not be given them*. The Lord is waiting to be very gracious unto this people, and to pour out upon them riches, honor, glory, and power, even that they may *possess all things* according to the promises he has made through his Apostles and Prophets." (*JD 11:114*) **All** things! That's a lot of power.

But how will we know what we should do with such power (parenthesis & italics added)? ". . . if ye will enter in by the way, and receive the Holy Ghost (the Baptism of Fire), *it will show unto you all things what ye should do*." (*II Nephi 32:5*) So a Born Again person is told by the spirit, all things that they should do. They are one with the spirit of truth, namely the Holy Ghost. No more guess work. No more trial and error. No more petitioning God to know what to do when faced with those difficult decisions. In fact one who is Born Again need only to ask and it will be given him. "—If thou wilt turn unto me, and hearken unto my voice, and believe, and repent of all thy transgressions, and be baptized, even in water in the name of mine Only Begotten Son,—ye shall receive the gift of the Holy Ghost, *asking all things in his name, and whatsoever ye shall ask, it shall be given you*." (*Moses 6:52* see also *Moroni 10:8-34* and *D&C 84:64-76*)

Power Now

Can it really be true that God will give into our hands that kind of power? Yes, yes, a thousand times yes! "But" you say, "Don't you mean after this life when we are glorified in the Celestial kingdom? **No, I mean here and now!**

When we are born of the spirit we not only become aware of a whole new dimension of life, we are that new life. We discover how much more powerful are the properties of spirit-matter than gross-matter. We are no longer subject to the temporal, mortal laws of physics, etc. We will have what we would presently be pleased to call supernatural powers. Let us read again (parentheses added), "Wherefore he is *possessor of all things*; for *all things are subject unto him*, both in heaven and on the earth, the life and the light, the spirit and the power, sent forth by the will of the Father through Jesus Christ, his son. But no man is possessor of all things except he be purified and cleansed from all sin (through the cleansing of the Baptism of Fire). And *if ye are purified and cleansed from all sin, ye shall ask whatsoever you will in the name of Jesus and it shall be done . . .*" (*D&C 50:27-29*) When we are Born Again we are then **possessor of all things** and those "all things" are subject to us. WHEN WE ARE BORN OF THE SPIRIT WE WILL HAVE POWER OVER **ALL THINGS** BOTH IN HEAVEN AND EARTH.

There are ample scriptural references that exemplify the great powers of the spirit. Power to discern the truth of all things; power to read the minds of others; power to overcome your enemies; power to heal the sick, blind, deaf, lame, and etc.; power to move mountains; power to see things never before revealed; power to know the mysteries of God; power to travel through space and time; power to create or otherwise organize the elements or whatever we have need of; power to prophesy; power to converse with angels and those beyond the veil; power to speak and understand foreign languages; power to move about unseen or detected; power over life and death; power to do greater things than Christ has done (see *John 14:12*); power to get whatever you ask God for; and yes even power over ourselves and sin. As a Born Again, you have that power because you have lost all desire to sin. "Now they, after being sanctified by the Holy Ghost, having their garments made white, being pure and spotless before God, *could not look upon sin save it were with abhorrence*; and there were many, exceedingly great many, who were made pure and entered into the rest of the Lord their God." (*Alma 13:12*) "—because of the Spirit of the Lord Omnipotent, which has wrought a mighty change in us, or in our hearts, that we have no more disposition to do evil, but to do good continually." (*Mosiah 5:2*)

"Therefore if any man be *in Christ*, he is a new creature: old things are passed away; behold all things are become new." (*II Cor. 5:17*) You will note that the term "in Christ" or "with Christ" is another way of saying "Born Again." "Therefore we are buried with Him by baptism into death: that like as Christ was raised from the dead by the glory of the Father, even so we also should walk in newness of life. . . . our old man is crucified with Him, that the body of sin might be destroyed, that henceforth we should not serve sin. For he that is dead is free from sin. Now if we be dead with Christ, we believe that we shall also live with him." (*Rom. 6:4, 6-8*)

You will also note, that "*there were many, exceedingly great many, who were made pure and entered into the rest of the Lord their God.*" "*Entering into the "rest of God" or "the glory of God*" is another way of saying "Born Again."

Other Words And Phrases For Being Born of God, Born Again, Baptism of Fire, or Baptism of Holy Ghost

When we become aware of the true, deep meaning of being Born Again we find that the scriptures are abounding with references to this event. So often is it referred to, that there are many other phrases and words besides Born Again, Baptism of Fire and the Holy Ghost. The following list is but a few references of the probably thousands that could be mentioned.

— filled with the Spirit or Holy Ghost (*Acts 2:1-4, III Nephi 26:17-18* and *Alma 36:24*)

— filled with joy or exceedingly great joy (*Mosiah 4:20, Alma 36:24, Helaman 5:44-45* and *Alma 22:15*)

— filled with love or God's love (*Moroni 7:48*)

— filled with light (*D&C 88:67-68*)

— filled with glory, fullness of glory, or fullness of God (*Ephesians 3:19, Helaman 5:44*, and *D&C 84:32*)

— fullness of joy or everlasting joy (*III Nephi 28:10*)

— joy of the Lord (*Matthew 25:21*)

— joy in the Holy Ghost (*Romans 14:17*)

— given a new name or sacred name (*Mosiah 1:12*)

— taking the name of Christ (*Mosiah 59-12*)

— in Christ, in the Lord, or abiding or dwelling in Christ (*I Cor 1:2, II Cor. 3:14, II Cor. 5:17, John 15:8, Alma 5:44*, and *1 John 4:12-13, 15-16*)

— one in God (*D&C 35:2* and *John 17:20-21*)

— perfected in Christ (*Moroni 10:33*)

— crucified with Christ or dead with Christ (*Rom. 6:4, 6-8*)

— receive remission of sins (*Mosiah 3:13*)

— rest in the Lord or entering into the Lord's rest or God's rest (*Alma 13:16* and *Moroni 7:3*)

— sanctification or sanctified in Christ (*I Cor 1:2, III Nephi 27:20,* and *Moroni 10: 33*)

— entering the holy order of God (*Alma 5:54*)

— unspeakable joy, unspeakable things, or unspeakable gift (*I Peter 1:8, III Nephi 28:14, Helaman 5:44,* and *D&C 121:26*)

— mighty change of heart (*Mosiah 5:2, Mosiah 5:7, Alma 5:14*)

— having the image of Christ in ones self (*Alma 5:14*)

— renewing of your body (*D&C 84:33*)

— Gift of the Holy Ghost (*Act 2:38* and *Moses 6:52*)

— coming to Christ (*Moroni 10:30 & 32*)

— redeemed of the Lord, Christ or God (*2 Nephi 1:15, Moses 5:10,* and *Mosiah 27:25-26*)

— possessing all truth or all things (*John 16:13* and *D&C 93:28*)

— having a hope in Christ (*1 Cor. 15:19-20*)

— made perfect in Christ (*Hebrews 12:22-24, Ephesians 4:11-14,* and *Moroni 10:32-33*)

— receive the Second Comforter (*John 14:16, 17, 18, 21, 23*)

— quickened in the inner man (*D&C 67:11-12, Moses 6:64*)

— name written in heaven or Lamb's book of life (*Alma 5:58* and *D&C 76:68*)

— become a new creature (*Mosiah 27:25-26*)

— wrapped in the power and glory of your maker (*TPJS pg 51*)

— putting off the natural man (*Mosiah 3:19*)

When we grasp what it means to be Born Again we begin to recognize these key words or phrases throughout the scriptures and we see how common, how often people were Born Again down through the history of this earth. As we take note of such references we realize that these and many more are synonymous with the Baptism of Fire and the Holy Ghost or being Born Again and we begin to comprehend the magnitude, the import, of this subject. It is a principle so profound, so basic to our eternal salvation that we **cannot** give it enough attention. The power of this event in our lives virtually takes us out of this world to a celestial level of thought and experience.

How Did We Do?

We need to look at the above list of evidences of being Born Again and ask ourselves if we have any of these powers? If we have any at all, do we have them all the time; twenty four seven, upon demand?

If not, have we really experienced the Baptism of Fire in our own lives? Are we new creatures in Christ having lost all desire to sin? I submit that we, not just as a church but as individuals, **have not** been "Born Again," received the "Gift of the Holy Ghost," or had the "Baptism of Fire."

I'm Not There Yet

Losing our desire to sin blows most of us out of the water. I can only speak for myself when I admit that I still desire to sin. Also, fear, doubt, despair, and guilt still fill my heart from time to time. I am seldom at peace either with myself or this world and the things that happen in it. Notwithstanding the many spiritual experiences, revelations, and powers I have had on occasion, sadly, at the date of this writing, I have not experienced the Baptism of Fire by the Holy Ghost nor have I received the Second Comforter through having my Calling and Election made sure (more on this in a moment).

Employs No Servant

I know this too because I have not seen God or Christ face to face. In the granting of this endowment the Lord employs no servant. It is administered by the Lord Himself. "O then, my beloved brethren, come unto the Lord, the Holy One. Remember that his paths are righteous. Behold, the way for man is narrow, but it lieth in a straight course before him, and *the keeper of the gate is the Holy One of Israel; and he employeth no servant there*; and there is none other way save it be by the gate; for he cannot be deceived, for the Lord God is his name." (*II Nephi 9:41*) ". . . and whoso believeth in me believeth in the Father also; and unto him will the Father bear record of me, *for* ***He*** *will visit him with fire and with the Holy Ghost*." (*III Nephi 11:35*) ". . . and unto them I have given power that they may baptize you with water; and after that ye are baptized with water, behold, ***I*** *will baptize you with fire and with the Holy Ghost*;—" (*III Nephi 12:1*) "And every one that hearkeneth to the voice of the Spirit cometh unto God, even the Father. And ***the Father*** *teacheth him of the covenant* which He has renewed and confirmed upon you . . . ." (*D&C 84:47-48*) "Jesus therefore answered and said unto them, Murmur not among yourselves. No man can come to me, except the Father which hath sent me draw him: and I will raise him up at the last day. It is written in the prophets, And *they shall be all taught of God* . . . ." (*John 6:43-45*)

Again let me emphatically state, this endowment does not come any other way but by the hand of God Himself. ". . . For the gate by which ye should enter is repentance and baptism by water; and *then cometh a remission of your sins by fire and by the Holy Ghost* . . . Wherefore, now after I have spoken these words, if ye cannot understand them it will be because ye ask not, neither do ye knock; wherefore, ye are not brought into the light, but must perish in the dark. For behold, again I say unto you that if ye will enter in by the way, and receive the Holy Ghost, it will show unto you all things what ye should do. Behold, *this is the doctrine of Christ, and there will be no more doctrine given until after he shall* ***manifest himself unto you in the flesh***. *And when he shall* ***manifest himself unto you in the flesh,*** *the things which he shall say unto you shall ye observe to do.* And now I, Nephi, cannot say more; the Spirit stoppeth mine utterance, and I am left to mourn because of the unbelief, and the wickedness, and the ignorance, and the stiffneckedness of men; for they will not search knowledge, nor understand great knowledge, when it is given unto them in plainness, even as plain as word can be." (*II Nephi 31:17, 32:4-7*) Nephi minced no words in his description of the mind and heart of men, not only in those days, but also in our day. Unbelief, failing to search after knowledge, wickedness, ignorance, stiffneckedness, does any of his portrayal fit us? God forbid, I fear it does. Further, what we fail to realize is that the above stated appearance of Christ Himself *manifesting "himself unto you in the flesh"* is not a generalization of His coming in glory, to all who remain as prophesied, but a personal, individual **visitation** at the time we receive the Holy Ghost.

Some Technical Background

The above scriptures outline the keys of both the greater, Melchizedek priesthood holding the keys of the mysteries of heaven and the knowledge of God and the lesser, Aaronic priesthood, holding the keys of the preparatory gospel of repentance and of baptism, and the remission of sins, the law of carnal commandments, and the ministering of angels. Let me restate that those who receive these two priesthoods and are faithful in them will be *sanctified by the Spirit unto the renewing of their bodies.* What does this mean?

In the days of Enoch and his Zion City of righteousness, he and all his people were translated (see *Hebrews 11:5*). It says that it was so they would not taste death but there was more to it than that. It was so they could dwell in the presence of God. Remember that to see God requires a change in us or Him. The change in us is called "translation." Apparently, though it does not say how long, Enoch's city was held suspended above the earth. It says, "angels descending out of heaven, bearing testimony of the Father and Son; and the Holy Ghost fell on many, and they were caught up by the powers of heaven into Zion." (*Moses 7:27*)

Translation

Back then, when a person repented and was baptized by water they were translated, baptized by fire and the Holy Ghost, and caught up to the Zion City. Although later on they were not caught up to the city of Zion (Zion fled), they were still translated. Translation not only happened at the time of Enoch but was the course of mans spiritual and physical progression down through the ages. When a person achieved that level of spiritual righteousness he or she was sanctified of the spirit (forgiven, cleansed of all sin and desire for sin) and translated of the body (taken from a mortal state to one of immortality), freed from the fall of Adam and the trials and buffetings of this mortal world, including being given power over death. Again, this is why the ancients like Adam and Methuselah lived so long. They had power over death and did not die until, according to the spirit of truth that was in them, it was time for them to do so.

I am trying here to say that translation of the body and sanctification of the spirit is simultaneous and synonymous with the Baptism of Fire.

Translation was common at various other times down through the history of man. In Alma's time the Lord said, ". . . he would rather suffer that the Lamanites might destroy all his people who are called the people of Nephi, if it were possible that they could fall into sins and transgressions, after having had so much light and so much knowledge given unto them of the Lord their God.—Having been visited by the Spirit of God; having conversed with angels, and having been spoken unto by the voice of the Lord; and having the spirit of prophecy, and the spirit of revelation and also many gifts, the gift of speaking with tongues, and gift of preaching, and gift of the Holy Ghost, and *the gift of translation*;" (*Alma 9:19, 21*)

Translation is the course of man's progression bringing him into the presence of God while in the flesh. ***We need to understand that this endowment, sanctification and translation, is synonymous with the Baptism of Fire, of receiving the gift of the Holy Ghost.*** It, translation, will become commonplace again or Zion cannot be established for that is the city of the living God and we will need the gift of translation in order to be in His presence.

A Moratorium On Translation

In our day, the Lord has seen fit not to translate those who achieve such a level of righteousness. He put a moratorium on translation for now. Apparently those keys were one of the two not restored to the earth through the prophet Joseph Smith. The keys of translation and the keys of resurrection are yet to be restored. Why is this so? **This is the curse, the scourge, and judgment we are under because of our vanity and unbelief and because we have treated lightly the things of God, namely His great priesthood powers** (see *D&C 84:55-58 & 95:6*).

Although the keys of resurrection may probably wait until the millennial era, the keys and powers of translation will be, in fact ***must be***, restored to the Zion people of the New Jerusalem or it cannot be established. Said John Taylor, (italics added) "Everything that (Enoch's people) had revealed to them pertaining to the organization of the church of God, also pertaining to doctrine and ordinances, we have had revealed to us, excepting one thing, and that is *the principle and power of translation*; That, however, will in due time be restored also." (*JD 23:32-33*) "*The principle of translation* was a principle which at that time (the time of Enoch) existed in the church, and is one of the principles of the gospel, and which will exist in the latter day." (*JD 26:90*)

Calling And Election—A Rain Check

Apparently at various times through the history of man, the Lord has opted not to endow people with the Baptism of Fire who merited such a state. Such an endowment of power, as noted above virtually and practically removes one from this world and the Lord, for reasons of his own, wants them to remain in a mortal fallen state. As a consolation however, he has made their Calling and Election Sure. We in The Church who think we know something about Calling and Election, have it backwards. We think to have one's Calling and Election made sure is to receive the greater gift when in fact it is a *consolation prize*, a *rain check* as it were. Although the level of endowment is the same, it is short of receiving the power and glory of the Baptism of Fire and translation. This is the state of many of the early saints as well as many of the latter-day saints.

Peter counseled us to work for this fullness. "And beside this, giving all diligence, add to your faith virtue, and to virtue, knowledge; And to knowledge temperance; and to temperance patience; and to patience, godliness: And to godliness brotherly kindness; and to brotherly kindness charity. For if these things be in you, and abound, they make you that ye shall neither be barren nor unfruitful in the knowledge of our Lord Jesus Christ. But he that lacketh these things is blind, and cannot see afar off, and hath forgotten that he was purged from his old sins. *Wherefore the rather, brethren, give diligence to make your calling and election sure*: for if ye do these things, ye shall never fall." (*2 Peter 1:5-10*) "We have also a *more sure word of prophecy*; whereunto ye do well that ye take heed, as unto a light that shineth in a dark place, until the day dawn, and the day star arise in your hearts." (*2 Peter 1:19*)

What is Calling and Election? What is the More Sure Word of Prophecy and who is the Second Comforter? The Lord explained these phrases to Joseph Smith. "The more sure word of Prophecy means a man's knowing that he is sealed up unto eternal life, by revelation and the spirit of prophecy, through the power of the Holy Priesthood." (*D&C 131:5*) "Wherefore, I now send upon you another Comforter, even upon you my friends, that it may abide in your hearts, even the Holy Spirit of promise; which other Comforter is the same that I promised unto my disciples, as is recorded in the testimony of John. This Comforter is the promise which I give unto you of eternal life, even the glory of the celestial kingdom; Which glory is that of the church of the Firstborn, even of God, the holiest of all, through Jesus Christ His Son . . . ." (*D&C 88:3-5*) Said Joseph Smith (italics for emphasis), "Now, there is some grand secret here, and keys to unlock the subject. Notwithstanding the apostle exhorts them to add to their faith, virtue, knowledge, temperance, etc., yet he exhorts them to *make their calling and election sure*. And though they had heard an audible voice from heaven bearing testimony that Jesus was the Son of God, yet he says we have a more sure word of prophecy, whereunto ye do well that ye take heed as unto a light shining in a dark place. Now, wherein could they have a more sure word of prophecy than to hear the voice of God saying, this is my beloved Son.

"Now for the secret and grand key. Though they might hear the voice of God and know that Jesus was the Son of God, this would be no evidence that their election and calling was made sure, that they had part with Christ, and were joint heirs with Him. They then would want that more sure word of prophecy, *that they were sealed in the heavens and had the promise of eternal life in the kingdom of God.* Then, having this promise sealed unto them, it was an anchor to the soul, sure and steadfast. Though the thunders might roll and lightnings flash, and earthquakes bellow, and war gather thick around, yet this hope and knowledge would support the soul in every hour of trial, trouble and tribulation. *Then knowledge through our Lord and Savior Jesus Christ is the grand key that unlocks the glories and mysteries of the kingdom of heaven.*

"Compare this principle with Christendom at the present day, and where are they, with all their boasted religion, piety and sacredness while at the same time they are crying out against prophets, apostles, angels, revelations, prophesying and visions, etc. Why, they are just ripening for the damnation of hell. They will be damned, for they reject the most glorious principles of the Gospel of Jesus Christ and treat with disdain and trample under foot the key that unlocks the heavens and puts in our possession the glories of the celestial world. Yes, I say, such will be damned, with all their professed godliness. Then I would exhort you to go on and continue to *call upon God until you make your calling and election surer for yourselves*, by obtaining this more sure word of prophecy, and *wait patiently for the promise until you obtain it*, etc." (*TPJS pg. 298*)

We must ask ourselves if we are not found in this boat? Do we profess a Godliness but "deny the power thereof?" In all our obedience to the carnal commandments and performances do we damn ourselves by saying "we have enough?" (see *II Nep 28:20-30*) Do we "fly to pieces like glass" when presented with higher celestial concepts? Are we "treating lightly" the power and keys to the mysteries and knowledge of God? Are we "rejecting the good gifts," even the greatest of all, eternal life? Hey, I'm just asking. Don't kill the messenger.

To receive the Second Comforter (Christ Himself), the more Sure Word of Prophesy, or Calling and Election is a glorious experience to be sure and we would be extremely grateful should we obtain such a promise but we are still in this mortal travail and subject to its rigors. When born again, we are translated which virtually takes us out of this world and gives us all the power and glory of God. Again, this is the greatest endowment man on earth can receive at the hand of God.

His Own Time

Whether or not we can conceive of this personal event, being Born Again, having the Baptism of Fire, of meeting Christ face to face, the scriptures make it clear that it is not only possible but the *end* we should all be working for. To deny that such a thing is possible is to throw God's gift of *knowing* Him, the greatest gift of eternal life, back in His face. If we will keep the commandments, become humble, and seek after the mysteries, we may, in God's due time, ***expect*** this great promise to be fulfilled, **even in this life**. Because the reception of the Holy Ghost is a gift (hence the Gift of the Holy Ghost), it will be given according to God's own good will and pleasure. It cannot be earned or it becomes a wage. It is a Gift.

Although it is true that according to God's will for us personally, *those who believe* ***may not*** have the mysteries of heaven opened to them or meet God face to face in this life, it is *for certain* it ***cannot*** happen to *those who do not believe.* We ***must*** *come to believe* that we may have this privilege of receiving the mysteries of the kingdom and be in the presence of the Father and Son, while in this life, or be condemned not to have it happen.

"It is the first principle of the Gospel to know for a certainty, the Character of God, and to know that we may converse with him as one man converses with another . . . ." (*TPJS, pg. 345-6*) "And if your eye be single to my glory, your whole bodies shall be filled with light, and there shall be no darkness in you; and that body which is filled with light comprehendeth all things. Therefore, sanctify yourselves that your minds become single to God, and *the days will come that you shall see Him; for He will unveil His face unto you, and it shall be in His own time, and in His own way, and according to His own will.*" (*D&C 88:67-68*)

Only Halfway There

Joseph Smith makes it abundantly clear that baptism of water without the Baptism of Fire is going only half way there. "You might as well baptize a bag of sand as a man, if not done in view of the remission of sins and getting the Holy Ghost. Baptism of water is but half a baptism, and is good for nothing without the other half—that is, the baptism of the Holy Ghost." *(TPJS pg. 314)* "The baptism of water, without the Baptism of Fire and the Holy Ghost attending it, is of no use; they are necessarily and inseparably connected. An individual must be born of the water **and** the spirit in order to get into the Kingdom of God." (bold added) *(TPJS pg. 360)*

Why don't we comprehend that **this is what it's all about**?!! Why do we muddle through life as if we haven't been told what our purpose and course are? Why do we act as though God is up there and we're down here and we may never meet? Don't we know that we can have it all, a fullness of all? Isn't this God's promise to us all? Why do we procrastinate? Do we not know it could just as well happen today as tomorrow? Said Joseph Smith, "We begin to learn the only true God, and what kind of being we have got to worship. Having a knowledge of God, we begin to know how to approach Him, and how to ask so as to receive an answer. When we understand the character of God, and know how to come to Him, He begins to unfold the heavens to us, and to tell us all about it. When we are ready to come to Him, He is ready to come to us." *(TPJS, pg. 350)*

You may wonder what all this has to do with charity, the pure love of Christ, but I am getting to that. Please be patient as I continue.

The Church of The Firstborn

In order to get the full picture we need to understand what is meant by references to the Church of the Firstborn or the General Assembly of the Church of the Firstborn. "And now, verily I say unto you, I was in the beginning with the Father, and am the Firstborn; And all those who are begotten through me are partakers of the glory of the same, and are the Church of The Firstborn." *(D&C 93:21-22)* Although Christ was the Firstborn of the Father in the flesh, that is not what the church of the firstborn has reference to. The church of the firstborn does not refer to Him as the title or name of a church. *The church of the firstborn or general assembly of the church of the firstborn has reference* ***to that group of people from all of God's offspring who are spiritually born first.***

Like Christ, they are legal heirs to all that God has. Like the Church of Enoch, it refers to a specific group of people. Of course the Church of Enoch alludes to those who entered into God's fullness at the time of Enoch. Accordingly, references to the Church or Assembly of the Firstborn refer to those who receive such an endowment first or before the remainder of the world.

The Big Brother

Historically, the firstborn of a family received the greatest portion of the family inheritance. It is also notable that they had the greatest responsibilities to the family, after the parents were gone, to maintain the traditions and priesthood keys. There is no chance associated with being the firstborn in a family, having the benefits and burdens of being so. "For whom he did foreknow, he also did predestinate to be conformed to the image of his Son, that he might be the firstborn among many brethren." (*Romans 8:28*) Likewise, there is no chance to being among the first to be *spiritually Born Again*. The Lord has chosen those first to receive this greater endowment of powers (before listed). Further, only those *Born Again* and endowed with these great powers will be called to establish the Zion Society, the New Jerusalem. "But ye are come unto mount Sion, and unto the city of the living God, the heavenly Jerusalem, and to an innumerable company of angels, To the *general assembly and church of the firstborn*, which are written in heaven, and to God the Judge of all, and to the spirits of just men made perfect, and to Jesus the mediator of the new covenant,—" (*Hebrews 12:22-24*) They are those who have already been sanctified through the Baptism of Fire. At least for them, the Church of Jesus Christ of Latter-day Saints, as we know it, will have no further purpose and will have passed away.

Notwithstanding this, The Church of Jesus Christ of Latter-day Saints is Christ's established church on earth. On the other hand, it is just that, His church *on earth*. Like all things earthly, it will pass away when it has filled its role in the salvation of man. "And He gave some, apostles; and some, prophets; and some, evangelists; and some, pastors and teachers; For the perfecting of the saints, for the work of the ministry, for the edifying of the body of Christ: **Till** *we all come in the unity of the faith, and of the knowledge of the Son of God, unto a perfect man, unto the measure of the stature of the fulness of Christ:* That we henceforth be no more children, tossed to and fro, and carried about with every wind of doctrine, by the sleight of men, and cunning craftiness, whereby they lie in wait to deceive." (*Ephesians 4:11-14*)

The purpose of the *earthly* LDS Church is the same as that church established by Christ when he walked the earth; that is for *perfecting of the saints, for the work of the ministry, for the edifying of the body of Christ.* That perfection comes at our Baptism of Fire and the Holy Ghost. We become *perfect men and women* and we will then measure up to the *stature of the fullness of Christ;* or in other words, we receive His fullness. We have then become members of that *heavenly* church that has been around since the beginning, the Church or Assembly of the Firstborn of Christ, made up of those who are first to be reborn, sons and daughters of God. This eternal organization, being heavenly, will never pass away.

When you think about it, it only follows that since salvation is such a personal thing (predicated on righteous character traits and the grace of God), acceptance into Gods *heavenly* church must come on an individual basis, not simply because one has joined any particular organized religious group. I mean, one does not, by default, find entrance into God's kingdom because they are members of Gods ordained *earthly* church, or because they marry a good person (even in the temple), have good children, or for any other like reason. Salvation is a blessing that is entirely individual.

So, we must realize that the LDS Church, as a church or unit, will not grow into the Zion Society. In fact, because we have so fully assimilated Babylonian characteristics, we are further from it now than when The Church was first restored by God to Joseph Smith. However, a group of people will be brought out from among the LDS Church to redeem Zion.

This is not a new concept. Much is said about it by the brethren in the Journal of Discourses. It says (parenthesis added), "There will be a people raised up, if we will not be that people there will yet be a people raised up whose lives will embody in perfection the revelations contained in this book (his reference here was probably to the D&C), who will live as the doctrines here taught require, as the laws here revealed show unto us, and they will be raised up, too, in this generation, and such a people will have to be raised up before Zion can be fully redeemed—." (*George Q. Cannon JD 24:144*) "The day will come when the Lord will choose a people out of this people, upon whom he will bestow his choicest blessings—." (*Heber C. Kimball JD 11:145*) "God will preserve a portion of this people, the meek and the humble, to bear off the kingdom to the inhabitants of the earth and will defend his priesthood; for it is the last time, the last gathering time." (*The Contributor Vol. 10 l pg 362*) "—the kingdom will not be taken from this people and given to another, but a people will come forth from among us who will be zealous of good works—." (*Daniel H. Wells JD 18:99*) "There will come up from the midst of this people that people that has been talked so much about—." (*Daniel H. Wells JD 23:305b*)

Tares & Wheat

Until such time of redemption, the tares will be found amongst the wheat. "—the tares choke the wheat and drive the church into the wilderness. But behold, in the last days, even now while the Lord is beginning to bring forth the word, and the blade is springing up and is yet tender—Behold, verily I say unto you, the angels are crying unto the Lord day and night, who are ready and waiting to be sent forth to reap down the fields; But the Lord saith unto them pluck not up the tares while the blade is yet tender (for verily your faith is weak), lest you destroy the wheat also. Therefore, let the wheat and the tares grow together until the harvest is fully ripe; then ye shall first gather out the wheat from among the tares, and after the gathering of the wheat, behold and lo, the tares are bound in bundles, and the field remaineth to be burned." (*D&C 86:4-7*) "Yes, within the Church today there are tares among the wheat and wolves within the flock. As President J. Reuben Clark, Jr., stated: 'The ravening wolves are amongst us, from our own membership, and they, more than any other, are clothed in sheep's clothing because they wear the habiliments of the priesthood. We should be careful of them.' (*Conference Report April 1949, pg. 163*) The wolves amongst our flock are more numerous and devious today than when President Clark made this statement.—President David O. McKay said that 'the Church is little, if at all, injured by persecution, and calumnies from ignorant, misinformed, or malicious enemies. A greater hindrance to its progress comes from faultfinders, shirkers, commandment-breakers, and apostate cliques within its own ecclesiastical and quorum groups.'" (*President Benson Conference Report 1967, pg. 9*)

Who are these wolves in sheep's clothing? I think they will make themselves manifest soon enough. I am more worried about those of us who are "walking in darkness at noonday" as a result of our "vanity and unbelief". I couldn't agree more with James Custer's analysis of who these tares are within The Church. Said he, "There is a tendency to regard the active members of the church as the wheat and the inactive members as the tares. Nevertheless, a thoughtful examination of the latter-day application of the parable will bring one to the realization that the inactive have virtually no influence in church affairs and, therefore, no significant ability to choke the wheat and drive the church into the 'wilderness'. (The wilderness being a state of general apostasy among the membership.)

"The tares must then include those who are active but whose primary focus and participation is in worldly Babylon rather than a quest for Zion. Their hearts are set upon their riches, their popularity, their social lives, their careers and their success in the world. The tares may also be those who are deeply in debt and can barely meet the demands placed upon them. They complain against God, the church and other members. The tares may be those who complain that the Lord doesn't hear their prayers and doesn't care about them so they have given up hope and faith. The tares are surely those apathetic passive members who are satisfied with the status quo and the milk of the gospel, who reject further light and knowledge. They go to church, perform in their callings, may even attend the temple, pay tithes as premiums on 'fire insurance' but have no personal relationship with their Savior or the Holy Spirit. They are those with shallow or vacant testimonies, they testify that the church is true. They worship the visible church in the name of Jesus Christ while placing their trust and confidence solely in the arm of flesh." (M. *James Custer, The Unspeakable Gift pg. 120-121*)

So which ones are the wheat? In the 76th Section of the D&C we find a detailed description of those who will inherit a Celestial glory. "They are they who are the church of the Firstborn. They are they into whose hands the Father *has* given all things . . . These are they who are come unto mount Zion, and unto the city of the living God, the heavenly place, the holiest of all. These are they who *have* come to an innumerable company of angels, to the general assembly and the church of Enoch, and of the Firstborn." (*D&C 76:54,55, 66,67*) For a full description read D&C 76:50-70, and note the past tense in this case. Those who will build Zion will already have been sanctified and called to that calling. Remember, Zion cannot be established except upon the principles of the Celestial Kingdom (see *D&C 105*) and only a Celestial people can do that. Also, only those who are *Born Again*, new creatures with changed bodies will be able to abide the presence of God in "the city of the living God".

144,000

Further, once Zion is established, the missionaries sent out, namely the 144,000 (12,000 from each of the 12 tribes), will proselytize directly to the Church of the Firstborn (not the LDS church). "Question. What are we to understand by sealing the one hundred and forty-four thousand, out of all the tribes of Israel—twelve thousand out of every tribe? Answer. We are to understand that those who are sealed are high priests, ordained unto the holy order of God, to administer the everlasting gospel; for they are they who are ordained out of every nation, kindred, tongue, and people, by the angels to whom is given power over the nations of the earth, to bring as many as will come to the church of the Firstborn." (*D&C 77:11*)

When we realize the significance of being spiritually Born Again; that it puts us among the *church of the firstborn*; that it is ***the greatest endowment of power ordained for man on this earth;*** that it is the means of entering into

God's kingdom—into His presence, into His "rest;" that it is the means of becoming sons and daughters of God, members of the royal eternal family; that it is the administration of the New and Everlasting Covenant; that it is a granting of all power and glory; that it is the renewing, the literal translation, of our bodies; then we begin to realize how far we have to go. Such a realization might just break our hearts and force us to contriteness.

The New Covenant, The Heavenly Gift

What is this *New and Everlasting Covenant*? It is being Born Again. It is ***the heavenly gift,*** that through the priesthood ordinances we not only *may*, but *must* **behold the face of God, hear His voice**, and **enter into His rest**, which rest, as Moses said is the ***fullness of His glory***! (see *D&C 84:24*) "For those who were once enlightened, and have *tasted of the heavenly gift*, and were made partakers of the Holy Ghost, and have tasted the good word of God, and the powers of the world to come." (*Hebrews 6:5-6*, see also *4 Nephi 1:3*, and *Ether 12:8*) It is the holy priesthood of God, with its powerful ordinances of not just salvation, but exaltation. This is the *marvelous work and a wonder* the Lord promised, through the Prophet Isaiah, to do in the last days when some men are drawing near Him with their mouths but removing their hearts far from Him (see *Isaiah 29:13-14* and *2 Nephi 25:17*). This is not just the restoration of The Church of Christ but a wonderful event worked by God in the lives of those who will seek Him diligently and obey His will.

The Law of Christ Is Freedom

"But," you say, "I am a baptized member of The Church, I have the Melchizedek priesthood, the higher priesthood, so why have I not seen the face of God? Why has He not taught me the mysteries of the kingdom?" Well, of course you must answer that question for yourself, the answer to which will likely and hopefully humble you and break your heart. My *answer* is you have treated lightly that which you have been given. You are vain, prideful, and unbelieving. You are still trusting in your own arm of flesh, still struggling to live the preparatory laws (repentance, baptism, tithing, the Word of Wisdom, and etc.) thinking that they will do the job. Though necessary, they will not! You must live the *Law of Christ* (see *D&C 88:21*). Again you say, "But I thought I was. Isn't that what repentance and baptism are all about?" Repentance and baptism of water yes, Baptism of Fire and the Holy Ghost a thousand times no! Repentance and baptism of water is the preparatory gospel, the schoolmaster, the keys of the lesser priesthood, not the law of Christ. Well then, what is the Law of Christ? It is the New and Everlasting Covenant. But what is this New and Everlasting Covenant?

To attempt to definitively answer those questions, and they are really the same question; to bring it all into focus, I must refer back to our discussion on law. You will remember we said that Christ lives *without law,* or rather, as stated before; He lives *with all law*. He can pick and choose which geometry or law (and the truths associated therewith) that He, according to His own good will and pleasure, will work within. God enjoys ultimate freedom. I must here expand a little more on this concept of *ultimate freedom*. Unlike God, with our finite minds, we do not have the ability to comprehend even a small portion of the laws governing all things, so we are left to work within one geometry or very few of the geometries, at most. However, God would like us to be totally free. This is the whole purpose of His plan of life and salvation, *to free us*. The Law of Christ, as spoken of in D&C 88:29-38 does just that. It will free us to live *without law* (or with all law). In other words, our final aim should be to live in this state of ultimate freedom, to choose which law (with its relative truths) we want. How can that be? With finite minds, how can we possibly learn all the infinite realms of law, let alone the truths that apply to them? Isn't this entirely beyond our reach? No, it is not. You see, you need not know *all*, you need only become one with truth, that mass of matter that is in all things, through all things, which gives life to all things, which is the light of truth. ". . . if ye will enter in by the way, and receive the Holy Ghost (the Baptism of Fire), it will show unto you all things what ye should do." (*II Nephi 32:5*) Said Joseph Smith, "I am learned, and know more than all the world put together. The Holy Ghost does, anyhow, and He is within me, and comprehends more than all the world; and I will associate myself with Him." (*TPJS pg. 350*) You must come to a oneness with that great spirit of truth. Here we are, back to the *oneness doctrine* again. Oh how great this *spiritual oneness*, this Holy Ghost, and how necessary to our *knowing* God.

What am I saying here? I am saying that, ***if we would live by the spirit of truth we would not need law!*** We must live "by every word that proceedeth out of the mouth of God" (*Matthew 4:4,* also *D&C 84:44* and *98:11*) "For all the law is fulfilled in one word, even in this; Thou shalt love thy neighbour as thyself. But if ye be led of the Spirit, ye are not under the law. But the fruit of the Spirit is love, joy, peace, longsuffering, gentleness, goodness, faith, meekness, temperance: against such there is no law." (*Galatians 5:14, 18, 22-23*) Why? Why is there no law? Because righteous people don't need written laws to coerce them into doing the right things. Because as we tap into *all law* as well as *all truth*, the Holy Ghost would then testify of the truth of all things as we need them. This is the celestial Law of Christ. This is ***no law*** (or as explained before, all law and all freedom). This is the ***New Law***.

But you say, "God is bound by law. We know this to be true." Yes, but to which law is He bound? Which ever He chooses! Therefore He is *not bound* by the law, but *freed* by it and we may be also. "Now we know that what things soever the law saith, it saith to them who are under the law: that every mouth may be stopped, and all the world may become guilty before God. Therefore by the deeds of the law there shall no flesh be justified in His sight: for by the law is the knowledge of sin. *But now the righteousness of God* ***without the law*** *is manifested, being witnessed by the law and the prophets; Even the righteousness of God which is by faith of Jesus Christ unto all and upon all them that believe:* for there is no difference: *For all have sinned, and come short of the glory of God* . . . ." (*Romans 3:19-23*) Since truth shines and that light is also the law that governs all things, the law, like truth, or rather which is truth, can make you free. (see *D&C 88:7-16* and *John 8:31-32*)

The Prophets Taught Us How

The prophets taught us how. It is by the ordinance (and it is an ordinance) of becoming one with truth, receiving a fullness of God's glory, entering into His rest. What rest? Rest from struggling to know which laws and truths apply and how to live them? You see; the law cannot save us. In fact, the law will condemn us. Said Nephi (italics for emphasis), "And men are instructed sufficiently that they know good from evil. And the law is given unto men. And *by the law no flesh is justified; or, by the law men are cut off. Yea, by the temporal law they were cut off; and also, by the spiritual law they perish from that which is good, and become miserable forever.* Wherefore, redemption cometh in and through the Holy Messiah; for He is full of grace and truth. Behold, He offereth himself a sacrifice for sin, to answer the ends of the law, unto all those who have a broken heart and a contrite spirit; and unto none else can the ends of the law be answered." (*2 Nephi 2:5-7*) You will note, there is that broken heart and a contrite spirit again. Some would argue that the temporal law cannot save us, but the spiritual laws can. Bear in mind, the Lord makes no distinction between temporal and spiritual law. "Wherefore, verily I say unto you that all things unto me are spiritual . . . ." (*D&C 29:34*) Since we tend to separate laws into temporal and spiritual, Nephi makes it plain that neither temporal law nor spiritual law will get us to eternal joy. He said we are given the law to teach us good from evil.

The Dead Law

Notwithstanding the need of the law and knowledge (man cannot be saved in ignorance), *knowledge will not save us, nor will* ***doing*** *save us*, that is, obeying the laws of carnal commandments and outward ordinances. What will? Redemption comes *only* in and through the Holy Messiah who is full of grace and truth. He answered the ends of the law. To those upon whom the redemption applies, the law becomes useless. For whom did He answer the ends of the law and to whom does the redemption apply? Only those who have a *broken heart and a contrite spirit*; ***unto none else*** *can the ends of the law be answered* (see *2 Nephi 2:5-7* and *D&C 59:8*). Nephi tells us (italics for emphasis), "For we labor diligently to write, to persuade our children, and also our brethren, to believe in Christ, and to be reconciled to God; for we know that it is by grace that we are saved, after all we can do. And, notwithstanding we believe in Christ, we keep the law of Moses, and look forward with steadfastness unto Christ, until the law shall be fulfilled. For, for this end was the law given; wherefore the *law hath become dead unto us*, and *we are made alive in Christ* (Born Again) because of our faith; yet we keep the law because of the commandments. And we talk of Christ, we rejoice in Christ, we preach of Christ, we prophesy of Christ, and we write according to our prophecies, that our children may know to what source they may look for a remission of their sins. Wherefore, we speak concerning the law *that our children may know the deadness of the law*; and they, by knowing the *deadness of the law, may look forward unto that life which is in Christ*, and know for what end the law was given. And after the law is fulfilled in Christ, that they need not harden their hearts against him when the law ought to be done away. And now behold, my people, ye are a stiffnecked people; wherefore, I have spoken plainly unto you, that ye cannot misunderstand. And the words which I have spoken shall stand as a testimony against you; for they are sufficient to teach any man the right way; for the right way is to believe in Christ and deny him not; for by denying him ye also deny the prophets and the law. And now behold, I say unto you that the right way is to believe in Christ, and deny him not; and Christ is the Holy One of Israel; wherefore ye must bow down before Him, and worship him with all your might, mind, and strength, and your whole soul; and if ye do this ye shall in nowise be cast out. And, *inasmuch as it shall be expedient*, ye must keep the performances and ordinances of God until the law shall be fulfilled which was given unto Moses." (*2 Nephi 25:23-30*)

The Only Way

What is the way, the *only* way? To believe in Christ, deny Him not, and worship Him with all our hearts. When Christ came, the law was indeed fulfilled in Him. "Behold, I am He that gave the law, and I am He who covenanted with my people Israel; therefore, *the law in me is fulfilled, for I have come to fulfil the law; therefore it hath an end.* Behold, I do not destroy the prophets, for as many as have not been fulfilled in me, verily I say unto you, shall all be fulfilled. And because I said unto you that old things have passed away, I do not destroy that which hath been spoken concerning things which are to come. For behold, the covenant which I have made with my people is not all fulfilled; but the law which was given unto Moses hath an end in me. Behold, *I am the law, and the light. Look unto me, and endure to the end, and ye shall live*; for unto him that endureth to the end will I give eternal life." *(3 Nephi 15:5-9)* So what was the old law fulfilled by?—the new law in Christ, and what is the new law and covenant?—Charity, the pure love of Christ. Are we beginning to get the picture?

Laws, Laws, And More Laws

Down through time, the Lord has repeatedly tried to get us to receive His gift, His New Law. Instead we seem to want a bunch of lesser ones. As I said before, The Children of Israel, who had the chance to receive the New Law, the celestial Law of Christ, to see His face, opted to be governed by temporal laws, carnal commandments, and performances. Are we not doing the same thing? We not only want the laws of the Word of Wisdom, Sabbath day observance, tithing, moral code, and etc., but we, like the children of Israel, want it all spelled out. We are even told when to fast (the first Sunday of the month), as apparently we can't determine, on our own, when it is necessary. The problem with spelling out laws is the same that plagued The Children of Israel. The more specific you get, the more loopholes you create and before long you are filling huge law libraries with volume after volume, and on it goes. Do we think that the heavens are filled with law libraries and practitioners of law, namely lawyers? Heaven forbid! That sounds more like hell to me.

Yet notwithstanding the constraints of law, just like the children of Israel, we want laws, laws, and more laws. Why do we want laws? Is it so we can obey them all perfectly and thereby become righteous? I don't think so. In fact, after giving this a great deal of thought, I have come to the conclusion that we want laws for two reasons, neither of which are virtuous. First, we want laws because *we do not want to be responsible for ourselves*. That's right. We want someone else to tell us what to do and just how to do it. The outcome is then the lawgiver's fault, not ours. Quite often, we really don't want to be responsible for our own decisions. Second, we want law *so we can judge when we are righteous and when others are not*. With laws in place, we can continually compare ourselves and others to what we think is right and good according to the law; then we can rationalize, condemn, or justify ourselves and others. In the Law of Christ, that is, a state of *no law*, you neither condemn nor rationalize. Not only is there no point in doing so, but no longer the desire to do so.

I have often heard others say how they love law and feel freed by obeying laws. I am afraid I do not share their feelings. I have always felt confined by law. Of course to protect others and ourselves, in our present society and on our limited spiritual plane, laws are an absolute necessity. Notwithstanding the propriety of laws, they limit us to a greater or lesser degree. I firmly believe that law does not free us, it imprisons us. It is knowing the laws, the truth, that sets us free. It is truth that sets us free "Then said Jesus to those Jews which believed on Him, If ye continue in my word, then are ye my disciples indeed; And ye shall know the truth, and the truth shall make you free." (*John 8:31-32*). This seems obvious to me. The irony is, and this seems equally obvious to me, that the more laws we break the more imprisoned we become and the more laws we obey the more liberated we become. This may be why we say that "the first law of heaven is *obedience*" but it is not. The first law of heaven is the law of Christ or love. "Jesus said unto him, Thou shalt love the Lord thy God with all thy heart, and with all thy soul, and with all thy mind. This is the first and great commandment. And the second is like unto it, Thou shalt love thy neighbour as thyself. On these two commandments hang all the law and the prophets." (*Matthew 22:38-40*) It is upon the principle of love that all the laws hang. Of course I appreciate the fact that without law our society would be in a complete state of chaos, but I can't help looking forward to a society where love is the governing principle, not law.

We Can Keep Them All!

If you still think you can keep all the laws and commandments by working hard enough, let me tell you of one of the most memorable classes I ever taught on this subject one Sunday some years ago. I first asked for a show of hands of those who believed we could keep all the laws and commandments. Nearly the entire class raised their hands. I then asked them to list all the laws and commandments they knew they were to live. I wrote them on the chalkboard as fast as they gave them to me. It seemed we started with what they deemed the most important and continued to what they considered the lesser ones. I wrote very small and we spent nearly the entire class period listing commandments. Before long, I was writing in between the lines, even smaller, and still the commandments came. The list looked a little like this: love the Lord, love your neighbor, don't deny the Holy Ghost, have no gods before me, make no graven images, take not the Lord's name in vain, keep the Sabbath day holy, honor our father and mother, don't kill, don't commit adultery, don't steal, don't bear false witness, don't covet, rid ourselves of vanity and pride, don't hold malice, don't be greedy, always speak the truth, be brave, be thankful, be reverent, be thrifty, be hospitable, forgive everyone (especially family members), don't use profanity, don't gossip, don't backbite, don't envy, no evil speaking, no sexual perversions (masturbation, petting, fornicating, homosexuality) or other unholy or impure practices, don't think evil thoughts, read the scriptures each day, pray often, be kind, don't get angry, don't yell at your kids, be patient, be merciful, be humble, have faith, have hope, don't get discouraged or depressed, no foolishness or loud laughter, don't overeat, do your genealogy, attend all your meetings, provide a living for your family, have family home evening each Monday,[113] keep a clean and neat house, plant a garden, think wholesome thoughts, multiply and replenish the earth (have children), get involved in good community affairs, spend quality time with your family, don't watch too much TV, pay tithing, follow the Word of Wisdom (in its completeness), go to the temple at least once a month, fast often, fulfill a church calling, beautify your yard and house, do random acts of kindness, don't abuse animals, take your wife out often, visit your extended family, donate fast offerings, donate to the missionary fund, give to the poor, stay out of debt, deal honestly with our fellowman, get an education, go on missions, get married, work at the welfare farm or cannery,[114] and etc. The list went on and on. As I listened to the members of my class recite what was expected of them, it became painfully obvious they were all just admitting to sins of commission or omission for which they were feeling guilty.

At the end of the class I asked again, (by a show of hands) who thought they could keep all the laws and commandments that were written on the board". To my amazement, no one raised a hand. Without trying to, I had effectively annihilated their hopes of making it to heaven. The consensus was that even if we were strong enough (which is a *big if*), there simply is not enough time, energy, or means to do it all. At least for that few minutes, we were humbled to an understanding that eternal life is not within our own ability to grasp, that if we are to make it, at all, it ***must*** be a gift of God and only through His grace and good pleasure will we enjoy this gift.

The Schoolmaster

Law is the Schoolmaster. "But before faith came, we were kept under the law, shut up unto the faith which should afterwards be revealed. Wherefore the law was our schoolmaster *to bring us* unto Christ, that we might be justified by faith. But after that faith is come, we are no longer under a schoolmaster." (*Galatians 3:23-25*) You will remember the scripture quoted earlier about how after the children of Israel rejected the higher celestial law of love and a fullness of God's glory they were given the lesser law of carnal commandments and performances (see *D&C 84:22-25*). Although we have moved past the Mosaic Laws, the laws we live by today are still carnal commandments and performances.

Such laws were never meant to save us to the celestial kingdom directly; they haven't the power, as they are laws of lesser kingdoms. Such laws will only sanctify us to those lesser kingdoms. These lesser laws were meant to school us, to teach us about ourselves, about God, and our relationship to Him. To love these carnal commandments and performances (or should I say *to love our ability to obey them*) to the extent that we refuse to move on to the higher Law of Christ is to doom ourselves to being consigned to a lesser kingdom. I realize that it is safer or more comfortable, especially for those of us who have been relatively successful at living these carnal commandments and performances. And why shouldn't potentially celestial people be able to obey most of them, as they are carnal or lesser laws. When we do obey them we can call ourselves righteous and worthy. That feels good. But can't we see that this is only taking pride in being righteous? Such pride takes us away from that "broken heart and contrite spirit" necessary for God's grace to take effect in our lives.

Still, I suspect that not one of us is all that successful at keeping all of God's commandments. This is a good thing if we are honest enough with ourselves to admit it. It might even humiliate us to that point of a broken heart and contrite spirit.

Please remember that God did not say redemption cometh to all those who can obey my carnal commandments and performances to perfection! He said, "redemption cometh in and through the Holy Messiah; for He is full of grace and truth. Behold, He offereth himself a sacrifice for sin, to answer the ends of the law, unto all those who have a *broken heart and a contrite spirit*; and ***unto none else*** *can the ends of the law be answered.*" (*2 Nephi 2:6-7*)

"None else" can be saved in the celestial world. It is only through the grace of Christ after our heart is broken (we lose our pride) that we are open to His love, His rest, His glory His New Law of Charity. **Isn't it curious that should we be successful at obeying the laws, even all of them, the most we can hope for is a place in a lesser kingdom when the inability to obey coupled with a hope in Christ will get us to the Celestial Kingdom**. There truly is something more wonderful, more glorious, more magnificent and more splendid than the sense of pride we get from obedience to carnal commandments and performances. It behooves us to find out what that is and look forward to it.

Not A Cop-out

Though the lesser preparatory law of carnal commandments and performances will not save us, this is no Cop-out on obeying those laws. We are not saying here that we should not try, with every fiber of our being, to keep the laws and commandments. On the contrary, it is only by so doing that we learn we cannot and, out of humility, we must then turn to Christ who makes weak things strong. We must keep trying, as we do not know if God has, or when He will, give us power to overcome.

Even when we are Born Again, when the law has become dead to us, we will keep the laws, performances, and ordinances because, as Nephi said (see *2 Nephi 25:30*), it is expedient to do so. It is right according to the truth that is in us, according to the geometry we are in. Should that geometry change, it would become expedient to keep a different set of laws. Of course when we have a fullness of all laws, the laws, as we have known them, may be done away with. We are then effectively *without law*.

When we live the Law of Christ, we, like God, are free to do whatever we choose. Christ told Nicodemus that we can become as free as the wind. "That which is born of the flesh is flesh; and that which is born of the Spirit is spirit. Marvel not that I said unto thee, Ye must be Born Again. The wind bloweth where it listeth, and thou hearest the sound thereof, but canst not tell whence it cometh, and whither it goeth: *so is every one that is born of the Spirit.*" (*John 3:6-8*) Surely that is freedom indeed, to be like the wind, *live* like the wind, and be lead by the spirit, not the rigidity of the written laws and commandments. The spirit will testify of the geometry we are in and of the laws that apply thereto. Once again, ". . . if ye will enter in by the way, and receive the Holy Ghost (the Baptism of Fire), it will show unto you all things what ye should do." (*II Nephi 32:5*)

You see; when we are truly "Born Again of the Spirit," when we live by the spirit of truth on a moment-to-moment basis, we are no longer subject to the law. The spirit of truth prepares the way for us to say and do all things that are expedient to be said and done and we will **never** be in opposition to any law. In very fact, the law frees us to act (as God) according to our own good will and pleasure. We are not just beyond the law; we are freed by it. This is more than freedom; it is power. "And if ye are purified and cleansed from all sin, ye shall ask whatsoever you will in the name of Jesus and it shall be done." (*D&C 50:29*) This is freedom ***and*** power. And again, of course, when we are sanctified to such a degree we will only use that freedom and power to do that which is right and true; **not because the law commands,** but because **that's what we are. Truth!**

Free At Last—Free At Last

Of course, once we choose the realm or geometry, we are, like God, bound to keep the laws that apply thereto. Having this fullness we, like God, may choose to do whatever our own good will and pleasure dictates. This is the *Law of Christ* as recorded in D&C 88:21. This is the *New Law*, the *New Covenant*, that Jeremiah prophesied would be given (see *Jeremiah 31:31-34*). When Paul quotes Jeremiah he gives us a little more insight into the meaning (italics and brackets for emphasis). "For *the law made nothing perfect, but the bringing in of a better hope did*; by the which we draw nigh unto God. For if that first covenant had been faultless, then should no place have been sought for the second. For finding fault with them [the old laws and covenants], He saith, Behold, the days come, saith the Lord, when I will make a *new covenant* with the house of Israel and with the house of Judah: Not according to the covenant that I made with their fathers in the day when I took them by the hand to lead them out of the land of Egypt; because they continued not in my covenant, and I regarded them not, saith the Lord. For this is the covenant that I will make with the house of Israel after those days, saith the Lord; *I will put my laws into their mind, and write them in their hearts*: and I will be to them a God, and they shall be to me a people: And they shall not teach every man his neighbour, and every man his brother, saying, Know the Lord: for all shall know me, from the least to the greatest. For I will be merciful to their unrighteousness, and their sins and their iniquities will I remember no more. In that He saith, A new covenant, He hath made the first old. Now that which decayeth and waxeth old is ready to vanish away." (*Hebrews 7:19, 8:7-13*) And where will this New Law be written, in *The Holy Bible*, in *The Book of Mormon*, in *The Doctrine and Covenants*, in any other books? No, it will be written *in our minds* and *in our hearts*. Why? Because we will no longer need a written law of carnal commandments and outward performances. The spirit of truth, which will be in *all those who know the Lord*, will dictate according to expediency what law we must, at that moment, live. Further, it is said that no one will need to be taught by his brother, neighbor, or anyone else. Why? Because *the Father will have personally taught them* and put His *New Law* in their minds and hearts.

This all seems strange, especially to the Mormons, who have been teaching that salvation is in keeping the laws, performances, and carnal commandments.

We fail to realize that ***the commandments are only there to condemn those who refuse to live according to them, and to humble, to a broken heart and contrite sprit, those who will try.*** These laws bring us to a knowledge of good and evil, and humiliate us to a broken heart and a contrite spirit as we learn we cannot possibly, by ourselves, comply perfectly with them.

Sounds Like A No Win Game

Let's turn to Ether 12:26-27 again one more time (changes and additions made by author for emphasis). "if men come unto me I will show unto them their weakness, *I give unto men weakness* that they may be" **humiliated**; "and my grace is sufficient for all men that" are **humiliated** "before me; for if they" are adequately **humiliated** "before me, and have faith in me, then will I make weak things become strong unto them." (*Ether 12:26-27*) You will note that I changed the word *humble* to *humiliate*. They are virtually the same word but I have discovered that the word humble is too mild, over used, and without impact. I have nearly stopped using it myself. I try instead to use the word humiliation. It seems to drive the point home a little better. Still, as Alma said, "Blessed are they who humble themselves without being compelled to be humble." (*Alma 32:16*)

You are probably asking, "Why is God giving us laws and commandments and then giving us weakness so that we are unable to keep them? What is He trying to do?" He is trying to break our hearts and bring us to that state of contriteness where we are eligible to receive the gift of eternal life. Once again let me quote, "redemption cometh in and through the Holy Messiah; for He is full of grace and truth. Behold, He offereth himself a sacrifice for sin, to answer the ends of the law, unto all those who have a *broken heart and a contrite spirit*; and ***unto none else can the ends of the law be answered.***" (*2 Nephi 2:6-7*) So, in other words, the Lord is trying to **humiliate** us. Why? Because of our pride!—Our pride!—**Our pride!** Oh not pride again? Yes pride again.

One of the last, if not the last, council given by the prophet Ezra Taft Benson was given in April conference 1989, read by Gordon B. Hinckley because brother Benson was physically unable. His talk was titled "Beware of Pride" and it is perhaps the most powerful dissertation on the subject this author has ever heard. Although I give the following excerpts, I admonish all to look up and read his full thesis. It will inevitably give you a new perspective on pride, especially when you consider that out of all the subjects he could have chosen near the end of his life as parting words, he considered pride so important. He said, "The central feature of pride is enmity—enmity toward God and enmity toward our fellowmen, Enmity means 'hatred toward, hostility to, or a state of opposition.' It is the power by which Satan wished to dethrone God and reign over us.—Pride is essentially competitive in nature. We pit our will against God's.—My dear brethren and sisters, we must prepare to redeem Zion. It was essentially the sin of pride that kept us from establishing Zion in the days of the Prophet Joseph Smith. It was the same sin of pride that brought consecration to an end among the Nephites. (see *IV Nephi 1:24-25*) Pride is the great stumbling block to Zion. I repeat. Pride is the great stumbling block to Zion."

Pride is a self-centered thing. It keeps us separate from others and God Himself. It keeps us from recognizing the need for our Savior. It keeps us from admitting or confessing and repenting of our sins.

To overcome it we *must* become one with Christ, the power. Without this oneness, we will inevitably fall short (italics for emphasis) "*for all have sinned, and come short of the glory of God.*" (*Romans 3:23*) It is not about law. It is not about sin. It is about humiliation (humility). It is about contriteness.

The Tree, Flame, And A Sword

Because we sin, we gain a knowledge of good and evil. It is what we've been learning by eating from The Tree of Knowledge of Good And Evil. As discussed before, this knowledge of good and evil is absolutely necessary to our having joy. We must have opposition in all things, taste the bitter that we might know the sweet. We have come to this fallen state to experience aloneness, separateness from God and all things, that we may be able to comprehend our true oneness with God and all things.

"What is this Tree of Knowledge of Good and Evil?" you may ask. Adam and Eve, in the garden, partook of the forbidden fruit of The Tree of Knowledge of Good And Evil and became like the gods, knowing good from evil (hence the name, *The Tree of Knowledge of Good And Evil*). They were free to partake of the *Tree of Life* **before** they partook of the forbidden tree, but afterward were barred from partaking of The Tree of Life by a cherubim and flaming sword. We have all settled into the notion that since the flaming sword is there, we are absolutely prevented from partaking of The Tree of Life. **This is not so.** You will note from reading the great vision of Lehi and his son Nephi about the Tree of Life (see *1 Nephi 8:* and *11:*), that the fruit of The Tree of Life, which is the love of God, is free to all those who will cling to the rod of iron, which is the word of God, and follow the path leading to it. Note that we get knowledge along the way from eating the fruit of The Tree of Knowledge of Good And Evil and from the rod of iron, as we trek down the path to the

Tree of Life. Also note that the fruit of the Tree of Life is the *love of God*, not *more knowledge*, nor was it power or some other mysterious reward. **Experiencing a fullness of the love of God, spiritual oneness with Him, *is* the prize.**

Then what are the cherubim and flaming sword in the story of Adam and Eve all about? Well, they symbolize two things. First, the sword is the chastening of the Lord, the humiliation. "And ye have forgotten the exhortation which speaketh unto you as unto children, My son, despise not thou the chastening of the Lord, nor faint when thou art rebuked of Him: *For whom the Lord loveth He chasteneth, and scourgeth every son whom He receiveth.* If ye endure chastening, God dealeth with you as with sons; for what son is he whom the father chasteneth not? But if ye be without chastisement, whereof all are partakers, then are ye bastards, and not sons." (*Hebrews 12:5-8*) Such chastening is meant to humiliate you and break your heart. And second, the flame is the Baptism of Fire, the cleansing and sanctification by God Himself, necessary to go through in order to partake of life eternal and stand in His presence. "Yea, repent and be baptized, every one of you, for a remission of your sins; yea, be baptized even by water, and then cometh the Baptism of Fire and of the Holy Ghost." (*D&C 33:11*)

Charity

"Wait." you say, "When are you going to tell us about the great secret concerning charity?" Well, finally now! The point I am trying to make is that ever since the fall, we have been eating from The Tree of Knowledge of Good And Evil, struggling to gain more knowledge about the laws, determine which laws are which, which geometry we are in, and which truths belong to which geometry, as if knowing more will get us back to life with God. Though having "a knowledge" of good and evil is necessary to knowing joy, **we should be trying to get back to the Tree of Life,** the *love and knowledge of God*, and partake. The object is *not* to keep gaining knowledge, adding to our confusion and/or our pride in knowing so much, but rather to partake of the fruit of The Tree of Life which is sweet and delicious above all else, the pure love of Christ, charity. If we are willing to be chastened and cleansed, the fruit of the Tree of Life is there, free for the taking. The *Tree of Knowledge of Good And Evil* **is death.** It brought on the death of Adam and Eve and their posterity after them down to you and me. There is no life in that tree. The *Tree of Life* **is life**, even eternal life. Let us go forth and partake of the fruit thereof and live!

What has all this talk of dead laws to do with charity? Well, Christ's love is charity and that love is the fulfillment of the law! Christ, that is charity, is the New Law, the New and Everlasting Covenant. Charity, the pure love of Christ is the New and Everlasting Covenant. "Love worketh no ill to his neighbour: therefore love is the fulfilling of the law." (*Romans 13:10*) Again, "For all the law is fulfilled in one word, even in this; Thou shalt love thy neighbour as thyself." (*Galatians 5:14*) You don't need to be told **not** to do bad things to people you love. ***Because*** you love them, you would not hurt them.

And why is this *New and Everlasting Covenant* everlasting? Because it is the same law that God lives and He is everlasting. Because it is His love and His love is everlasting. It is His power and glory, which is everlasting. It is the same covenant that was from the beginning and will be forever.

The Same Covenant Made With Our Fathers

The last two verses of the Old Testament read, "Behold, I will send you Elijah the prophet before the coming of the great and dreadful day of the LORD: And he shall turn the heart of the fathers to the children, and the heart of the children to their fathers, lest I come and smite the earth with a curse." (*Malachi 4:5-6*) This scripture reference is generally accepted by the Mormons as being a scripture on the importance of genealogy, which it is, but it is much more. The Lord's restatement in the D&C gives us greater enlightenment (italics for emphasis). "Behold, I will reveal unto you the Priesthood, by the hand of Elijah the prophet, before the coming of the great and dreadful day of the Lord. And he shall plant in the hearts of the children *the promises made to the fathers*, and the hearts of the children shall turn to their fathers. If it were not so, the whole earth would be utterly wasted at his coming." (*D&C 2:1-3*) What were the promises made to our fathers? The New Covenant, which is the same covenant that was from the beginning. The promise; of Christ's love, His fullness. "*And as pertaining to the new and everlasting covenant, it was instituted for the* ***fulness of my glory****; and he that receiveth a fulness thereof must and shall abide the law, or he shall be damned, saith the Lord God.*" (*D&C 132:3-6*)

Let me explain further. You will remember back in the chapter on love we defined love as *spiritual oneness*, that *indwelling* of spirit-matter. We said there are two kinds of love, the Devil's love (or what he is spiritually one with) and Christ's love (or what He is spiritually one with). We said the latter, that is, Christ's love, is called charity. But it goes deeper than just a definition. So now I'll ask a few questions to see if we really know what is meant by the word charity. How is it that "Though I speak with the tongues of men and of angels, and have not charity, I am become as sounding brass, or a tinkling cymbal. And though I have the gift of prophecy, and understand all mysteries, and all knowledge; and though I have all faith, so that I could remove mountains, and have not charity, I am nothing. And though I bestow all my goods to feed the poor, and though I give my body to be burned, and have not charity, it profiteth me nothing . . . Charity never faileth: but whether there be prophecies, they shall fail; whether there be tongues, they shall cease; whether there be knowledge, it shall vanish away. For we know in part, and we prophesy in part. But when that which is perfect is come, then that which is in part shall be done away. When I was a child, I spake as a child, I understood as a child, I thought as a child: but when I became a man, I put away childish things. For now we see through a glass, darkly; but then face to face: now I know in part; but then shall I know even as also I am known. And now abideth faith, hope, charity, these three; but the greatest of these is charity." (*1 Corinthians 13:1-13*) Why is charity even greater than faith? How can the love of Christ, charity, surpass knowledge? "And to know the love of Christ, which passeth knowledge, that ye might be filled with all the fulness of God." (*Ephesians 3:19*) How can the love of Christ, charity, give you a fullness? Well, because **His love is the fullness! His love is the fullness**! I repeat. **His love is the fullness!**

Words Fail

Let me personally confide, I am sitting here in front of my computer struggling for a way to phrase my words so you will feel the signifecance of my meaning. I deeply concerned that the greatness, eminence, power, and glory of this concept will be too easily lost among my inadequate expressions. Please know I deem this principle of charity to be the greatest man can discover. But my words fall short. Even Joseph Smith said, and I will go back to his statement (italics for emphasis), "All men know that they must die. And it is important that we should understand the reasons and causes of our exposure to the vicissitudes of life and of death, and the designs and purposes of God in our coming into the world, our suffering here, and our departure hence. What is the object of our coming into existence, then dying and falling away, to be here no more? It is but reasonable to suppose that God would reveal something in reference to the matter, and it is a subject we ought to study more than any other. We ought to study it day and night, for the world is ignorant in reference to their true condition and relation. If we have any claim on our Heavenly Father for anything, it is for knowledge on this important subject. Could we read and comprehend all that has been written from the days of Adam, on the relation of man to God and angels in a future state, we should know very little about it. *Reading the experience of others, or the revelation given to them, can never give us a comprehensive view of our condition and true relation to God*. Knowledge of these things can only be obtained by experience through the ordinances of God set forth for that purpose. *Could you gaze into heaven five minutes*, you would know more than you would by reading all that ever was written on the subject." (*TPJS pg. 324*)

Since I cannot, through my words or the quoting of another's, hope to transfer to you the reader, the power of the meaning, I can only trust that my attempt will inspire you to seek, ask, and knock for yourself. If our true relationship with God is a subject we ought to study *more than any other*, even day and night, it behooves us to do so.

Notwithstanding the above confession of inadequacy, let me here ask some questions and attempt some answers. What does it mean, what is it like to receive a fullness, to receive charity, the love of Christ? What is it like to be one with truth, one with God? Perhaps I can say what it is not. It is not just *knowledge* that you get like when you attend a class, or read a book, or when a concept is explained to you and you are therefore given new information or understanding. That is knowledge you can get from eating from the Tree of Knowledge of Good and Evil. No, it is more. It is a *comprehension* of things, of all things. You don't just create things. You are the composition of the creation itself. It is made of you and you are it. You don't just perceive the cosmos and its contents. You comprehend it as though you are inside of every particle of it, and you are. It is not the good feeling you get when you obey a commandment. It is not just a feeling like those feelings of peace and great joy that you feel when the Holy Ghost has taken you to a spiritual high. It is not a feeling at all but a *state of being*. You don't just know truth; you *are* truth. You don't just feel joy; you *are* joy. You don't just feel love, you *are* love. You don't just feel peace, light, power, and glory, you *are* peace, light, power and glory. You are it! It is being! You don't just feel or see God, you are God.

I recognize that collection of words probably has little meaning to you and will not until you become a recipient of the oneness and of the fullness. I can say, however, that when (not if) this event occurs in your life, you will be a different being. You will no longer be on the outside, a separate observer, struggling to discover yourself and God, but you will be inside, not just a part of the great whole but you will be the whole itself.

Well, that's the best I can do at this point. Please forgive my ineptness. Let us go on.

Eat, Drink, Sleep, Or Know God

Regarding this most important subject of our relationship to God, Joseph Smith said (italics for emphasis), "There are but a very few beings in the world who understand rightly the character of God. The great majority of mankind does not comprehend anything, neither that which is past, or that which is to come, as in respect to their relationship to God. They do not know, nor do they understand the nature of that relationship; and consequently they know but little above the brute beast, or more than to eat, drink and sleep. This is all man knows about God or His existence, unless it is given by the inspiration of the Almighty.

"If a man learns nothing more than to eat, drink and sleep, and does not comprehend any of the designs of God, the beast comprehends the same things. It eats, drinks, sleeps, and knows nothing more about God; yet it knows as much as we, unless we are able to comprehend by the *inspiration of Almighty God*. If men do not comprehend the character of God, *they do not comprehend themselves*. I want to go back to the beginning, and so lift your minds into a loftier sphere and a more exalted understanding than what the human mind generally aspires to.

"I want to ask this congregation, every man, woman and child, to answer the question in their own heart, what kind of a being God is? Ask yourselves; turn your thought into your hearts, and say if any of you have seen, heard, or communed with Him. This is a question that may occupy your attention for a long time. I again repeat the question—What kind of a being is God? Does any man or woman know? Have any of you *seen Him, heard Him, or communed with Him?* Here is the question that will, peradventure, from this time henceforth occupy your attention. The Scriptures inform us that 'This is life eternal that they might *know thee*, the only true God, and Jesus Christ whom thou hast sent.'

"If any man does not know God, and inquires what kind of a being He is,—if he will search diligently his own heart—if the declaration of Jesus and the apostles be true, he will realize that he has not eternal life; for there can be eternal life on no other principle.

"It is the first principle of the Gospel to know for a certainty the Character of God, and to know that *we may converse with him as one man converses with another* . . . ." (*TPJS pg. 343-345*)

The prophet Joseph said that *if* we are to *know* God, not just know about Him, if we are to have a relationship with Him to the point that we actually *know* Him, it is *given by the inspiration of the Almighty*. What is even more amazing is that unless we comprehend the character of God, we do not comprehend ourselves. To press his point, the key, the secret to the mystery of knowing God, he asked us twice if we have *seen, heard, or communed with Him*. Then he tells us that if we haven't, we don't *know* Him and accordingly, do not have eternal life, for eternal life is based upon this very principle. He is not just asking; do you *know about* God? He is asking; do you ***know*** Him. Is He your personal friend? Have you seen him? Have you heard his voice? Have you talked with Him face to face? Have you been born of Him? Have you been spiritually begotten of Him? Have you received the Baptism of Fire? Have you had that physical and spiritual change? Are you a new person *in Christ*? Are you one with His spirit, the Holy Ghost? Have you entered into His rest? This **is** eternal life.

If you are to live with Him you must at the very least, *know* Him. If He is to be in you and you in Him, as Christ prayed to the Father that all those who believe on His word might be, you must *know* Him. To *know Him* is to be *one with Him*. This isn't even exaltation, it is salvation only. Exaltation, that is the highest glory in God's heavenly celestial kingdom, comes only *after* knowing Him.

The entire point of what is taught us about this endowment of power and glory in the Lord's sacred house is that we may be introduced to God; meet Him face to face.

A Little Hope Here Please

Does this put things in perspective for us or only cause us to lose hope? When we contemplate such a great principle, it should humiliate us, even to the point of a broken heart; however, we should not be depressed. Humility is not depression. On the contrary, it is the cleansing of the soul. It is the death of our separateness. It is the rebirth of our oneness of all things. It is the making ready of our spirits to actually commune with our Savior. If, in our *humiliated, nothingness* state, we turn to Christ, through belief (if not faith), confessing, repenting, and begging for His grace, He will *first bless us with faith, then hope, then in His due time, charity*, which is His perfect love, His fullness. "They did fast and pray oft, and did wax stronger and stronger in their *humility*, and firmer and firmer in the *faith of Christ*, unto the filling their souls with joy and consolation, yea, even to the purifying and the sanctification of their hearts, which sanctification cometh *because of their yielding their hearts unto God*." (*Helaman 3:35*)

"For the grace of God that bringeth salvation hath appeared to all men, Teaching us that, denying ungodliness and worldly lusts, we should live soberly, righteously, and godly, in this present world; Looking for that blessed hope, and the glorious appearing of the great God and our Savior Jesus Christ." (*Titus 2:11-13*) Again, this isn't a reference to Christ's coming a second time but rather a hope in His visitation to us personally. "He that hath my commandments and keepeth them, he it is that loveth me: and he that loveth me shall be loved of my Father, and I will love him, and will manifest myself to him. Judas saith unto him, not Iscariot, Lord, how is it that thou wilt manifest thyself unto us, and not unto the world? Jesus answered and said unto him, If a man love me, he will keep my words: and my Father will love him, and we will come unto him, and make our abode with him." (*John 14:21-23*) "John 14:23-The appearing of the Father and the Son, in that verse, is a personal appearance; and the idea that the Father and the Son dwell in a man's heart is an old sectarian notion, and is false." (*D&C 130:3*)

"We consider that God has created man with a mind capable of instruction, and a faculty which may be enlarged in proportion to the heed and diligence given to the light communicated from heaven to the intellect; and that the nearer man approaches perfection, the clearer are his views, and the greater his enjoyments, till he has overcome the evils of his life and lost every desire for sin; and like the ancients, arrives at that point of faith where he is *wrapped in the power and glory of his Maker and is caught up to dwell with Him*." (*TPJS pg. 51*)

When we are wrapped in the love of Christ and His power and glory, we will no longer be the natural man that is an enemy to God. We will have received the Baptism of Fire. Remember what Christ said to the people on the South American continent, "And ye shall offer for a sacrifice unto me a broken heart and a contrite spirit. And whoso cometh unto me with a *broken heart and a contrite spirit*, him will I baptize with fire and with the Holy Ghost, even as the Lamanites, because of their faith in me at the time of their conversion, were baptized with fire and with the Holy Ghost, and they knew it not." (*3 Nephi 9:20*) What did they experience as a result of this Baptism of Fire and the Holy Ghost? "Behold, they saw that they were encircled about, yea every soul, by a pillar of fire. And Nephi and Lehi were in the midst of them; yea, they were encircled about; yea, they were as if in the midst of a flaming fire, yet it did harm them not, neither did it take hold upon the walls of the prison; and they were filled with that joy which is unspeakable and full of glory. And behold, the Holy Spirit of God did come down from heaven, and did enter into their hearts, and they were filled as if with fire, and they could speak forth marvelous words." (*Helaman 5:43-45*) Like them, we will lose our desire to sin. We will be filled with *joy unspeakable*. "And it came to pass that when Ammon arose he also administered unto them, and also did all the servants of Lamoni; and they did all declare unto the people the selfsame thing—that their hearts had been changed; that they had no more desire to do evil. And behold, many did declare unto the people that they had seen angels and had conversed with them; and thus they had told them things of God, and of His righteousness." (*Alma 19:33-34*) This is what took place on the Day of Pentecost.

"And when the day of Pentecost was fully come, they were all with one accord in one place; And suddenly there came a sound from heaven as of a rushing mighty wind, and it filled all the house where they were sitting. And there appeared unto them cloven tongues like as of fire, and it sat upon each of them. And they were all filled with the Holy Ghost, and began to speak with other tongues, as the Spirit gave them utterance." (*Acts 2:1-4*)

Receiving A Fullness

Now this communion with Christ comes as The Baptism of Fire. It is the reception of the gift of the Holy Ghost. There is no greater endowment of the love of Christ, His power and glory ordained for man on earth. You may have visions, you may receive visitations of angels (keys of the lesser priesthood), or you may have some of the mysteries of heaven revealed to you but until you receive the Second Comforter spoken of in John 14:16-23 and have Jesus Christ Himself appear to you revealing the Father to you, your Calling and Election is not sure **nor** have you been Born Again.

The event of being Born Again has blessed the souls of many in times past as it has and will in these latter-days. It is not meant just for a special few, but is, in fact, the *wholeness* of the Gospel of Christ to all who will come to Him with a broken heart and contrite spirit. This is the answer to my old professor's riddle, the best kept secret of the Mormon Church, the Gospel of Christ. This is charity, the pure love of Christ. This is Christ's *fullness*, which He received from the Father (italics & bold for emphasis). "And I, John, bear record, and lo, the heavens were opened, and the Holy Ghost descended upon Him in the form of a dove, and sat upon Him, and there came a voice out of heaven saying: This is my beloved Son. And I, John, bear record that He received a fulness of the glory of the Father; And He received all power, both in heaven and on earth, and the glory of the Father was with Him, for He dwelt in Him." (*D&C 93:15-17*)

This is the same fullness that He is offering to us, to all men; that through the **oneness doctrine**, we may have. This is **joint heir-ship** with Christ, having it all. This is the "blessing hitherto unknown" promised us by the prophet Ezra Taft Benson, if we will but come out from under the condemnation and judgment. This is the fullness of the New and Everlasting Covenant. "Therefore it is given to abide in you; the record of heaven; the Comforter; the peaceable things of immortal glory; the truth of all things; that which quickeneth all things, which maketh alive all things; that which knoweth all things, and hath all power according to wisdom, mercy, truth, justice, and judgment. And now, behold, I say unto you: *This is the plan of salvation* **unto all men**, *through the blood of mine Only Begotten, who shall come in the meridian of time.*" (Moses 6:61)

The First And Last Commandment

Can we casually sit back, not seeking, not asking, not knocking, and expect that it will simply come to us? I think not. Or perhaps we believe this is not really a necessary part of the Gospel of Christ. It is not just a part; *it is the fullness of the Gospel of Jesus Christ.*

Let me press the point that the fullness of the Gospel of Jesus Christ is to be wrapped in His eternal love, charity. It is to become one with Him, spiritually one, literally, so that all He has becomes ours. John explains this love of Christ. "Beloved, let us love one another: for love is of God; and every one that loveth is born of God, and knoweth God. He that loveth not knoweth not God; for God is love . . . . If we love one another, *God dwelleth in us*, and His love is perfected in us. Hereby know we that we dwell in Him, and He in us, because He *hath given us of His Spirit* . . . Whosoever shall confess that Jesus is the Son of God, God *dwelleth in him, and He in God.* And we have known and believed the love that God hath to us. *God is love; and he that dwelleth in love dwelleth in God, and God in him.* Herein is our love made perfect, that we may have boldness in the day of judgment: because *as He is, so are we in this world.* There is no fear in love; but perfect love casteth out fear: because fear hath torment. He that feareth is not made perfect in love. We love Him, because He first loved us." (*1 John 4:7-13, 15-19* see also *Moroni 8:16*) Christ's love is everlasting. Charity never fails.

Can there be any question why *Thou shalt love the Lord thy God with all thy heart, and with all thy soul, and with all thy mind*, and to love our neighbor also, are the great commandments upon which hang all the law and the prophets? Becoming one with Christ is everything. Receiving His love is to receive all in all. It is to have all truth, all glory, all knowledge, all kindness, all patience, as well as all other of Christ's virtues. Once we have been wrapped in the love of our Savior, not just feel His love on occasion, but receive the fullness of His love, (charity), we will have no desire to sin, we will have no fear, and we cannot fall. For, though we may be called to suffer much and certainly endure to the end, "Until we have perfect love we are liable to fall and when we have a testimony that our names are sealed in the Lamb's book of life we have perfect love and then it is impossible for false Christs to deceive us . . . ." (*TPJS pg.* 9)

As He Is, So Are We

So, what shall we do to receive this great blessing of faith, hope, and charity, the love of God? "And again, behold I say unto you that he cannot have faith and hope, save he shall be meek, and lowly of heart. If so, his faith and hope is vain, for none is acceptable before God, save the meek and lowly in heart; and if a man be meek and lowly in heart, and confesses by the power of the Holy Ghost that Jesus is the Christ, he must needs have charity; for if he have not charity he is nothing; wherefore he must needs have charity . . . But charity is the pure love of Christ, and it endureth forever; and whoso is found possessed of it at the last day, it shall be well with him. Wherefore, my beloved brethren, pray unto the Father with all the energy of heart, that ye may be filled with this love, which He hath bestowed upon all who are true followers of His Son, Jesus Christ; that ye may become the sons of God; that when He shall appear we shall be like Him, for we shall see Him as He is; that we may have this hope; that we may be purified even as He is pure. Amen." (*Moroni 7:43-44, 47-48*)

What does it mean to see Him as He is? It means we will be able to see Him without any veil or filters to preserve our lives. We will see Him as He really is, in His power and great glory and we will be able to do that because we will be like Him. We will not only be able to withstand His glory without withering away, but we will have glory just like Him. To see Him *as He is,* is to be *like Him.* "Beloved, now are we the sons of God, and it doth not yet appear what we shall be: but we know that, when He shall appear, we shall be like Him; for we shall see him as He is." (*1 John 3:2*) We must also, "Let thy bowels also be full of *charity towards all men*, and to the household of faith, and *let virtue garnish thy thoughts unceasingly*; then shall thy confidence wax strong in the presence of God; and the doctrine of the priesthood shall distil upon thy soul as the dews from heaven. The Holy Ghost shall be thy constant companion, and thy scepter an unchanging scepter of righteousness and truth; and thy dominion shall be an everlasting dominion, and without compulsory means it shall flow unto thee forever and ever." (*D&C 121:45-46*) If we will do these things, that is, be meek, think virtuous thoughts, then not just our hope but our confidence before God will be strong, and the Holy Ghost, that spirit-matter of the Gods, will fill our souls with righteousness and truth. Power in the priesthood will flow unto our posterity and us forever, throughout time and eternity, without having to struggle for it. You don't struggle for it you let go. It's a gift; remember?

It Has Always Been With Us

Notwithstanding our unwitting attempts to keep it a secret, the wonderful thing is that this law, this *New Law*, this *New and Everlasting Covenant*, this charity, this love of Christ, this *Gospel of Jesus Christ,* is not really very far out of reach, nor has it ever been. "For this commandment which I command thee this day, it is not hidden from thee, neither is it far off. It is not in heaven, that thou shouldest say, Who shall go up for us to heaven, and bring it unto us, that we may hear it, and do it? Neither is it beyond the sea, that thou shouldest say, Who shall go over the sea for us, and bring it unto us, that we may hear it, and do it? But the word is very nigh unto thee, in thy mouth, and in thy heart, that thou mayest do it. See, I have set before thee this day life and good, and death and evil . . . . That thou mayest love the Lord thy God, and that thou mayest obey His voice, and that thou mayest cleave unto Him: for He is thy life . . . ." (*Deuteronomy 30:11-15, 20*)

Day And Night

Is this important or something we can *treat lightly*? "And I now give unto you a commandment to beware concerning yourselves, to give diligent heed to the words of eternal life. For you shall live by every word that proceedeth forth from the mouth of God. For the word of the Lord is truth, and whatsoever is truth is light, and whatsoever is light is Spirit, even the Spirit of Jesus Christ. And the Spirit giveth light to every man that cometh into the world; and the Spirit enlighteneth every man through the world, that hearkeneth to the voice of the Spirit. And every one that hearkeneth to the voice of the Spirit cometh unto God, even the Father. *And the Father teacheth him of the covenant* which He has renewed and confirmed upon you, which is confirmed upon you for your sakes, and not for your sakes only, but for the sake of the whole world. And the whole world lieth in sin, and groaneth under darkness and under the bondage of sin . . . Verily, verily, I say unto you, they who believe not on your words, and are not baptized in water in my name, for the remission of their sins, that they may receive the Holy Ghost, shall be damned, and shall not come into my Father's kingdom where my Father and I am." (*D&C 84:43-50*) These are the words of eternal life and woe be unto those who say they don't need these words. Joseph Smith tells us, "The Savior has the words of eternal life. Nothing else can profit us . . . I advise all to go on to perfection, and search deeper and deeper into the mysteries of Godliness. A man can do nothing for himself unless God direct him in the right way; and the Priesthood is for that purpose." (*TPJS pg. 364*) The Prophet Joseph goes on to say, "Here, then, is eternal life—to know the only wise and true God; and you have got to learn how to be Gods yourselves, and to be kings and priests to God, the same as all Gods have done before you, namely, by going from one small degree to another, and from a small capacity to a great one; from grace to grace, from exaltation to exaltation, until you attain to the resurrection of the dead, and are able to dwell in everlasting burnings, and to sit in glory, as do those who sit enthroned in everlasting power. And I want you to know that God, in the last days, while certain individuals are proclaiming His name, is not trifling with you or me." *(TPJS pg. 346)*

Why do we not seek, day and night, with every fiber of our beings, to see the face of God? Has God not said it enough times, in enough ways, to us all? The Lord said (italics for emphasis), "Verily, thus saith the Lord: It shall come to pass that ***every soul*** who forsaketh his sins and cometh unto me, and calleth on my name, and obeyeth my voice, and keepeth my commandments, shall *see my face* and *know that I am*; And that I am the true light that lighteth every man that cometh into the world; And that I am in the Father, and the Father in me, and the Father and I are one . . . And it shall come to pass, that if you are faithful you shall receive the fulness of the record of John. I give unto you these sayings that you may understand and know how to worship, and know what you worship, that you may come unto the Father in my name, and in due time receive of His fulness. For if you keep my commandments you shall receive of His fulness, and be glorified in me as I am in the Father; therefore, I say unto you, you shall receive grace for grace. He that keepeth His commandments receiveth truth and light, until he is glorified in truth and knoweth all things. Behold, here is the agency of man, and here is the condemnation of man; because that which was from the beginning is plainly manifest unto them, and they receive not the light. And every man whose spirit receiveth not the light is under condemnation. For man is spirit. The elements are eternal, and spirit and element, inseparably connected, receive a fulness of joy; And when separated, man cannot receive a fulness of joy. The elements are the tabernacle of God; yea, man is the tabernacle of God, even temples; and whatsoever temple is defiled, God shall destroy that temple." *(D&C 93:1-3, 18-20, 28, 31-35)* "And I will pray the Father, and He shall give you another Comforter, that He may abide with you forever; Even the Spirit of Truth; whom the world cannot receive, because it seeth Him not, neither knoweth Him; but ye know Him; for He dwelleth with you, and shall be in you. I will not leave you comfortless: *I will come to you*. He that hath my commandments, and keepeth them, he it is that loveth me: and he that loveth me shall be loved of my Father, and *I will love him*, and *will manifest myself to him . . . If a man love me, he will keep my word: and my Father will love him, and we will come unto him, and make our abode with him*." *(John 14:16, 17, 18, 21, 23)* Remember Joseph Smith explained that "the *Other Comforter is no more nor less than the Lord Jesus Christ Himself*; "and this is the sum and substance of the whole matter; that when any man obtains this last Comforter, *he will have the personage of Jesus Christ to attend him*, or *appear unto him from time to time*, and even *He will manifest the Father unto him*, and *they will take up their abode with him, and the visions of the heavens will be opened unto him, and the Lord will teach him face to* *face, and he may have a perfect knowledge of the mysteries of the Kingdom of God . . . .*" (*TPJS, pg. 150-1*) "This principle ought to be taught, for God hath not revealed anything to Joseph, but what He will make known unto the Twelve, and even the least Saint may know all things as fast as he is able to bear them, for the day must come when no man need say to his neighbor, know ye the Lord; for all shall know him from the least to the greatest." (*TPJS, pg. 149*)

THIS IS THE GOSPEL OF JESUS CHRIST. HOW DARE WE KEEP IT A SECRET!

Final Words

Who can say it more poetically than did Moroni in his last words to the world? "And again I would exhort you that ye would come unto Christ, and lay hold upon every good gift, and touch not the evil gift, nor the unclean thing. And awake, and arise from the dust, O Jerusalem; yea, and put on thy beautiful garments, O daughter of Zion; and strengthen thy stakes and enlarge thy borders forever, that thou mayest no more be confounded, that the covenants of the Eternal Father which He hath made unto thee, O house of Israel, may be fulfilled. Yea, come unto Christ, and be perfected in Him, and deny yourselves of all ungodliness; and if ye shall deny yourselves of all ungodliness and love God with all your might, mind and strength, then is His grace sufficient for you, that by His grace ye may be perfect in Christ; and if by the grace of God ye are perfect in Christ, ye can in nowise deny the power of God. And again, if ye by the grace of God are perfect in Christ, and deny not His power, then are ye sanctified in Christ by the grace of God, through the shedding of the blood of Christ, which is in the covenant of the Father unto the remission of your sins, that ye become holy, without spot." (*Moroni 10:30-33*)

If we are prepared, we will not reject the gifts. If we do all *we can do*, despite our weaknesses, and otherwise let our souls be full of love towards God and man, have faith, and let virtue garnish our thoughts unceasingly, then we will receive the offered gift of the Holy Ghost, thereby becoming one with the Gods. What more of a promise do we need? Have faith; He will keep His promise.

"If we will be true believers, have faith in the Lord Jesus Christ, love with all our hearts, serve Him, and ask of God, we will have revelations of the mysteries of heaven and enjoy the gifts such as signs, miracles, and prophecies. Our greatness and glory will not be measured in telestial or terrestrial terms, nor will our virtues be necessarily recognized and accepted by this world, but our mansions will be prepared in the celestial realm, which is, hopefully, the only realm in which we will be comfortable. We as baptized members have been given, on the principle of righteousness and faithfulness, the right to the constant companionship of an actual member of the Godhead, the Holy Ghost. It is well known among us that the Holy Ghost is a Revelator and a Sanctifier; that if we ask of God in faith, we shall receive revelation upon revelation, until the mysteries of the kingdom are unfolded in full; that faith precedes the miracle; and that signs always follow those who believe. Our obligation is to seek and obtain the Spirit so that all of these things will flow to us as they did to the ancients." (*Bruce R. McConkie, The Promised Messiah, pg. 571*)

The Gospel of Christ is simple and plain. It should be no secret to Mormons, non-Mormons, or anyone else. I have a hope that we may come to *know* God and His son Jesus Christ. My hope is that "the visions of the heavens will be opened unto [us], and the Lord will teach [us] face to face, and [we] may have a perfect knowledge of the mysteries of the Kingdom of God," (*TPJS pg. 150*).

This hope comes to me by the grace of our Savior Jesus Christ, who is the source of all gifts and power. I hope also that this may happen to us soon. "God hath not revealed anything to Joseph, but what He will make known unto [us], as even the least Saint may know all things as fast as he is able to bear them, for the day must come when no man need say to his neighbor, Know ye the Lord? For all shall know Him—from the least to the greatest." (*TPJS pg. 149*) "And this is life eternal, that they might know thee the only true God, and Jesus Christ, whom thou has sent." (*John 17:3*)

God is a very great being. He is greater, bigger, more wonderful than we can imagine. He wants to tell us His secrets, let us prepare ourselves to receive them, Him.

---

[111] **The Standard Works are the four books sanctioned by The Church as scripture, *The Book of Mormon*, *The Holy Bible*, *The Doctrine and Covenants*, and *The Pearl of Great Price.***

[112] **Approximately two-thirds of the gold plates, from which Joseph Smith translated *The Book of Mormon*, were sealed. Joseph Smith was instructed by the angel Moroni not to attempt to translate them as they were to be saved to come forth at a later time.**

[113] **The Church has set aside each Monday night as a time the family may get together for study or fun activities calculated to bring them closer as a family. No church meetings are scheduled on Monday nights.**

[114] **The Church has welfare farms and canneries where the members donate their labor to provide all manner of commodities for the poor and needy in The Church.**

Index

A

a blessing hitherto unknown...... 44, 338
about the author.. 17
agency 64, 65
  a matter of our desire 66
  bounds to 136, 139
  but Gods hand in all things 137, 140
    bad things also 141, 142
  choices not wrong................................. 66
  ultimate freedom 70
  we choose the law we will live 65
ask, seek, knock 28, 36, 37
Axioms
  10 of them 57
  foundation of all truth.......................... 58

B

Babylon 237, 243
  get thee out 276
Baptism of Fire. *See also* See Born Again
basics 25, 26, 34
  improve upon to progress 74
  remember 101
belief...199
Born Again 299, 309
  evidence of 338
  evidences of..302
  examples of..301
  greatest endowment............................318
  Holy Ghost will show you all things 303
  lose desire to sin 337
  no desire to do evil 304
  possesor of all things 301
  principle of power 303
  synonymous with translation ... 305, 309
broken heart, contrite spirit 278, 285, 328, 340
  only requirement for grace 282

C

Calling and Election 311
  a rain check 311
charity .... *See* love: See oneness or indwelling
  being wrapped in love of Christ 339
  being wrapped in the power and glory of God 337
  Christs love, a fullness of His glory 332
  Gods love never failing.......................333
  how do you get it 333
  same as recieving a fullness 338
  the New and Everlasting Covenant 292
Church of Firstborn 314
condemnation
  saints of Zion under 43, 298
  saints sin a very grievous sin...... 45, 240
  saints walk in darkness at noon-day..... 44
curse of Eve 173

D

damnation..... 19, 23, 47, 49, 100, 131, 312
darkness at noon-day 45, 240

Devil
void of truth 100
disclaimer. *See also* non-disclaimer
divorce 168

E

Electromagnetic Spectrum 94, 96
endless torment 131
essence motivation 134, 135
why we do what we do 134
eternal life 341
not far off 340
the meaning of 334
to know God 295, 335
eternal now
past, present, future 129
eternal punishment 131
Euclids Axioms 57
Euclids Elements 57

F

faith 193, 194, 203
a gift 196
in future events 197
no fruits no faith 200
to cross a footbridge 198
fear 46, 264
feelings 289
get off the pity pot 290
language of the spirit 166, 169
you made me feel bad 167
your responsibility, your choice 168
first great cause of things 32

G

General Authorities
excellent leaders 21
mysteries not just for 38
not source of all truth 79, 82, 90
geometry .... 53, 57. *See* truth
different geometry-different truth ....
62, 65, 69, 70
four major realms 62
our own personal 69
gifts 256
cannot be earned 256, 282
deny them not 256
God
attributes of 127, 128, 146
differences between God and man 130
His hand in all things 147
bad things also 144, 149
His job 130
is ultimately responsible 145
knows all 128, 133
how He knows all 133
life eternal to know him 110
lives in the Eternal Now 129, 133
must know Him 313
personal appearance 336
see Him as he is 340
see Him while in this life 294, 297
ultimately responsible 147
Godhead 109, 120
individuality of 111, 115
oneness of, or indwelling 112, 119, 125
oneness vs separate 110, 114
oneness with 125
Gods Priesthood or power
the honor of men 72
grace 273, 343
a gift from God 282
fulfillment of law 321
Gods grace is sufficient 274
requirements to receive 280, 282
gratitude 285
grievous sin 44
guilt
a feeling, a choice 289
is anti-Christ 287
is self-condemnation 288

H

half a baptism 47
hate 160
heir-ship 73, 115, 122, 338
Holy Ghost 116
available to all 121
denial of 98, 100
is spirit-matter 117
is shared by all who are one with God 121
is the oneness of the Gods 118
is the Spirit of the Lord 117
knows all truth 76
truth matter 116
will reveal all truth 79
humiliation 329, 336

I

indwelling .... *See oneness or indwelling, See also Godhead, See love*
inner peace
none if fighting truth 75
inspiration 205

J

joint heirs with Christ 73, 122, 338
judging 283
evil to be good or good to be evil 88
judge righteously 88
men by their hearts 85
justification by law 279
not possible 281

K

Karl Friedrich Gauss 58
knowledge 199

L

law. .... *See* geometry
cannot save us 321
celestial in telestial world 277
celestial will not pay off in telestial world 276
deadness of 322
four major realms 62, 63
like the wind 321
many geometries 62, 69
New and Everlasting Covenant fulfills 320
not fully perfect 74
sanctified by 64
the schoolmaster 46, 325
to condemn and break our hearts 329
ultimate freedom 71, 320, 328
we choose what level we will live 65, 68
why we want law 323
Law of Consecration and Stewardship
not a poverty program 248
letting go 290
life
meaning of
a test 188
gain a body 188
this world a deception 187
to know evil 189
to suffer .... 189, 204, 209. *See also* suffering
light
is matter 95
is truth matter in and through all things 96, 98
love .... 155. *See* charity
a one and only 178
benefits of 163
comes with no obligation 172
commanded to love all 174
definition of 156, 157

different kinds of relationships 161
free to love all 176
homosexual 176
is a choice 163
must love to help 165
only two kinds 157, 158
spiritual oneness 156, 158, 159
stranger 182
tapping into the Spirit of God 185
the cure for loneliness 181, 186
love vs relationships 161, 183
obligation comes with relationships, not love 172
lying
denying the Holy Ghost 100
never to ones self 99

M

marriage
criteria for 177
not a partnership 220
matter
gross-matter 93
spirit-matter 93
Melchizedek Priesthood
a high geometry 72
keys of mysteries, knowledge of God 36, 38, 44, 72, 295, 298
purpose of 45
receiving a fullness 72
milk vs. meat .... 26. *See* basics
Millennium 238
telestial destroyed 237
miracle 200, 201, 203
mysteries .... 31, 33, 37, 40. *See also* through a glass darkly
for whom 38, 42
keep sacred 38, 81
keys of 35, 36
know while in the flesh 42
known by Holy Ghost 89, 90
leave alone 33
looking beyond the mark 26
made known 37
none to exalted beings 33
search deeper into 36
search out the 40
treated lightly 43, 200
unwillingness to receive 18, 19, 23, 35, 37, 44, 45, 48
twinkie—fried froth—angel food cake 35
vain trifling conferences meetings 35

N

New and Everlasting Covenant 292, 319
a fullness 338
charity the new law 331
law put in hearts 328
taught by God 293, 308
non-disclaimer 15
Non-Euclidean geometry 59
a more accurate description of space 59
a revolution 60
truth 59

O

O wretched man
Nephis lament 278
Pauls lament 272
obedience 274
oneness or indwelling .... 122, 320, 339. *See also* love
opposition in all things 144
outward appearance 85

P

partnerships 213, 215
marriage is not a 220
none in heaven 215

they separate 215
perception
not truth 77
seeing through glass darkly 78
seems real to us 79
perdition 64, 123
perfection 278
not possible without Gods
grace 279, 24, 328
power 244
a gift from God 273
pride 282, 286
must sacrifice 283
prophecy 231
Prophet, Seer, Revelator
those who have Holy Ghost 81, 82

R

rewards 63, 123, 275, 331
parable of the laborers 208
riddlebest kept secret 30, 291

S

sacrifice 193, 207
letting go 283
our will 195
sanctified
by the law we live 64
scandalous 20
schoolmaster 319
scripture
definition of 84
Second Comforter 311, 342
secret, the great 291
speculation 33
spirit
is matter 93
is more powerful matter 94
spiritual death 123
stewardships 216
by assignment 218, 220
how they work 217
unifying 218, 225
suffering .... 145, 146, 148, 150, 179. *See also* life, meaning of
how to alleviate 210
joy in 204

T

the 144,000 318
translation
keys of 309
moratorium on 310
Tree of Knowledge of Good and Evil ... 330
Tree of Life 74, 330
truth .... 31, 197. *See also* geometry
a personal responsibility 80, 83, 85, 90
danger in not advancing in 48, 49
defined 54
discerning of 76
fighting against, is unhappiness 75
how it works 61
is eternal 20, 102
is everywhere 103, 106
heaven and hell 104
in other churches 104
is matter 93, 95
know by Holy Ghost 76
know, think, believe 90
only true church 105
relative vs. absolute 55, 61, 69, 70
unwillingness to
receive 18, 19, 23, 48, 200
vanity and unbelief 43
we believe what we choose 53
where is it 93
wo unto him that sayeth all is well,
we have enough 49

two gospels
greater gospel 47
lesser gospel 46

U

ultimate freedom
no law or rather all law 70
unbelief ....196. *See also* vanity and unbelief
United Order 247

V

vanity and
unbelief ...43, 105, 200, 239, 245, 266

W

walking dead 300
weakness
God-given 152, 272
Paul does what he would not 273
wheat and tares 316
will
must sacrifice 282, 283
work vs grace 270
saved by grace no matter
what we do 271

Z

Zion 263
all is well in 48
built by those Born Again 234
city of (New Jerusalem) 235
economy 246
no private ownership 246
established by people out
of this people 316
mountain of 235
not yet established 105
under condemnation 43
Zion Society 82, 225, 233
a state of power 244
built on Celestial law 236
church pass away 242
disobedience postponed it 247
living celestial laws now 263
lunch is free 253
must be celestial before entering 237
no competition 252
no fear 264
no loneliness 261
no suffering 251
no veil 260
not yet established 239, 243
one mind one heart 248, 263
only Born Again will be in 315
people taught by God personally 293
Queens and Priestesses 245
travel and communication 253
wo untoall is well 240

Made in the USA
Lexington, KY
21 March 2013